The
GATES
of
REPENTANCE

The
GATES
of
REPENTANCE

Rabbeinu Yonah

translation and commentary by
Yaakov Feldman

JASON ARONSON INC.
Northvale, New Jersey
Jerusalem

This book was set in 10 pt. Adobe Garamond by Alabama Book Composition of Deatsville, AL and printed and bound by Book-mart Press, Inc. of North Bergen, NJ.

Library of Congress Cataloging-in-Publication Data

Jonah ben Abraham Gerondi, ca. 1200–1263.
  [Sha'are teshuvah. English]
  The gates of repentance / by Rabbeinu Yonah ; translated and
commented upon by Yaakov Feldman.
     p.   cm.
  Includes bibliographical references and index.
  ISBN 0-7657-6085-1 (alk. paper)
  1. Ethics, Jewish—Early works to 1800. 2. Repentance—Judaism
—Early works to 1800. 3. Jonah ben Abraham Gerondi, ca. 1200–1263.
Sha'are teshuvah. I. Feldman, Yaakov. II. Title.
BJ1287.J653S5213 1999
296.3'6—dc21   98–54336
                                                      CIP

Printed in the United States of America on acid-free paper. For information and catalog write to Jason Aronson Inc., 230 Livingston Street, Northvale, NJ 07647-1726, or visit our website: www.aronson.com

לעליאת נשמת או״מ יצחק הערש בן רניאל ,ע״ה

In loving memory of my father,
Irving H. Feldman
of blessed memory

CONTENTS

Note on the Typesetting of This Book:

With the exception of his footnotes, material written by the translator has been set within ruled boxes. This way, the reader can easily distinguish between the translator's commentary and Ibn Pakuda's own words.

Translator's Introduction

1.

A moving and highly inspiring work, Rabbeinu Yonah's *The Gates of Repentance* seems difficult for the modern reader to swallow whole, so to speak. Its apparently stark and rigorous demands, and its full-throated advocacy of a venerable and Heaven-centered code of behavior and personal ethic, seem beyond us. And its challenge to redress all our wrongdoing and pettiness seems an unrealizable, nearly superhuman dream. In fact, its difficulty seems to compare to the one the modern reader would have with Moshe Chaim Luzzatto's *The Path of the Just*, as we indicated in our introduction to our treatment of it (Aronson: 1996).

But *The Gates of Repentance* is perhaps an especially challenging work for the modern reader, because the Jewish notion of repentance (tshuvah), which is the work's main thrust, is so highly misunderstood. So, what we'll try to do is clarify Rabbeinu Yonah's explanation of tshuvah here, in this introduction, as well as throughout the book. In order to do that, we'll need to present a fairly detailed sketch of the work itself, gate by gate, and then some.

2.

Although Rabbeinu Yonah didn't formally dedicate an introduction to *The Gates of Repentance*, the first gate's first 9 sections serve as one. Accordingly, it's there that Rabbeinu Yonah defines tshuvah, and declares it first off to be a means to "rise above our destructive acts, to avoid the traps we set by our acts of defiance, to ward off personal devastation, and to deflect (God's) anger" (1:1). But then Rabbeinu Yonah introduces yet another aspect of tshuvah, which we'll come to shortly, that we'd never have expected.

In the meanwhile, Rabbeinu Yonah goes on to refer to tshuvah as an "escape hatch" of sorts, which we'd be foolish to not take advantage of; he offers that it's smart to use that escape hatch as soon as possible; that there's a danger of getting into a rut about your sins and taking them for granted; that while sinning is only too natural and even understandable, not doing tshuvah for those sins is absurd, and shows an out-and-out obstinacy on your part; that each generation is susceptible to particular sins (our own included), which it must be sensitive to; and that tshuvah is always helpful, but the deeper and more heartfelt, the better and more effective it is.

Not much of this comes as a particular surprise to the reader. One would only expect there to be warnings about destruction, traps, devastation, Divine wrath, etc., in a book of ethical betterment and moral growth such as this. But what *does* surprise the reader is Rabbeinu Yonah's introduction of the idea of drawing close to God as an end product and full-face *aim* of tshuvah.

In fact, the idea of drawing close to God comes both at the beginning of Rabbeinu Yonah's introduction and at its end, it's that important to him. He reveals in the first section that tshuvah, "allows us to *return*" to God. And he points out in the last one (1:9) that "the greater the degree of your tshuvah, the *closer to God you get.*"

It will actually be our contention in the notes that a major key to understanding tshuvah and *The Gates of Repentance* itself will be our concentrating on the idea that we can have an intimate relationship with God (and that, in fact, we're encouraged to). But that that relationship can "go sour" and approach "divorce," or be dreadfully threatened just as a loving relationship with a person can be — with far, far deeper, immortal implications of course. And it will be seen that what "sin" is, is a personal affront and threat to that relationship with God; and that tshuvah is a reconciliation.

But it will also be seen that Rabbeinu Yonah's overarching point is that we're capable of greatness.[1] That as souls incarnate, we're well-suited to drawing close to God, and able to rise above human pettiness and error. That tshuvah enables us to do just that—yet, it's not *limited* to that. Because tshuvah allows us to become the people we're capable of being. And of drawing close to God as a consequence, as He's always wanted us to.[2]

So many people overlook that aspect of tshuvah when they talk about it. And tend to dwell instead upon the more dour and daunting fact of our

---

1. See, for example, 1:10's "For the Creator breathed a living soul into my nostrils, with a wise heart and good sense with which to be conscious of God and fear Him, and to reign over my body," 1:19's discussion of our being God's emissary on earth; 3:17's discussion of the noble virtues we're capable of attaining; and see 3:148, 158 about our abilities to sanctify God's name in the world.

2. See the very last paragraph of section three to this introduction that harkens back to that idea.

making mistakes, which need to be corrected. As a consequence the modern Jew is put off by so much of Musar literature that speaks of dark and ugly things like "sin," "retribution," "punishment," "vengeance," and the like. The reader would do well to take the love aspect of tshuvah into consideration when reading other Musar-related works as well.

Nonetheless, many, many people haven't any relationship whatsoever with God. And they can't even fathom the idea of fostering an *intimate* one with Him. They can't sense the urgency of such statements as, "Our souls await God" (Psalms 33:20), can't appreciate the restlessness and vulnerability expressed in, "We don't know what to do, for our eyes are fixed on You" (2 Chronicles 20:12). They certainly can't resonate with the High Love spoken of outright throughout "The Song of Songs," which the great Maimonides characterizes as a metaphor for that love.[3] And they know nothing of the reciprocal nature of that High Love.[4] So the realization that such a relationship isn't only possible but *suggested* is perhaps the reader's first task.

The reader's second task would be to grapple with Rabbeinu Yonah's seemingly "mixed message," if you will, about the nature of that relationship. Is it to be one of "fear," i.e., reserved, austere, and at a respectful, reverential distance; or one of love and adoration, intimacy, and inner passion?

Based on his prolific use of the terms, it would seem that Rabbeinu Yonah is referring to a relationship based on fear and dread.[5] But clear and unambiguous mention is made of the love of, and deep devotion to God, too.[6] So what are we to think?[7]

In response we'd point out that Rabbeinu Yonah most especially seems to be referring to fearing God outright. After all, he declares that we're to purify ourselves to the point where our sins are so forgiven that it's as if they'd never been committed in the first place.[8] And that alludes to doing tshuvah

---

3. See *Hilchot Tshuvah* 10:3.

4. See the statement in 1:12 that God "created you outright as an act of tenderness, takes you by the hand at all times, and watches over you moment by moment" as an allusion to that reciprocal lover-interest. And see, "He bountifully loves your returning to Him" (2:2), as well as our first and second notes to 1:1. Also see *Nepesh HaChaim* 1:8 (end).

5. See 1:4,10,11,17, 49; 3:7.

6. See 1:1; 2:22, 28; 3:17, 34, 191 (end).

7. We ourselves have gone to some pain to clarify these two concepts. See note 26 to 1:4; note 9 to 1:10; note 4 to 1:21; note 13 to 1:11; note 1 to 1:12; note 21 to 1:42. And see our many, many references to God as "The Beloved."

8. See 1:9, and especially 1:42.

out of the rank fear of God.[9] Yet Rabbeinu Yonah tells us that doing tshuvah will bring us to the love of Him, too.[10] So, what is his point?

We can clear that all up by pointing out that there are actually *two* sorts of "fear" of God— lower and higher. The lower sort is based on a fear of the harm that God can do you if you displease Him, and it's a rather primitive sort of fear at that. While higher "fear" is based on awe and thunder-struck reverence for Him[11]—*and is actually even greater than the love of Him!* Hence, Rabbeinu Yonah is referring to the latter sort of "fear."[12]

The reader's third task is then to find out exactly how to do tshuvah, and thus foster such a relationship to God. Rabbeinu Yonah begins the laying down and spelling out of the principles of tshuvah from 1:10 to the end of the first gate.

It should be noted at the outset that Rabbeinu Yonah says outright in 1:19 that "There are actually three essential principles of tshuvah—remorse, confession, and ridding yourself of the sin." And that "remorse and confession

---

9. See *Yomah* 86B where it's written, "Resh Lakish said: Tshuvah is great, for thanks to it, purposeful sins are considered accidental sins (i.e., as if they hadn't really been committed) . . . But Resh Lakish said that tshuvah is so great that purposeful sins are considered (like) merits! . . . That's not a contradiction: (The latter) refers to (tshuvah) done in love, and the (former refers) to (tshuvah) done in fear."

10. See 1:1.

11. See Ch.'s. 4 (near end) and 24 of *The Path of the Just*, and Maimonides' *Hilchot Tshuvah*. 10:1−2 and *Yesodei HaTorah* 2:1−2, 4:12.

12. One indication of that lies in the fact that in another work, *The Book of Fear*, Rabbeinu Yonah offers his plan of what we're to do daily, in our Divine service. And he makes his suggestions in *ascending* order of importance. Significantly, he places taking the love of God upon yourself before the fear of Him. (In fact, in his commentary there, the *M'kor HaYirah* equates the form of fear Rabbeinu Yonah speaks of there with *d'vekut*, which alludes to adhesion onto God in a mystical sense.)

Needless to say, the fact that the work itself is called *The Book of Fear* rather than *The Book of Love* underscores the significance of the fear of God.

It's also important to note that it's written in 2:28 that, "Time is getting shorter, yet there's a lot of work to do—work on Torah, on self-improvement and on achieving personal qualities like *love, fear* and *devotion* to God," where fear once again follows love, and is right before devotion, the Hebrew for which is the aforementioned *d'vekut*. (We've translated it "devotion" for clarity of understanding, and for simplicity's sake. See note 58 to 3:17.)

It's interesting to note that the first Slonomer Rebbe illustrated how fear can in fact be rooted in love—when you love someone so much that you wouldn't dare do anything to offend him for fear that you might threaten your relationship to him (*Yesod HaAvodah*, cited in the third chapter of the introduction to the first volume of *Netivot Shalom*).

are incorporated in 'admission.'" So, there could be said to be *two* fundamental principles of tshuvah. Nonetheless what this section does is disclose the elements of *full* tshuvah—full reconciliation with the Beloved after sin and separation.

The principles don't necessarily follow in order,[13] and they're to be taken on as befitting and needed. They're to be ingested slowly and at intervals; then set down for a time before being partaken of again, in order to be digested well.[14] It's also important to realize that these principles are both prods to tshuvah, as well as marks of the depths of your tshuvah, and indexes of how much further you'd have to go.[15]

Nonetheless, each component of each principle is meant to pierce and petition the sinner's core. To challenge his or her will and love. For at the point of sin the individual stands at a nexus of choices, and can embrace either sin and separation, or reconciliation and the high fear and adhesion that is tshuvah. Practice these principles and you allow for that reconciliation. Know as well that, "The sensible, with eyes open wide, would take this all to heart and internalize it" (1:12).[16]

The end of the gate (1:51–52) then addresses the twenty-four traits that may hinder tshuvah when carried out irresponsibly and stubbornly, but which nonetheless never preclude it.

3.

While the first gate was concerned with expounding on and defining tshuvah, the second is concerned with what it is that would inspire us to do it, as well as with what's to follow tshuvah.

Rabbeinu Yonah says in 2:1 that there are "six instances in which a person can be moved to do tshuvah." And he goes on to cite and explicate them in the course of this gate. But Rabbeinu Yonah is quick to point out in the first section, though, that it's eminently important, "to do tshuvah every day and to purify yourself . . . whether you sense anything inspiring you to or not." That is, on your own. For, "It would be known . . . that your tshuvah came from within"—that is, that it was heartfelt and genuine—"if you're not impelled by one of these (external) instances, which move people to

---

13. See Supplementary Note to 1:40.

14. See Supplementary Note to 1:17.

15. See Supplementary Note to 1:29. And see our comments at the beginning of section 6 below, as well.

16. See our comments about the seeming rigorousness and other-worldliness of the principles in section 6 of this Introduction, below.

tshuvah, but are drawn to it of your own volition." He then offers how to do that in 2:26, advising you to build upon the words of criticism offered in these six instances, and "take them to heart, think about them all the time, expand upon them yourself, say things about them that come from your own heart, meditate upon them in the depths of your soul . . ." (See 2:26).

And the gate ends with an analysis of what Rabbeinu Yonah refers to as a "venerable dictum," Hillel's famous statement that, "If I am not for myself, who will be? But when I alone am for myself, what am I? And if not now, when?" (*Pirke Avot* 1:14). That analysis turns upon the ideas that it's not enough to be motivated by others, you're to come to tshuvah on your own (as indicated above), and do it as quickly as possible, for there are always a lot of impediments.

One of the book's most important points is brought up in 2:28.[17] As we indicate in our note there, it's that the goal of tshuvah is not merely to rescind wrong and return to a spiritual status quo. Its goal is to allow us to rescind that wrong *in order to go on from there to spiritual excellence, and further and deeper intimacy with the Beloved.*

4.

The third is the largest of the four gates, and has been said to be a book unto itself. It addresses the importance of knowing just how consequential each sin is, in order to be appalled and unsettled enough by it not to commit it. And in order to realize how important it is to do tshuvah if you *have* committed it. As such, the gate serves as what we in modernity would see as something of a "warning label" on the "side" of each sin.

The themes and issues raised here are themselves a revelation to the modern mind. For we're ordinarily insensitive to the problems cited herein, and unaware of the very real worldly and/or spiritual ramifications and consequences of being guilty of them. Hence, it's essential for us to identify our own actions within these off-deeds, and catch ourselves among the wrongdoers when that's applicable. So that we, too, might be motivated to do tshuvah for our errors, and re-establish our relationship to God.

It should be noted that while this gate serves as an amalgam of the *mitzvot* Rabbeinu Yonah indicated his generation is lax in (see 3:2, 23, and 26), which our generation is apparently lax in as well, it's still more than that. For we'll have accomplished nothing if we just understand and acknowledge what's said here. Instead, we're to be moved to live the righteous life Rabbeinu

---

17. See note 2.

Yonah advocates here; and to recognize how far our inclinations are from the elements of full goodness expressed here, be stunned by that fact, and try to rectify ourselves.

That's to say, we're to see the motifs cited here as "flash points," if you will—as allusions to the issues that tend to separate us specifically from God. And to use that information as a means of drawing closer to Him than we'd been before. And the gate as a whole should be seen as a plea for exquisite sensitivity toward the other.

Aside from the points mentioned, the reader will also discover many captivating spiritual and philosophical byways peppered throughout the gate.

Perhaps the most telling statement of all, though, is made at the very end of this gate, at 3:231. Rabbeinu Yonah warns us there are never to be inveterate faultfinders, people who "always complain, grumble about, and find fault in others' deeds and words, even when the other person is perfectly innocent, and does . . . no harm," who "see everything as wrong rather than right, and all mistakes as intentional sins."[18] Perhaps what Rabbeinu Yonah is saying is that while we're certainly to be on the lookout for sin and wrongdoing, and to purge ourselves and others of it, we're nonetheless obliged to be even-handed and fair about it. And to judge others—and ourselves— equitably.

5.

Rabbeinu Yonah draws our attention to the fourth and last gate at several points in the first one, because the two gates are linked.[19] For while that first gate instructs us in the art of tshuvah,[20] the fourth directs our attention to what we'd have to do if we were guilty of offenses that tshuvah alone couldn't eradicate. Hence, Rabbeinu Yonah begins this gate by likening sin and faults to illness and disease, and then speaks of the "bitter pill" a *seriously* ill patient would have to take in order to be healed.

Essentially, though, the import of this gate is this: tshuvah is certainly the "way to rise above our destructive acts, to avoid the traps we set by our acts of defiance, to ward off personal devastation, and to deflect His anger," as well as the best means of "return(ing) to Him" (1:1). But sometimes a person needs to scrub long and hard to remove a stain imbedded in his being;[21] oftentimes

---

18. See the end of 3:177 as well.

19. See 1:46, 47, 48, 51.

20. . . . the second persuades us in it, and the third informs of just what we'd have to do tshuvah for...

21. See 1:9.

there are hindrances to tshuvah;[22] and there are even instances in which tshuvah alone simply won't lead to full atonement.

Nonetheless, Rabbeinu Yonah is quick to illustrate in this gate that just as God "never closes the doors to tshuvah to us, even when we're very defiant and rebellious, and utterly unfaithful" (1:1), He also never closes the door to atonement. And he chooses to conclude this most remarkable book with just such a message, in this last gate, in order to continue enlightening us about all the great "favors God has done for us" (1:1). For that is indeed the dominant point.

6.

Some concluding words. As to the seeming rigorousness and other-worldliness of the twenty principles of tshuvah enunciated in the first gate, we'd say the following. It might seem rather extreme to have to experience such dire and intense emotions when doing tshuvah. But the truth is, if we were faced with the consequences of a personal or financial loss that affected us deeply (God forbid), we'd certainly experience remorse, sadness, anguish, worry, shame, and more. And we'd consider that perfectly "normal." The point is that if we took God and our relationship to Him seriously, we'd suffer just as deeply when faced with the "loss" of Him in our lives as we would facing other terrible losses.[23]

The other point to be made about that is that such emotions should be understood to be one corner in the heart of an individual who is otherwise chock-full of a *joie de vivre*, as well as a full, deep, and healthy sense of self and purpose. To say nothing of the aforementioned closeness to God Almighty.

Rabbeinu Yonah's proddings toward nobility, his underlying message of hope and great grace, shouldn't go unnoticed either.[24] Nor should his warnings of the sad but undeniable near-inevitability of sin even in the best of

---

22. See 1:51–52.

23. See 1:12, "For if you'd find it hard losing a small amount of money, and you'd mourn and moan deeply and bitterly losing your whole fortune catastrophically; and if you'd be hopelessly wounded over many and serious troubles, and you'd express sorrow for them day after day—you should all the more so be troubled and moan for having rebelled against God." And see note 51 to 2:20.

We later found this approach corroborated in Rabbi Zohn's *Pirkei Tshuvah*, Ch. 3, p. 20.

24. See 1:28 (at end); note 21 to 1:42; note 13 to 1:38; note 14 to 1:45; note 18 to 2:11; note 3 to 2:13; note 18 to 2:28; note 60 to 3:17; and 3:73 (at end).

human hearts.[25] Because seen in the right light, those warnings can be understood as a calming reassurance that "it happens to the best of us," but that tshuvah can undo those errors.

And with that in mind we would especially want to underscore Rabbeinu Yonah's deep and abiding convictions about the ever-availability of tshuvah,[26] and the great love God has for us which that evidences.

We've taken some liberties with the original text of *The Gates of Repentance*, as we did with our treatments of *The Path of the Just* and *The Duties of the Heart* (Aronson: 1996). We've used the second-person rather than the third-person case in most instances (i.e., saying *you* instead of *he, she,* or *they* in translation), in the belief that the author would've constructed his sentences that way had he written his work today. And unlike our other works, we've used contractions in this translation and its comments (*it's* rather than *it is, wouldn't* rather than *would not*, etc.), in an effort to make the work more approachable to the modern reader who does that automatically when reading anyway, and might have been slowed in his approach to the original if we hadn't used them.[27]

We also made use of several Hebrew editions and classical commentaries to the work, both for the text, and for external as well as internal citations and references. They include the edition offered by The Institute for the Dissemination of Torah and Musar; the anonymous *Biur,* the *Me'or HaShaar, Ohr HaTshuvah* (with its quotes from the holy Rav Yechezkel Levenstein, of blessed memory), and the *Shaarei Tshuvah Ha'Mephurash.*

The reader should be alerted to the fact that for reasons of clarity and ease of understanding, we've not included some few confusing sections of the original text (though we've always placed those missing sections in our notes at the bottom of that very page).[28]

We also feel it's important for the reader to follow the citations found in our Supplementary Notes of other places in the work where Rabbeinu Yonah speaks about the very same subject in other ways, in order to get a full flavor of his statements (as well as to get a deeper understanding of certain ideas, as expressed there). And that it's equally as important to refer to the

---

25. See 1:6, 17; 2:9; and 3:143, 149, 215; 4:21.

26. See 1:1, note 3 to 1:51; note 10 to 3:2; 3:17; note 46 to 4:21; and note 59 to 4:22.

27. But we haven't used contractions when we quoted from biblical, talmudic, or midrashic sources.

28. See note 23 to 1:4 for a full explanation and the first instance.

synopsis we've provided at the end of each gate in order to allow for a more sweeping, "global" view of that gate, and the entire work.

I offer heartfelt thanks to my mother, Mrs. S. Feldman, and to my mother- and father-in-law, Dr. and Mrs. S. Morris Goldberg, for all their love, encouragement, and support. And I extend my gratitude to Rabbi Betzion Kokis for his learned and sensitive suggestions, as well as his encouragement.

And I especially want to express my deepest gratitude and appreciation to my life partner and *zivug*, my dear wife, Sara. And wish us both many, many years of service to God Almighty and partnership in health and well-being. And great and holy *nachas* from Nechama, Aryeh, and Dina, our dear and much-loved children.

Gate One

AN EXPLANATION OF THE MITZVAH OF TSHUVAH

&02&02&02&02&02&02&02&02&02&02&02&02

   As we said in our own introduction above, these first nine sections of the first gate serve as an overall introduction to *The Gates of Repentance*. For it is here that Rabbeinu Yonah introduces the concept of tshuvah, adjures us to correct our errors, to avert retribution, to take advantage of the "escape hatch" that tshuvah provides us with as soon as possible, and to avoid falling into a spiritual rut of sorts by sinning again and again.

   But it is here, too, that Rabbeinu Yonah introduces us to that glorious theme that underscores the entire work—that tshuvah allows us to draw closer and closer to God, and to enter into a deeper and more committed relationship with Him as a consequence.

1. Among the favors God has done for us, His creations,[1] has been to provide us with a way to rise above our destructive acts, to avoid the traps we set by our acts of defiance, to ward off personal devastation, and to deflect His anger.[2] By kindly and justly teaching us how to return to Him,[3] and alerting us to do that when we sin against Him.[4] Because He knows our impulses.[5] And so it's said, "God is kind and just, so He teaches the way to sinners" (Psalms 25:8).

In fact, He never closes the doors to tshuvah to us,[6] even when we're very defiant and rebellious, and utterly unfaithful.[7] As it's said, "Return to Him whom the Children of Israel have profoundly revolted against" (Isaiah 31:6) and, "Return, unfaithful children, and I will heal your faithlessness" (Jeremiah 3:22).[8]

---

1. The original can quite literally be translated, "Among the good things God has done *with* us, His creations . . .," which would immediately usher us into the idea that tshuvah is a means of solidifying and deepening our's and God's mutual love.

2. A few very important points are being made here: First, that tshuvah is a favor, rather than a price to pay for our sins, as most think. Second, that it's "a way to rise above," to transcend our errors. Third, that it's a way for us "to avoid the traps" that *we ourselves* set. For we set traps for ourselves all the time, either purposefully or subliminally—banally or deeply. Fourth, that if we're capable of bringing full, serious, personal, existential devastation upon ourselves (God forbid!) as a consequence of our mistakes, we're obviously just as capable of drawing closer and closer to God Almighty, and clinging onto Him steadfastly through our goodness and our tshuvah—since it's only natural to have such a relationship, as it's written, "If you seek Him, you will find Him" (1 Chronicles 28:9). And fifth, that God is sometimes said to "get angry" at us, or better yet, to "be disappointed" in us, as a result of our moral failings—because He feels so close to us, and seems to have so much invested in us. But doing tshuvah averts that, restores God's "faith" in us, and reaffirms His sure and abiding love of us.

3. Hence tshuvah involves our returning to God.

4. What would *ever* move a person to sin against God and threaten his precious relationship with Him? In fact, what would ever move a person to threaten any precious, loving relationship? All in all, it's a person's cold and near-brutal "need" to have things his own way, and to assert self and self-serving demand. What tshuvah is, then, is the realization of that, and of its consequences. And a taking of a deep breath, blushing, and reconciling.

In fact, it's our contention, as we'll lay out in the course of the commentary, that we can learn a lot about restoring our relationship with God—that is, about doing tshuvah—from the process of restoring a wholesome, loving relationship to a loved one. Because every loving relationship is not only inherently precious, it's also meant to teach us how deeply we can love God. And each and every breach and consequent healing in that loving relationship is meant to teach us how to heal our relationship to God, which is tshuvah.

5. See Supplementary Notes.

6. See Supplementary Notes.

7. See Supplementary Notes.

8. This paragraph includes the first mention of tshuvah. Like "yetzer harah" (see our

The Torah often warns us to do tshuvah, and makes it clear that it's accepted[9] even when you do it in response to a lot of suffering,[10] though more so if you do it out of the fear or love of God.[11] As it's said, "When you suffer, and all these things befall you in the end of days, and you return to God your Lord, and listen to His voice . . ." (Deuteronomy 4:30).

And it's explained in the Torah that God helps those who do tshuvah and are otherwise restricted by their nature, by fostering a purity of spirit within them that enables them to love Him. For it's said, "You will return to God your Lord, and listen to His voice in accordance with all I have commanded you today, you and your children, with all your heart, and all your soul" (Ibid. 30:2). And it's said later on that "God will circumcise your heart, and the hearts of your children that you might love God your Lord with all your heart . . ." (Ibid. 30:6). That's to say, since you

---

first Supplementary Note), we've also not translated tshuvah (which is usually translated as "repentance," "penitence," "penance," and the like), because the English terms connote dire and stark acts of self-flagellation for serious, mortal, and barbarous acts of *evil*. As such, we wouldn't think it necessary to "do penance" for many of the apparently minor sins enunciated in the course of the book (see 3:14–15 below). We retained the title, *The Gates of Repentance*, though, because of its familiarity.

As indicated here, tshuvah is best translated as "returning"—returning to God, after having been either "defiant and rebellious, and utterly unfaithful" to Him, or after having disappointed Him on a smaller level, and not been sensitive to His presence, or to the needs our relationship with Him would place upon us. Hence the use of the verse, "Return to Him. . . ."

The fact that access to tshuvah is never denied us, as indicated here, gives us great comfort as well. It reminds us that God's way is to forgive, and to try once again to refresh the relationship between us—when we, too, want it refreshed.

9. By God.

10. See Supplementary Notes.

11. There are two ways of understanding this statement. One is in keeping with the tradition that each and every member of the Jewish Nation will return to God by the time of the Great Redemption. Some by inspired choice, "out of the fear or love of God" cited here. Others by dint of horrible circumstances (God forbid!), "in response to a lot of suffering."

On a less ominous level, though, it also comes to allow us our human frailties. And to say that while some may be moved to return to God and to do tshuvah on a very sublime level, others will only be brought to it in the face of calamity and rank fear. But all instances will help (see ¶9 above). That's very much the way some people are moved to reconcile a relationship with another person gone sour—either by a realization of the depth and importance of the relationship in the first place, or by a realization of the possibility of a rupture.

and your children didn't reach the level of loving Him "with all your heart and all your soul," God will circumcise your hearts in order to enable you to.[12]

In fact, the Books of the Prophets and the Writings so routinely speak about tshuvah that all of its principles are explained in them, as we'll show.

2. Know, however, that the consequences you'd have to suffer for your sins grow more and more serious the longer you postpone tshuvah.[13] Because you'd know you've brought resentment upon yourself, and that you had an escape hatch to run to, which is tshuvah. Yet you insisted on rebelling and doing wrong, when you had the wherewithal to walk away from the tumult. And you weren't afraid of the anger and outrage.[14] You'd be very, very wrong for doing that.[15]

Our sages compared that in Midrash *Kohelet* (7:15) to the situation of the

---

12. We're told here that the means God will use to nourish the heart-purity we'd need to love Him is referred to as a "circumcision" of the heart. What that implies is that our hearts are often covered over and sheathed. And that like eyes stopped shut that only need to have their covering lifted to see and be aware, our hearts only need their outer sheathing of blindness circumcised and removed for us to be sensitized to the real presence of God in the world. So, too, when it comes to our relationship to others: we need our hearts to be sensitized in those instances as well to be aware of love. And we can only come to both instances of sensitization through tshuvah.

13. We'll be using the expression "to suffer the consequences of our sins" for the Hebrew word עונש found here, which would ordinarily be translated as "punishment."

And that is part of the problem people would have with *The Gates of Repentance*—the "hellfire and brimstone" aspect it seems to flaunt. But perhaps the best representative explanation we have of the Torah perspective on "punishment" is the one offered by a near-contemporary of Rabbeinu Yonah, Rabbeinu Nissim (in *Drashot HaRan*, Tenth Discourse), who states that God doesn't have people experience punishments "for His own purposes" or to serve a need He might be perceived to have to "take revenge," and to hurt sinners, or get back at them. After all, He Himself forbade such behavior when He said, "Do not take revenge, or bear a grudge against your people" (Leviticus 19:18). Instead, His intentions are always to make us righteous, and to encourage us to do tshuvah.

And as to "punishment" in the afterlife, Rabbeinu Nissim continues, that's a natural outcome of having rebelled against God, much like the pain one would just naturally suffer had he torn a limb. For after all, there in the afterlife, one cannot improve, and no one else could learn from any "punishment" anyone would get there. It would then serve no end. So, again, it's just a natural outcome.

The other point to be made is that *everything* we do yields consequences, which we either suffer or enjoy. And that's all the more so true of everything we do in our relationships, where the consequences are often deeper and more heartfelt. (See Supplementary Notes.)

14. . . . you'd brought on.

15. Again, if we take sins to be things we do that vex and threaten our relationship

band of robbers sent to prison by the king, who all then dug an escape hatch and fled through it—except for one of them. When the jailkeeper came by and saw the escape hatch, and saw the one remaining prisoner, he began to club him with his stick and to say, "Imbecile! There's an escape hatch right in front of you, and yet you aren't rushing to save your own life!"[16]

3. But only the unlearned, who are "asleep" and inert, always oblivious,[17] and have neither the know-how nor the sense to quickly save themselves, would postpone tshuvah. Included among them, too, would be those so alienated from God that they don't believe there are consequences to sinning.

For as our sages said, "If you see a scholar sinning at night, give no thought to it by morning, because he actually already did tshuvah" (*Berachot* 19A).[18]

---

with God. And if we see them as akin to the silly or even deranged things we'd do or say that would likewise vex or threaten our relationship with a mortal loved one, then it's only reasonable to expect that we'd want to undo our error in short order, if only just to show God or that person how sorry we were for having done that. And it's also only logical that the longer we'd wait, the more trouble we'd be in—the more serious the consequences we'd have to suffer.

As Rabbeinu Yonah put it, "you'd know you've brought resentment upon yourself" by doing what you did—as soon as you came to your senses. And, "that you had an escape hatch to run to"—that is, that you could make amends easily enough. "Yet you insisted on rebelling and doing wrong" in all obstinacy. And you thus show you don't care—that "you weren't afraid of the anger and outrage" you yourself brought on. In fact, you *would* be, "very, very wrong for doing that." That is, you'd be making a serious mistake. So, you'd have to suffer the consequences of that, which boils down to a threat to your relationship.

16. It might be wondered why the cooperative, compliant prisoner is denigrated rather than the defiant ones who escaped. Isn't he better for having not tried to escape, and for obeying the rules? The point being made, though, is that God *wants* you to do tshuvah. Because He wants you not to suffer. I might think it would be good and pious of me to acquiesce to the punishment I have coming to me for what I did. But God says otherwise. He wants us to do tshuvah, and to go on from there. Much as someone who loves us would want us to draw close to them again, rather than to continue to pull away by avoiding them.

17. The original reads, "ולא ישיבו אל לבבם." That can more literally be translated as, "They don't return to their heart," which is a metaphor for tshuvah. Since tshuvah involves readdressing or revisiting the heart, coming to realizations, and acting upon them.

18. That's to say, only the oblivious or naive, and downright foolish, would procrastinate if a relationship they treasured was threatened. Because the price to pay would be too great. The wise react quickly.

4. Consider again how very wrong it is to postpone tshuvah. For if instead of vacillating in it you'd do tshuvah then and there, by sighing bitterly, trembling, worrying,[19] and crying sorrowfully[20] — then when your impulses would approach you a second time with sin in hand, you'd prevail over them by recalling the cup of bitterness that had already been passed to you, and you wouldn't[21] drink from it again. For it's said, "Tremble and do not sin" (Psalms 4:5), which is to say, tremble and be troubled by your sins, and you won't sin again.[22,23]

But if you postpone tshuvah, then when sin comes upon you again, you'll fall into its trap as you first did. This new sin would then be even greater, and your guilt would ascend before God Himself.[24] Because, while you didn't give thought to how quickly your yetzer harah[25] could consume you the first time; nonetheless this time, after seeing for yourself how weak you were, and how much more aggressive and stronger than you your impulses were, you should have realized how intractable you were being. And you should have gone about looking for advice on how to grow in

---

19. See Supplementary Notes.

20. See Supplementary Notes.

21. . . . want to . . .

22. If you took your tshuvah seriously, because it suddenly occurred to you that you were seriously threatening your relationship with God or a loved one, and you were, "sighing bitterly, trembling, worrying, and crying sorrowfully" as a result, you'd remember having experienced that later on. But better yet, you'd remember the heart-numbing and chilling sudden prospect of profound loss that would have set all that off in you — referred to here as "the cup of bitterness." For it was the latter that set off the sighing, trembling, etc. And you wouldn't want to do anything whatsoever to threaten that relationship again.

23. Oftentimes Rabbeinu Yonah will cite proofs for his particular use and understanding of certain terms from other or parallel instances of it. Those proofs will often be based on wordplays and points of grammar. They thus demand excessive interpolation and explanation, and can be an impediment to the English-speaking reader's appreciation of the work. We've thus decided to place those instances here, in our notes, so the reader will get the full text of *The Gates of Repentance* without being bogged down by wordy explanations. This is the first instance of that, and the text reads as follows (with our explanation in brackets):

> [We know this to be the meaning of "tremble" — i.e., that it implies that you're to tremble over sins you've already committed] since the Psalm cited their sin earlier on by saying, "How long will you . . . search for untruth?" (Psalms 4:3). And that's further confirmed by the use of the [same] term in "Do not tremble on the way" (Genesis 45:24) and "I tremble at my place" (Habbakuk 3:6), which refers to being troubled by something in the past or the present, as opposed to [use of the terms] "Be afraid" or "Be frightened" [which refers to being troubled by something that might happen in the future].

24. That is, you'd have offended God so, that if He were human we'd say that "He couldn't help but notice it."

25. Here we translate this as "your yetzer harah" rather than "your impulses." See our supplementary note to ¶1.

you[48] prevail over your impulses.[49] But, all acts of tshuvah help. As it's said, "You return man to the dust and say, 'Return, mankind!'" (Psalms 90:3), which our sages indicate means[50] until he is utterly obliterated[51] (J. T., *Chagigah* 2:1).

We will now explain the principles of tshuvah.

---

48. . . . nonetheless . . .

49. And the sin-patterns set out, discussed above, aren't quite so set and definitive as they can be in old age. (See Supplementary Notes.)

50. . . . one can do tshuvah . . .

51. . . . and returns "to the dust."

The Principles of Tshuvah

Herein begins the laying down and spelling out of the principles of tshuvah. They include:

1. **Expressing remorse** for having abandoned God and not having kept Him in mind, for having been callous to your body and soul, for having forsaken The World to Come, and for having degraded yourself (¶10).
2. **Ridding yourself of the sin** by resolving never to commit it again. But there are actually two phases to that. If you tend to lapse by impulsively succumbing to temptation, begin tshuvah by expressing remorse and augmenting your commitment to God. But if you always want to satisfy your cravings, begin tshuvah by first ridding yourself of the sin and determining never to commit it again. Then regret what you did and return to God (¶11).
3. **Being sad** and reiterating over and over again how wrong it was to have thwarted God. In fact, the more bitter-hearted and sad you are for having done that; the more you want to serve God; and the more you worry about your shortcomings in His service—the more effective will your tshuvah be (¶12–14).
4. **Manifesting anguish** by sighing and expressing bitterness and contrition for the sins instigated by your heart, and by weeping for the sins instigated by your eyes (¶15).
5. **Worrying** about your sins, and fearing their consequences. And about being lackadaisical in tshuvah's requisite anguish, bitterness, fasting, weeping, as well as in your overall service to God. Worry, too, about being overtaken again by your yetzer harah, about the harm you did to others, and about profaning God's name (¶16–20).
6. **Feeling ashamed** to sin in God's presence to the same degree you'd be to sin in the presence of others, by meditating upon God's greatness and recalling that He's always watching over you, examining your innermost being, and scrutinizing your thoughts (¶21–22).
7. **Surrendering wholeheartedly and being humble** in order to express your awareness of God and your realization of how base anyone who sins against him actually is, in order to please Him, and to rid yourself of traits that lead to sin. By augmenting your service to God and taking no credit for it, serving Him demurely and in private, and by avoiding arrogance and anger (¶23–28).

8. **Manifesting surrender** by responding gently, being indifferent to attractive clothing and ornaments, and lowering your eyes, all of which will remind you to be humble (¶29).

9. **Overcoming your physical cravings** (even those for permitted things) by eating to stay healthy, and being intimate to procreate and fulfill your obligations to your spouse, which will prove how well-meaning your intent to do tshuvah really was, and how true a "disciple of Abraham" you really are (¶30–34).

10. **Correcting your actions through the agent used to sin** by using the very one used to sin to do *mitzvot* with instead. By always keeping your eyes lowered if you've stared pruriently, for example; by studying Torah if you've slandered, etc. (¶35).

11. **Scrutinizing your ways** in order to remember what to confess to, to realize how many sins you committed and thus come to true humility, and in order to set up safeguards against "relapse" (¶36).

12. **Examining, knowing, and recognizing the seriousness of each sin,** for by doing that you'll come to realize how serious each one is, and will thus be moved to tears, be humbled, and fear sinning (¶37).

13. **Taking your minor sins seriously** and worrying about not fulfilling a mitzvah, in order to concentrate upon the greatness of Him who warned you not to sin because minor sins easily add up to the equivalent of serious ones, in order not to repeat them, and in order to conquer your yetzer harah (¶38–39).

14. **Confessing** to and articulating your ancestors' sins, besides your own, since you'd be punished for those, too, if you followed in your ancestors' ways (¶40).

15. **Praying** to God for mercy, for all your sins to be forgiven, for your good deeds to no longer be overlaid by sin, for Him to be as pleased with you now as He was before you sinned, and for help in tshuvah itself (¶41–43).

16. **Amending your misdeeds as much as possible** before you confess to God, by returning what you stole from anyone, or asking one you oppressed, shamed, or slandered to forgive you, after which God will then forgive you (¶44–46).

17. **Expressing kindness and truth** to avoid the tribulations that would come your way for having committed certain sins, and to undo your profanation of God's name. For while God won't be "bribed" by acts of kindness and the like, His anger will nonetheless be mollified by them (¶47).

18. **Keeping your sin before you all the time** by remembering them to the day you die (¶48).

19. **Shunning a sin when faced with it and still fully craving it** and fully capable of committing it again, out of the fear of God, is the highest form of tshuvah. But if you're never faced with such a situation head on, you'd have achieved full tshuvah, nonetheless, by having grown so much in the fear of God that He knows you would have resisted it (¶49).

20. **Turning others away from sin as much as you can,** that is, not only doing

tshuvah yourself, but bringing others to tshuvah by criticizing them when they sin (¶50).

The end of the gate (¶51–52) addresses the twenty-four traits that may hinder tshuvah when carried out irresponsibly and stubbornly, but which nonetheless never preclude it.

Chapter One

10. First Principle: Expressing Remorse

Realize how bitterly wrong it was of you to have abandoned God.[1] And impress upon your heart the fact that there are consequences to be suffered for sins, as well as retribution and amends to be made.[2] And so it's said, "Retribution and amends belong to Me" (Deuteronomy 32:35) and, "Fear the sword, for[3] wrath brings on the punishment of the sword" (Job 19:29).

Regret your wrongdoings and say to yourself, "What have I done? How could I not have feared God outright, or been frightened by all His criticisms of sin, or by all the serious rulings brought against the guilty, who suffer so?[4]

---

1. See our second note to ¶ 11.

2. What this means to set off is a quick and cold realization of some basic truths: First, that you've abandoned and foresaken God outright by toying with things that estrange you from Him. Two, that there are consequences to that, as would only be expected. And three, that you'd now have to enrich and renew your trustworthiness to Him.

Arriving at such realizations requires sophistication and acumen, and would be beyond the abilities of the ignorant spoken of in ¶3. Those who are "alienated from God," and hence without the necessary sophistication built on spiritual insight. Those who "don't believe there are consequences to sinning," and thus haven't the acumen to realize that *everything* either done, said, or thought has its consequences.

3. . . . God's . . .

4. So the first step to tshuvah is taking yourself seriously, and stepping back and taking a look at yourself from a critical distance.

We all ask and say things like, "What have I done?," "How could I've been such a fool?," "I can't believe I actually . . . ," "What I wouldn't do to go back to that moment, and . . . ," "If only I knew then what I know now," "I only wish someone had told me . . . ," "I don't know what came over me," "I should have known better," etc., when we

"For the sake of a moment's satisfaction, I was callous and merciless to my body by not seeing to its being protected from ruin. I was like the thief who robbed and assaulted, then ate a meal, knowing full well that when he'd be finished eating and drinking, a judge would order his teeth smashed! As it's said, 'The bread of guile is sweet to a man, but his mouth will be filled with gravel afterwards!' (Proverbs 20:17).

"Worse than that, I've been cruel to my precious soul, which has become contaminated by the effects of my impulses. For what use would all its accomplishments be if it were guilty in the eyes of its Master?[5]

"How could I have exchanged an everlasting world for an ever-changing one? And how could I have become so animal-like by following my impulses like a dim-witted horse or mule, and strayed so from the path of reason?

"For the Creator breathed a living soul into my nostrils, with a wise heart and good sense[6] with which to be conscious of God and fear Him, and to reign over my body and all its effects the way it would reign over any other base creature, as I was created to do[7] (for God honors those He holds most precious that way[8]). So, if I was created to do that, and I'm doing just the opposite, what point is there in my living? As it's written, 'The man who strays from the path of reason will abide in the assembly of the dead' (Proverbs 21:16)![9]

"Not only that, but I haven't even lived up to the tenets of the animals and am even more abase than they. For while 'An ox knows its owner and a donkey knows its master's stall' (Isaiah 1:3), I neither know nor have ever considered.[10]

---

make mistakes that have serious consequences. The most vital point to be made here, again, is that we blunder when we sin. And that it has broad implications for our well-being. The second-most vital point is that we need to realize that.

5. See Supplementary Notes.

6. See Supplementary Notes.

7. See Supplementary Notes.

8. i.e., by giving them that ability.

9. What we have here is nothing less than a statement outright of what's expected of us in life, and what we're capable of. We're "to be conscious of God" and "to fear Him," which is to say, to foster a deep and vital relationship with Him, which we're to dwell on at all times. And we're to "reign over [our] body and all its effects the way [we] would reign over any other base creature," which is to say, we're to master our passions, and be the overarching overseer of our every move and deed.

The two actually go hand in hand. For it's only by becoming the overseer of our movements and deeds that we can realize that God Almighty is the overarching Overseer of the universe. For man is known as a "miniature universe." When our souls are in control of that miniature universe, we're reminded of the ways of Him who controls the great universe. And being reminded of that by being lesser exemplars of it enables us to "be conscious of God and fear Him," as well as to live up to the injunction to "go in His ways" (Deuteronomy 28:9), which Rabbeinu Yonah cites in 3:17, 36.

10. . . . either.

"I've absolved myself from my Master's service, sampled nectar without thought of the consequences, robbed and assaulted, and trampled upon the poor. And I haven't confronted the day of death,[11] when the only thing left behind beside my soul will be my corpse, and dust."

Jeremiah referred to what we just illustrated when he said, "No man regretted his wrongdoing enough to say, 'What have I done?'" (Jeremiah 8:6).

---

11. See Supplementary Notes.

Chapter Two

11. Second Principle: Ridding Yourself of the Sin

Rid yourself of your wrongful ways and wholeheartedly resolve never to act that way again,[1] or to ever commit a particular sin again.[2] As it's said, "Turn, turn away from your wrongful ways" (Ezekiel 33:11).

Understand that when you sin unwittingly, it's because you craved something, your impulses intensified and overwhelmed you, and your thoughts and feelings couldn't combat such an onslaught by quickly admonishing the ocean of cravings and drying it up. Your impulses fooled you, you fell into their trap for the moment, and you were ravaged by the winds of the yetzer harah.[3] It's not as if you wanted to transgress, or had it in mind to ever do that again.[4]

The first thing to do for tshuvah in such an instance is suffer remorse. And to

---

1. See Supplementary Notes.

2. The Hebrew term for "getting rid of" used here in relation to sins, and "abandoning" used in ¶10, in relation to God, is the same, עזיבה. The underlying implication is that it's a choice between God and your sin, in many, many instances. Hold onto your sins, and you'll have abandoned God; let go of them, and you'll have attached yourself onto Him.

3. This could also be translated as, "you were ravaged by the *spirit* (רוח) of the yetzer harah." What's the spirit of the yetzer harah? The extolling of physical satisfaction over spiritual satisfaction. The yetzer harah harasses us with the idea that if we do without a particular worldly delight we'll deny ourselves pleasure, and we'll get nothing in return for it, because spiritual satisfaction is questionable at best. So why not indulge, it reasons. Sadly, we succumb to that because one of our greatest misgivings is that we might be doing something for no good reason. But that's as if to say that it would do you no good to be in love and have a full and sincere relationship. Because true love is "questionable at best" or meaningless, while petty affectations are all one can ever hope for.

4. The actual physical experience of sinning impulsively, as Rabbeinu Yonah depicts it

grow sorrowful, spirit-laden, and as bitter[5] as gall for having sinned. Then you're to instill more and more of the fear of God within you each day, and place the dread of God in your heart at all times,[6] until your heart is surely and securely with Him.

Then, if your yetzer harah continues to confront you and goad you on again and again, and your cravings grow as they did originally, you won't be seduced by them, and would have rid yourself of your former ways. For as it's said, "Whoever admits[7] and rids himself[8] will be shown mercy" (Proverbs 28:13), where "admits" is mentioned first because it refers to remorse and confession, and is followed by ridding yourself of them.[9]

But if you're entrenched in a path that isn't good, and you sin again and again, you repeat your transgressions daily, you return to them energetically over and over again, love doing wrong all along, and purposefully set the pitfalls to sins—cravings and your yetzer harah—before you. And all you want and aspire to is that nothing you'd ever think of doing be denied you.[10] Then the first thing to do for tshuvah in that instance is to abandon such a path and such wrongful thoughts. And agree to take upon yourself not to sin again.[11]

And then you're to regret what you did that was so corrupt, confess, and return to God.[12] As it's said, "Let the wrongdoer abandon his ways, and the sinful man his thoughts; and let him return to God, who will pity him" (Isaiah 55:7).

---

here, involves your being suddenly "fooled" and quickly "ravaged" by an "onslaught" and "ocean of cravings," as you're swept along by "the winds of the yetzer harah," which suddenly intensifies and overwhelms you. And which you can neither "combat" nor "dry up" either intellectually or emotionally. This is obviously a very hurried, unforeseen, and furious wave of events out of your control at the moment.

5. See Supplementary Notes.

6. "Dread" would imply taking something very, very seriously, and making every effort to ensure that the individual or thing taken so seriously is satisfied and not displeased.

7. . . . to his sins . . .

8. . . . of them . . .

9. Rabbeinu Yonah is explaining that an instant immersion into remorse (¶10) isn't always right. For if you were an entrenched sinner, you'd have another route to follow, as we'll soon see. But if you're the kind of person who sins unwittingly, spoken of here, you'd be expected to experience remorse right off, followed by sorrow, woe, and grief. And those would be natural reactions to what had just happened. What you'd have to do to never suffer such remorse, sorrow, etc., *again* is "instill more and more of the fear of God within you each day, and place the dread of God in your heart at all times." Because if you don't, you yourself will become the sort of inveterate sinner soon to be discussed. And you'd have to follow *that* route.

10. We'd call the kind of person whose every want and aspiration in the world is that he get whatever he wants, a "spoiled brat." And in a very true sense that's exactly what an irascible sinner is.

11. See Supplementary Notes.

12. For the first thing an inveterate sinner must learn to do is drop the sin pattern he'd fallen into, addressed in ¶5. For only then can he be expected to know true, heartfelt remorse, which leads to confession and a full emotional recommitment to the Beloved.

It's like the situation of the individual who was holding onto a reptile while he immersed[13] to purify himself, who'd indeed purify himself if he'd drop the reptile right away and then immerse. But who'd remain impure, and would immerse in vain, as long as he held onto the reptile and immersed.[14] Ridding yourself of the thought of sin is[15] dropping the reptile. And regretting your sin, confessing, and praying, stand for immersing yourself.

If you then find yourself being tried and made to suffer when you're doing wrong and thinking about nothing but sinning and sinning, first be admonished, do tshuvah for your bad idea, and stop what you're doing. And you'd be like a calf whose herder had struck him with his rod to keep him in line. That is, accept the admonishment in order to abandon the ways of death, and head onto the straight path when you're entrenched in a path that isn't good.[16] As it's said, "I have surely heard Ephraim groaning; 'You have admonished me, and I was admonished like an untrained calf'" (Jeremiah 31:17), which is followed by, "Afterwards I returned, I regretted" (Ibid. v. 18). That means to say that after you admonished me and I accepted the admonishment, and did tshuvah for my wrongful ways, I then regretted and had remorse for my past transgressions.

That now explains everything we set out to explain.[17]

---

13. . . . in a *mikveh* (ritual immersion bath) . . .

14. See Supplementary Notes.

15. . . . analogous to . . .

16. That's to say, if you're the sort of bred-in-the-bone sinner spoken of, and you notice yourself wracked with pain and vexed by troubles, don't assume that's just a coincidence. For you'd be one of those, spoken of in ¶3, who are "so alienated from God that they don't believe there are consequences to sinning." Take quick stock, realize something is wrong for a reason, and live a Godly life.

17. . . . about the relationship between feeling remorseful and abandoning sin.

Chapter Three

ᘓᘓᘓᘓᘓᘓᘓᘓᘓᘓᘓᘓ

12. Third Principle: Being Sad

Impress upon yourself just how very wrong it was to have rebelled against your Creator. Then grow heart-sad,[1] let a storm brew in your mind, and moan bitterly.[2] Because it's possible to have remorse and to acknowledge how wrong you were to sin, and yet not make the sort of amends you'd have to.[3]

For if you'd find it hard losing a small amount of money; if you'd mourn and moan deeply and bitterly losing your whole fortune catastrophically; and if you'd be hopelessly wounded over many and serious troubles, and you'd express sorrow for them day after day—you should all the more so be troubled and moan for having rebelled against God[4] by having acted so depravedly and abhorrently, and not remembering that He created you outright as an act of tenderness, takes you by the hand at all times, and watches over you moment by moment.[5] How could you have

---

1. It should be pointed out that it isn't mere dolor we're talking about here. The sadness spoken of here alludes to a sorry "wistfulness" and "homesickness" of the soul for familiarity with the Beloved once again. And it's rooted in spiritual delight and joy. In the longed-for fulfillment of the verse, "We will rejoice and gladden in His salvation" (Isaiah 25:9), i.e., in His closeness. As opposed to the usual sort of sadness, which is sometimes rooted in missed chances to fulfill fantasies, or in Godlessness.

2. See Supplementary Notes.

3. To use our ongoing analogy, your beloved would likely forgive you if you expressed remorse for your hurtful ways, stated outright that what you did was wrong, and thus conceded your guilt. And you stopped acting that way and promised never to again. But you'd have to experience far more growth and change utterly in order to grow closer to your beloved—which is the thrust of full, out-and-out reconciliation.

4. . . . . and threatened your relationship to Him. (See Translator's Introduction for reference to this statement.)

5. We reject it, but it's true: there was never a burning need for any one of us to have been created. And the world could very easily have done without us, as it eventually will. As

been so self-absorbed to have angered Him?[6] And how could you not have seen clearly enough to understand?

The sensible, with eyes open wide, would take this all to heart and internalize it.

13. In fact, the bitterer and sadder you feel, the more effective and profound will be your tshuvah.[7] Because your tshuvah would be the result of the refinement of your soul, and the purifying of your mind. And because[8] a lot of serious, sorrowful thinking about your many sins depends on the quality of your mind, and upon your opening your eyes to your many sins.[9]

Thus it's said, "For I will not argue forever, nor will I always be so angry that the spirit and the souls I made would faint before Me" (Isaiah 57:16), meaning, "I will no longer argue or be angry when the spirit, which is before Me and so sublime, faints and is pained, and when the souls I Myself made, faint. For how could I not feel for and have mercy on the precious spirit before Me, or the souls I Myself made?"[10]

As such, the harder you work at sighing about it, the less significant your sin then becomes. Because sorrow originates in a refined, sublime soul, which makes itself more favorable with sighing than with a lot of physical torment and pain. For a king would have more compassion on a disciple born in his own household, who was close to him and a well-respected nobleman,[11] than he would on lesser, more distant subjects.[12] And he would show him more mercy.[13]

---

such, our having been created is a gift outright rather than an expectation fulfilled, or a right. Hence, everything we have and actually are is from God, and continues to be from Him. And though it so humbles us as people to do so (which is exactly the point!) it behooves us to acknowledge our rank and brutish, absolute dependence upon Him. Yet, we resist that, and hold very high opinions of ourselves, think ourselves imperative, and believe we have every right to do whatever we care to. Therein lies the root of sin.

6. See Supplementary Notes.

7. See Supplementary Notes.

8. . . . the ability to do . . .

9. That's to say, the more seriously you take your relationship, the deeper will be your shock and abhorrence for the fact that you actually did something—and something petty at that!—to threaten it. And the longer will you sit stunned, amazed, and bereaved by the fact that the relationship is now imperiled. For only such a realization will lead to the degree of change and growth called for in tshuvah. Such rumination and resolve hurts very much, and undoes a person. But that, too, is the point. Because the individual who will come out the other side after having gone through it will have refined his soul and purified his mind, as is enunciated here.

So, a stark realization of our utter dependence upon God, as indicated above, followed by another stark realization of this threat to our connection to Him should truly lead to profound change.

10. See Supplementary Notes.

11. i.e., a refined soul.

12. i.e., tormented and pained bodies.

14. As King David put it, "My craving is fully before You, God, and my sighing is not concealed from You" (Psalms 38:10). That is, "As You know, the only thing I long to do is serve You.[14] And my sighs have nothing to do with worldly or ephemeral things, but rather with my sins and my shortcomings in Your service."[15] As a supplicant once put it so pointedly, "Since I sigh in fear of You, remove[16] sighs from me; and since I worry about my shortcomings in Your service, remove[17] worries from me."

---

13. The text continues as follows:

Because both the body and everything else is His handiwork, the verse refers to "the souls I Myself made," in order to equate the soul more precisely with the Celestial Beings. As such, it's like the statement, "The tablets were God's handiwork" (Exodus 32:16). [That is, like the tablets upon which the Ten Commandments were written, the soul is unique and stellar, too.] And because our sages said that, "Three partners join in the making of man—his father, his mother, and God" (*Niddah* 31A), though the father and mother play no part in the creation of the soul, it's therefore also said, "the souls that I Myself made," alluding to the expression, "the spirit which is before Me," which means what we said above.

14. See Supplementary Notes.

15. The righteous are far more autonomous and fully free than we. We crave untold millions of things that we're beholden to for our happiness, while they crave one thing alone. We moan and sigh woefully, with the intangible feeling we've been cheated, for untold numbers of reasons, and they sigh for things they can make amends for.

16. . . . all other . . .

17. . . . all other . . .

Chapter Four

⚣⚣⚣⚣⚣⚣⚣⚣⚣⚣⚣⚣⚣

15. Fourth Principle: Manifesting Anguish

It's said, "'Even now,' says God, 'Return to Me with all your heart, by fasting, weeping, and mourning'" (Joel 2:12); our sages said, "The heart and eyes are both agitators of sin" (J. T., *Berachot* 1:5); and it's written, "Do not go about after your own heart and eyes" (Numbers 15:39).[1] Hence the sins your heart and eyes bring on are forgiven when those agitators are used for tshuvah[2] rather than for further descent.[3]

Accordingly, your sins of the heart would be forgiven through the heartbreak that bitterness and sighing bring on. As it's written, "The spirit will faint before Me" (Isaiah 57:16) and, "You would not disdain a broken and contrite heart, God" (Psalms 51:19). And you'd then be like a defiled vessel that becomes pure when broken, as it's said, "An oven and ranges for pots should be broken" (Leviticus 11:35).[4]

---

1. See Supplementary Notes.

2. See Supplementary Notes

3. The logical sequence here is as follows: You best demonstrate tshuvah through concrete action. And since your heart and eyes foment sin, it follows that you're to use them as tools to manifest tshuvah, measure for measure.

4. In it's entirety, the verse reads, "Everything on which any part of their carcass falls shall be unclean. . . ." That is, when even part of a carcass, which is inherently defiled and spiritually unclean, falls onto something, "whether it is an oven, or ranges for pots," they then become defiled and "should be broken" to undo their defilement. And so analogously, you too should be "broken"—broken-hearted—when you become defiled, to be purified.

And your sins of the eyes would be forgiven through tears.[5] As such it's said, "Rivers of water stream down my eyes, because they do not keep Your Torah" (Psalms 119:136).[6]

---

5. Why are sins of the heart forgiven through "the heartbreak that bitterness and sighing bring on," which seem so onerous, while the sins of the eyes are "forgiven through tears" alone? Because the heart touches upon the very core, so it requires bitterness, sighing, etc., when it sins, which induce an existential shift. While the eyes only touch the surface, so they merely need to be awash in tears when they sin, to undo their illusions.

6. The text continues with:

Rather than say, "because I do not keep Your Torah," it says, "because *they* do not" instead. Since they incited the sin. And that is why "rivers of water stream down."

Chapter Five

੶੬੭੩੬੭੩੬੭੩੬੭੩੬੭੩੬੭੩੬੭੩੬੭੩੬੭੩੬੭੩੬੭੩

16. Fifth Principle: Worrying

Worry about your sins and fear their consequences.[1] Because sometimes atonement is held in abeyance, despite tshuvah, and only tribulations will purge.[2] As it's said, "For I will tell of my transgression; I will worry about my sin" (Psalms 38:19). And while sorrow[3] touches upon the past, worry touches upon the future.

You should also worry about being negligent in the sort of anguish and embitterment over your sins, and fasting and weeping for them that tshuvah would require. For while you might very well have anguished and cried a lot over them, you should still wonder and worry if you'd grown otherwise guilty despite that, and not carried out all the crying and fasting your sins would have required.

In fact, when you consider how obliged we, God's creations, are to serve Him, and how inordinately wrong it is to rebel against Him, you'd even be disappointed with whatever extra you'd do to serve Him or to do tshuvah, and it would seem so trivial to you.[4]

---

1. That is, realize that what you did wrong is now alienating you from your Beloved. And worry about that.

2. . . . you of them. (See Supplementary Notes.)

3. See ¶12.

4. Two causes for concern are cited here (more will come): First, that you might soon suffer the consequences of your sins despite your tshuvah. And second, that you might not have done enough of it. The first could actually be based on a subliminal fear that tshuvah just might not help. After all, if you're to suffer *despite your tshuvah*, it would seem to be of no avail. But in point of fact, you'd have to suffer only if you'd done something serious enough to incur a death sentence or the penalty of excision (see 4:11–12). And besides, tshuvah works on a subtle, subliminal, and existential level without your knowing it even when it seems not to.

And the second cause for concern is based on a firm and sober realization that you

As King Solomon said, "A sage fears, and withdraws from wrongdoing" (Proverbs 14:16), which means to say that even though a sage withdraws as much as he can from wrongdoing, he nonetheless worries and wonders whether he'd actually fulfilled his obligations, or been careful enough to do all that he should.[5] (It's likewise said, "Better is the poor who walks in his uprightness, than a rich man who is perverse in his ways" [Proverbs 28:6], despite his riches.) The sages remarked, though, that you're not to interpret it[6] to mean that a sage *first* fears, and *then* withdraws from wrongdoing. Rather that he first withdraws from wrongdoing, and then fears (*Tanchuma, Lech* 15).[7]

17.   Also worry about your yetzer harah possibly overtaking you[8] even after you'd done tshuvah. For as our sages said, "Do not trust yourself till the day of your death" (*Pirke Avot* 2:4), which is all the more true of one whose impulses have already gotten the best of him.[9] For you should watch out for the yetzer harah, which sits in ambush[10] all the time, by instilling more and more of the fear of God

---

could never actually do enough to make amends to God if you'd so ungratefully forsaken Him. But this second fear is utterly groundless. Because God yearns for our tshuvah, despite the apparent logic of that fear. For, as is pointed out in Ezekiel 18:23, God doesn't want us to suffer inexorably for our sins, but to do tshuvah and live on.

5. But why would a sage really have to worry "whether he'd actually fulfilled his obligations, or been careful to *do all he should*," we might ask. After all, he's tried his hardest, no doubt, and probably always will. And he's only human. But it's our spiritual mediocrity that would have us even ask such a question, sadly enough. The truth is, though, we'd try our utmost to do everything we could to excel at something we cared very, very deeply about. So, the sage who cares most for attachment to God tries his utmost to excel at that. And would settle for nothing less.

6. i.e., the verse, "A sage fears, and withdraws from wrongdoing."

7. The text continues with the following:

The end of that verse proves that [i.e., that a sage first withdraws from wrongdoing, then fears]. It reads, "A sage fears and withdraws from wrongdoing; *while the fool rages, and is confident*" (Proverbs 14:16), contrasting the fool and the sage [i.e., the structure of the second part of the verse proves that the entire verse is contrasting the fool and the sage]. For it says that when a fool rages, he's confident that he won't sin or come to harm [i.e., just as the fool *first* feels confident that no harm will come to him and *then* rages; the sage *first* withdraws from wrongdoing and *then* fears], even though angry people are prone to defiance and susceptible to harm. For it's said, "A furious man abounds in acts of defiance" (Proverbs 29:22) and, "One without self-control is like a city in ruins and without walls" (Proverbs 25:28).

8. . . . again . . .

9. There's a real and tragic possibility that you wouldn't have learned your ultimate lesson, and would have only learned the lesson of the moment. That is, you might have learned that your beloved is offended by one thing or another you've done, and stop doing that. But you wouldn't have come to realize how important your relationship with your beloved is.

10. . . . for you . . .

in your heart each day. That will serve as a stronghold against whatever new waves the yetzer harah may roll over you.[11]

18. When King Solomon spoke about tshuvah, he cited this trait[12] specifically. He started by saying, "When the righteous rejoice, there is great honor; but when wrongdoers arise, people are sought out" (Proverbs 28:12). Which means to say that the righteous honor and respect people for their good qualities, while wrongdoers always look for faults in others and mistakes in order to disparage them,[13] even after those people would have rejected what they[14] had done, and did tshuvah.[15]

He then followed that with, "One who conceals his acts of defiance will never succeed; but one who admits[16] and rids himself[17] will be shown mercy" (Ibid. v. 13). That's to say, while you shouldn't publicize your sins in the process of doing tshuvah, which we understand from the statement that, "when wrongdoers arise, people are sought out,"[18] you're nonetheless obliged to confess to them.[19] As it's said, "I acknowledged my sin to You, and did not hide my transgression" (Psalms 32:5), as well as, "Behold, I will bring you to judgment[20] because you said, 'I have not sinned'" (Jeremiah 2:35).

Our sages explain that to mean that there are times when someone who conceals his sins won't succeed (*Yomah* 86B)—as when it comes to sins against another person. Since a person isn't forgiven[21] until he returns what he stole, confiscated, or extorted, and until he asks for forgiveness from the person he victimized, disgraced, or slandered.[22] And when it comes to sins against God that become well-known. Because a person who sins publicly profanes God's name,[23] and

---

11. See Supplementary Notes.
12. i.e., worrying.
13. See Supplementary Notes.
14. . . . themselves . . .
15. There seems to be no connection between what had been said before about this principle—that you should worry about not having been successful in tshuvah—and this. Apparently, though, Rabbeinu Yonah's point is that while the righteous never overlook their own shortcomings, they nonetheless always see the good in others. While the very opposite is true of wrongdoers.
16. . . . to them . . .
17. . . . of them . . .
18. That is, by virtue of the fact that wrongdoers seek out others in order to publicize their sinful ways, we understand that we shouldn't publicize our past sins when we do tshuvah.
19. . . . to God, and to the person you wronged, as will soon be illustrated. (See Supplementary Notes.)
20. (says God)
21. . . . for those sins . . .
22. See Supplementary Notes.
23. See Supplementary Notes.

must bemoan and grieve for those sins before others in order to *sanctify* God's name.[24]

So it's written, "For after I turned, I lamented" (Jeremiah 31:18), with "lamented" referring to remorse and anguish, because tshuvah is essentially the expression of heartfelt bitterness, as we explained. And then it's said, "After I was informed, I struck my thigh" (Ibid.), which indicates that after others discovered my sin, which had then become so well-known, I grieved over what had become so obvious (as in, "strike your thigh" [Ezekiel 21:17] and, "He should assemble a row of men and say, 'I have sinned and perverted what was right" [Job 33:27]).

19. "Whoever admits[25] and rids himself[26] will be shown mercy" (Proverbs 28:13) means to say that there are actually three essential elements to tshuvah— remorse, confession, and ridding yourself of the sin[27] (though remorse and confession are incorporated in "admission," because when you confess to something, you express remorse for it[28]).

And in fact, there can be no tshuvah without these three. Because if you regret and confess to what you did, but don't rid yourself of the sin, you'd be like the individual who immersed[29] with a reptile in his hand, and thus immersed in vain.[30] That's why you'll be shown mercy if you admit to and rid yourself of your sins. Because you'd have done tshuvah, though there are many levels to it, as we've explained.

20. Then it says, "One who is always fearful is fortunate. But one who hardens his heart will stumble into wrongdoing" (Proverbs 28:14). That's to say, even when you do "admit and rid" you should nonetheless always be afraid that you might not have fulfilled all the tenets of tshuvah, because there are many levels to it, and you should be more determined every day to reach them.

Also be afraid that new impulses may arise, which you should always take precautions against. So, always augment your fear of God, and constantly pray to Him for His help in tshuvah, and for help with your impulses.[31]

---

24. This follows the idea introduced in ¶15 of doing tshuvah through the very mechanisms you sinned with.

25. . . . to them . . .

26. . . . of them . . .

27. See Supplementary Notes.

28. Remorse is to confession, what wishing is to praying. That is, while the former is internal and can be vague, the latter is external and explicit.

29. . . . in a *mikveh* (a ritual immersion bath) . . .

30. See Supplementary Notes.

31. There's somehow an odd reticence within us about praying to God to ask Him for help in tshuvah. As if that were "cheating," somehow; as if you were on your own when it came to tshuvah, since it's so personal; or, as if you'd be expected to be "less juvenile" about it, and just do it, somehow. But the truth is, you can't really be said to have done tshuvah if you don't ask for God's help in the process. Because, again, the point of tshuvah is to deepen

What the phrase, "But one who hardens his heart will stumble into wrong-doing" means is, if you convince yourself that you've already fulfilled all the tenets of tshuvah rather than try to continue advancing in them and amassing more fear in your heart, you'd have to suffer the consequences of that. Because you'd have been pretentious, and would have had no idea of how base you really were. You'd also have been oblivious to how obliged you really are to correct your ways as much as possible before God. And you'd have taken no precautions against your impulses, which always sit in ambush for you, and would fall into their hands as a consequence.[32]

---

and solidify your devotion to God, and you best do that not only by rectifying what had gone wrong, but by collaborating and sharing more and more with your Beloved about issues that matter to the two of you. (See Supplementary Notes.)

32. See Supplementary Notes.

Chapter Six

❧❧❧❧❧❧❧❧❧❧❧❧❧❧❧❧❧❧❧

21. Sixth Principle: Feeling Ashamed

As it's said, "I was ashamed, utterly mortified, because I bore the disgrace of my youth" (Jeremiah 31:18).

Why aren't you ashamed to sin before God, when you're so ashamed to sin in front of others and would be mortified to learn that they had an inkling or knew of your sins? Because God is removed from your innermost being.[1] That's why you experience shame in front of His creations but not in front of the Creator Himself.[2] And so our sages said that, "When Rabbi Yochanan Ben Zakkai was about to die, his disciples said to him, 'Bless us, master!' And he said, 'May it be God's will that you fear Heaven as much as you fear flesh and blood.' They said, 'And no more than that, master?' To which he said, 'I only wish! You should know that when a person sins in private he[3] says, "No one sees me!"'" (*Berachot* 28B).[4]

---

1. A friend once remarked that a person without God has a hole in his heart the size of God. But the truth is, God is always in our innermost beings, despite ourselves. And it is we alone who "remove" Him from it, which is to say, who overlook Him. (See Supplementary Notes.)

2. That is, we're aware of others when we do wrong because we're emotionally and personally tied to society and to particular people. But we're not aware of God when we do wrong, because we're emotionally and personally removed from Him.

But what about being aware of *ourselves* at the time? The point seems to be that when a person is disassociated from God, he's also dissociated from himself on a very profound level. And that he can't be said to be truly aware of himself in his core being if he's not aware of God.

3. . . . . invariably . . .

4. That is, "I can get away with it because no one sees me." The implication is that

22. The ultimate degree in this is your being *mortified* for having sinned before God,[5] which involves feeling shame and blushing.[6] As in, "Our faces are covered over with humiliation" (Jeremiah 51:51).[7]

Become deeply[8] ashamed when you sense God overlooking your sins, extending you a reprieve, not penalizing you, not reacting to your sins, and not requiting you for your transgressions. After all, wouldn't someone disobeying and deceiving a mortal king be shamefaced if the king forgave him? As it's written, "That you may remember and be ashamed . . . when I forgave everything you did" (Ezekiel 16:63).

Our sages said, "A person who does something[9] which he is then ashamed of is forgiven for all his sins" (*Berachot* 12B).[10] As such, it's said that Saul remarked, "God has departed from me and does not answer me any more, either through prophets, or in dreams" (1 Samuel 28:15), yet he didn't mention[11] the Urim and Tumim.[12] Because he was too ashamed to, after killing the people of Nob, the city

---

if someone were watching him, he'd stop. Rabbi Yochanan's blessing was that all his students (and all of us, too) always be as aware of God's presence as we are of the presence of people all around us. For what the fear of God is, on one level, is a charged and rabid realization of God's presence.

5. See Supplementary Notes.

6. For, just as one would have to demonstrate his anguish (see ¶15), he'd also have to *demonstrate* his shame to prove himself truly affected by his realizations.

7. The text continues with the following:

Humiliation is always mentioned after shame, because it's more serious than it, as in, "We were ashamed *and* mortified" (Ezekiel 36:32) and, "I was ashamed as *well* as mortified" (Jeremiah 31:18).

8. i.e., especially . . .

9. . . . wrong . . .

10. The clear, simple explanation is as we've presented it—that when a person is ashamed of some specific wrong he did, the shame itself comes to cleanse him, and to thus prepare him for forgiveness of that sin. The original, however, does not include the word "wrong." And could legitimately imply that "A person who does something" —*anything*— "which he is then ashamed of is forgiven for *all his sins.*" The clear implication of that is that true, heartfelt shame and humiliation are such strong emotions, and such clear indicators of an epiphany and a true willingness to change (whether they're warranted or not), that they're thus powerful enough to remove all sins.

How sad to remark that in our day, shame—as well as the sense of responsibility inherent to it—is balked at, ridiculed, and seen as proof of low self-esteem, which is itself deemed a dread modern affliction. While its opposite, chutzpah (audacity), is lauded, as our sages told us it would be in the days before the coming of the *Moshiach.* (See Supplementary Notes.)

11. . . . the possibility of his being answered through . . .

12. See Supplementary Notes.

of Cohanim. And yet Samuel said to him, "Tomorrow you and your sons will be with me" (Ibid. v. 19)—i.e., in my environs.[13]

But you only achieve such a level of shame by secluding yourself and reflecting upon God's greatness,[14] and upon how very wrong it is to rebel against Him. And by recalling that God observes all your actions, examines your innermost being, and scrutinizes your thoughts.[15]

---

13. That is, in Heaven, where Samuel was speaking to him from.

14. The usual suggestion that a person seclude himself and reflect upon God's greatness, as offered here, is not in order to arrive at shame. But rather, in order to arrive at an all-encompassing, cosmic love and high fear of Him (see Rambam's *Yesodei HaTorah* 2:1–2, 4:12). As such, the sort of shame being spoken of here isn't an instance of piddling, meek, foppish embarrassment. Instead, it's an experience of a stunning, bold, and coldly undoing realization of God's full greatness and our own true paltriness. (Hence our choice of the word "mortification" rather than abashment, humiliation, and the like, to allude to our mortality and limitedness.)

15. On one level, this is a daunting, loud, and numbing thought—which it's actually meant to be, in order to remind us of a numinous truth. On another level, though, it's actually a very comforting and safeguarding reminder of God's imminence and regard.

Chapter Seven

𝕰𝕺𝕾𝕰𝕺𝕾𝕰𝕺𝕾𝕰𝕺𝕾𝕰𝕺𝕾𝕰𝕺𝕾𝕰𝕺𝕾𝕰𝕺𝕾𝕰𝕺𝕾𝕰𝕺𝕾𝕰𝕺𝕾

23. Seventh Principle: Surrendering Wholeheartedly and Being Humble[1]

Anyone aware of his Creator would realize how lowly, base,[2] and of low worth anyone who sins against Him actually is.[3] As it's said, "Who will abide in your tent, God? Who will dwell in Your holy mountain? . . . One in whose eyes a vile person is despised" (Psalms 15:1–4), "(God) puts no trust in . . . anyone who is abominable and filthy—anyone who drinks iniquity like water" (Job 15:15–16),

---

1. See Supplementary Notes.

2. What we've translated as "base" in this context is the same word used for "humble" throughout—שׁפל. We've translated it here thusly in order to make the concept clear in context. Nonetheless, that's to say that while sinners *debase* themselves with their acts, you're to purposefully *belittle* yourself and your deeds when you do tshuvah.

3. How breathtaking a statement, "Anyone aware of His Creator. . . ." Who among us is truly aware of God and of His presence in our midst? In fact, the whole of Torah could be said to be a means of growing more and more aware of God all the time. As such we find the Zohar (2, 82B) characterizing the Torah's 613 *mitzvot* as 613 pieces of advice on how to draw closer to God.

Nonetheless, the point is that anyone who *is* aware of Him would certainly also be aware of several basic, existential truths. Including the fact that a person who'd sin against God—which is to say, who'd distance himself from Him—could only be characterized as "lowly, base, and of low worth." Simply because he wouldn't have recognized how much more delightful drawing close to Him is than anything physical. For by settling for mere physical delight we're like the peasant who'd serendipitously wound up in the king's chamber and was allowed to choose anything from the king's treasury he'd care for, who chose a worthless trinket, out of ignorance.

and, "They will call them 'base silver' because God has rejected them" (Jeremiah 6:30). So surrender and humble yourself before Him.[4]

As such, when David confessed to his sin when Nathan the Prophet approached him he finished with, "A broken spirit . . ." (that is, a forlorn spirit) ". . . is[5] a sacrifice to God. And You would never despise a broken and contrite heart, God" (Psalms 51:19). Thus we learn that humility is one of the principles of tshuvah (since this Psalm is a source of the principles of tshuvah.[6])

And you please God when you surrender to Him.[7] As it's said, "I will look to him who is poor and of a contrite spirit, and trembles at My word" (Isaiah 66:2). And it's said in the context of tshuvah, "I dwell upon the high and holy place, as well as with one who is of a contrite and humble spirit, to resuscitate the spirit of the humble, and to resuscitate the heart of the contrite" (Isaiah 57:14–18). Thus we learn that surrender is one of the principles of tshuvah.[8]

24. Understand that there are many degrees of surrender, as we'll illustrate in

---

4. . . . for having sinned and thus degraded yourself so.

5. . . . like . . .

6. Hence we learn that broken-spiritedness, along with forlornness and contrition, are the primary elements of surrender. But that's not to suggest depression and hopelessness, God forbid. The kind of broken-spritedness spoken of here is the kind a raging horse might come to after being tamed. A sort of soft, sober calm, born in resignation to reality.

7. Surrender is a principle of tshuvah and it pleases God so because its opposite, audacity, is an inherent factor in sin, as well as a mortal threat to your relationship to God. Because audacity is rooted in a higher-than-befitting sense of self, and too *much* self-esteem (see our note to ¶12). The audacious person regards himself as very, very worthy, and expects others to consider him so, as well. And if they don't, he's bedeviled by that, and lashes out at them for their "insensitivity." Then he does whatever he cares to do, since he'd have come to see it as his "right." Which is just the sort of rationalization that feeds sin.

Audacity is a mortal threat to your relationship to God because it necessarily causes a rift, or disallows for intimacy, between *any* two parties. The audacious person lets it be known from the outset that he wants nothing to do with the other, and only cares to get his point across or to have his way. And the other feels assaulted and insulted, and wants nothing other than to retaliate or simply leave.

Surrender, on the other hand, is rooted in vulnerability and a deeply felt connection to the other.

8. The text continues with the following:

In fact, the rest of that section addresses those who do tshuvah: [It says,] "I will not argue forever, nor will I always be so angry, that the spirit and the souls I made would faint before Me . . . for I was angry about his sin of greed . . . (but) I have seen his ways, and will heal him; I will guide him as well" (vv. 16–18). "I have seen *his* ways" alludes to his humility (as in, "I will look to him who is poor and of a contrite spirit") and to his becoming bitter-hearted (as in, "to resuscitate the heart of the contrite"). "I will heal him" alludes to God's forgiving a person's sins (as in, "I will heal their transgression" [Hosea 14:5], and "return, and be healed" [Isaiah 6:10]). . . . And "I will guide him as well" alludes to God's helping a person rid himself of his sins and conquer his impulses.

The Gates of Humility, with God's help.[9] But the greatest degree of it, when it comes to tshuvah's demands, is arrived at by augmenting and intensifying your Divine service without taking credit for it. For one should deprecate whatever he does in light of what we should all really be doing to serve God.

So surrender yourself to God and serve Him demurely. Don't long for honor for all the honorable things you do, and don't ask for glory from others for all the glorious things you do. And hide them as much as you can from them.[10]

25. This principle of tshuvah is best illustrated by the following words of the prophet: "With what shall I come before God, and prostrate myself before God on high?" (Micah 6:6). Meaning, with what shall I come before God, in light of all His kindness[11] (which is mentioned just previously in the section); and, with what shall I prostrate myself before God on high, in light of all my sins (referring to "God on high" in order to convey and demonstrate how important it is to prostrate and surrender yourself to Him when you rebel against God on high).

It then goes on to explain, "Shall I come before Him with burnt-offerings, with year-old calves? Would God care for thousands of rams,[12] or for tens of thousands of rivers of oil?" (v. 7), which I would come before Him with, for all His kindness.

"Should I give my firstborn[13] for my acts of defiance?" (cited in response to, "With what shall I . . . prostrate myself before God on high?") in order to prove that I've surrendered and abased myself in light of all my sins, and that I realize how grave my acts of defiance were, and how they warrant my sacrificing my firstborn,[14] they were that great and serious? Should I offer "the fruit of my body for the sin of my soul?" (Ibid.)[15]

---

9. To our great regret, *The Gates of Humility* no longer exists.

10. Nothing perhaps is as odious as a husband or wife who brags about his or her marriage. But it's especially offensive if the partner goes on and on about how much better things are in the marriage, and about all he or she is doing to enhance and intensify it. Listeners would invariably turn quickly skeptical, they'd be sure there were things being left unsaid, and they'd be offended by the boastfulness that they'd be sure would itself threaten the marriage. For in fact a couple that had drifted apart and then come together again after the sort of soul-searching, metamorphoses, and self-improvement referred to here as "augmenting and intensifying" their relationship would not boast. Everything lovely they'd recovered in their marriage would be left unsaid to others, and neither husband or wife alone would claim credit for what he or she did. That certainly is all the more true of one who returns to God.

11. . . . toward me . . .

12. i.e., After all, would God care for thousands of lambs . . .

13. . . . as recompense . . .

14. . . . as recompense . . .

15. The text continues with the following:

"Acts of defiance" corresponds to "my firstborn" [in the expression, "I realize how grave my acts *of defiance* were, and how they warrant my sacrificing *my firstborn*"], and "sin" corresponds to "the

But the response to that is, "He has told you, O man, what is good, and what God requires of you—to act justly and to love kindness"[16] (Micah 6:8), because that's better than bringing burnt-offerings or gift-offerings to God for all His kindness. ". . . And to go about demurely with your God" (Ibid.)—since serving God demurely is the essence of surrendering and abasing yourself to Him.[17]

For by doing so you convey your humility, and that you don't covet honor[18] for your honorable deeds (to say nothing of those of your qualities that your Creator doesn't care for, because they aren't[19] commendable, like wealth, strength, or erudition), only for your understanding and knowledge of God Himself. For it's written, "Let not the sage glory in his wisdom, the strong man glory in his strength, or the rich man glory in his riches. But let him who glories glory in this: that he understands and knows Me" (Jeremiah 9:22–23).[20]

26. You're also obliged to surrender yourself[21] when you do tshuvah in order to fulfill your obligation to rid yourself of all the traits that caused you to sin and act defiantly.[22]

---

fruit of my body" [in the expression, "(Should I offer) *the fruit of my body* for the *sin* of my soul"], because, as our sages explain, acts of defiance, which are acts of rebellion, are more serious than sins (*Yomah* 36B).

16. See Supplementary Notes.

17. The righteous have a clandestine relationship with God, as well as a public one. While their public relationship with Him is much like the one any citizen would be expected to have with a leader he'd come before on state business, their secret relationship is like that of a minister of state and a confidant. That is, the righteous carry on their external service to God the same way all of us do. But they meet in private with Him besides, so to speak. They confide in Him, expose their vulnerability to Him in ways they'd never do in front of others, and they cry and laugh with Him, so to speak. As such, they enjoy a far greater intimacy and closeness to God than we.

18. i.e., you refuse to accept credit . . .

19. . . . really . . .

20. The Torah expects us to use all our knowledge to understand God and His ways in the world. That is, to refer everything we know back to the Initiator of it all, the One who intended it to be just that way, and to wonder what each thing says about Him and our relationship to Him. For, God could be said to be the Protagonist of the universe. And *everything* among the details of the great novel of reality can be said to harken back to that Protagonist. Knowing Him, we know the world and its purposes, just as by knowing the world and its purposes we know a great deal (but certainly not everything) about Him. (See Supplementary Notes.)

21. . . . to God . . .

22. Renouncing and giving up personal predilections and traits is indeed an act of surrender and self-sacrifice. Since they seem to be an essential feature of our very beings (when they really aren't). In fact, see ¶32 where a similar demand—renouncing your urges—is compared to being "broken-hearted." (See Supplementary Notes.)

27. For arrogance[23] encourages many sins and puts you under the sway of your impulses. As it's said, "Your heart becomes haughty, and you forget God your Lord" (Deuteronomy 8:14),[24] "Haughty eyes and a proud heart are fertile fields of sin for wrongdoers" (Proverbs 21:4) (which means to say that arrogance is a "fertile field" for wrongdoers, because sins ripen as a result of it, and, "Your heart becomes haughty, and you forget God"). As It's said, "The wrongdoer persecutes the poor in his arrogance" (Psalms 10:2), "Let the wrongdoers be ashamed, . . . who speak insolent words arrogantly and contemptuously against the righteous" (Psalms 31:18–19), and, "(Arrogant nations have) . . . struck terror in the land of the living" (Ezekiel 32:26).[25]

For like one who'd prepare a fertile field for seeds to ripen in, or to harvest a lot of produce, wrongdoers prepare fertile fields of arrogance in their hearts, in which they plant wrongful thoughts, in order to produce and foster the sins that are the fruit of those thoughts. And so the prophet said metaphorically, "Judgment springs up like wormwood in the furrows of the field"[26] (Hosea 10:4).[27]

That's so because beside causing you to sin, arrogance is itself a sin. As it's said, "Everyone proud-hearted is an abomination to God" (Proverbs 16:5). For when you're arrogant, you subjugate yourself to your impulses.[28] And God no longer helps you,[29] because you're abominable to Him.

---

23. See Supplementary Notes.

24. The term for "haughty" in this verse is רם לבב, literally "high-hearted." The next verse cited refers to a pride as, רחב לב, literally, "wide-hearted." As such, arrogance entails hoisting up and expanding one's sense of self far beyond its natural reach. Like a child hoisted up on shoulders to see the Mardi Gras parade at greater range. The thrill is real, and the scan is panoramic, but the rank truth is the child is little and life is not the Mardi Gras. Forget that and you discount the greatest truth, "you forget (that) God (is) your Lord."

25. See Supplementary Notes.

26. i.e., in the field of arrogance.

27. The text continues with the following:

As to its saying, "Haughty eyes and a proud heart are fertile fields of sin for wrongdoers," that means to say that the fertile fields are themselves wrong and replete with sin [i.e., the term "*for* wrongdoers" is ambiguous enough to also mean "*are* the wrongdoers"]. As in, "Sin of Judah, written with a pen of iron, and with the point of a diamond" (Jeremiah 17:1) rather than "*The* sin of Judah . . .". And as in "Sun and moon stood still in their habitation" (Habbakuk 3:11), rather than "*The* sun and moon."

28. It's said here that "when you're arrogant (literally, a בעל גזה, which is to say, "a confirmed egotist"), you subjugate yourself to your impulses." While at the very beginning of this ¶ it's written, "Arrogance (itself, גאוה) . . . puts you under the sway of your impulses." As such we see that when you first start to "dabble" in arrogance, so to speak, you start to come "under the sway of your impulses," and you're courted and wooed by them, in a way. But once you become a confirmed egotist, your whole self is subjugated to the whims and caprice of your impulses, and you're enslaved.

29. See Supplementary Notes.

28. You're also obliged to surrender yourself when you do tshuvah in order to fulfill the words of the sages that one should, "be humble-spirited before everyone" (*Pirke Avot* 4:10). For by doing that you'll avoid being angry at or short-tempered with others.[30] And you'll disregard what you hear, and rise above your nature.[31] Do *that* and you'll merit having your sins forgiven. For as our sages said, "All acts of defiance of the person who rises above his nature are disregarded" (*Rosh Hashanah* 17A), measure for measure.[32] In fact, doing that offers a very important source of hope, as it's said, "Let him set his mouth in the dust; because there may be hope. Let him offer his cheek to whoever strikes him; let him take his fill of insults" (Lamentations 3:29–30).

---

30. i.e., you'll manage to avoid trying to have the "upper hand" or control over another person, which the angry and short-tempered try to have. For domination over another is noxious to emotional closeness, and certainly to the sort of reconciliation that tshuvah is. (See Supplementary Notes.)

31. Because when you take everything to heart and give in to your baser nature by seeking revenge or bearing a grudge, you not only transgress those prohibitions (see Leviticus 19:18), you also make it as impossible to draw emotionally close or to reconcile as the domineering sort of person just spoken of.

32. (This refers to the principle of the punishment fitting the crime; see *Sanhedrin* 100A.) For by learning to rise above your nature and to be a greater-hearted person than you'd been, by overlooking wrongs done you, you prove you're no longer the impetuous brat the "defiant" person would have been. You prove you've changed to the core. And that allows the sins of your past to slough off your back.

Chapter Eight

᭙᭖᭙᭖᭙᭖᭙᭖᭙᭖᭙᭖᭙᭖᭙᭖᭙᭖᭙᭖᭙

29. Eighth Principle: Manifesting Surrender

Respond gently to others (as it's said, "A gentle response turns away wrath" [Proverbs 15:1]), and in a low voice. Because that's the way of the humble. As it's said, "And you will be humbled, and will speak[1] from the ground, and your speech will be low[2] from the dust" (Isaiah 29:4). Which is the opposite of what's said of an arrogant rich person—which is that "the rich person answers audaciously" (Proverbs 18:23).[3]

Don't concern yourself with attractive clothing or ornaments. As it's said, "You are a stiff-necked people . . . remove your ornaments" (Exodus 33:5). And it's said of Ahab that he "fasted, lay in sackcloth, and went about softly" (1 Kings 21:27), about which God said,[4] "Do you see how Ahab surrenders himself?" (Ibid. v. 29), since his going about softly was diametrically opposite to the way kings go about, with an entourage, and full-throated.

And always keep your eyes lowered, for it's said, "He will save those with lowered eyes" (Job 22:29).[5]

---

1. . . . as if . . .

2. . . . as if . . .

3. The implication is that you're not even to initiate a conversation yourself. Only to *respond*, and in a low, restrained, perhaps mournful tone at that.

4. . . . approvingly . . .

5. The implication here is not only that you not buy attractive clothing or ornaments, but that you're to remove the ones you have, bear homely ones, and go about with them in a preoccupied, nomadic, and sorrowful way, perhaps aimlessly and despondently. But see the following note.

These outward signs of surrender—a gentle response, a tender voice, lowered eyes—will remind you to surrender your heart.[6]

---

6. There are two vital points to be made here. The first is that the impression made by our two previous observations are of a poor woebegone soul wandering about the outskirts of things, preoccupied with his memories, and hopeless about the future. This is all a rather off-putting portrayal of one who would do tshuvah. It in fact evokes an image of a cliché "penitent" who goes about in sackcloth and ashes aimlessly and listlessly. It reminds us of Cain, who became "a fugitive and a wanderer" (Genesis 4:12) after he killed Abel, and lived for years repenting just that way. And it once again raises the issue of what tshuvah is.

But as we've been stressing all along, tshuvah is a stark and heartfelt reaction to a threat to a relationship that's utterly vital in one's life—one's relationship to God Himself. As such, Cain could perhaps be said to have been a "penitent" rather than one who did tshuvah. Because he first complained to God in Genesis 4:14 about having been driven "from the face of the earth"—which is to say, from his everyday life and career (Cain was a farmer; see Genesis 4:2). And only then, as a second thought, did he say, "I will be hidden from Your face" (4:14). As such, his priorities were askew, because he cared more for himself than for his relationship to God. But the individual who'd follow the principle enunciated here would be motivated by the aforementioned longing to restore the love relationship he'd had with God. And would be doing tshuvah.

Our second point, however, is even more vital. And perhaps goes a long way toward explaining the principles enunciated in this gate. As Rabbeinu Yonah just put it, "these outward signs of surrender" are meant to "*remind* you to surrender your heart." That's to say, they're meant to be outside "agitators" of tshuvah (see ¶15, for reference to agitators of sin). As such, the implication is that the principles of tshuvah enunciated here in this gate are "prods" toward tshuvah (with the exception of the essential three required by *halacha* itself, see ¶19). And also something akin to barometers or read-outs of your degree of tshuvah.

That's to say, if I did something to seriously threaten my relationship to my beloved (human or Divine), and the reality of that—with its concomitant heartfelt sadness, fear, etc.—struck me, I'd *certainly* be expected to exhibit all the signs of surrender and humility spoken of, including belittling and taking no credit for my deeds (¶'s 24 and 25) and not taking things that don't pertain to my relationship too seriously (¶28). For how could I think of past accomplishments and side issues when what's most important to me could be taken away! And I'd certainly also be expected to exhibit all the other "symptoms" spoken of throughout this gate, including worry, shame, etc.

We also contend that the principle of surrender and humility spoken of here serves as the paradigm for all the other principles, because its opposite, audacity, is *the* greatest threat to a relationship, since it "encourages many sins," and subjugates you to your impulses (¶27), which is to say, to your own needs, rather than to God and your relationship to Him. In fact, we learn our greatest lessons about drawing closer to God, and reconciling with Him after having "left" Him, from this principle. (See Supplementary Notes.)

Chapter Nine

ᏦᎿᏗᏦᎿᏗᏦᎿᏗᏦᎿᏗᏦᎿᏗᏦᎿᏗᏦᎿᏗᏦᎿᏗᏦᎿᏗᏦᎿᏗᏦᎿᏗ

30. Ninth Principle: Overcoming Your Physical Cravings[1]

Keep in mind that it's your cravings that have you sin, and draw transgressions along by ropes of guile. So set up barriers to protect the road to tshuvah by denying yourself your pleasures,[2] and by not even acceding to your cravings for permitted things. Practice abstinence and only eat to satisfy your needs and to stay healthy. As it's written, "The righteous man eats to satisfy his soul" (Proverbs 13:25). And only approach your wife to fulfill the *mitzvot* of procreation and of allotting her her time.[3]

Because when you indulge your cravings, you're pulled toward your baser nature,[4] severed from reason, and overwhelmed by your impulses.[5] As it's said,

---

1. See Supplementary Notes.

2. i.e., the objects of your cravings.

3. See Supplementary Notes

4. Literally, "you're pulled toward the consequences of being physical." That is to say, eating, drinking, and the like, are all natural consequences of being a human being, rather than of being a soul. When you're in the habit of "indulging your cravings," you become drawn toward such consequences of physical life rather than to soul drives, concerns, and longings. See next note.

5. First, that's to say that the pull toward physical satisfaction detracts from and outshouts the pull toward spiritual satisfaction. And it lends further credence to the apparent, aboveboard, and mundane over the invisible, inscrutable, inferred, and holy, which has such trouble asserting itself anyway, in our tumultuous and distracting lives.

Second, in regard to the contrast between reason and our cravings and impulses: It's well-known that if we were lucid all the time, we'd avoid a world of heartache, and live more temperate, virtuous lives. Yet we're so often irrational and "get carried away." We blame the irrationality on our "raw emotions" and "animal instincts," and envision a wild and jagged

"Jeshurun became fat and scoffed" (Deuteronomy 32:15), "Lest you eat and become full . . . , and your heart becomes haughty" (Ibid. 8:12–14), and, "Lest I become full and deny You and say, Who is God?" (Proverbs 30:9). As our sages put it, "Man has a certain small organ which hungers when fed, and is satisfied when left hungry" (*Sukkah* 52B).

31.   The cravings that lay fixed in your heart are the root of[6] all your actions. So if you'd adjust those cravings to the point where your limbs, which serve them, were to comply with, follow, and serve reason,[7] then everything you'd do would be proper.[8] As it's said, "But as for the pure, his actions are right" (Proverbs 21:8).

It's said, "A craving indulged in is sweet to the soul. It is an abomination to fools to depart from wrong" (Proverbs 13:19). But "indulged in"[9] is to be read "broken"[10] in this instance, as in, "I was broken[11] and sick" (Daniel 8:27). For when you overcome your cravings for permitted things, you[12] triumph, and find the ability to give reason the upper hand sweet.

That's followed by, "It is an abomination to fools to depart from wrong" because fools—those who can't overcome their urges, and indulge in all sorts of common cravings all the time instead—don't flee when those cravings have them sin

---

beast of sorts deep within us raging and ranting, clawing away brutishly at things it rejects, and sweeping things it craves ravishingly toward it.

But Rabbeinu Yonah's point is that it's not anything alien and mad within us that makes us irrational and has us do things we'd rather not do if we thought about it. Instead, it's the very things that are closest to our hearts, and which we use to define ourselves—our cravings, i.e., *our tastes and proclivities*—that do. For as everyone knows, if a person craves sweets, he'd often do some extraordinary things to allow himself sweets. And he'd forgo a lot of otherwise important things to not have to do without them. In fact, he might sacrifice his health and well-being—or his very life—for sweets. And many, many do.

So it stands to reason that the first step toward lucidity is the art of tempering nearly all your cravings (nearly all, because there are healthy and holy cravings, too, as is known. Including cravings for health and holiness!).

Yet, to be sure, most of us are taken aback at this point, and have some ready, seemingly lucid responses of our own. "Where's the fun?" and "If that's what I have to do, I don't want it," etc. But Rabbeinu Yonah will address them shortly.

6. i.e., the impetus behind.

7. . . . rather than impulse . . .

8. The primary implication is that the body (and by extension, you yourself) will sheepishly follow one thing or another. If drawn to reason, you'd comply with it; if not, you'd just naturally defer to blind cravings.

And there's the further implication that we can, in fact, "adjust" our cravings, which many would deny.

9. נהיה

10. נהייתי

11. נהייתי

12. . . . experience a sense of . . .

or do wrong. In fact, they're called fools because they pursue pleasure.[13] As it's said, "Costly things and oil are treasured in the home of the wise; but a fool uses it all" (Proverbs 21:20), "Woe to those who rise up early in the morning to chase after strong drink. The lyre and the lute . . . are in their feasts, but they disregard God's work" (Isaiah 5:11–12), "The belly of the wrongdoer lacks"[14] (Proverbs 13:25), and, "I will strew dung upon your faces, the dung of your festivals" (Malachi 2:3), which our sages said refers to those whose whole lives are like festivals (*Shabbat* 151B).

It's also said, "One who seperates himself wants to indulge his own cravings; he grumbles about wisdom" (Proverbs 18:1). That means to say that if you set out to indulge your cravings and whims, you'll separate yourself from others, and reject all who'd love and befriend you.[15] Because people have different cravings and

---

13. It's here that Rabbeinu Yonah starts to address the resistance raised earlier, in a previous note. He speaks of the "triumph" and "sweetness" of giving reason the upper hand—which we'd never expect. And by extension he dismisses or belittles the usual triumph and sense of sweetness we assume ourselves to have when we indulge our cravings. But Rabbeinu Yonah is very right, and *dashingly* insightful.

Because the truth is, we all know only too well the instinctive discomfort, disappointment, and sense of personal defeat we experience when we indulge. And we've all at least had glimpses of the real glee, satisfaction, and subtle personal jubilation had when we conquer an unwanted, seemingly irresistible force within. But we tend to rationalize a personal failing with a coquettish and sly waving of the hand, and by repressing the feeling held deep that we've gone wrong. (Contrast this with the commonly held notion of so-called "unhealthy" supression of untoward impulses!)

But the man or woman of reason, who is capable of boldly taking charge of self, knows well of that "sweet savor to God" (Leviticus 1:9) that is self-mastery. And understands the import of "Those who search for God will be heart-glad" (1 Chronicles 16:10). While the itinerant occupant of a self who is a veritable tenant of his being and not the "lord of the realm"—i.e., the indulgent individual Rabbeinu Yonah refers to as the "fool"—knows nothing of that satisfaction, and searches for it nearly everywhere else.

14. i.e., always seems to need to be filled more and more.

15. It's here that Rabbeinu Yonah draws us back to the subject at hand, tshuvah. Otherwise it might be asked what overcoming your urges has to do with it specifically. After all, the theme of abstinence itself is discussed in nearly all Musar works (many of which, in fact, including *The Path of the Just*, *The Duties of the Heart*, *The Ways of the Righteous*, etc., dedicate entire sections to it). And it's held to be an essential element of a Jewish life (see ¶34, where it's pointed out that a disciple of Abraham—any Jew—would be expected to live by such a code). For as Nachmanides points out in his comments to Leviticus 19:2, one can manage to live a technically kosher life and still actually be a boor and a lout in practice by overindulging himself in all sorts of kosher foods and drinks. So it's always important to practice some abstinence.

But Rabbeinu Yonah's point apparently here is that, "if you set out to indulge your cravings and whims, you'll separate yourself from others" since you'll be seen to be the self-serving, self-absorbed debaucher you essentially are, and you'll be spurned. And you'd have "rejected all who'd love and befriend you," God Himself included!

character traits, and want different things.[16] So if you follow the ways of reason, you'll have friends, and many people will love you. As it's said in Musar literature, "People are always captivated by a pleasant person."

As to the idea itself that, "One who separates himself wants to indulge his own cravings," that means to say that anyone who separates himself from friends and family does that to indulge his own cravings, and hence distances himself from others in order to do what he wants to do.[17] As in, "The poor man is separated from his neighbor" (Proverbs 19:4).

And, "He grumbles about wisdom" means to say that when you indulge your cravings, you not only sin in one area, you also "grumble about" all of the Torah's prohibitions, and sin against all of them, as in, "Every fool will grumble" (Proverbs 20:3).

32. There's another benefit to overcoming your physical cravings.[18] For should you then crave something wanton or sinful, you'd be able to say to yourself, "I don't even indulge my cravings for permitted things. Why should I even extend a hand toward something forbidden?"[19]

33. There's yet another great and enormous benefit to overcoming your cravings. When you do, you reveal just how virtuous and well-meaning your intent to do tshuvah really was, since you now abhor the very inclination that drove you

---

As such, the underlying implication is that one who has done things to threaten his relationship to God would have to no longer be so self-absorbed. And he'd have to learn to fully temper himself if he's to prove himself faithful to his Beloved once again.

16. Apparently, then, companionship seems to be a sign that a person is reasonable and well-adjusted enough to acquiesce to the wishes of others. But, in fact, we see many indulgent people with friends. So the truth must be that they acquiesce more of their cravings to the demands of their friends than they're willing to admit when they're with them (which goes to explain "the honor of thieves," i.e., the code of behavior accepted by even the most lowly when among friends). And that people only truly indulge their cravings fully when they're alone.

17. A simple, everyday example might be the young person who moves far way from home to indulge in things he'd be too embarrassed to indulge in closer to home. Another, more apt, example might be the husband or wife who leaves the family to indulge his or her cravings, who'd certainly be said to have done tshuvah if he or she spurned those indulgences and came home in a state of remorse for the sake of reconciliation.

18. The specific expression "*physical* cravings" used not only here, but in ¶'s 30 (in the heading) and 34 underscores the point made in note 5 that there are holy and spiritual cravings as well.

19. For if you'd been forced to avoid salt at the table, for example, for your health, which you'd gotten used to, and you were then offered an oversalted exotic dish, you'd find it easier than the next person to refuse it (though it would do you both good to avoid it), since that other person had never limited his salt intake, and you'd be aghast to take in that much salt at one sitting, thanks to your training.

to sin.[20] That pleases God and finds favor in His eyes.[21] As it's written, "To God, a broken spirit . . . ," a forlorn and submissive spirit, ". . . is[22] a sacrifice. For You, God, would never despise a broken and contrite heart" (Psalms 51:19), which refers to overcoming your physical cravings, since cravings are implanted in the heart. As it's said, "You have granted him his heart's craving" (Psalms 21:3).

And we learn from the fact that the expression, "You, God, would never despise a broken and contrite heart" is contained in the "Tshuvah Psalm" that you please God when you overcome your physical cravings in the process of doing tshuvah. And that doing so is one of the principles of tshuvah. It's also said in regard to tshuvah that God "resuscitates the spirit of the humble, and resuscitates the heart of the contrite" (Isaiah 57:15).[23]

34. Our sages said, "Whoever has these three traits is among the disciples of our father Abraham: A gracious eye, a forlorn spirit, and a humble soul" (*Pirke Avot* 5:19). A "humble soul" doesn't even accede to his physical cravings for permitted things, as was true of Abraham, who said,[24] "Now I know that you are an attractive woman" (Genesis 12:11). For until that very day he had never looked closely enough at her to determine just how attractive she was.

And our sages said about the verse, "They were shut in up to the day of their death, 'widows' of a living husband:" (2 Samuel 20:3) that "David would order that their hair[25] be set every day and that they be well-groomed, in order to arouse cravings within him, which he would then subjugate, and thusly prevail over his yetzer harah, in order to be forgiven for the incident with Bathsheba" (J. T., *Sanhedrin* 2:3).[26]

---

20. It's as if you'd come awake and realized what *you've* done, and what *it's* done, as well as how much you actually abhor it now—the way a smoker or a drunk might suddenly come to see the truth.

21. That's to say, if you change so much that you no longer crave the things you once craved, which so distracted you from your Beloved. And you're in fact repelled by those very things. That demonstrates how much you've matured, and how much the relationship matters to you now, which draws you ever closer to Him.

22. . . . like . . .

23. Because Rabbeinu Yonah uses the modifier "physical" for cravings and "resuscitation" in relation to tshuvah we can infer that he understands sin and cravings as a form of death, and tshuvah as a form of resurrection. In fact it's said that "Wrongdoers are called 'dead' in their lifetimes" (*Berachot* 18B). After all, wouldn't we call a relationship gone sour "dead," and a renewed one, "resurrected"?

24. . . . to his wife, Sarah . . .

25. i.e., his concubines' hair.

26. See Supplementary Notes.

Chapter Ten

35. Tenth Principle: Correcting Your Actions Through the Agent Used to Sin

If you've stared at instances of nudity, accustom yourself to lowering your eyes; if you sinned by slandering someone, engross yourself in Torah.[1] That is, try to fulfill a mitzvah with each limb you sinned with. As our sages put it, "The righteous become pleasing through the very thing they sinned with" (*Shemot Rabbah* 23:3).[2]

They also said, "If you committed bunches of sins, then fulfill bunches and bunches of corresponding *mitzvot*. So, if your 'feet hurried to do wrong' (Proverbs 6:18), have them hurry to do a mitzvah. If you have 'a lying tongue' (Ibid. v. 17), then speak the truth, only express wisdom, and allow only Torah-kindness to come from your lips. If your 'hands shed blood' (Ibid.), then always open your hands to your poor brothers. If you have 'an arrogant look' (Ibid.), then be meek, and lower your eyes. If you have 'a heart that plots sinister plans' (v. 18), then keep words of Torah sequestered in your heart, and meditate upon[3] thoughts. And if you 'sow discord among brothers' (v. 19), then search for peace and pursue it" (*Vayikrah Rabbah* 21:4).

---

1. See Supplementary Notes.
2. That is, in order to draw close to your beloved once again, then be warm and loving if you'd been uncaring. And praise if you'd belittled. Because it's not only a compensating *deed* that Rabbeinu Yonah is talking about, but a compensating emotion or quality as well.
3. . . . serious . . .

Chapter Eleven

36. Eleventh Principle: Scrutinizing Your Ways

As it's said, "Let us scrutinize and examine our ways, and return to God" (Lamentations 3:40).[1] Do so for three reasons: first, in order to remember all your sins and thus confess to them all, since confession is one of the principles of forgiveness.[2]

Second, in order to know just how many sins and transgressions you've committed, and to thus be even more submissive.[3]

And third, because even though you'd have taken to ridding yourself of each sin, you'd still have to know how you sinned in order to set up safeguards against them. And to protect yourself from the snares of the yetzer harah.[4] Because you'd be susceptible to those sins since they'd have become insignificant in your eyes,[5] and

---

1. See Supplementary Notes.

2. See Supplementary Notes.

3. We're very often stunned and put off by what others say about us, because we view ourselves in an existential context we understand and favor, while they view us in their own such context. But if we agree we've been wrong, and start to see ourselves in our beloved's context (as lovers do), we become humbled by raw realization and remorse, rather than stunned and put off.

4. That is, even though you'd no longer be staying abreast of the details of those sins and would have taken them out of your mind, you should nonetheless recall them in general in order to know how to offset them. The way a reformed thief might recall some of his old maneuvers in order to foil active thieves.

5. See Supplementary Notes.

your impulses would have had command over them.[6] After all, you'd been "infected"[7] by those deeds, and like anyone hoping to be healed, you'd need to be cautious about a lot of things to not "relapse."[8]

---

6. See Supplementary Notes.

7. Literally, "made sick."

8. That is, you're vulnerable in that area, so you'd need to not only take every reasonable precaution, like rest, exercise, vitamins, and healthy food. You'd also have to follow a regimen of preventive medicine.

Chapter Twelve

37. Twelfth Principle: Examining, Knowing, and Recognizing the Seriousness of Each Sin

Know which sins, for example, would incur flogging; which, excision; and which, a court-imposed death sentence. In order to know just how serious your sin was when you confess to it,[1] and in order to weep bitterly for having so embittered God, grow more submissive, and fear your sins.[2] For when it comes to significant sins, forgiveness is held in abeyance despite tshuvah, and only tribulations purge you of them.[3] As it's written, "How can you say, I am not polluted? . . . See your way in the valley, know what you have done" (Jeremiah 2:23).

This principle will be expanded upon in[4] the third gate.

---

1. That is, know just how wrong you were, and how serious a blunder you committed in God's eyes (or the eyes of the person you offended). In order to avoid the offense of being nonchalant and emotionally removed when apologizing for it.

2. i.e., fear either the consequences of your sins, or fear ever committing them again. Or fear the daunting fact that "when it comes to significant sins, forgiveness is suspended *despite* tshuvah, and only tribulations cleanse you of them" as Rabbeinu Yonah is about to say. (See Supplementary Notes.)

3. See Supplementary Notes.

4. i.e., throughout . . .

Chapter Thirteen

38. Thirteenth Principle: Taking Your Minor Sins Seriously

Do so for four reasons: First, because rather than concentrate on the "insignificance" of the sin itself, you should concentrate instead on the significance of the One who warned you about it.[1]

Second, because your yetzer harah rules[2] when it comes to minor sins, which might cause you to commit them over and over again.[3] And then the consequences to be suffered for the combination of them would be the same as for serious sins (like a strand of delicate silk, which becomes a thick cord when doubled over itself again and again[4]).

Third, because when you commit the same sin all the time, it comes to seem acceptable to you, you cast off its yoke and become careless in it. And you then fall

---

1. That is, remember—it's your relationship to God that matters, not the "pettiness" of what would threaten it. For the sensitive soul would care for his beloved's feelings above all if she would be offended, hurt, or put off by something he said or did. The other point to be made is that it was forgetting God that brought you to sin in the first place. Having Him loom large in your life now is the reparation. (See Supplementary Notes.)

2. . . . over your will . . .

3. Your yetzer harah wouldn't dare suggest loud and full-bodied violations right out—the first time you're faced with them, at least. Because you'd simply reject them out of hand as coarse, unthinkable, or at least unreasonable. What it does is make simple, tiny suggestions to us all the time, which seem actually quite bright, quite tasteful, and quite reasonable. And we follow through on them all the time, believing as we do that we certainly "deserve it." That's how we go on doing wrong so often quite blithely.

4. See Supplementary Notes.

into the category of those who cast off their yoke[5] and are "apostates in one area."[6]

And fourth, because if the yetzer harah can prevail over you today when it comes to something insignificant, it will[7] prevail over you tomorrow when it comes to something significant. For, as our sages said, "Consider a person who breaks dishes when he gets angry an idol worshipper" (*Shabbat* 105B). Because, in fact, that's the way of the yetzer harah. Today it tells you to do one thing, and the next day it tells you to worship idols.[8]

For it's said, "Will you not be accepted if you do well? . . ." (Genesis 4:7), which means: Why be downcast? Will you not be accepted if you improve your ways and return to Me?[9] "But if you do not well, sin crouches at the door" (Ibid.)—if you don't do tshuvah for your sins, not only will that sin remain with you, but the yetzer harah will "crouch at the door" and cause you to sin wherever you go. It will prevail over you all the time, because it has already prevailed over you, ensnared you, and trapped you before, and you didn't do tshuvah.

"And it will desire you" (Ibid.)—that is, it will want you to be rejected.[10] And will lie in wait for you all the time.[11] "But you can rule over it" (Ibid.)—if you want to rule over it. But because I gave you the ability to prevail over it,[12] you will suffer the consequences of that sin.[13]

39. When Solomon said, "One who scorns something will be destroyed by

---

5. . . . of Divine service in its entirety . . .
6. See Supplementary Notes.
7. . . . certainly . . .
8. See note 3.
9. The text continues with the following:

"Accepted" [אשׂנ] in this case both implies having reason to lift your face, as in "Surely then you will lift up [אשׂנ] your face without blemish" (Job 11:15), and it implies being forgiven.

10. . . . by God.
11. . . . in order to be a part of that.
12. . . . and you didn't. Hence we see that we can prevail over our impulses. And that you'd not only have to suffer the consequences of committing a sin itself. But you'd have to answer for the fact that you decided not to master your yetzer harah.
13. This whole quote from Genesis 4:7 and its analysis seems out of place here. What connection has it with the discussion right before it, which centered on why it's so important to take even your minor sins seriously, let alone your serious ones?

Simply this. The sensitive soul can shrink in despair and sorrow catching sight of its many errors. And lose all hope of ever reconciling with his Beloved. How fully miserable a sorrow; and how eternally wretched a prospect! So Rabbeinu Yonah feels compelled to remind us here of the ever-availability of tshuvah. And of the great hope that should provide us with. Yes, we're susceptible to sin, even inclined by nature to it. But there is always, always tshuvah.

God "never closes the doors to tshuvah to us, even when we're very defiant and rebellious, and utterly unfaithful" Rabbeinu Yonah told us in the very first ¶ of the book. And while the yetzer harah may want to have you rejected by God, as it's said here, God never-

it. But one who fears a mitzvah will be repaid" (Proverbs 13:13), he was referring to scorning[14] minor sins. For if you do that, you will bring the sort of destruction spoken of upon yourself.[15] "But one who fears a mitzvah," that is, if you're just as afraid to not do a mitzvah as you are to commit a serious sin, you "will be repaid."[16] That is, you're destined to enjoy a full reward. As our sages said, "Be as cautious with a minor mitzvah as you would with a significant one" (*Pirke Avot* 2:1) and, "Each mitzvah impels another mitzvah, and each sin impels another sin. And the reward for a mitzvah is a mitzvah, while the reward for a sin is a sin" (Ibid. 4:2).[17]

---

theless "devises means that none of us be rejected" (2 Samuel 14:14), as the Baal Shem Tov and his disciples were wont to underscore, time and time again.

14. i.e., belittling, discounting, etc. . . .

15. i.e., of having to suffer the incremental and ever-deepening influence of the yetzer harah.

16. See Supplementary Notes.

17. That is, actions build upon themselves quite naturally, and patterns are easily established. So, be aware of each little thing you do, in order not to set up a pattern of wrongdoing.

Chapter Fourteen

CRACRACRACRACRACRACRACRACRACRACRA

40. Fourteenth Principle: Confessing

As it's said, "And it will be, when he will be guilty of one of these things, that he should confess that he has sinned in that thing" (Leviticus 5:5).

Articulate your sins,[1] as well as the sins of your ancestors. Because you'll suffer the consequences of their sins if you follow in their ways.[2] And so it's written, "They should confess their transgressions, and the transgressions of their fathers" (Ibid. 26:40).

---

1. Nothing so cleanses the soul and unburdens it as the outpouring of the heart in admission of wrong. For, despite our vision of ourselves in modernity as utterly free and independent entities, we often take various emotional "yokes" upon ourselves—through our sins. In fact, if you're perceptive, you can sense those yokes pressing deeply upon your heart. Such yokes need to be shucked off if we're to take the Yoke of the Kingdom of Heaven upon ourselves in their place. And confession most especially allows for that.

2. That's to say, if you merely play out the habits, learned responses and predilections you inherited from your family, you'll make the same mistakes they made. And you'd be worshipping God outwardly only, and by rote (see Isaiah 29:13), rather than by choice (see 3:17). This also alludes to the sin patterns you might have established for yourself, which must be avoided, referred to in our notes to ¶'s 5 (at end) and 7–9. (See Supplementary Notes.)

Chapter Fifteen

ⵣⵣⵣⵣⵣⵣⵣⵣⵣⵣⵣ

41. Fifteenth Principle: Praying

Pray to God and ask to be mercifully forgiven for all your sins.[1] As it's said, "Take with you words and return to God. Say to Him: Forgive all iniquity and accept us graciously; and we will offer the words of our lips instead of calves" (Hosea 14:3).

"Take with you words and return to God" refers to confession, and "Say to Him: Forgive all iniquity and receive us graciously" refers to prayer.[2] What, "accept us graciously"[3] means is, accept the good we've done.[4] For our sages said, "A sin douses a mitzvah" (*Sukkah* 21A). But when you do tshuvah, your sins are forgiven,[5] the merit accrued from your *mitzvot*[6] is bestirred, and their lights shine in ways they hadn't before you did tshuvah.[7]

It's likewise written, "If you are pure and upright; surely now He will rouse Himself for you, and make the habitation of your righteousness prosperous" (Job 8:6). Our sages point out that it isn't worded, "If you *were* pure and upright;" rather,

---

1. See Supplementary Notes.
2. See Supplementary Notes.
3. Which is more literally translated as "accept the good."
4. That is, we ask God to accept the good things we've done in the past despite our sins. But, why would we have to ask that of Him? Because . . .
5. That is, not only are your sins forgiven, but . . .
6. . . . that had been doused . . .
7. That is, your *mitzvot*—the things you did for God's own sake, to please Him and draw closer to Him—are doused when you sin. The same way everything good and considerate you did for your beloved in the past would be overshadowed by what you did to hurt your beloved's feelings. Nonetheless, when you do tshuvah, not only will you be forgiven, but those same *mitzvot* will be bestirred and reignited. The same way your past favors and acts of love will come to the fore once again in your beloved's mind once you'd reconciled with her. (See Supplementary Notes.)

"If you *are* pure and upright." Which is to say that He will only rouse Himself for you now that you've done tshuvah (*Breishit Rabbah* 79:3).[8]

That is, now that you've done tshuvah, all the acts of charity you did before, like keeping your house wide open[9] and setting up a lodging place (for it's written, "I opened my doors to the traveler" [Job 31:32]), will be roused for you. For, while your acts of charity wouldn't have shielded you before you did tshuvah, now that you've done tshuvah and fled from sin, your merit[10] has been bestirred. Thus, "He will . . . make the habitation of your righteousness prosperous."[11]

What "we will offer the words of our lips instead of calves"[12] refers to is the fact that your confessions will now be like calf-offerings brought to become acceptable to God. Calves are specified because they were offered in the inner courtyard, and their blood was sprinkled onto the curtain as well as onto the golden altar.[13]

42. Also pray, when you do tshuvah, that God scatter about your acts of defiance and sins like clouds. And that He favor and be as pleased with your prayers[14] now as He would have been had you not sinned. As Elihu said of someone who did tshuvah after suffering tribulations, "He should pray to God, and He will favor him" (Job 33:26).[15] For though your sins may have been forgiven, and you'd been spared tribulation and judgment, God may nonetheless not be pleased with

---

8. The language here calls for some explanation. The verse that immediately precedes this one reads, "If you will seek God, and make your supplication to the Almighty." It too clearly speaks of prayer and tshuvah. So what the verse here, which reads, "If you are pure and upright; surely now He will rouse Himself for you, and make the habitation of your righteousness prosperous," means is as follows, according to Rabbeinu Yonah:

"If you are pure and upright," that is, now that you're pure and upright, by virtue of your having done tshuvah, "surely now He will rouse it," the mitzvah (for the term in the original, "יעיר," is ambiguous and could be read either "He will rouse Himself" or "He will rouse it"). And as a consequence, God will "make the habitation of your righteousness prosperous," which Rabbeinu Yonah is about to explain.

9. . . . for guests . . .

10. i.e., the merit you originally accrued from that mitzvah.

11. i.e., God will reignite the merit you will have accrued for establishing "habitations of righteousness" (charitable lodging places).

12. . . . which is the last section of the verse cited at the beginning of this ¶, "Take with you words, and return to God. Say to Him: Forgive all iniquity and accept us graciously; And we will offer the words of our lips instead of calves." . . .

13. Mention of "the inner courtyard" and "the curtain" alludes to the great intimacy and familiarity you'd share with God after reconciliation, which will be expanded on in the following ¶.

14. . . . and hence, you . . .

15. The less-than-common term for prayer here, עתר, can also mean "smoke." Hence the reference to scattering your sins about like "clouds" at the beginning of the ¶.

you,[16] or favor your guilt-offerings.[17] When, in fact, the only accomplishment the righteous crave is winning God's approval and favor.[18] For His favor is the true life everlasting, and the great light that encompasses all delight. As it's said, "Being in His favor is life" (Psalms 30:6), "Accept us, God, Lord of Hosts! Shine Your countenance[19] and we will be saved" (Ibid. 80:20), about which our sages said, "For, all we have is the shining of Your countenance!" (Midrash *Tehillim* 80) referring to His favor, as we've explained.[20]

And so we find David first praying upon doing tshuvah, "Wash me thoroughly from my transgression, and cleanse me from my sin" (Psalms 51:4), then praying to find God's favor—for God to be as pleased with him then as He was before he sinned.[21]

That is, he first said, "Do not cast me away from You, and do not take Your spirit of holiness away from me" (Ibid. v. 13). Then, "Have me return to the glee of Your salvation" (Ibid. v. 14)—thus asking that God's miracles and salvation remain with him, and that he succeed at experiencing God's spirit as he once did.[22] That's followed by, "Uphold me with a willing spirit" (Ibid.), which means to say, though I've degraded myself by my acts of defiance and don't deserve miracles or revelations

---

16. See Supplementary Notes.

17. For like any beloved who is sinned against, God might "forgive" you for what you did, and spare you any further "arguments" or unpleasantries if you'd done some modicum of tshuvah. But like that lover, He still might not quite trust you as much as He had in the past, or feel as close to you.

18. . . . alone.

19. . . . upon us . . .

20. This alludes to the great intimacy and closeness to God known as The World to Come, "the true life everlasting," the experience of which is the "great light that encompasses all delight," as Rabbeinu Yonah puts it here.

It's described as the experience of, "delight(ing) in God and enjoy(ing) the radiance of His Divine presence" in *The Path of the Just*, where it's revealed to be "the true delight, the greatest enjoyment of all." In *Hilchot Tshuvah*, Rambam describes it as "a form of life without death (which) entails goodness without evil" (8:1), where "the righteous . . . bask in God's Glory" (8:2). Rambam also lets us know that "The great good that the soul will encounter in The World to Come can in no way be fathomed or known in this world . . . (and that it) is so exceedingly great that it can only be likened to the good things in this world metaphorically . . . (But it) is unfathomably, incomparably, and unparalleledly greater" (8:6). In other words, that is our reward, and the promised satisfaction due those who love and draw as close to God as they can. And it's likened metaphorically to the sort of "marital bliss" young lovers yearn for and can enjoy in this world when they partake in a marriage based on emotional, spiritual closeness and fusion. (See 3:143–171 for more about The World to Come.)

21. See Supplementary Notes.

22. Here is an allusion to the idea that one can have a World to Come experience in this world, though it's usually limited to the extraterrestrial, soul realm.

of Your holy authority. And though You've tolerated my iniquity, and I don't deserve to be as beloved and favored as I'd been before. Nonetheless, 'Uphold me with a willing spirit,' for Your generosity and goodness is everlasting."[23,24]

Hosea likewise said, "I will heal their backsliding, I will love them freely" (Hosea 14:5), which conforms to David's "Uphold me with a willing spirit."

43. Also pray to God, when you do tshuvah, to always help you with it.[25] As it's said, "Turn me back, and I will return. For You are God my Lord" (Jeremiah 31:17).

---

23. God Almighty is so loving and kind that He not only provides us with tshuvah as a gift outright, He also lovingly and generously helps us with it. The way a beloved would not only hear out your apologies, but would "coach" you in them, and make the circumstances surrounding them comfortable for you and welcoming.

24. The text continues with the following:

> It's actually written, "uphold me *and* a willing spirit" rather than "*with* a willing spirit." But that corresponds to "and (i.e., *with*) grain and wine have I sustained him" (Genesis 27:37).

25. See note 31 to 1:20.

Chapter Sixteen

ꙮꙮꙮꙮꙮꙮꙮꙮꙮꙮꙮ

44. Sixteenth Principle: Amending Your Misdeeds as Much as Possible[1]

It's said, "And God saw[2] their deeds that they had turned from their wrongful way" (Jonah 3:10), and,[3] "Let everyone turn from his wrongful way, and from the plunder that is in their hands" (Ibid. v. 8).[4] Because sins between one person and another, like theft and plunder, are only atoned for[5] when you return the stolen item.[6] That's also true if you aggrieved, tyrannized, disgraced, or slandered someone. You're not atoned for that until you ask your victim for forgiveness.[7]

As our sages put it, "Even after you will have paid your victim for his shame, troubles, and for the harm done him, you would not be atoned for the shame, troubles, and harm[8] until you ask him to forgive you. As it's said, 'Now, return the man's wife, for he is a prophet, and if he prays for you, you will live.' (Genesis 20:7)" (*Babba Kama* 92A).[9]

---

1. See Supplementary Notes.
2. . . . from . . .
3. . . . it's said before that . . .
4. That is, they plundered. Then they "turned" (שבו) from their guilty ways, "and from the plunder that is in their hands," which could also be translated to mean they "returned" (שבו) the plunder in their hands.
5. . . . by God . . .
6. . . . to your victim.
7. See Supplementary Notes.
8. . . . you caused him . . .
9. For it's only logical that animosity would linger as long as any wrong done wasn't

45. It's important to do this before confessing[10] when you do tshuvah, in order to make your confession acceptable. David did as much when he did tshuvah, before he confessed, as it's said, "I have sinned against You alone and done what is wrong in Your eyes; that You be justified in Your sentence, and right in Your judgment" (Psalms 51:6). That means to say, I am considered a sinner by You alone, and all I need is Your forgiveness. For if I sinned against another, I already asked him for forgiveness, and have been atoned for.[11]

Or else it means, "I have sinned against You alone"—I haven't sinned against another person, nor pleaded with him. Nor have I taken anything from anyone I'd need to be forgiven by, or return a stolen item to. My atonement depends on Your forgiveness alone. "So that You are justified in Your sentence, and right in Your judgment"[12]—to show the nations how just You are, and how very forgiving You are when you speak to, judge, and sentence me.

It's also written, "So that You are justified in Your sentence . . ." to indicate

---

made right. But what has that to do with my being atoned for by God? And what's the point of mentioning how wise it would be to return Abraham's wife, Sarah, since he might pray for you if you did? Or the fact that his prayers are propitious, since he's a prophet?

Apparently there are two points being made here, and the first is this: It's relatively easy to confess your wrongdoings to God. Primarily because you realize He knows of them already, and that your uttering them is only the last, practical step of a long, inner process of realization, rejection, and remorse. But confessing and making amends to another person is a whole other matter. He likely had no idea what you did, and your admitting to it undoes his opinion of you (which is always so threatening). Or if he did know, your affirming it rankles at his being and sets off an animal need for revenge. So, the soul who would confess and make amends to another person, then confess his having wronged that person to God, too, is beloved. And almost cannot help but be atoned for.

The second point is this: As is known, victims of crimes or insult feel utterly vulnerable. As if suddenly kidnapped, and abruptly subject to the schemes of strangers. And like anyone kidnapped then rescued and brought home again, victims who've then had their property—or their dignity—restored, are buoyant and seemingly invincible for a time. In fact, though, few souls are actually so vulnerable, and not one human being is invincible. Grasp that fully, and you approach truth, brush against prophecy, and are likely to have your prayers answered.

10. . . . to God . . .

11. The text continues with the following:

It's like, "I will have sinned against my father for ever" (Genesis 44:32), that is, I'll always be considered a sinner by my father because of this sin, since he wouldn't have forgiven me for it. As the *Targum* put it, "I will be a sinner to my father." [This refers to Judah's promise to his father, Jacob, that Judah himself would ensure that Benjamin (Jacob's youngest son) is returned to him from Egypt. And that if he didn't, then Judah would always be wrong in his father's eyes.]

12. i.e., And I did that, "So that You are justified in Your sentence . . ."

that the greater the sin, the greater the realization of how charitable[13] God is when He forgives you.[14] Hence it's as if to say that the sin was committed in the first place to reveal God's generosity and righteousness when He forgives as He judges. It's thus like, "They made idols for themselves from their silver and gold, to be cut off" (Hosea 8:4). In fact, they cut[15] silver and gold in order to make idols. But it's worded to seem as if they made idols in order to be cut off.

As such, "so that You are justified in Your sentence and right in Your judgment" could also mean, So that You are justified regardless of whether You absolve or indict. And, "that they may be cut off" could also mean, So that they may be cut off for doing that.

46. Our sages said about the first interpretation[16] that, "It is like the situation of the doctor who looked at a wound and said, 'This is a terrible wound!', to which his patient replied, 'I was only made to suffer such a terrible wound in order to demonstrate how justified your healing methods are, and to prove your abilities!'" (Midrash *Tehillim* 51).[17]

But we'll expand upon this principle in the fourth gate.[18]

---

13. The roots of "just" and "charitable" are the same, צדק. Hence, the double meaning.

14. Mention of God's charity and forgiveness here here once again reminds us of the seeming leniency of tshuvah. Why should anyone who commits a crime be forgiven in the first place? And why through tshuvah alone? In fact, one Midrash calls tshuvah a "bribe" (*Shocher Tov, Tehillim* 17), since a person seems to be paying off the True Judge with it to avoid the consequences of his sins. As it's stated in *The Path of the Just* (Ch. 4, p. 40), "According to the strict letter of the law, the sinner should be punished immediately . . . and the punishment itself should be meted out with great anger, as we would expect in the case of one who rebels against the word of the Creator." Nonetheless, God has granted us tshuvah, and it's always available to us. And just as the greater the depth of depravity a person returns from wholeheartedly, the more righteous he appears after the fact. So, too, the more serious the crime forgiven through tshuvah, the more generous God is seen to be. In fact, this mechanism of darkness followed by light and the like is, at bottom, the very workings of the universe, and God's own tool for revelation (see Moshe Chaim Luzzatto's *Da'at T'vunot*).

15. i.e., quarried . . .

16. i.e., that "the greater the sin, the greater the realization of how charitable God is when He forgives you."

17. That is, just as a doctor is proven great by his ability to heal a dread wound, God is proven merciful and charitable by His willingness to forgive a person's serious transgressions.

18. See 4:18–19.

Chapter Seventeen

47. Seventeenth Principle: Expressing Kindness and Truth

It's said, "Sins are atoned for through kindness and truth; and one turns from wrongdoing by fearing God" (Proverbs 16:6). Reflect, now, on the inner import of this verse.

In truth, if you sin and don't return to God, your sin won't be forgiven by any act of kindness on your part. As it's said, "(God) favors no one,[1] and takes no bribes" (Deuteronomy 10:17), which our sages explained to mean that He will not be bribed by *mitzvot* to forgive or bypass sins (*Yalkut Mishle* 11:947).[2] They also said, "Whoever says that God overlooks sins will be overlooked by Him" (*Babba Kama* 50A).[3] But God *will hold back His wrath.*[4] Yet He'll nonetheless exact payment for your actions directly upon you if you don't listen.[5]

So when Solomon says that "Sins are atoned for through kindness and truth," he's referring to one who'd done tshuvah. For there are instances of sin where tshuvah and Yom Kippur are held in abeyance, and tribulations purge the sin, as we'll explain in the fourth gate.[6] So what acts of kindness do is shield you,[7] and protect you from

---

1. . . . person over another, unjustly . . .

2. See Supplementary Notes.

3. That is, whoever thinks God doesn't care enough about him to notice *everything* about him, will in fact *not* be cared for to that degree by God. (See Supplementary Notes.)

4. . . . as a consequence of your acts of kindness.

5. i.e., if you continue not to listen to Him. That is, while the True Judge won't waive charges against you because of your record of good deeds, He'll defer judgment in light of them, to allow you time for tshuvah. But if you don't do tshuvah, He'll sentence you soon enough.

6. See 4:11–13.

7. . . . in such instances . . .

tribulations. They also deliver you from death, as it's written, "Charity will save you from death" (Proverbs 10:2).

There's one sin, however—profaning God's name[8]—in whose case both tshuvah and tribulations are held in abeyance, and death purges. As it's said, "Surely this sin will not be forgiven you till you die" (Isaiah 22:14). Try, in that instance,[9] to champion truth, to bolster it, and to be encouraged by it, as well as to convey truth's light to other Jews by upholding men of truth and exalting them, while denigrating liars and casting them to the ground.[10]

For that's how you sanctify God's name, and lend glory and splendor to the belief in Him, and to the service of Him in the world. And how you strengthen and glorify the Sanctuary of His Torah. So do as much as you can to sanctify God's name, to encourage the truth, to accommodate it and come to its aid, and you'll be forgiven for your sinful profanation of His name with your tshuvah. Because you substituted truth for your blameworthy profanation.[11] And your tshuvah corresponded to your lapses.[12] That's what's meant by "Sins are forgiven through kindness and truth."

---

8. See Supplementary Notes.

9. i.e., if you're guilty of having profaned God's name.

10. A word about the structure of this section. Rabbeinu Yonah spent the beginning of this explaining how "Sin is forgiven through kindness . . ." (only after tshuvah), this paragraph explains how "Sin (i.e., the sin of profaning God's name) is forgiven through . . . truth." The rest of the verse, ". . . and one turns from wrongdoing by fearing God," will be discussed in ¶49.

11. . . . of God's name.

12. There's a fundamental identification of God and Torah with truth. Malachi 2:6 refers to "The Torah of truth." And Psalms 31:6 speaks of God as being "The God of truth." So when a person profanes or "*hollows*" (מחלל) God's "name," i.e., His reputation, he removes the ring of truth and dependability from God Himself, and His Torah. And endows untruth with a reputation for honesty.

Two things alone would undo such a sin. Either the death of the person who committed it, which would show that he, too, was mortal, and hence rooted in relativity and untruth, rather than in the Absolute and in utter truth. Or his tshuvah and public lambasting of untruth, and extolling of truth. (See Supplementary Notes.)

Chapter Eighteen

48. Eighteenth Principle: Keeping Your Sin Before You All the Time

It's important to always remember your sins, and to never forget them for the rest of your life or allow them to leave your heart till the day of your death.[1] As it's said, "I know my acts of defiance, and my sin is always before me" (Psalms 51:5).[2] This principle will be expanded upon in the fourth gate.[3]

---

1. This last phrase, "ומלבבו לא יחליפו עד בא חליפתו," can be translated more literally as "don't supplant (the memories of your sins) from your heart until you are supplanted"; "don't have them vanish from your heart until you vanish"; or "don't displace them from your heart until you're displaced." As if Rabbeinu Yonah were equating a person himself with his memories (by using parallel language for your memories and your self), as we often do. In fact, a common horror associated with the possibility of losing one's memory is the notion of losing all sense of self. As the expression goes, "After all, what am I, if not my memories?" And as is also often said when a person is incapacitated, God forbid, or removed from a situation he once loved, "Well, at least I have my memories," as if that were the essential factor.

But the truth is, Rabbeinu Yonah is not saying that at all. Instead he's alluding to a much deeper notion that touches upon the nature of reality, God's intentions for the universe, our true being's make-up, and the like—all of which is far beyond the scope of this analysis. Suffice it to say now, though, that the point is that with the exception of our immortal soul, we're as impermanent as a mere memory (as is alluded to in the verse, "There are many thoughts in man's heart, but God's advice endures forever" [Proverbs 19:21]), and made of the same stuff. That alone should give us pause and humble us. The God-fearing would be moved to tshuvah with it in mind, while others will simply not care. (See Supplementary Notes.)

2. That is, if you're to truly reconcile with your beloved and change your ways, you'd need to always remember how wrong or insensitive you'd been in the past, and how obtuse you could be in the future as a consequence. Holding that in mind will keep you alert, and humble you. And will remind you of how precious your relationship to your beloved is.

3. See 4:21.

Chapter Nineteen

ᕫᕬᕫᕬᕫᕬᕫᕬᕫᕬᕫᕬᕫᕬᕫᕬᕫᕬᕫᕬᕫᕬ

49. Nineteenth Principle: Shunning a Sin When Faced With It and Still Fully Craving It[1]

Our sages said, "Whose tshuvah reaches the very Throne of Glory? One who is tested[2] under the very same circumstances, in the very same place, and with the very same woman,[3] and remains blameless" (*Yomah* 86B). That is, one who's faced with the very same[4] sin, while his impulses are just as strong and powerfully situated in his being as they were when he first sinned, who nonetheless prevails over them and avoids sin, through the strength of his fear of God and dread of His glory.[5]

But if[6] that doesn't avail itself to you[7] then if you'd instill more and more of the fear of God in your heart day after day, for the rest of your life. And would have

---

1. See Supplementary Notes.

2. . . . again . . .

3. i.e., the very same temptation.

4. . . . chance to . . .

5. That is, you'll have proven yourself to have fully changed and matured if the external circumstances were somehow reproduced, and you show yourself to be the sort of person who wouldn't sin in those circumstances. But for no other reason than for your committment to your Beloved. Not because you were afraid of being caught, of losing face, of becoming guilt-laden, or because you knew that sinning again would make life too uncomfortable. Only because it would adversely affect, even ruin, your relationship to your Beloved.

6. . . . the opportunity to do . . .

7. . . . you'll nonetheless prove yourself blameless . . .

substituted the capacity for fear[8] for the need to fulfill the demands of your impulses, and have overcome your urges. Then He who scrutinizes hearts would grasp; He who fashioned you would know then that if you were to be tested by being placed in that original situation that you'd be spared from[9] your impulses. And you'd be considered by God to have reached the highest level of tshuvah.[10]

That's what Solomon was referring to when he said, "Sins are atoned for through kindness and truth; and one turns from wrongdoing by fearing God" (Proverbs 16:6).[11] That is, that you can turn from wrongdoing when faced with it through the fear of God.[12,13]

As our sages put it, "If you stay in place rather than sin, you are accredited with having fulfilled a mitzvah" (*Makkot* 23B), as would be the case if you came upon a sin and were spared from[14] it.

---

8. . . . of God . . .

9. . . . acting out on . . .

10. And that's to say that you'd still prove yourself to have changed essentially even if you weren't actually put to the test. If you nonetheless devoted yourself to so deepening and widening your relationship to your Beloved all along, that it became patently clear that you'd pass the test if it came your way.

11. See ¶47, where this verse is first cited, as well as our notes there.

12. See Supplementary Notes.

13. The text continues with the following:

In fact, the word "turns" is used in the infinitive here, which lends credence to our explanation, since it could have said "Turn from wrongdoing by fearing God" [rather than, "One turns from wrongdoing by fearing God," as Rabbeinu Yonah understands it]. As to the expressions, "Turn from wrongdoing and do good" (Psalms 34:15) and "He fears God and turns from wrongdoing" (Job 1:8), they imply that you're to turn away from wrongdoing when you're faced with it. Because it wouldn't say "turn from" something or another unless you were very close to doing it.

14. . . . committing . . .

Chapter Twenty

෯෯෯෯෯෯෯෯෯෯෯෯෯෯

50. Twentieth Principle: Turning Others Away From Sin as Much as You Can[1]

It's said, "Return, and have yourselves turn from all your defiances"[2] (Ezekiel 18:30), which teaches us that doing that is one of the principles of tshuvah.

And it's said, "Criticize your neighbor diligently, and do not bear sin on his account" (Leviticus 19:17) to teach you that if you don't criticize him, you'll suffer the consequences of his sin.[3] As David said in the "Tshuvah Psalm," "I will teach the defiant Your ways, so[4] sinners will return to You" (Psalms 51:15).[5]

---

1. See Supplementary Notes.

2. That is, not only must you return to God, but you must have others of "yourselves" (i.e., others of your people) return to Him as well.

3. See Supplementary Notes.

4. . . . that we two . . .

5. Just as there's no better advocate for sobriety than a drunk come to sobriety, and no better champion of religion than a renegade come to faith, there's no better proponent of love restored than a once-disenchanted lover. And while many would sneer at such a person (even call him a "hypocrite" and a charlatan), others who are like him would know him to be honest and full of conviction. And to be fortunate enough to have seen "both sides," and to know the difference firsthand. In fact, if such a person were not to try to convince others he'd once been like to change, he'd be assumed to lack depth of conviction. And his newfound sobriety, etc., could legitimately be questioned.

Chapter Twenty-one

51. The Hindrances to Tshuvah[1]

We've thus concluded our explanation of the principles of tshuvah. Reflect now upon the things that hinder it. For tshuvah becomes difficult for you when you cast off your yoke[2] and constantly stumble in one of these areas.[3]

If, in fact, you do stumble in one,[4] then be strong, and enunciate[5] fearlessly, pray and plead a lot, muster all your strength and satisfy all of the principles of tshuvah, as well as the suggestions to be offered in the fourth gate. You'll be shown sympathy, and mercy will be conferred upon you.[6]

52. I'll now tell you what our sages added about this. They said (Rif, *Yomah* Ch. 8), "Twenty-four things hinder tshuvah:[7] 1) rumor-mongering,[8] 2)

---

1. This phrase isn't included in the text, and was inserted here for ease of reference.

2. i.e., you commitment—to God . . . (see our comment to ¶6)

3. For while God "never closes the doors to tshuvah to us, even when we're very defiant and rebellious, and utterly unfaithful" (¶1), and while you'll "be shown sympathy, and mercy will be conferred upon you" (end of this ¶) if you follow the advice given here, nonetheless there are hindrances to tshuvah. Things that make it difficult to achieve. But not impossible. And even then, you'd have to have dismissed your commitment altogether, and to have *constantly* stumbled in one of the instances to be suggested shortly. And even then, tshuvah would only be "difficult for you."

The underlying message is that nothing will stand in the way of tshuvah, if you're intent on doing it. Nothing. As it's put in *The Duties of the Heart* (The Gate of Repentance, p. 339), "In truth, only your mind and your scheming heart prevent you from repenting. For the gates of repentance will never be closed to you, and nothing will ever deter you if you truly want to draw closer to God."

4. . . . constantly (see previous note) . . .

5. . . . your confessions and remorse . . .

6. . . . by your once estranged Beloved, God.

7. See Supplementary Notes.

8. It's so difficult to do tshuvah for this because of the complications and all the people involved. As Rabbeinu Yonah says in 3:222, "it's impossible to estimate the damage done by

slander,[9] 3) fury,[10] 4) thinking untoward thoughts,[11] 5) associating with wrong-doers,[12] 6) regularly accepting food from those who don't have enough,[13] 7) staring at instances of nudity,[14] 8) sharing in stolen property,[15] 9) saying, 'I will sin and then do tshuvah,' for it is said in the Mishna, 'Whoever says, "I will sin and then do tshuvah" is not given the chance to do tshuvah. And whoever says, "I will sin and

---

rumor-mongering, for it's boundless. It compounds hatred in the world . . . (And) it kills three: those who practice it, those who listen to it, and those who are spoken about."

9. It's written in 3:204, "it's very hard for a slanderer to do tshuvah. For after having trained his tongue to speak lies, consigned his lips to evil, and been in the habit for so long, he can no longer control himself."

10. See notes 30 and 31 to ¶28 above.

11. See 3:27, where it's written, "You're also obliged to try to embrace the sorts of practises that would automatically have you keep God in mind, like . . . ennobling your thoughts. . . . For the Nation of Israel can achieve all sorts of lovely traits, which will then distinguish it, when it keeps God in mind." So you'd find it difficult doing tshuvah and thus getting close to God if you were in the habit of "thinking untoward thoughts."

12. As it's explained in 3:198, "You're obliged to leave the company of wrongdoers. Because you'd have to suffer the consequences of always hearing their evil words and being reticent about responding to them. . . . (And because) you yourself will incur a transgression through their sins by always listening to their evil words and remaining silent." So, associating with wrongdoers is a hindrance to tshuvah because you'd be in a situation where you'd be too discomfited to return to the side of good, since you'd be outnumbered and have a hard time withstanding social pressures.

13. For the utmost seriousness of this and any other insensitivities to the poor see 3:15, "In fact, we find in the case of the people of Sodom, who were very wicked and sinful in God's eyes, and committed many nefarious crimes including robbery, brutality, miscarriage of justice, and having illicit relations (cf. *Sanhedrin* 109), . . . that the only reason they were brought to ruin and devastation was for the sin of not being charitable!" So the sort of person who'd *take* from the poor would be more sinful yet, and would find it exceedingly hard to do tshuvah.

14. One reason could be based on the statement in 3:64, "(Do not) stare at a married woman, or at any other woman forbidden of you. Because you might go astray as a result," which is all the more so true if you stare at nudity. But there's another point to be made. When one stares at nudity he's inexorably seduced by the allure and magic of the physical, visible, and concrete. All abstract notions, lofty thoughts, philosophical ideals, and the like go by the wayside at the moment. And it becomes very, very hard to return to God. In fact, sins associated with that trait are said by the Zohar (1:188A, 219B; see *Even Ha'Ezer* 23:1) to make tshuvah impossible. Nonetheless many righteous and great souls dispute that, and underscore that tshuvah is always possible (see *Sichot HaRan* 71, *Netivot Shalom*, vol. 1, and *Chelkat M'Chukok* to *Even Ha'Ezer* 23:1). (See our Supplementary Note to ¶35 as well, which speaks of the *high* arrogance of this sin, which in itself hinders tshuvah.)

15. Because you'd never know whom the goods were stolen from, since you didn't steal it yourself. So it would be very hard to return it and make amends. And as it's said in ¶44, "sins between one person and another, like theft and plunder, are only atoned for when you return the stolen item . . . (and) ask (your victim) for forgiveness."

Yom Kippur will atone for my sins" will not be atoned for by Yom Kippur' (*Yomah* 85B),[16] 10) achieving honor at another's expense,[17] 11) separating yourself from the congregation,[18] 12) belittling your ancestors or teachers,[19] 13) cursing the masses,[20] 14) preventing the masses from doing a mitzvah,[21] 15) causing another to deviate from the path of good and to follow a bad one instead,[22] 16) using a pauper's pledge

---

16. For though tshuvah is characterized as "an escape hatch" in ¶2. And though Rabbeinu Yonah cites a Midrash there about the guard at a jail that was escaped from who "came by and saw the escape hatch, and he saw the one remaining prisoner, (and) began to club him with his stick and to say, 'Imbecile! There's an escape hatch right in front of you, and yet you aren't rushing to save your own life!'" Nonetheless, one who'd sneak into the jail the night before he committed his crime to dig an escape hatch would certainly not be praised. And any cohort who refused to be a part of such a plot would certainly not be chastised by the guard.

17. This is equivalent to shaming someone, about which Rabbeinu Yonah said, "The person who makes another person blanch (with shame) doesn't realize the seriousness of his sin, so he doesn't grow bitter as a result of his transgression. . . . He's too (emotionally) removed to do tshuvah" (3:141). And he'd have a hard time mustering the wherewithal to do tshuvah.

18. "Those who separate themselves from the community by not accepting the decisions community leaders instituted, discourage the hesitant, and cause the multitude to sin" (3:168) with their defiance. So they'd have a hard time convincing all those they'd affected negatively that they'd been wrong (as they would have to, to do tshuvah).

19. See all the harm done by those who belittle ancestors and teachers who all transmit the tradition. As Rabbeinu Yonah put it in 3:148, "As everyone knows, among the ways to sanctify God's name is to show with everything you say, every wink of your eye, and every use and move of your hand that what underlies man's existence, where his prominence lies, and what is so becoming, important, exalted and valuable about him is his service to and fear of God and His Torah. . . . That brings honors upon God. But when you demean scholars and those who fear God, you undermine this whole idea, and express its opposite in everything you do. It's as if you were saying that Divine service isn't primary, that honor and glory are based on worldly achievements, and that something other than serving God is essential." It would thus be very hard to undo all the harm done to others' attitudes and perspectives about what's primary in life and what's not, as you would have to to do tshuvah.

20. If, "No servant who loved his master's enemies and became close to those who distanced themselves from him could ever love the master himself" (3:191), it stands to reason that no one who cursed his Master's servants could ever love Him either, and would have trouble doing tshuvah.

21. Rabbeinu Yonah speaks of people who not only "can't bear (the thought of) other people studying Torah. Or . . . serving and fearing God," who then "put those thoughts into action, and actually discourage others from studying Torah or doing *mitzvot*, out of their hate for God" (3:160). And he refers to them as "God's enemies," who lose their place in The World to Come, whose spirits are destroyed, and whose sins "are visited on their children, grandchildren, and great-grandchildren" (3:159). Such people would clearly find it hard establishing the fast and sure bond to God that tshuvah is.

22. You'd certainly have trouble fulfilling the twentieth principle, of "turning others

for personal gain,[23] 17) taking a bribe to pervert justice,[24] 18) finding a lost object and not returning it to its owner,[25] 19) seeing your child going bad and not objecting,[26] 20) eating from the sustenance of paupers, orphans, and widows,[27] 21) arguing against the words of sages,[28] 22) suspecting the innocent,[29] 23) hating criticism,[30] and 24) maligning *mitzvot*.[31]

---

away from sin as much as you can" (¶50), if you were prone toward drawing them away from the path of goodness in the first place. And you'd certainly be thought to be someone "alienated from God" who doesn't believe there are consequences to sins (¶3) if you were guilty of this sin, too. Because you obviously didn't think there were consequences to your friend's sins either, since you encouraged him in them. And how could one alienated from God find it easy to do tshuvah? (See 3:37 as well.)

23. See note 13 above and apply it here. Also see Deuteronomy 24:12, "And if a man is poor, you must not go to sleep holding his pledge."

24. Any judge doing that would have trouble doing tshuvah simply because it would prove him to be thoroughly alienated from God, the True Judge, his exemplar, who "favors no one, and takes no bribes" (Deuteronomy 10:17), as cited in 47 above.

25. For if you yourself would "find it hard losing a small amount of money" (¶12), yet wouldn't sympathize with someone else who'd lost something that you found. You'd certainly find it hard regretting having "lost" and threatened your relationship to God (see our notes there), and doing tshuvah.

26. In his comments to Proverbs 1:4 Rabbeinu Yonah explains that this trait hinders tshuvah, "because (the child) was under your control . . . and there was always a chance that he could have restrained his urges, and changed his character" with your input. But you did nothing to help. And thus all that he and you did wrong would have to be rectified if you're to do tshuvah, which is thus doubly difficult to ensure.

27. A person guilty of that would be closely associated with those "culpable for death at the hands of Heaven" (see 3:108–118), so alienated is he from God. So he'd find it very hard reconciling with Him and doing tshuvah.

28. If you'd argue against the words of the sages you'd be "unlikely to do tshuvah, since what you did (wrong) doesn't matter enough to you" (3:6).

29. Those who suspect the innocent are likely to be slanderers (see 3:211), who are "considered deniers of God's existence" (3:200). They'd therefore find it very hard to do tshuvah. (Also see 3:217.)

30. See 2:11 where Rabbeinu Yonah writes, "The person who hates being criticized is worse than (an out and out sinner), for he'd be hopeless and incorrigible even with serious admonishment, and would be doomed to die. . . . (In fact) his hate for criticism expresses a hate for the words of God" and God Himself. So he'd certainly find it hard doing tshuvah.

31. Rabbeinu Yonah speaks of maligners in 3:174–177. He associates their ways with arrogance (¶175), and points out that they're so arrogant that they "even demean the holy ones or prophets," needless to say, the *mitzvot* (see ¶176). And that such a person "enrages his Maker" who will then "malign those maligners" who are "beyond hope" (Ibid.). In fact, to further illustrate how far gone such individuals are, Rabbeinu Yonah adds that "the habit of maligning only becomes a part of you when you cast off the yoke of Heaven" (177). Is there any wonder then why one who maligns God's *mitzvot* will have trouble doing tshuvah?

Synopsis

⧼decorative ornament⧽

Tshuvah is a chance to rise above your wrongful deeds, and to avoid suffering their consequences. God Himself taught us how to do it, exhorted us to, and never closes the doors to it. And while it's better to do tshuvah out of the fear and love of Him, it's still and all accepted in response to suffering. It also enables you to transcend your nature, and imbues you with a spirit of purity, which brings on the love of God (¶1). But the longer you'd postpone avoiding God's resentment, the guiltier you'd be. Since you had the chance to avoid it through tshuvah, your escape hatch, and you didn't take advantage of it (¶2). But only the oblivious and naive, and those who don't believe there are consequences to sinning, would postpone tshuvah. Not the learned (¶3).

Do tshuvah immediately by sighing, trembling, worrying, and crying. And then, when you're next faced with the chance to sin, you'll remember all that, and you won't sin. But you'd grow more and more guilty if you delay tshuvah, because you wouldn't have learned your lesson, learned how to augment your fear of God, or been alert to your impulses (¶4). And because repeating a sin makes it seem allowable, which is a very serious mistake. In fact, if you repeat a sin again and again, and you intend to do it one other time but you get waylaid, the act is ascribed to you anyway (¶5).

In truth, the righteous sometimes sin. But they prevail over their impulses, and never repeat it. But if you don't take precautions against a well-known sin you'd still be considered an "apostate in one area." Since you'd have decided what to observe, and what not to, of your own volition (¶6). It's also important to realize that the same sin committed ten times over is considered ten distinct sins (not one blanket sin) (¶7).

Many people mean to be careful about certain known sins but aren't, because those sins become "allowable" to them, including worthless oaths; cursing by the use of God's name; taking His name in vain or mentioning it in unclean places or with dirty hands; turning away from the poor; slandering; hating for no reason; being arrogant; evoking terror; staring pruriently; neglecting Torah study, etc. So it's important for you to record your sins and to review them daily when you do tshuvah (¶8). Nonetheless, the deeper you go in tshuvah, the closer you get to God. And while every attempt at it brings forgiveness, your soul is only thoroughly purified and your sins undone when you purify and prepare yourself in the ways about to be enunciated (¶9).

First: Expressing Remorse. Know that abandoning God is wrong, that there are consequences to doing that, and that sins are avenged for. And ask yourself what you've done, and how you could have not feared God. Realize how callous you've been to your body; how mean you've been to your soul; that you've overlooked The World to Come; that you've become animal-like, or lower yet; and that you've disregarded your very reason for living, as well as the reality of death (¶10).

Second: Ridding Yourself of the Sin. Resolve never to commit it again. If you tend to sin only when ensnared by your impulses, begin tshuvah with remorse, then augment your fear of God. But if you always want to satisfy your cravings, begin doing tshuvah by ridding yourself of that sin, and determining never to commit it again. *Then* regret what you did, and return to God. If troubles come upon you then, accept them right off, and abandon your mistaken ways (¶11).

Third: Being Sad. Reiterate how wrong it is to defy God. Grow sadder and sadder, until you're caught in a whirlwind of sighs and bitterness. For if you would mourn, sigh, etc., losing your money, you should all the more so do that "losing" God, who created you, has been generous to you, and supports and protects you (¶12). In fact, the efficacy of your tshuvah is measured by how bitter and sad you are about your sins, which is more valuable than torment and pain (¶13). So, focus your desires onto the service of God; your sighs onto concern for your sins; and your worries onto your shortcomings in the service of God (¶14).

Fourth: Manifesting Anguish. The heart and eyes are agitators of sin. The sins relevant to the heart are atoned for by bitterness, sighing, and contrition. And the sins relevant to the eyes are atoned for by tears (¶15).

Fifth: Worrying. Worry about your sins, and fear their consequences. And about being negligent in your anguish, bitterness, fasting, and weeping. As well as in your over-all service to God. (¶16). Worry about being overtaken again by your yetzer harah, and augment your fear of God to avoid that (¶17). As a rule, don't expose your sins to others. But you must admit to what you did to the person you sinned against, recompense him, and apologize. And you're to confess to and lament your sins against God, which have profaned His name (¶18). Tshuvah is essentially based on remorse, confession, and ridding yourself of your sin, though there are many levels of tshuvah (¶19). Worry as well about not having fulfilled the various levels of tshuvah, and about new impulses arising. Regularly augment your fear of God, and pray for help in tshuvah and in continuing to resist your impulses. If you think you've met your requirements, you're being pretentious. and are acknowledging neither your lowliness nor your obligation to improve as much as possible (¶20).

Sixth: Feeling Ashamed. The only reason you're ashamed to sin in front of other people, and yet you're not ashamed to sin in front of God, is because He's not on your mind (¶21). The highest level of shame is being mortified when you find God overlooking your sins, extending you a reprieve, not penalizing you, and not reacting to your sins for the moment. But you only achieve such a level of shame by meditating upon God's greatness and by recalling that He's always watching over you, examining your innermost being, and scrutinizing your thoughts (¶22).

Seventh: Surrendering Wholeheartedly and Being Humble. Express your awareness of God and your realization of how base one who sins against him actually is by surrendering and being humble in His presence, and thus pleasing Him (¶23). While there are many degrees of surrender, the greatest one for tshuvah's sake consists of augmenting your service to God and taking no credit for it. As well as serving Him demurely and in private (¶24). As such, never accept honor for your honorable accomplishments, to say nothing of those which God doesn't honor, like wealth, strength and knowledge of anything other than of Him (¶25). Surrender in order to rid yourself of personal traits that lead to sin and rebellion, as well (¶26). And avoid arrogance, because it brings on many sins, and is itself a sin. It also has you serve your impulses rather than God (¶27). Also be humble to avoid being angry or short-tempered, in order not to take things said to heart, and to overlook things. Doing that will atone for your sins and will be a great source of hope for you (¶28).

Eight: Manifesting Surrender. Respond gently, be indifferent to attractive clothing and ornaments, and lower your eyes. That will remind you to be humble (¶29).

Ninth: Overcoming Your Physical Cravings. Since it's your cravings that have you sin, establish barriers to them by abstaining and not acceding to your cravings even for permitted things. Eat to stay healthy, and be intimate to procreate and to fulfill your obligations to your spouse. Otherwise you'll be overwhelmed by your impulses (¶30). Adjust the cravings that are under your control, subsume them to reason, and you'll correct your deeds. Because they're rooted in your cravings, which affect all you do. Know as well that you won't get along with others if you always indulge your cravings, but you will if you act through reason. And that if you always indulge your cravings, you'll surely sin in all areas (¶31). Then you can reason, "Why give in to this forbidden urge, when I deny myself permitted things?" (¶32). Overcoming your urges also proves how righteous and well-meaning your intent to do tshuvah really was, since you've come to despise the very inclination that brought you to sin, which pleases God (¶33). In fact, to be a true "disciple of Abraham" you'd have to overcome cravings for permitted things (¶34).

Tenth: Correcting Your Actions Through the Agent Used to Sin. If you stared pruriently, always keep your eyes lowered; if you slandered, study Torah; etc. All in all, use the very agent used to sin to do *mitzvot* with instead (¶35).

Eleventh: Scrutinizing Your Ways. For three reasons: to remember what to confess to, in order to realize how many sins you committed and thus come to true humility, and in order to set up safeguards, since you might "relapse" (¶36).

Twelfth: Examining, Knowing, and Recognizing the Seriousness of Each Sin. For by discovering the consequences for each, you'll realize how serious each is. And that will provoke bitter tears, humility, and the fear of sinning (¶37).

Thirteenth: Taking Your Minor Sins Seriously. Because you should concen-trrate upon the greatness of Him who warned you not to do it, rather than on the smallness of the sin anyway; because minor sins easily add up to the equivalent of serious ones; because when you repeat them, you start to see them as acceptable and become careless; and because if you can't conquer your yetzer harah with a lesser sin, you won't be able to conquer it with serious ones (¶38). Worrying about *not* doing a mitzvah is just as important as worrying about committing a serious sin (¶39).

Fourteenth: Confessing. Articulate your ancestors' sins, besides your own. Because you'd be punished for them, too, if you followed in their ways (¶40).

Fifteenth: Praying. Ask God to have mercy on you, and to forgive you for your sins. For your good deeds will only be rewarded and shielded you when you've done tshuvah, otherwise they'll be overlaid by sin (¶41). Pray that God be as pleased with you now, that you've done tshuvah, as He was before you sinned. Because it's possible for your sins to have been forgiven and for you to have been spared tribulations, and still not be accepted by God (¶42). Also pray to God to always help you with tshuvah (¶43).

Sixteenth: Amending Your Misdeeds as Much as Possible. Your crime won't be forgiven until you return what you stole, or ask the person you oppressed, shamed, or slandered to forgive you (¶44). And ask his forgiveness before you confess to God (¶45). Like a doctor whose greatness is best evidenced when a patient is cured of a dread disease, God's mercy and charity are best evidenced when a sinner is forgiven for a serious transgression (¶46).

Seventeenth: Expressing Kindness and Truth. While God won't be bribed by your acts of kindness to forgive sins, He'll nonetheless be slow to anger as a consequence of them. So, what acts of kindness will do is shield you from tribulations in certain instances, after you'd done tshuvah. And your exalting Torah and its scholars, and denigrating those who pursue untruth in addition to your tshuvah, will atone for your having profaned God's name (¶47).

Eighteenth: Keeping Your Sin Before You All the Time. Remember your sins to the day of your death (¶48).

Nineteenth: Shunning a Sin When Faced With It and Still Fully Craving It. You've clearly achieved the highest form of tshuvah when you're faced with the opportunity to commit a sin again, which you're still drawn to and capable of, which you nonetheless don't commit because of your fear of God. But even if you never face that situation, yet you grow so much so in the fear of God daily that you *would* resist, then God accepts that. And you'd have achieved the highest level of tshuvah (¶49).

Twentieth: Turning Others Away From Sin as Much as You Can. Not only should you do tshuvah, but you should have others do so, too, by criticizing them when they sin (¶50).

Consider the following hindrances to tshuvah. If you cast off all responsibility and stumble in one of them all the time, it will be difficult for you to do tshuvah. You'd need to pray and plead a lot, and to fulfill the above principles of tshuvah as well as to accept the suggestions offered in the fourth gate. You'll be shown mercy if you do (¶51).

The hindrances: 1) rumor-mongering, 2) slander, 3) fury, 4) thinking untoward thoughts, 5) associating with wrongdoers, 6) regularly accepting food from those who don't have enough, 7) staring at instances of nudity, 8) sharing in stolen property, 9) planning to repent after sinning, 10) achieving honor at another's expense, 11) seperating yourself from the congregation, 12) belittling your ancestors or teachers, 13) cursing the masses, 14) preventing the masses from doing a mitzvah, 15) causing another to deviate from the path of good and to follow the bad one instead, 16) using a pauper's pledge for personal gain, 17) taking a bribe to pervert justice, 18) finding a lost object and not returning it, 19) seeing your child going bad and not objecting, 20) eating from the sustenance of paupers, orphans, and widows, 21) arguing against the words of sages, 22) suspecting the innocent, 23) hating criticism, and 24) maligning *mitzvot* (¶52).

Gate Two

GUIDANCE IN THE INSTANCES IN WHICH YOU CAN BE MOVED TO RETURN TO GOD

The six instances in which you're likely to be moved to tshuvah are as follows:

1. **When you're overrun by troubles,** and you realize that it's your sinning ways that brought that all on. What you should do then is examine your ways, and return to God, realize that tribulations atone for sins and undo damage done, and trust that they are the "darkness before the (great) light." But if you come upon troubles when you're genuinely free of sin, know that those troubles will increase your eternal reward, and are actually a product of God's love (¶'s 2–6).
2. **When you grow old,** and you reflect upon the approach of death. But, don't presuppose yourself to be righteous then, by taking your sins lightly or forgetting them. And stop focusing on your bodily needs and upon ephemeris. Focus instead upon the fear of God, self-examination and -improvement, Torah and *mitzvot,* and on grateful prayer (¶'s 7–9).
3. **When you're admonished by a sage,** and you take it upon yourself to do everything he says, and utterly transform yourself. For by doing that, you'll instantly accrue upon yourself the merit associated with all the *mitzvot.* Hearing out reproach also fulfills the function of the ears which, as vital organs, are certainly expected to serve God their own way (¶'s 10–12).
4. **When delving into Torah,** and you start to take its admonishments and warnings to heart, and you resolve to improve your ways (¶13).
5. **When you face the onset of the Ten Days of Repentance,** and you realize that your actions are about to be recorded and judged. What you should do then is what you'd do if you were about to be judged by a king. That is, whatever you could to be judged favorably, and avoiding everything that would distract you from accomplishing that. As well as reflecting, scrutinizing your ways, pouring out your heart to God, and doing tshuvah (¶14).
6. **When you realize how vulnerable and mortal you are,** and you ready yourself

to greet God at any time by scrutinizing your ways, confessing, experiencing the fear of God all the time, doing new *mitzvot* every day, studying Torah, correcting character flaws, and making yourself a repository of Torah and *mitzvot*. Have confidence in the fact that the souls of the righteous dwell with God after death. Perceive of this world as a temporary dwelling-place, as the quarters in which you're able to serve God best. And be hunbled by that realization (¶'s15–25).

Chapter One

⬡⬡⬡⬡⬡⬡⬡⬡⬡⬡⬡⬡

1. The Rationale[1]

Know that there are six instances in which a person can be moved to do tshuvah for his wrongful ways. Each gives us insight into how people differ, how to understand their thinking, and how to convince them to listen to reason. These invaluable principles are sought after and delved into by all who love them.[2]

But more importantly,[3] be sure to do tshuvah every day and to purify yourself, my child, whether you sense anything inspiring you to or not. And despite all the distracting circumstances of the day. Because you're to[4] remember your Creator, and by remembering Him you'll be spared the repercussions of being a lump of clay.[5]

So, unsheathe your bow and arrow of know-how, and adjust the jagged edges of your nature. Advance ever upward by fearing and loving God, and being abashed in His presence. Strive for innocence,[6] remove any idea of rebellion from your mind, and purify your limbs. By thus remembering your Creator,[7] you'll become engaging

---

1. This phrase isn't included in the text, and has been inserted here for ease of reference.

2. That is, by all who come to love them for their capacity to move us to tshuvah.

3. That is, what's even more important than delving into and making use of these invaluable tools would be for you to . . .

4. . . . always . . .

5. That's to say, don't depend on a logical grasp of your motivations, or on an external prod. Simply draw close to God every day by transcending petty diversions, and consigning time to your relationship with Him. As one would be expected to do if he wanted to sustain any loving relationship. (See our comments to 1:30 about the consequences of physicality.)

6. Literally, "clean hands," which is to say, avoid dishonesty.

7. Sin is the natural result of rank animality, the whisking away of sense and soul, and the subsequent forgetting of God. Remember Him and you undo all that—you set soul back in place, and rise above animality. (See Supplementary Notes.)

and more comely.[8] As it's said, "The Nation of Israel will be made righteous and laudable through God" (Isaiah 45:25).[9] Then be brave and motivate yourself through the six instances we're about to illustrate. But if you haven't reached that level,[10] let your uncircumcised[11] heart be humbled by other means or by the many other things you'd see.[12]

It would be known, though, that your tshuvah came from within if instead of being impelled by one of these instances that[13] move people to tshuvah, you were drawn to it of your own volition.[14]

---

8. . . . to Him.

9. Rabbeinu Yonah seems to be depicting tshuvah here as the best way to become "engaging and more comely" to your Beloved. And the means of being spared "the repercussions" of being mortal, as well as of avoiding being blindsided by the world. He's also pointing out that you achieve tshuvah not only by bettering yourself morally and personally, but by concentrating on the stunning reality of God's very real presence in the world as well. That's to say, that at bottom, tshuvah is the fulfillment and embodiment of the mitzvah of remembering God all the time (see 3:27). (See our note to ¶28.)

10. That is, if you haven't managed to "advance ever upward by fearing and loving God, and by being abashed in His presence," as was just advised. And you thus haven't been inspired to do tshuvah that way, then at least . . .

11. i.e., insensitive.

12. . . . all around you that might inspire you to tshuvah. For the events of the day evidence the broad and wide presence of God in the world, and should move you to tshuvah in themselves.

13. . . . ordinarily . . .

14. That is, if you're self-motivated toward tshuvah rather than externally motivated, it would be coming from your heart and would hence be deeper. Nonetheless, as Rabbeinu Yonah pointed out earlier on, tshuvah "is accepted even when you do it in response to a lot of suffering" (1:1), to say nothing of other motivating factors. (See Supplementary Notes.)

Chapter Two

CRICRICRICRICRICRICRICRICRICRICRI

2. The First Instance

If you find yourself suffering, take it to heart and say, "This has all come upon me because of my behavior and deeds, and the sins I've committed!" and return to God, who will have mercy on you.[1] As it's said, "Many misfortunes and troubles will befall

---

1. There are two points to be made here. First, that many of us seem to stroll blithely about our own lives, completely unaware of the causes and effects all about us. As if things just "happened," and our moral decisions had nothing to do with them. *When they're central to them.* And, we act as if God Almighty were at our beck and call, and a kindly but preoccupied wealthy father in a far-off suburb who sends money as soon as we ask him to. But who's otherwise indifferent to what we do. As a consequence we disregard the interplay between us and Him.

And it's all of that—our jaunty ignorance of our own moral input into our lives, our belittling of God's role in the universe, and our indifference to the moral collaboration He and we engage in—that lays us open to utter shock when we're faced with disaster or tribulation. When the truth is, who we *are* affects what becomes of us. And God plays a visceral and intimate part in the playing out of all that.

The second point is this: Don't most people take suffering to heart? Aren't they very concerned? So why is Rabbeinu Yonah cajoling us to do just that? Because the kind of concern Rabbeinu Yonah is talking about here is concern for the *metaphysical* reason for one's suffering. That is, not for the particular germ, faulty investment, bad idea, etc., that might seem to have caused the dilemma. But the trait, deed, or perspective on life that actually did.

In fact, most people's initial reaction to trouble is to address just that point. They'll say things like, "Why's this happening to me?" "What did I do to deserve this?" and thus immediately refer to their moral status. But they very quickly lapse into a more mundane view (usually after someone offers a pat, banal response like, "I'm sure it's nothing you did"). And they then look for a more "rational" explanation, saying something like, "But after all, didn't this-or-that happen?" What would better serve would be to continue taking stock of ourselves, and to unearth the personal causes of our troubles.

them, and they will say on that day, 'Have not these misfortunes come upon me because God is not within me?'" (Deuteronomy 31:17).[2]

For though human nature is such that any remorse or subservience that the person who wronged another would start to express to his victim, in order to get his help when he was in trouble, would be taken lightly by the victim (as Jeptha said, "Why come to me now, when you are suffering?" [Judges 11:7]); nonetheless, one of God's many favors[3] is that He accepts tshuvah that's prompted by suffering, that it pleases Him, and that He bountifully loves your returning to Him on the day of reproach, in the midst of troubles. As it's said, "Return to God your Lord, Israel, for you have stumbled in your transgression. Take words with you . . . I will heal their backsliding, I will love them bountifully" (Hosea 14 : 2–5), and, "God criticizes those He loves, like a father does with a son He's pleased with" (Proverbs 3:12).[4]

If you don't do tshuvah for your wrongful ways when misfortune strikes and you're criticized through suffering, and you don't return to the One criticizing you, you'd be transgressing even more so, and the consequences[5] would double. For would a human king admonishing someone who'd sinned against him, who then didn't take his admonishment to heart, not admonish him even more so then, and make his burden even heavier? As it's written, "If you will continue not to listen to Me, I will admonish you more" (Leviticus 26:18), and "But the flatterers heap up wrath, they do not cry out when He admonishes them" (Job 36:13).

But if you don't realize and ponder the fact that all your hardships are a result of your sins. And like the Philistines you say, "It is not His hand that struck us—that happened to us by chance"[6] (1 Samuel 6:9), then God will cast His ire upon you. And your sin in that instance would be even greater than it would've been in the first.[7,8]

---

2. That's to say that we only sin when God isn't "within" us; that is, when our relationship to Him isn't our primary concern.

3. . . . to us . . .

4. See Supplementary Notes.

5. . . . of your actions you'd have to suffer . . .

6. See Supplementary Notes.

7. In terms of relationships again, if you don't realize that your own mistakes and misjudgments have contributed to your estrangement, and you blame your mate entirely, then all that you'd already done wrong would be more offensive yet in your mate's eyes. And your relationship would be further estranged.

8. The text continues with the following:

That's why it's said initially, about the first instance of sinning, "I will chastise you more" (Leviticus 26:18). And why it's said, "But if you walk contrary to Me, and will not want to listen to Me, I will bring seven times more plagues upon you for your sins" (Ibid. v. 21) about the second. Because the sins of each succeeding instance [mentioned] in the section is more serious than the first.

And that's why it's written, "If you will not be admonished by Me in these instances but will walk contrary to Me, then I will also walk contrary to you" (Ibid. vv. 23–24) as well as "And

If you don't know what you did or how you sinned, then examine your deeds and explore your ways. As it's said, "Let us scrutinize and examine our ways" (Lamentations 3:40). But if you close your eyes instead, remain foolish and wrong enough not to recognize your ways or to realize what you did with your very own hands, and you say, "I didn't sin,"[9] then you'd be sinning very seriously.[10] As it's said, "Behold, I will bring you to judgment, because you said, 'I have not sinned!'" (Jeremiah 2:35), "It set him aflame all around, and he did not know. It burned him, and he did not take it to heart" (Isaiah 42:25) and, "A man's own foolishness perverts his way, and his heart rages against God" (Proverbs 19:3).[11]

3. But understand that when God admonishes you when you sin before Him and do what's wrong in His eyes, it's for your own good. In fact, there are two benefits to His chastising you.

First, it atones for your sins and pardons your transgressions. As it's said, "Look upon my affliction and pain, and remove my sins" (Psalms 25:18). For the physical ailments God brings upon you heal spiritual ailments,[12] and sins are spiritual ailments.[13] As it's said, "Heal my soul, for I have sinned against You" (Psalms 41:5) and, "The inhabitant should not say, 'It is I who is sick. The sin of the people living there should be forgiven!'" (Isaiah 33:24).

And second, it will criticize you[14] and have you do tshuvah for your wrongful ways, as it's written, "Surely you will fear Me and accept admonishment" (Zephaniah 3:7).

---

if you will not listen to Me in these instances, but walk contrary to Me, then I will walk contrary to you also in My ire" (Ibid. vv. 27–28) afterward. For, "If you will . . . walk contrary [קֶרִי] to Me" means "If you will . . . say, 'That happened to us by chance [מִקְרֶה, grammatically related to קֶרִי, just cited, making the expression a double entendre].'"

9. . . . to what you did . . .

10. That is, if you realize that it must have been something you did that brought on your troubles, but you can't determine what it is at the outset, then search your ways until you find out. But you'd be very wrong to deny your blunders, and go on making mistake after mistake, without ever coming to an understanding, or ever changing if you did err.

11. That's to say, we sometimes make terrible, terrible errors in judgment. And succumb to all sorts of rationalizations in utter denial of the teeming, naked truth before our eyes. Then we're stunned by the natural consequences of our actions, and call out to God in righteous indignation, asking Him how He could have been so unfair and coldhearted.

12. The mystery of inflicting the body to treat the soul is somewhat akin to taking a bitter little pill to somehow or another treat an inner organ. (See Supplementary Notes.)

13. Understand that Rabbeinu Yonah is not only talking about physical ailments, but emotional, existential ones like fear, anguish, loneliness, despair, etc., as well.

But all in all, the underlying idea behind that is that the woe, dread, and humiliation, etc., you'd suffer as a consequence of your travails will do you nearly as much good as what you'd bring upon yourself by following the twenty principles of tshuvah enunciated in the first gate. (See Supplementary Notes.)

14. i.e., offer you criticism . . .

But if you don't accept God's admonishments, if you're not put in your place by His criticism, and you don't circumcise[15] your heart then, Woe is to you! For you'd have suffered and borne sin, and not been forgiven for that sin.[16] And the consequences for it would have doubled too, as we explained.[17]

4. But when you take God's admonishments to heart and improve your ways and deeds, it's then important for you to be happy about your troubles.[18] Because they will advance you dramatically. In fact, you should actually thank God for them as much as you would for any other windfall.[19] As it's said, "How can I repay God for all His favors to me? I will lift the cup of salvation, and call upon the name of God" (Psalms 116:12–13); "I found trouble and sorrow, and called upon the name of God" (Ibid. vv. 3–4).

As our sages put it, "Rabbi Eliezer Ben Yaakov said, 'As long as a person enjoys good fortune,[20] not a single one of his transgressions is atoned for.[21] But when he suffers with troubles he is pleasing to God.[22] As it is said, "For God criticizes those He loves like a father does with a son He is pleased with" (Proverbs 3:12)'" (*Sifre, V'etchanan* 6).

That means to say that, as a father would be with a son he's pleased with, God is pleased with those He criticizes who then take His admonishments to heart. And like a father, He continues to be pleased with His son after criticizing him. We could

---

15. i.e., sensitize.

16. That is, if you sin and suffer as a consequence, and you don't draw the lesson about bettering yourself and drawing closer to God meant for you to draw from your pain. Then not only would you have sinned and suffered, but you'd have done so for no good reason. You'd remain the fool you'd been all along, as a consequence, and would be wounded besides.

17. See ¶2, "But if you don't do tshuvah for your wrongful ways when misfortune strikes and you're criticized through suffering, and you don't turn to the One criticizing you, you'd be transgressing even more so, and the consequences would double."

18. Truthfully, one can *only* be happy about his troubles after reaching the high level of taking God's interplay in his life so seriously that he's moved to change his ways. Anyone who claims to be happy about his troubles who hasn't such a God-centered perspective on life is either a liar, deviant, or fool.

19. Such a person would see his "sorry lot" as a personal windfall, after the fact, in light of all the spiritual good it's actually done him. After all, how many people are "grateful" for their heart attacks, for example, for having taught them how to live sensibly and with more spiritual intent, and for putting the fear of Heaven in them.

20. i.e., apparent or so-called "good fortune."

21. Notice the ironic use of "windfall" in the previous paragraph and "good fortune" here. We'd consider a material windfall an instance of good fortune. But the righteous consider tribulations auspicious. And that's because while we're narrow-visioned and fixed upon the physical, they're visionary and transcendent.

22. That can either mean that he *becomes* pleasing to God as he draws closer to Him as a result of his suffering. Or it can mean that his suffering is a sign that he's *already* pleasing to God, since "God (only) criticizes those He loves."

also explain it to mean that[23] God is like a father who criticizes a son he's pleased with, but who doesn't criticize the children he expects little from, whom he knows wouldn't benefit from criticism.

It's said about people who don't realize how actually good and advantageous it is to be criticized, "I would have redeemed them, but they would have spoken lies against Me" (Hosea 7:13), "I have chastised them and strengthened their arms, yet they plan wrongdoing against Me" (Ibid. v. 15) and, "I trained Ephraim to walk, taking them by their arms. But they did not know that I healed them" (Ibid. 11:3).

5. One who trusts in God would hope that this all-consuming anguish would at least be the darkness that brings on the light. As it's written, "Do not rejoice over me, my enemy, because I have fallen, as I will rise up. For even when I sit in darkness, God is my light" (Micah 7:8), which our sages explained as follows: "Had I not fallen, I would never have risen. Had I not sat in darkness, He would never have been my light" (Midrash *Tehillim* 5).

In fact, each and every person should try to understand why he's come upon suffering when he does. He should fast, do tshuvah, and pray—just as a congregation is obliged to fast in times of trouble, as our sages decreed. In fact, that would be a special fast, and a day of favor.[24]

But if God's admonishments come upon you when you're pure and upright,[25] they're a test,[26] and will increase your merit in The World to Come. As it's said, "That He might afflict you, and that He might test you, to do you good in the end" (Deuteronomy 8:16). As our sages said, "Search through your deeds when you suffer. If you scrutinize and examine them and find no sins, your suffering is a product of[27] love" (*Berachot* 5A).

6. Included in this category is doing tshuvah on the day of your death,[28] when you'd realize that wrongdoing[29] is coming to an end, and all hope is gone.[30] As it's written, "All hope is gone when a wrongdoer dies" (Proverbs 11:7). You should

---

23. . . . in this instance . . .

24. Hence, the point of fasting, doing tshuvah, and praying is twofold: to undo your sins in expiation, as *well* as to arrive at the presence of mind and clarity that would allow you to "understand why (you've) come upon suffering" in the first place.

25. . . . for, indeed, sometimes the righteous *do* suffer in this world. Nonetheless know that . . .

26. . . . of your mettle, to determine whether or not you can maintain your righteousness within adversity . . .

27. . . . God's . . .

28. See Supplementary Notes.

29. i.e., your ability to do wrong.

30. That is, you realize that your life is coming to end, you can no longer do the wrong you'd enjoyed so. And all of the great hopes and dreams you'd attached to those things are already gone, as you yourself will soon be. (See Supplementary Notes.)

confess at that point, and return to God wholeheartedly.[31] For this form of tshuvah helps, though it doesn't compare to the sort of tshuvah you'd come to in all simplicity, as we explained in the first gate.[32]

---

31. This can be understood two ways. Either, confess at that point, and "return to God wholeheartedly," which is to say, and do tshuvah wholeheartedly. Or, confess (and do tshuvah) at that point, after you'll have come to realize that your wrongdoing days are over and all your material hopes are gone, and you'll "return to God wholeheartedly" as a consequence.

32. See 1:19.

Chapter Three

ଊଡ଼ଌଊଡ଼ଌଊଡ଼ଌଊଡ଼ଌଊଡ଼ଌଊଡ଼ଌଊଡ଼ଌଊଡ଼ଌଊଡ଼ଌଊଡ଼ଌ

7. The Second Instance

Return to God when you reach old age and become elderly, and your strength fails you and wanes, when your impulses have crumpled, and you start to recall that the end is near and what your fate is, and He will have mercy on you.[1,2]

But if you don't return[3] through tshuvah when you become old, then the consequences you'd have to suffer would double, and you'd be more repulsive to Him. As our sages said, "God despises three:[4] the arrogant poor, the scoffing rich, and the adulterous old" (*Pesachim* 113B),[5] and as it's written, "Strangers have

---

1. Must our strength fail and our impulses crumble before it finally occurs to us we're mortal? Apparently it takes that to have us at least "*recall*" it. So when did we forget it? In middle age, apparently, which Rabbeinu Yonah is going to talk about at the end of this ¶. For most young people are well aware of their mortality, and are sometimes morbidly taken by the idea of deterioration. But it's when we're in our prime that we think ourselves immortal and omnipotent—unless we suffer in that period of life and are reminded even then of death, which harkens back to the first instance (¶'s 2–6), as well as to our next note.

2. The point that God will have mercy on you when you're inspired to do tshuvah is only made here and in the previous section (¶'s 2–6), not in the other instances to come. That's because those later instances involve being inspired more intellectually (i.e., when you're reproached; when you read Torah passages that remind you of what you're doing wrong; during the days between Rosh Hashanah and Yom Kippur, when you realize that your deeds are all being recorded; and any other time, when you realize your own mortality). But the immediately preceding instance (when you're subsumed by troubles or at the point of death), and this one (when you're old and inevitably close to death) both touch the very core, and so move you to a deeper level of tshuvah. And hence draw you ever so much closer to your Beloved, who will have mercy on you.

3. . . . to God . . .

4. . . . sorts of people . . .

5. That is, if you will not have reconciled with your mate by the time you're old, you'd

consumed his strength, and he does not know. Gray hairs have sprung up on him, and he does not know" (Hosea 7:9).

In fact, it's always astonishing and dumbfounding to behold someone middle-aged—who sees the years passing and fading, sees his edifice beginning to deteriorate, his constitution declining, and he himself withering away (as it's said, "My days are like a lengthening shadow; and I am withered like grass" [Psalms 102:12])—who nonetheless refuses to see and to grasp, and to notice that he's heading closer and closer to his final resting place day after day![6]

8. There are many from whom the light of tshuvah is withheld[7] because they see themselves as spotless and pure, and don't think of improving their ways, since they think they're perfect.[8] But they're actually sinning very seriously against God. For isn't it written, "There is not a man on earth so righteous that he does[9] good without sinning" (Ecclesiastes 7:20).[10]

They've either minimized their sins, grown insensitive to them, and misunderstand them. Or else they've forgotten about them after knowing about them. As

---

have to suffer the consequences of fierce alienation, and you'd become utterly repulsive to her—both because you no longer have the animal allure you had when young. And also because you'd have grown as repugnant in her eyes as a luckless, poor fool who has nothing to his name but an absurd braggadocio ("the arrogant poor"), a sardonic lucky buffoon who might as well have inherited his fortune for his part in the Divine Plan that allowed him it ("the scoffing rich"), and a piteously over-embellished old man out of touch with reality ("the adulterous old").

Another point being made is that one who has become old, who still hasn't come to tshuvah or transcended his worldly passions is nothing but an "adulterous" old person. Because he's flirting and consorting with things out of his domain.

6. This touches a very sore point in the modern soul, which, truth be known, will not concede to old age, idolizes stamina, and takes decades to mature and wizen (if ever). The rank truth is that we age, we weaken and decline, and we eventually die. The long-lived lie we tell ourselves now that we're not really getting older while middle-aged, is often far more long-lived than ourselves, or friends around us.

7. See note 30 to ¶ 9.

8. Why isn't this outlook one of the traits that interferes with tshuvah, as enunciated at the end of the first gate? Apparently because a person who feels this way could actually go through the motions of tshuvah, since there's nothing to make it hard for him to do it (as is the case of the traits cited there). Nonetheless, "the light of tshuvah"—i.e., the great delight and giddy rapprochement that comes along with it—will be beyond his reach. Because his heart was indifferent.

9. . . . only . . .

10. That is, if you think you're beyond reproach, you're wrong. Because it's an existential "given" that *everyone* sins—everyone offends God and others by what he says, does, or thinks at some time. But don't we know that? We claim to. But we act as if we don't. And strut about in utter self-assurance as a result. The individual of personal integrity and humility, though, would be only too aware of his own failings, and would allow the other person his due. (See Supplementary Note.)

such they're like ill people who don't feel ill and don't give a thought to being cured, whose illness then worsens until it becomes incurable.

That's often because of a lack of understanding, since they don't inquire of God, and don't care to know His ways. So they don't diligently stand at the doors of sages or their disciples.[11] As it's written, "A maligner does not like his critics, he would not go to the wise" (Proverbs 15:12).[12]

9. But those who are genuinely righteous and upright[13] find their thoughts roaring like a lion all the time, and thundering like the sea about their sins and about how negligent they'd been in their service to God.[14] Because, in fact, a person expresses as much defiance and is as wrong the latter way[15] as he'd be by committing serious sins.[16] For as our sages said, "God will overlook licentiousness and murder, but He will not overlook the sin of being negligent in Torah study" (J. T., *Chagigah* 1:7),[17] despite how very wrong those who are physically and mentally preoccupied with satisfying their bodily needs and on all sorts of passing fancies are.[18]

They[19] never enter into the inner realms of the fear of God, never ruminate

---

11. . . . in order to understand the error of their ways.

12. This point is a highlight of this entire gate, as well as much of the book itself. For while it's true that one has to "inquire of God" in order to "know His ways." And that the only way to do that is to "diligently stand at the doors of sages or their disciples," who'll both hand you the solutions, and inspire you enough to advance in your inquiries. Nonetheless, what is it that has you *want* to inquire of God and to know of His ways in order to be moved enough to inquire of the sages? As this gate illustrates, it's either one or more of these six instances of inspiration, or your own spiritual inquiry and growth. (See ¶1's suggestion that in lieu of these motivators you're to "advance ever upward by fearing and loving God, and being abashed in His presence. . . ." And see ¶'s 26–34, which discuss self-motivation.)

13. See Supplementary Notes.

14. i.e., about how less than enthusiastic they'd been about taking things upon themselves to proactively serve God, aside from avoiding what's prohibited. Contrast this with the reaction of those who hold themselves to be righteous, who go about blithely unaware of the truth, cited in ¶8. (See Supplementary Notes.)

15. i.e., being negligent in the service of God.

16. That's to say, if I only shun things that offend my mate but do nothing to please her, not only would our relationship be lackluster and skin-deep. I'd also prove myself to be loveless, which would hurt her as much as any offense I might commit.

17. . . . which is the most significant proactive mitzvah. For Torah study (as well as prayer) is also the way we maintain a relationship with our Beloved. Since it involves communicating and *communing* with Him, which is vital to the relationship. (See Supplementary Notes.)

18. That is, the licentious and self-indulgent ("those who are physically and mentally preoccupied with satisfying their bodily needs, and on all sorts of passing fancies") are very wrong, and will never come to know the depths of their beings, as will soon be discussed. But they're still-and-all not as irksome and unforgivable to the Beloved as one who won't commune with Him (see previous note).

19. i.e., "those who are physically and mentally preoccupied with satisfying their

deeply about it, and their souls never converge into the innermost chambers of their hearts or dwell therein for any length of time. Nor do they set aside time for Torah study in their day. They've[20] lost their sense of self, become a "people lacking counsel" (Deuteronomy 32:28), and are on a very low level.[21]

Our sages said, "A person of sixty is old, one of seventy is elderly, one of eighty is powerful, one of ninety is prayerful, and one of a hundred is considered dead, gone and departed from the world" (*Pirke Avot* 5:21). What they meant by saying that was to alert you to do tshuvah, and to think about your ultimate destiny when you become old, if you didn't merit doing that while you were young. To renounce the wants and cravings of the body when your time starts to approach, and to perfect yourself.[22]

And to withdraw yourself even more so from worldly things when you become elderly.[23] So that the older you get, the less involved in the world you'd be, and the more dedicated you'd be all the time to contemplating the fear of God, communing with yourself, perfecting your character, and pursuing Torah and *mitzvot*.[24]

Solomon told us not to be lax in Divine service in old age. As he put it, "Sow your seed in the morning, and do not withhold your hand in the evening. For you never know which will prosper, this or that one, or if both will be good" (Ecclesiastes 11:6), likening childhood and youth to morning, old age to evening, and seed to children and disciples. For as our sages said, "One who married[25] when young, should marry[26] when old; and one who trained disciples when young, should train

---

bodily needs and on all sorts of passing fancies"—not "those who are genuinely righteous and upright."

20. . . . consequently . . .

21. That is, one who'd never commune with his Beloved by "enter(ing) into the inner realm of the fear of God," by "ruminat(ing) deeply about it," by "converging into the inner chambers of (his) heart," by "dwell(ing) upon it," and by "set(ting) aside time for Torah study" will not only lose "all sense of self." He'd also be "lacking (for) advice" and be "on a very low level," which is to say, loveless and alone.

22. Rabbeinu Yonah is now returning to the main theme of this section—being moved to do tshuvah upon the approach of old age. To this immediate point we'd been taken upon a foray into the difference between those who perceive themselves to be righteous, and those who truly are.

23. See Supplementary Notes.

24. The text continues with the following:

As to the statement that "One of ninety is prayerful [לשוח]"—that's derived from "(He) poured out his prayers [שיחו]" (Psalms 102:1) and "To pray [לשוח] in the field" (Genesis 24:63), which our sages explain alludes to the fact that "Isaac instituted the Afternoon Prayer, as it's said, 'And Isaac went out to *pray* [לשוח] in the field'" (*Berachot* 26B). Because after you reach ninety it's important for you to concentrate upon praying to and praising God, and to enunciating [לשיח] His wonders.

25. . . . and bore children . . .

26. . . . again . . .

disciples when old. Because perhaps the ones he produced in old age will be more successful in Torah and *mitzvot* than the ones produced in his youth. Or perhaps the disciples he trained when he was old will either be more successful than the first, or just as much so" (*Yevamot* 62B).[27]

He then said, "Light is sweet, and it is good for the eyes to behold the sun" (Ecclesiastes 11:7). That is, returning to old age, which he likened to evening, he offers that since an old person can no longer enjoy the taste of what he eats or drinks, as Barzilai the Gilead put it,[28] he should enjoy the light of the sun, rather than be irritable. Because being so interferes with one's Divine service.[29]

He should then find the light of the sun sweet, in the face of coming darkness,[30] as is then mentioned in the next verse, "And if a man lives many years, let him rejoice in them all; yet let him remember the days of darkness, which will be many. For a lot of what is to come will[31] be meaningless" (Ibid. v. 8).

What that means is that even growing very old shouldn't be burdensome to you. You should be happy your whole life long, so that not a single one of your years will be wasted, and so that you never stop serving God. So, "let him remember the days of darkness, which will be many" because he won't be able to serve God then. As it's said, 'Who can thank You[32] in the nether world?'" (Psalms 6:6)

In fact, the righteous[33] bolster themselves in old age, gird themselves for battle, and rejuvenate themselves in order to serve God. As our sages put it, "The older sages get, the wiser they become" (*Shabbat* 152A), as it's said, "They will still pour forth fruit in old age; they will be fat and flourish" (Psalms 92:15), and as it's said before that, "A righteous person flourishes like a palm tree; he grows like a cedar in Lebanon. Those that are planted in God's house flourish in God's courts" (Ibid. vv. 13–14). Since the righteous "flourish in God's courts" from the time they're young, and grow up in the *Beit Midrash*[34] from youth like a palm tree that flourishes, or a cedar tree that grows in Lebanon. And so our sages said, "'(They) flourish in God's court' refers to children" (Midrash *Tehillim* 92:10), in accordance with "May our sons be like plants grown up in their youth!" (Psalms 144:12).

---

27. This comes to reiterate the point that one shouldn't be lax in his Divine service in old age. For his service then will also bear fruit.

28. . . . when he said, "I am eighty years old today. Can your servant taste what I eat or what I drink?" (2 Samuel 19:36).

29. What Rabbeinu Yonah is doing at this point is continuing to follow the gist of Solomon's statements about old age, and explaining them.

30. The reference to light here alludes back to the mention of the "light of tshuvah" in ¶8.

31. . . . otherwise . . .

32. i.e., serve you.

33. This is now a return to the discussion at the beginning of the ¶ about the truly righteous.

34. i.e., the Study Hall in a yeshivah, "God's house."

It nonetheless then goes on to say that in another sense they're not like trees. Because while trees no longer produce when they mature, the righteous "still pour forth fruit in old age."[35]

He also said, "And also now when I am old and elderly, God, do not forsake me. So that I might proclaim Your might to this generation, and Your power to every one to come" (Psalms 71:18).

---

35. i.e., they still study Torah and fulfill *mitzvot*, which bear spiritual fruit.

Chapter Four

10. *The Third Instance*

Listen well, surrender yourself, and return[1] in tshuvah when you're admonished by sages and those who criticize you.[2] Take each word of criticism to heart without exception. By doing that you will go from darkness to great light in an instant.[3]

Because if you listen and internalize, understand in your heart and do tshuvah, take the words of those who criticize you to heart as soon as you hear them, take it upon yourself to fulfill all you're taught by those who grasp Torah from that day onward, and to be cautious about the things those who know alert you about from then on—your tshuvah will take effect, and you'll become a whole other person. In fact, the very moment you accept those words in such a way in your mind and take them to heart, you'll earn the merit and reward of *all* the *mitzvot* and admonishments.[4]

---

1. . . . to God . . .
2. . . . for Godly reasons. For while there are many critics—many who even offer criticism professionally (like therapists, counselors, consultants, and the like)—Musar-type criticism, which will have your full well-being in mind, will serve you best. For while the former is often material- and self-centered and questionably motivated, the latter is Heaven-centered.
3. See Supplementary Notes
4. Apparently going "from darkness to great light *in an instant*" (see end of previous paragraph) would have to be quite a feat. Because you'd have to listen well, surrender yourself, do tshuvah, and take every single word of criticism to heart, as cited here, in that one instant! Rabbeinu Yonah's point seems to be, then, that if you're so struck by what you hear that you experience a quick and utter metamorphosis (i.e., you "become a whole other person"), on the heels of stark surrender and self-abnegation, then you're sure to go through the rest of the process afterward. And you'll certainly go from darkness to great light *as a result* of that instant of metamorphosis.

How fortunate you'd be—for you'd have exonerated yourself in short order![5]
And so our sages said, "(It is written) 'The Nation of Israel went to do as God commanded' (Exodus 12:28). But did they actually do it right away? Did they not do it twenty-four months later? However, since they took it upon themselves to do it,[6] the text credits them with having done it right away" (*Mechiltah, Bo* 12:28).

It's also said in *Avot D'Rebbe Natan* (Ch. 22), "Only the wisdom of one who has more deeds than wisdom, is sustained,[7] as it is written, 'We will do, then we will listen' (Exodus 24:7)." What that means to say is that as soon as you wholeheartedly take it upon yourself to observe and conform to the instructions and decisions those who are qualified to judge give you, you're accredited from that day on with the merit of *all* of the *mitzvot*—for the words of Torah you've already heard and understood, as well as for those you hadn't yet been exposed to. You'd have cloaked yourself in righteousness, and earned merit both for those that were revealed to you and those[8] that were not.[9]

So, search hard for those who'd offer you criticism from that day on, and learn from whoever would teach you.[10] You'd thus become one "who has more deeds than wisdom" by earning merit for doing something before even knowing about it. Which was the case with the Jewish Nation at Mount Sinai, when they said, "We will do, then we will listen" and thus took the deed upon themselves before even hearing about it. For it's otherwise impossible for a person to do more than he's aware of.[11]

---

5. That's to say, if you truly internalize the suggestions offered you by those who want only to rectify you. And you quickly realize the truth of what they say then, as well as the implication that anything else they'd say in the future would make as much sense. You'll act righteously from then on, and would thus be credited with the merits you're sure to earn in the future, *right there and then*. (See Supplementary Notes.)

6. . . . at that point . . .

7. i.e., rather than the wisdom of one who has more wisdom than deeds, as will be explained.

8. . . . *mitzvot* . . .

9. What this means to say is that if you're so inspired by what you hear that you say to yourself "I will do" (i.e., "I hereby take it upon myself to do" whatever I'll learn about in the future) even before you say "I will listen" (i.e., even before you're told what to do), you'll "have more deeds than wisdom" (i.e., you'll be accredited with having done more than you know about), and your wisdom will be broader and longer-lived than others'.

10. Apparently this is the one stipulation behind the glorious promise of this ¶ that you can garner credit before the fact. And that stipulation is that you go back again and again to those who'd offer you criticism, to learn more. For otherwise you'd lose all the merit you'd just then accrued, because you'd invariably backslide. (See Supplementary Notes.)

11. That is, it's impossible to understand how a person could be said to have accomplished things even before he knew about them unless you explain the statement as Rabbeinu Yonah did. For as we explained his idea here in our note above, you'll have earned

11. But your sin[12] becomes compounded if you're not moved by what those who criticize you say.[13] Because they'd have warned you, yet you hardened your heart and didn't take heed. As it's said, "Criticism enters more deeply into one who understands than a hundred blows[14] into a fool. A wrongdoer wants only to rebel, so a cruel angel will be sent against him" (Proverbs 17:10–11). What that means to say is that a wrongdoer would never acquiesce to what his critics say; he'd only care to rebel. And so because he didn't accept what a criticizing "angel" said, "a cruel angel will be sent against him," measure for measure.[15,16]

Solomon also said, "One who abandons the way will be admonished seriously, but one who hates criticism will die" (Proverbs 15:10). That means to say that while "one who abandons the way" and sins against the Torah certainly deserves to be "seriously admonished," there's nonetheless still the hope that he'll be admonished and do tshuvah for his wrongful ways.[17] But anyone who hates criticism is worse off than he, for he'd be hopeless and incorrigible even with serious admonishment, and would be doomed to die.[18]

Because[19] people sin when they're overtaken by their cravings and urged on by their yetzer harah,[20] and they're likely to be bitter-hearted for not resisting their impulses, and to even long for criticism or admonishment. But the sort of person who hates criticism is beyond hope. Because his hate for criticism implies a hate for the words of God.[21]

---

credit for *mitzvot* before you even know about them if you change so entirely that you accept right there and then everything your teachers would ever say to you in the future.

12. . . . only . . .

13. The implication is that listening to criticism is a double-edged sword. It can bring you to great purity, if you listen in all innocence and accept what's said. Or it can cause you great harm if you don't take it to heart, as we'll soon see. But the latter is only to be expected. Because nothing would irritate and alienate a mate more than if her words of (constructive!) criticism were constantly ignored.

14. . . . would penetrate . . .

15. The expression "measure for measure" refers to the principle of the punishment fitting the crime (see *Sanhedrin* 100A).

16. The text continues with the following:

Critics are referred to as "angels," as in "They mocked the angels [or "messengers"] of God . . . and ridiculed His prophets" (2 Chronicles 36:16).

17. . . . as a result.

18. The idea that a sinner deserves to be seriously admonished, which will then bring him to tshuvah, is of course the very bedrock of and rationale behind the writing of *The Gates of Repentance*.

19. . . . as a rule . . .

20. See Supplementary Notes.

21. This is perfectly logical. For what Torah (תורה) is, is "instruction" (הוראה), and all instruction is criticism, at bottom. In that it's a critique of your mistakes, and an offer of truth

12.   He also said, "The heart is gladdened by the light of the eyes, and good news fattens bones. But an ear that accepts persistant criticism dwells among sages" (Proverbs 15:30–31). Any wise person would understand that Solomon, who was adjudged "wiser than all men" (1 Kings 5:11), couldn't possibly have included something as frivolous and worthless as this[22] amidst his ethics and[23] fear of God.[24]

This, then, is the solution. "The heart is gladdened by the light of the eyes" implies that eyes are very valuable organs, since they enable you to see the luminaries,[25] which then gladdens your heart. But ears are even more valuable, since they make it possible for you to hear good news, which then fattens[26] bones that are insensient,[27] and can only grow fat from the light of the eyes at times of intense pleasure.[28] As such our sages said, "The ear is the most valuable[29] organ. For if you were to blind someone, you'd only have to pay him the value of his eyes.[30] While if you were to make someone deaf, you'd have to pay him the value of his entire body" (*Babba Kama* 85B).

Now, if you're required to serve God with each one of your organs and component parts, since they were created to serve Him (as it's written, "God made all things for His sake" [Proverbs 16:4]), then you're especially required to serve Him with the most valuable organ you were created with.[31] In fact, you'd have to suffer much more serious consequences for not using them to do *mitzvot* and serving God. Because you'd have not repaid God for them, when He did you a very great favor through your valuable organs,[32] and crowned you with honor and glory through them.[33]

---

in its place. (For example, if I'm learning how to saw wood, I need to learn that whatever I might have thought before was the way to do it, was wrong. And that I was about to learn the right way.) So if you hate criticism, you hate instruction and Torah. (See Supplementary Notes.)

22. . . . appears to be . . .
23. . . . instruction in the . . .
24. See Supplementary Notes.
25. i.e., the sun and moon, which illuminate the sky.
26. i.e., fully gladdens and satisfies . . .
27. . . . as a rule.
28. i.e., bones (like anything else dry and unfeelling) can only be gladdened and fully satisfied at times of intense pleasure, since they're far less affected emotionally than the heart. So, if ears can gladden them (and hence make such a deep impression), they're obviously very valuable
29. i.e., highly valued.
30. . . . in a legal settlement for damages.
31. See Supplementary Notes.
32. i.e., by granting you valuable organs.
33. The text then continues with the following:

Solomon first mentioned one of the benefits to having ears, in order to show you how obliged they are to serve God. And then explained that the service of the ears involves listening to criticism

And our sages said that "A person who falls off a roof and injures himself needs a bandage or cast for each thing he broke or wounded. But a sinner is like someone who injured his entire body, from head to toe, since he sinned with his whole body. As in, 'There is no soundness to it, from the sole of its foot to its head' (Isaiah 1:6). Yet God can heal all his wounds with just one bandage—a listening ear. As it's said, 'Incline your ears, and come to Me. Hear, and your souls will live (Ibid. 55:3)' (*Shemot Rabbah, Yitro* 27)."[34]

---

by saying, "An ear that accepts persistant criticism dwells among sages," which means to say that it's important to dwell among sages in order to hear their criticism.

34. Since a listening ear is a bandage for all of a sinner's spiritual wounds, it's clear that criticism is effective both before *and* after sinning. That's to say, not only are you sure to avoid sins in the future if you take criticism to heart right now (as is pointed out in ¶10), but you'll also undo *past* sins when you internalize criticism and have full remorse for what you did wrong in retrospect.

Chapter Five

ξ◊ξξ◊ξξ◊ξξ◊ξξ◊ξξ◊ξξ◊ξξ◊ξξ◊ξξ◊ξξ◊ξ

13. The Fourth Instance

When you delve into God's Torah and read the Prophets and Writings, and understand how agreeable admonishment is,[1] and you see[2] the warnings and the consequences to be suffered, you should tremble, and determine to improve your ways and deeds, and endear yourself to God.[3]

As it's said, "But I will look to this one, to the poor and contrite, who trembles at My word" (Isaiah 66:2). And as it's written of Josiah, "When the king heard the

---

1. See Supplementary Notes.

2. i.e., you read about and "see" for yourself . . .

3. But why do most people vehemently oppose having their perceptions of truth critiqued? Apparently because they believe that their perceptions (and their personality quirks) are *them*. That those ideas and traits are all they have, besides their bodies, in this world. And that if you threaten to take those perceptions away by arguing against them, you threaten their very being.

But the person of faith understands that his essential being is his immortal soul. That everything else accrued onto it is as malleable and repairable as his body, and as mortal. And is there only to help his soul in its life's work. He'd care most about his soul's standing as a consequence, and he'd do whatever he'd have to, to adjust those perceptions, traits, etc., to best nourish his immortal soul. As such, he'd welcome any sage advice along those lines, which is essentially what Torah is all about.

So, in order to succeed at all that, you'd first have to come to realize the make-up of your soul. Which you'd do by "delv(ing) into God's Torah and read(ing) the Prophets and Writings." Once you'd done that reverently for a while, and had come to "see (for yourself the reality of) the warnings (of what to avoid if you're to nourish your immortal soul) and the consequences to be suffered (i.e., the impediments to that soul's progress you'd have to experience if you sin)," you'll then come to "understand how agreeable admonishment (i.e., spiritual instruction) is." And you'll set out to nourish that immortal soul by "improv(ing) your ways and deeds" and rectifying your character and perceptions. And you'll thus "endear yourself to God."

words of the Book of the Torah he tore his clothes" (2 Kings 22:11), and about what happened through Ezra, when, "All the people wept when they heard the words of the Torah" (Nehemiah 8:9).[4]

In fact, you'd have defied God even more seriously if you don't dwell upon His word then.[5] As it's said, "They were not afraid, and they did not tear their garments" (Jeremiah 36:24). As our sages said, "It would have been better for the person who studies[6] and does not fulfill[7] to have had his face turned over in his afterbirth than to have been born"[8] (J. T., *Berachot* 1:2). And as it's said, "Though I write for him the great things of My Torah, they are regarded as strange" (Hosea 8:12) and, "How can you say, 'We are sages and God's Torah is with us?' Behold, certainly the quill has written lies, and the scribes lied" (Jeremiah 8:8).[9]

---

4. The previous instance (cited in ¶'s 10–12) focused on the importance of hearing and accepting criticism from others. And yet while this instance focuses on reading about and concentrating on Torah, which will itself criticize you—Rabbeinu Yonah nonetheless offers as proof verses that read, "When the king *heard* the words of the Book of the Torah . . ." and, "All the people wept when they *heard* the words of the Torah." Apparently, then, Rabbeinu Yonah is equating listening to criticism with arriving at in on your own through Torah study. As such, we would suggest that the best way to come to tshuvah is through a combination of the two—by attending Musar-based lectures and taking in what's said.

5. See Supplementary Notes.

6. . . . Torah . . .

7. . . . what he learned there about how to improve himself, and nourish his soul that way . . .

8. . . . since for all intents and purposes he wouldn't have succeeded at his life's work.

9. See Supplementary Notes.

Chapter Six

14. *The Fifth Instance*

Your heart should agonize, if you fear the word of God, during the Ten Days of Repentance, knowing that your deeds are being recorded in a book, and that God is subjecting everything you do, inside and out,[1] good and bad, to judgment just then. For man is judged on Rosh Hashanah, and his judgment is sealed on Yom Kippur.[2]

For if you knew your case was being brought before a mortal king, wouldn't you shudder and tremble, mull over ideas, and do everything you possibly could, as quickly as you could, to rescue yourself? You wouldn't think of digressing,[3] or of attending to anything else. You wouldn't bother seeing to it that your field is plowed or furrowed, or tend to your vineyard.[4] Nor would you dare be lax about preparing to flee like a deer in an instant if you then came upon troubles.[5]

---

1. Literally, "each deed, and everything hidden."

2. Rabbeinu Yonah will point out toward the end of the ¶ that the Ten Days of Repentance is a very auspicious time. It's when the very highest Heavens are unbolted and accessible, when your prayers are accepted, and God can be found. Nonetheless there's still the sheer reality of the fact that "your deeds are being recorded in a book, and that God is subjecting everything you do . . . to judgment" just then, too—which is quite a stupefying thought!

As such the Ten Days of Repentance can perhaps be likened to a period of reconciliation you and your beloved arranged for, in the hopes of fixing what went wrong in your relationship. And while it's heady to realize that your mate is fixing all of her attention upon you, that she's receptive to your every word and move, and hoping love will be renewed, it's also daunting to realize that she's considering everything you say and do, and wondering as well if you've failed her, and doomed the relationship, all in all.

3. Literally, "of turning either to the right or to the left."

4. Acknowledging the fact that we'd take a summons by the government very seriously and anxiously, and the summons by God that is the Ten Days of Repentance lightly will be one of the discomfiting truths we'll have to face, after death, when we're asked if we believed in God in life.

How foolish you'd be, then, to go about your business until the very eve of the Days of Awe, the days of judgment and sentencing, without knowing your verdict![6] Shouldn't you be reflecting on how you'd respond when spoken about?[7] As it's said, "What will we do for our sister on the day she will be spoken about" (Song of Songs 8:8)?[8]

It's important for you then, as a God-fearing person, to restrict your activities, to block out all other thoughts, to set aside periods of time in the course of the day and night to be alone in your room[9] and scrutinize and examine your ways, to rise up in the early morning in order to do tshuvah and rectify your deeds, and to pour out supplications,[10] pray, implore, and plead.[11]

For that is a favorable period of time, and your prayers are listened to then.[12]

For, in truth, we all take the world so very seriously. And seem to be intimidated by the serious parts of it right "on key" — that is, to the degree expected, and about the things we're expected to be intimidated by, as if by reflex. But, few of us are intimidated by (i.e., *truly* believe in and sense the presence of) God. And we essentially dismiss Him from our lives. For if we truly "fear(ed) the word of God," as it's put at the beginning of this paragraph. And we truly believed in the presence of a living God, we'd be *routinely* awestruck. And we'd automatically make far more allowances for His presence in our lives than we do.

5. That's to say, if you were then faced with the prospect of conviction, you'd certainly make every effort to come up with an escape plan. But as was pointed out in 1:2, tshuvah itself is an "escape hatch." And that's certainly what Rabbeinu Yonah is alluding to.

6. That is, how can you go about your business so nonchalantly until the very last moment before Rosh Hashanah, when so much is going on in the setting of your destiny?

7. . . . in the Heavenly Tribunal. That is, shouldn't you prepare your case ever so much more intensely, in light of the fact that it's fast approaching?

8. Our soul is likened to a sister here. Because, like a sister, the soul is well aware of everything fundamental about us. And because she mourns along with us at times of shared loss, as well as rejoices with us at times of shared joy.

9. See Supplementary Notes.

10. i.e., to pour out your heart in supplication.

11. Compare the directives offered in this paragraph with the way you'd react if you were about to face a mortal judge, cited above. You're advised here to "restrict your activities, to block out all other thoughts" when about to be judged by God. For if you knew you were about to respond to a governmental summons you'd avoid "digressing, or . . . attending to anything else" or "seeing to it that your field is plowed or furrowed, or tend to your vineyard." You're advised here to "set aside periods of time . . . to be alone in your room and scrutinize and examine your ways, to rise up in the early morning in order to do tshuvah and rectify your deeds, and to pour out supplications, pray, implore, and plead" during the Ten Days of Repentance. For you'd "shudder and tremble, mull over ideas, and do everything you possibly could, as quickly as you could, to rescue yourself" when about to come to trial.

The point is to use the same energy, and to demonstrate the same alacrity and dedication to cause when facing God as you would when facing anyone or anything of this world having great influence upon your life and affecting your well-being.

12. A Jew can sense deep in his heart that there are mystically propitious times. That

As it's said, "I responded to you at a favorable time . . ." (Isaiah 49:8). And as our sages said, "The verse, 'Seek out God when He can be found' (Isaiah 55:6) refers to the ten days between Rosh Hashanah and Yom Kippur" (*Yevamot* 49B).

In fact, it's a Torah imperative to rouse yourself to return to God on Yom Kippur.[13] For it's said, "You will be cleansed of all your sins before God" (Leviticus 16:30), which our sages explained means, "Since Yom Kippur atones when accompanied by tshuvah, the verse is thus warning us to purify ourselves before God through tshuvah, and that He will forgive us on that day in order to purify us" (*Yomah* 86A).[14]

---

is, times when both he and his prayers are accepted, almost despite himself. By virtue of the fact that he's a Jew, and all of that is part of our covenant with God. So he might slacken off at times and "plow or furrow his field, or tend to his vineyard." Which is to say, he might occupy himself with his work and satisfying his urges as usual, rather than dedicate himself to his soul's growth. But unfortunately that is a product of the mistaken belief that he doesn't have to do *anything* to be acceptable to God, either because of the favorableness of the time, or because of his intrinsic closeness to Him.

But as we saw in 1:42, being acceptable to God is a very high level of achievement. Hence, to enjoy the benefits of these "ten days of acceptance" we ourselves would have to draw ourselves closer to God in the ways described in the paragraph before this one—rather than rely on the intrinsic closeness to God we enjoy. Because while we *are* intrinsically close to Him as Jews, we can nonetheless endear ourselves to Him even more deeply by actively drawing *ourselves* closer to Him "when He can be found" (to be cited shortly).

13. See Supplementary Notes.

14. i.e., the verse, "You will be cleansed of all your sins before God" could also be explicated to mean, "Be sure to be cleansed of all your sins when you face Him during this propitious time."

Chapter Seven

෯෯෯෯෯෯෯෯෯෯෯෯෯෯

15. The Sixth Instance

Be ready to greet God at any moment, because you never know when your time will come.[1] So, hone your conscience[2] and supply yourself with enough virtues to return your spirit in purity to God, who gave it to you. Scrutinize your ways and deeds every day. Revisit them each morning, and test them all the time.[3]

As our sages say, "Rabbi Eliezer said, 'Do tshuvah the day before you die.' His disciples asked, 'But, can a person know when he is to die, Master?' And he responded, 'All the more so, then! Do tshuvah today because you may die tomorrow. That way you will do tshuvah your whole life long'" (*Shabbat* 153A).

It's also said, "Let your garments always be white, and let your head not lack for oil" (Ecclesiastes 9:8), where the "whiteness" of your clothing symbolizes the personal purity that comes with tshuvah,[4] and "oil" symbolizes good deeds and a

---

1. As Ibn Pakudah put it in *The Duties of the Heart* ("The Reproach," p. 463), "Know that the chalice will soon pass to you as well, and . . . you will depart instantly from your room at the inn, to return to your eternal home." The gist of Rabbeinu Yonah's statement here and Ibn Pakudah's is both that life is very tenuous and never guaranteed. As well as that everyone will have his turn at death. But where Ibn Pakudah stresses the moment of death, Rabbeinu Yonah stresses the moment *after* death. For it is then that your eternity begins, and you must acclimate yourself to your new surroundings. And the first thing you'll notice to be different there will be the palpable presence of God Almighty (see *Pirke D'Rebbe Eliezer* 34).

2. Literally, "your kidneys," which are referred to as a person's "advisors"; hence our translation.

3. This refers to the keen and subtle degree of self-knowledge required of us all if we're ever to succeed at growth. It's not enough to know that you're selfish, for example. You'd have to know if you're being selfish now. And how to transcend that in this very instance, and the like.

4. See Supplementary Notes.

good reputation. As it's said, "A good reputation is better than precious oil" (Ecclesiastes 7:1).

Our sages also said, "It is like the situation of the sailor's wife who was dressed up and made up, even though her husband was overseas. Her neighbors asked, 'Has your husband not gone very far away? Why are you making yourself attractive for no reason?' And she replied, 'My husband is a sailor. The winds might reverse at sea, and he could easily come right home to find me. So I am dressed up'" (*Kohelet Rabbah* 9:8).[5]

So, try to imagine, whenever you're alert and relaxed, how worried and afraid you'd be and how you'd shiver, coming upon your day of death[6] and about to ascend upward to give a reckoning.[7] Just imagine how broken-heartedly you'd confess at the time of your death. Thus, confess with a contrite heart every day, and let the fear of Heaven be upon you.[8]

16. Do new *mitzvot* every day since your turn to die might come and you'd thus not lack for those *mitzvot*. As our sages said, "Whoever fulfills a mitzvah close

---

5. On one level, this Midrash comes to simply though elegantly illustrate how important it is to always be ready to greet God (the "sailor"), to do tshuvah all the time and thus adorn yourself with the fine clothing, make-up, and perfume-oil of good deeds. And to retain your good name by remaining faithful to God, your Beloved, even when He is "far away." As such, the Midrash is straightforward. Yet on another level it's curious. Isn't it *we* who are about to greet the Other—to return to the Beloved? Aren't *we* the one's who've left home (Heaven) to go off in the distance of this world for a lifetime, who are nonetheless sure to come home, as soon as "the winds . . . reverse at sea" and we die?

As such, the sailor-husband can be death itself, to whom we're all married, who's often off in the distance, and bound to come to greet us at any turn. Or he could represent God, in another sense. By virtue of the fact that He reveals Himself and "greets" us in the world itself from time to time from the great sea of Heaven, to which He returns again and again, in hiding. See our supplementary note to ¶ 21 for another perspective.

6. . . . then and there . . .

7. . . . of your life to God.

8. That's to say, always remember that you're mortal, do tshuvah now in life, while you can. Picture how sorry and remorseful you'd be in Heaven while confessing for your sins, and be as sorry and as full of regret now as you confess. And you'll thus lessen your soul's burden.

But there's another point to be made as well. We're often very self-assured and at peace in the world. And are able to accomplish and plan things as a consequence. But crisis will sometime strike swiftly and mercilessly (God forbid). When we suddenly find ourselves hapless and desperate, and to have gone from great light to darkness in an instant (contrast this with ¶10). One who's able to at least realize how vulnerable life is will take stock of and appreciate what he has, and carry on, enjoying it even more now than he did before. But the wise would keep the tenuousness of it all before him at all times, would take nothing for granted, and would undertake to do whatever good he could do as soon as he could. He'd also be self-aware enough to know when he was fooling himself and *not* doing good, and would admit to that directly to God now, rather than later.

to death is credited with keeping every mitzvah of the Torah but that one.[9] While whoever commits a sin close to death is considered to have abrogated the entire Torah" (*Kohelet Rabbah* 3:18).[10]

17. Some people are so oblivious to death that they neither store provisions for the way, nor correct their deeds. And the reality of death doesn't occur to them until it comes upon them.[11] As such, they're like animals who are oblivious to death until the day they're slaughtered.[12] And thus it's said, "They are assigned to the grave like sheep. Death will be their shepherd, and the upright will rule over them in the morning. Their form will waste away in the grave, leaving their dwelling-place behind" (Psalms 49:15).

That's to say, they'll be lead to the grave like sheep because they're oblivious to the fact of their death until it suddenly comes upon them.[13]

"Death will be their shepherd"[14]—death is different for wrongdoers than it is for animals. For while an animal dies only once, death "shepherds" wrongdoers every single day[15] (as in, "Shepherd your people with your staff" [Micah 7:14][16] and "Death's firstborn will devour his own limbs" [Job 18:13[17]]). Because havoc and ruin take hold of wrongdoers all the time, until they finally molder, wither away, and become extinct.[18]

---

9. . . . until that point. (See Supplementary Notes.)

10. The original reads, "יש על האדם לחדש לו מצוה בבל יום," which can also be translated as "You're to *revive mitzvot* every day." Which is to say, do *mitzvot* you'd done all along in remarkable and new-sprung ways every day. "Since your turn to die might come," it goes on to say, "and you'd thus not lack for those *mitzvot*." That is, and you'd have really done those *mitzvot* in a heartfelt way, rather than by rote. (See Supplementary Notes.)

11. See Supplementary Notes.

12. Rabbeinu Yonah is discussing wrongdoers here, as we'll see. Not only are they oblivious to the reality of death, they also only care about satisfying their bodily cravings, as will be pointed out in ¶18. They're consequently likened to animals here. They'll prove to be more pitiable than animals, though. Because unlike them, wrongdoers are aware. But their awareness will cause them grief, as we'll see. (Compare this with the statement, "I haven't even lived up to the tenets of the animals and I'm even more abase than they" in 1:10).

13. That is, like sheep, they're passive rather than active participants in their destiny.

14. . . . alludes to the fact that . . .

15. i.e., death guides and provides for them, and affects their life all the time.

16. This verse alludes to several verses before it, which describe the need wrongoders will have to be shepherded (see Micah 1–14).

17. This verse also alludes to several verses before it (as well as one after it), which describe the terror of the wrongdoers (see Job 5–14).

18. Death can be said to "haunt" wrongdoers and obsess them, as Rabbeinu Yonah is implying here, for two reasons. First, because they know only too well that they'll no longer be able to satisfy their cravings then, as is pointed out at the end of the ¶. So they live with a deep seated, lifelong dread of having to do without everything they love. And second,

"And the upright will rule over them in the morning"[19]—The Resurrection of the Dead[20] is likened to morning, when people will be awakened from their "sleep"[21] (as it's said, "Many who sleep in the dust of the earth will awaken" [Daniel 12:2]), and the upright will rule over wrongdoers. As it's said, "You will trample upon wrongdoers, who will be ash under the soles of your feet" (Malachi 3:21); and as our sages said about the Day of Judgment in conjunction with the Resurrection of the Dead, "After twelve months their bodies will decompose and their souls will burn until they become 'ash under the soles of the feet' of the righteous. As it's said, 'You will trample upon wrongdoers . . . ' " (*Rosh Hashanah* 17A).[22,23]

The point of the matter is that the soul of wrongdoers will wither away in the grave, which will then be its "dwelling-place." For, while the soul is derived from a celestial dwelling-place (as in, "From the dwelling-place of Your holiness" [Isaiah 63:15]), the wrongdoer nonetheless causes his precious soul to abandon its celestial dwelling-place[24] with his sins, and to wither away in the grave below.

How difficult death becomes, then, for those who won't detach themselves from their earthly cravings until death itself detaches those cravings from them.[25] As such, our sages said, "If you want to never die, then die until you no longer die" (*Derech Eretz*), which means to say that if you want death to lead you to everlasting life, then reason with yourself that since you're destined to leave this world and to leave behind all your bodily desires,[26] and to come to despise and renounce them in

---

because they're wracked with guilt for all the wrong they've done, and are distraught with fear of their judgment (sometimes consciously so, but often times quite unconsciously).

19. i.e., the expression, "in the morning" in the phrase, "And the upright will rule over them in the morning" alludes to . . .

20. . . . which is . . .

21. The Resurrection of the Dead itself will be the "dawning" of The World to Come.

22. See Supplementary Notes.

23. The text continues with the following:

"Their form [צוּרף] will waste away in the grave" is like, "their essential form [צוּרתם] will waste away in the grave" (as in, "According to their own understanding [בתבונם]" [Hosea 13:2], rather than "According to their own understanding [בתבונתם]"). Because while the "spirit" is often taken to refer to man's [physical] "form," others conversant in it refer to it as man's "essential [or spiritual] form."

24. i.e., its place in Heaven.

25. This refers to the stunned and stubborn resistance of the newly dead to the loss of this world, when that was all they had to begin with (or so they thought). Their's is like the situation of the child who has a glorious time at a circus or fair—a far better time than any of the adults, in fact. But who suffers far worse than they do for having to leave the circus at the end of the day. And cries for days on end afterward.

26. . . . anyway . . .

the end—then leave them behind now,[27] in life. And only make use of worldly things to serve God with. Death will then lead you on to everlasting life.[28,29]

18. Understand that all wrongdoers ever want their whole lives long is to satisfy their bodily cravings.[30] But since those cravings are incompatible with the service of God, and those wrongdoers are[31] utterly severed from their Root, they plummet down to the ground, the site of all their cravings, when they die.[32] Like earth, which descends rather than ascends by nature—though they[33] ascend upward to be judged and sentenced, and to see[34] how they traded Heaven for the nether world.[35] Or like a stone that's shot upward by slingshot, which just naturally falls to the ground after having ascended, or as any stone would fall after having been tossed.

---

27. i.e., both literally and figuratively (by becoming emotionally detached from them).

28. That is, then your realizations about the reality of death and its ramifications will free you from death's emotional toll.

29. That's to say, most people dread and feel hopeless when they think of death because they perceive it to be the end of everything they hold important, pleasant, and dear. And the beginning of either bitter torture (God forbid) or some vague angelic tedium. And that's all because they've come to believe that the only delight is physical delight. If only they'd learn of the delights of the spirit! If only they'd come to grasp the truth of Moshe Chaim Luzzatto's statement that "we were created to delight in God and enjoy the radiance of His Divine presence" in The World to Come. And that that is "the true delight, the greatest enjoyment of all" (*The Path of the Just*, Ch. 1).

30. See our statement in the previous ¶ about this remark. We can also understand this to be saying either that wrongdoers sin because at bottom all they want to do is satisfy their bodily urges. Or it could be saying that what a "wrongdoer" (a רשע, which is usually translated as "a wicked person") is, is someone who only wants to satisfy his bodily urges—even though he does nothing else wrong. That's to say, he may be an otherwise moral, honest person who does everything else right. But he's nonetheless essentially temporal and self-indulgent, and never strives for intimacy with God. And is thus to be taken as essentially "wrong." (See Supplementary Notes.)

That's both a warning and a consolation. For, if you strive toward Godliness, but occasionally lapse, you're nonetheless essentially not a wrongdoer, and are likely to enjoy God's presence. But if you're an otherwise "good" person who's self-indulgent, and you think you're fundamentally good, take heed!

31. . . . thus . . .

32. Of course there are cravings that are perfectly compatible with the service of God. As cravings per se are neither inherently good or bad. Only their applications are. Those who apply their cravings to God and the quest for holiness will soar ever upward, in life and in death, to the Object of their cravings.

33. . . . must first . . .

34. . . . for themselves . . .

35. Not only are they to see for themselves that they had forgone their chance for bliss and adhesion onto God's presence, but to see *how* they did that, which was by dedicating themselves to living for moments of quick "ascent," i.e., of easy sensual fulfillment and delight. Which invariably end in equally quick "descent."

As it's said, "My master's soul will be bound in the bundle of life with God your Lord. But He will sling the souls of your enemies from a slingshot" (1 Samuel 25:29). And as our sages said, "Both the souls of the righteous and the souls of wrongdoers ascend upward.[36] But the souls of wrongdoers turn round, descend, and are flung back to earth, as it's said, 'But He will sling the souls of your enemies from a slingshot'" (*Kohelet Rabbah* 3:21).

It's also said, "All hope is lost when a wrongdoer dies" (Proverbs 11:7)[37] because a wrongdoer could never hope to pass from darkness to light,[38] since it's said of a wrongdoer that, "He will join the generation of his forefathers who will never see light" (Psalms 49:20).

19. It's thus clear from the verses and the sayings of the sages cited that the souls of wrongdoers descend to the nether world. It's likewise said, "The way of life leads upward for the wise, that he may escape from the netherworld below" (Proverbs 15:24).

But it's also said, "Who knows the spirit of man which ascends upward, and the spirit of the animal that descends downward to the earth?" (Ecclesiastes 3:21). That means to say, who can identify[39] righteous people and wrongdoers in this world? For there are wrongdoers whose deeds are hidden and go unnoticed. And there are people who are secretly God-fearing, in keeping with, "Walk demurely with your God" (Micah 6:8).[40]

The wrongdoer's soul is referred to as "the spirit of the animal" because, like an animal, it's drawn toward physical craving. As it's written, ". . . people who cannot discern between right and left, and a lot of animals" (Jonah 4:11).[41] And the soul of the righteous is called "the spirit of man," as in, "You, My flock . . . are men"[42] (Ezekiel 34:31).

So, what the verse means is, "Who knows the spirit of man," that is, the righteous, "which ascends upward." Because there are many righteous people in the world whom others wouldn't know to be truly righteous, who will ascend upward.

---

36. . . . after death.
37. See Supplementary Notes.
38. . . . unless he experiences the "light of tshuvah" (see ¶8).
39. i.e., differentiate between . . .
40. Aside from the obvious point that one never knows what others do in secret—good or bad, Rabbeinu Yonah is also underscoring the point he made in the previous ¶ that one's moral status is determined more by his attitude toward this world, which no one but God Himself can truly know, than by his actions. But by virtue of the fact that Rabbeinu Yonah inserted the verse, "Walk demurely with your God," we see that he's also encouraging us to serve God in secret, not just openly. And is thus tantalizing us with the possibility of having the sort of intimate and animated relationship with God in the recesses of our beings, away from the scrutiny of others, that satisfies like no other. (See Supplementary Notes.)
41. That's to say, it's as if the verse reads, ". . . people who cannot discern between right and left"—right and wrong, who are thus like—"a lot of animals."
42. i.e., though in a sense you're a flock of "sheep," you're in fact men.

Because, as it's said, "Man looks at what he can see, while God looks at the heart" (1 Samuel 16:7). Also because many of the righteous are secretly God-fearing, and aren't known to be righteous, as it's said, "Walk demurely with your God" (Micah 6:8). "And[43] the spirit of the animal . . .", because there are also many wrongdoers whose deeds go unnoticed. As it's said, "Their works are in the dark, and they say, 'Who sees us? And who knows us?'" (Isaiah 29:15). In fact, our sages agree that "the spirit of man" refers to the righteous, and "the spirit of the animal" refers to wrongdoers (*Kohelet Rabbah* 3:21).

No one could ever doubt that a man's soul ascends upward. For it's written, "The spirit returns to God who gave it" (Ecclesiastes 12:7). And how could anyone ever doubt that an animal's soul descends below? Is an animal's soul not derived from earth? So how could it ascend upward?

It's also revealed in the Torah that man's soul is supernal, and that an animal's soul is derived from the earth. As it's said, "Let the earth bring forth the soul of creatures by its kind" (Genesis 1:24), while it's written about man's soul that "(God) breathed a living soul into his nostrils" (Ibid. 2:7).[44] So, man's soul ascends upward with the death of the body, since everything returns to its source. As it's said, "Dust returns to the earth where it had been; and the spirit returns to God who gave it" (Ecclesiastes 12:7).

It's also said about the souls of the righteous, "I will give you access among these who stand by" (Zechariah 3:7) that is, among the angels, who forever "stand."[45] As it's said, "And He established them[46] for ever and ever" (Psalms 148:6) and, "I came near to one of those who stood by" (Daniel 7:16). And as our sages put it, "The souls of the righteous are sequestered beneath the Place of Honor, as it's said, 'My master's soul will be bound in the bundle of life' (1 Samuel 25:29)" (*Shabbat* 152B).

If you're wise, you'll consider this world a temporary dwelling-place, and will only make use of it to serve God and prepare supplies for your soul.[47] For even if

---

43. . . . who knows . . .

44. And, as the *Sefer Hakanah* points out, "When one exhales, he breathes out something of his very self." (See Rabbi Chevel's notes on Nachmanides' comments on this verse.)

45. The angels forever "stand" in place, spiritually speaking, by neither deviating nor bettering their status. While man can surpass himself (as well as lapse, unfortunately).

46. Literally, "stood them up" . . .

47. How is this statement, which is about to be expanded upon, connected to the above theme that there are often hidden righteous and guilty people? The underlying point is, this world is not at all what it appears to be — even on a moral level. So, all in all, "do not search about after your heart and after your eyes, which lead you astray" (Numbers 15:39). That's to say, don't take anything about this world at face value. And don't settle upon it as the pinnacle of eternity. For just as you were elsewhere before you were here, you'll be elsewhere afterward, as well. (See Supplementary Notes.)

you were to live for many years—even two thousand—eventually those years would come to an end, and would ultimately seem to have never been.

The world of reward, on the other hand, is everlasting. As it's said, "For after a few years will have passed, I will take the path from which I will never return" (Job 16:22). While man's days are like a passing shadow. As it's said, "The days of our years are seventy . . ." (Psalms 90:10) and, "His days are like a passing shadow" (Ibid. 144:4). And as our sages put it, "Not like the shadow of a tree or the shadow of a wall, but rather like the shadow of a passing bird" (*Kohelet Rabbah* 1:3).

What they mean to say is that you're obliged to liken this world to the shadow of a passing bird, and a split second.[48] For you never know if you'll be here today and in the grave tomorrow. Or if all your efforts and troubles for the next day will prove to be an instance of taking pains over a world not your own.[49] As our sages put it, "Do not take pains for the next day, for you never know what the day will bring" (*Sanhedrin* 100B).

20. In fact, Solomon's main intention in writing Ecclesiastes was to impress upon us the fact that the world is utterly vacuous,[50] and that we're only to make use of it to serve God.[51]

---

48. Notice that we're *obliged* "to liken this world to the shadow of a passing bird, and a split second" and to realize that "even if you were to live . . . two thousand years, eventually those years would come to an end, and would ultimately seem to have never been" as was said above. We're not just to "think of it" as such.

49. A materialistic sort of person would respond to this with, "So, why bother doing anything, when you'll get nothing out of it anyway," which will then draw him away from the world. Although not on a transcendent level. While a spiritual person would respond by saying, "So, I'll contribute to others' well-being," which will then draw him into the world. But not on a selfish level.

50. i.e., utterly unreliable for anything other than the most ephemeral of things.

51. There may be times, in the course of the reading of this section in particular, when the reader will be discouraged by the tone and import of what Rabbeinu Yonah is saying. The reader may put this work down and wonder what is so bad about this world, after all! And he may turn away, God forbid, and take the art of Musar and spiritual accomplishment as "anti-life," sullen, and the product of dour old men.

But it's vitally important to know that the point that's being made here is that mere physicality—rank adoration of the material, the obvious, the coarse, and superficial—is what's being discouraged. Not life itself, God forbid, which certainly has goodness, richness, abundant beauty, and holiness. The other point, however, is that all that goodness lies in potential, and only comes to the fore when we apply its elements to the life of the spirit, of the family, of goodness, and of full ethical self-expression.

In that light, and in keeping with our ongoing attempt to explain *The Gates of Repentance* in terms of a relationship with God Almighty, we would point out the following. If we take Heaven to be "home" (i.e., where we come from, and where we're certainly due to return), and this world as "away from home," and if our Beloved is "still home" while we're "away for a while"—then it only makes sense that we'd be expected to "miss" and to long for

And he let his intention be known in the book's beginning and end, by beginning it with, " 'Utterly vacuous!,' declared Ecclesiastes. 'Utterly vacuous! Everything is utterly vacuous!' " (1:2). About which our sages said, "Had anyone else said that, we would have retorted, 'He probably doesn't have a penny to his name, and that's why he considers the world vacuous.' But it was said of Solomon, 'And the king made silver as common in Jerusalem as stones' (1 Kings 10:27), so he was qualified to say that the world is utterly vacuous" (*Kohelet Rabbah* 3:11).[52]

And by ending his book with,[53] "The end of the matter, everything[54] having been heard, is this: Fear God and observe His *mitzvot*. For that is the whole of man" (Ibid. 12:13).

21. If God granted you understanding, then keep in mind the fact that He sent you to this world to keep His charge, and to observe His Torah, decrees, and *mitzvot*. Don't set your eyes upon anything other than on what has to do with your mission, and you'll return to Him at the end of days with glee and everlasting joy, because you carried out your mission faithfully. And you'd be like the servant, sent abroad by his king, who only set his eyes and heart upon things that had to do with his mission, up to the very day he returned to the king. As Solomon said, "I taught you in the way of wisdom" (Proverbs 4:11) . . . "that your trust be in God. . . . That I might make you know the certainty of the words of truth; that you might answer the words of truth to those who send you" (Ibid. 22:19–21).[55]

---

home. And that we not take where we are all that seriously—despite all its luscious beauty. Could a homesick lover be blamed for not quite enjoying the scenery, and for spending his time on the phone to his beloved, or reading and rereading her notes to him?

That is the attitude Rabbeinu Yonah is expressing.

52. That is, if anyone else had said that, we could have argued that he obviously hadn't done or seen this or that, etc. But since Solomon had done and seen everything, his assessment could be counted on.

53. i.e., He let his intentions be known by ending his book with . . . (see beginning of preceding paragraph).

54. . . . else . . .

55. Rabbeinu Yonah speaks of the "glee and everlasting joy" the soul experiences when rejoining God. That parallels Luzzatto's aforementioned statement at the beginning of *The Path of the Just* that we were created to "delight in God and enjoy the radiance of His Divine presence" then (as we pointed out in note 29, above). Thus, that seems to be the ultimate goal. What, however, does that have to do with the trust of God underscored in the verses cited? Apparently, Rabbeinu Yonah's point is that true, studied trust in God is a worldly taste of the bliss the righteous will enjoy in the afterlife. Interestingly, Rabbeinu Yonah said in his commentary to Proverbs (22:19), "My whole intent in offering Musar is to bring you to trust in God."

But we misunderstand the idea of trusting in God. We think of it as a *requirement* of the faith, a "duty of the heart," with a stress on the word "duty," which we're to accomplish here and now much like we'd accomplish any other tenet of the faith. No different than eating matzoh on Passover. And we assume that trusting in God demands that we deny all human

22. Among the other reasons you're obliged to recall the day of death is in order not to forsake your service of God, or slacken off in it. So, deny yourself sleep in order to delve into Torah, to ruminate on the fear of God, to improve your character, achieve high levels of fear and love,[56] and in order to think about how to maximize and enhance *mitzvot* so that they become a bounty and treasure trove for your soul.[57] As it's said, "The wise-hearted will take *mitzvot*" (Proverbs 10:8). Understand and always recall that your days are limited. As our sages said, "The day

---

and to-be-expected anxiety and fear. Because to be anxious or afraid is equivalent in our minds to violating Passover.

The truth is that trusting God is a skill. A duty of *the heart*, which is to say, an *inner process*. And while we're certainly duty-bound to engage in that process, we're certainly, clearly not expected or obliged to have already achieved its end at the outset! In fact, it's comparable to the *process* of swallowing matzoh on Passover. The Torah doesn't expect you to have already eaten matzoh. But rather to set out to do just that. The difference is, of course, that trusting in God is, again, an *inner* process.

Trust in God will be found to be its own reward, though. For what it denotes is blissful liberation and realization of the highest order—nothing less than the stunning realization that God alone is in charge of the universe. That His will is always, invariably carried out. And that the verse, "God is good to all, and merciful to all He created" (Psalms 145:9), is to be taken quite literally, and to be seen as a rock-bottom truism, and a universal axiom.

It also promises nothing less than the liberation that comes with the knowledge that I myself am not in charge of the universe. That while I have my mission, I also have my limitations. And that He who sent me on it is ultimately responsible for the success of my mission.

The process involves the following, as Rabbeinu Yonah lays it out: First, keeping in mind the fact that your life has meaning, and that you were sent to this world for a purpose—"to keep (God's) charge, and to observe His Torah, decrees, and *mitzvot*." Nothing less. And that you're consequently an emissary of God Almighty Himself in this world.

The second step involves bypassing the distractions, and keeping your mission in mind at all times, as would be expected of anyone with a special assignment. That involves focusing "on what has to do with your mission" (as well as on things that obviously feed into the success of the mission, like food, clothing, personal needs, etc.).

And the third involves studying your mission statement, i.e., Torah, all the time. Because the Torah is in fact that—a statement of your mission, as well as a mission plan. And unless you read and reread your mission plan and statement all the time, you're bound to forget, first, that you're on a mission. And second, what that mission entails.

Only then, after you'll have followed through on that process and eventually succeeded in your mission, will you have achieved your goal. And will you experience the great "glee and everlasting joy"; the "delight in God and enjoy(ment of) the radiance of His Divine presence" spoken of. For only then will you be able to affirm and acknowledge "the certainty of the words of truth" you'd have studied all along in Torah. (See Supplementary Notes.)

56. . . . of God . . .

57. . . . after death.

is short, there is a lot of work to do, the workers are lazy, and the Master impels"
(*Pirke Avot* 2:15).[58]

23. But if you don't always keep the reality of death in mind, you'll think
you have all the time and latitude you need to accomplish what you'd want to.[59] Our
sages said, "A single hour spent doing tshuvah and good deeds in this world is more
satisfying than the whole of the World to Come. And a single hour of spiritual
satisfaction in the World to Come is more satisfying than the whole of this world"
(*Pirke Avot* 4:22).[60]

24. When Solomon said, "There is hope for anyone at all connected to life.
For a living dog is better than a dead lion" (Ecclesiastes 9:4), he was praising life in
this world when it comes to doing tshuvah,[61] fulfilling *mitzvot*, and progressing
spiritually. For that's the hope associated with anyone connected to life.[62] And so, "A
living dog is better than a dead lion," because even the coarsest of people can
progress spiritually while alive, while even a sage or a righteous person can't do that
in death.

At another point, however, Solomon belittled and degraded this world, when

---

58. Notice the different sorts of contemplation spoken of here: delving (עמלות) into
Torah, ruminating (התבוננות) on the fear and love of God, and thinking (מחשבה) about how
to maximize and enhance *mitzvot*. And all are meant to bring you to the point where you
"*understand* and always *recall* that your days are limited."

What that tells us is that despite all your delvings, which would involve struggling with
ideas, considering and rejecting some, then proposing and dwelling upon others; despite all
your ruminations, which would involve in-depth thought, taking things to heart, arriving at
convictions; and despite all your thinking, which would involve coming up with original,
creative ideas — you're still not likely to have yet come to "understand and always recall" your
own mortality. Why?

Because the act of "*understand*(ing) . . . that your days are limited," which implies all
three sorts of contemplation, is the result of a series of realizations and epiphanies that can
vanish or fade. While the act of "*recall*(ing) that your days are limited" implies a sort of
ongoing resuscitation of that "understanding" by constantly repeating and reaffirming that
indeed, "The day is short, there is a lot of work to do, the workers are lazy, and the Master
impels." (See Supplementary Notes.)

59. i.e., once you realize that you were indeed created to study Torah, fear God,
improve your character, and to fulfill *mitzvot* (as was said in the previous ¶), you'll want to
do just that. But, "if you don't always keep the reality of death in mind, you'll think you have
all the time and latitude you need" to do just that. But you don't. So, keep the reality of death
in mind, since. . . .

60. i.e., so, spend your time doing the things spoken of in the previous note, since the
effort will be so richly rewarded. See note 55 and note 20 to 1:42, which discuss the spiritual
satisfaction that characterizes The World to Come.

61. i.e., for the opportunity it avails us to do tshuvah . . .

62. That is, as long as you're alive there's hope — i.e., a chance — you'll come to
tshuvah, that you'll do more and more *mitzvot*, and that you'll grow spiritually as a
consequence.

it comes to satisfying your cravings and looking for honor. He said, "How does a man profit from all his labor under the sun?" (Ecclesiastes 1:3) and, "So I praised the dead, who are already dead, more than the living, who are still alive" (Ibid. 4:2).[63]

25. Our sages said, "Observe three things and you will never come to sin: Where you came from—from a murky droplet; where you are heading—to a place of dust, worms, and maggots; and before Whom you are due to give a reckoning—before the King of kings, the Holy One, blessed be He" (*Pirke Avot* 3:1).[64]

That means to say, you'll humble yourself and come to disdain arrogance once you consider where you came from. You'll belittle this world and recognize how worthless its excesses are once you remember where you're heading, and you'd only use them to serve God. And the fear of Heaven will be upon you once you consider before Whom you're destined to give a reckoning.

Our sages also said, "The verse, 'God saw that all that He had done was very good' (Genesis 1:31) refers to death" (*Breishit Rabbah* 9:5). Because death is also good—for humbling you, for affixing the dread of God in your heart, and for having you not make this world primary.[65]

Some people never give themselves the chance to realize just what will ultimately come out of all their struggles to acquire worldly things. As it's said, "Has their profit not departed from them? They will die without wisdom" (Job 4:21). That means to say, has their profit—their money—not departed from them, despite all their travels?[66] Because, in truth, there's no advantage to having it, and it actually undoes a lot of good, by causing them to die without wisdom. In that[67] they don't acquire the wisdom to understand their destiny, to improve themselves, or to store provisions for the way. As it's written, "Would that they were wise, that they would grasp this, that they would understand their destiny" (Deuteronomy 32:29).

---

63. Rabbeinu Yonah's point is that like all sages, Solomon is ambivalent about life in this world. After all, God seems to be missing here, and there are so many ludicrous and pointless things to contend with. Yet, it's here alone that you can prepare so much of what you'll need for your situation in infinity. As such, life in this world is like a college career: the process itself is often trying and noisome, and is not itself what you're striving for (after all, no one goes to medical school to be a medical student, but to eventually be a doctor!). But there is so much you can accomplish here and now, while you have the opportunity, which you'll never be able to accomplish afterward.

64. See Supplementary Notes.

65. . . . in your eyes. Because this world is a house you're renting, which you'd be wise not to invest more than you actually have to in, and which you should be ready to vacate at any time. (See Supplementary Notes.)

66. i.e., despite all their departures, which is to say, all their travels and travails.

67. . . . as a direct result of their travels . . .

Chapter Eight

26. The Venerable Dictum[1]

We'll now conclude this subject with a venerable dictum from our sages. "Hillel would say, If I am not for myself, who will be? But even when I am for myself, what am I? And if not now, when?" (*Pirke Avot* 1:14).

What that means to say is, what good do all the admonishments do if you don't motivate yourself?[2] For while they[3] might penetrate your heart the day you hear them, the yetzer harah will[4] have you forget them, and pass them from your heart.[5] As it's said, "Your piety is like the morning mist" (Hosea 6:4).[6]

It's also said, "The tongue of the righteous is like choice silver; but the heart of the wrongdoer is worth little" (Proverbs 10:20). What that means is that the

---

1. This phrase isn't included in the text, and was inserted here for ease of reference.

2. Rabbeinu Yonah is now returning to a theme he presented in ¶1. As he put it there, "Understand that there are six instances in which a person can be moved to do tshuvah for his wrongful ways," and he goes on to list them in ¶'s 2–25. He then adds, "But more importantly, be sure to do tshuvah every day and to purify yourself, my child, whether you sense anything inspiring you to or not," that is, whether you're moved to do tshuvah in those instances or not. And he concludes that it's actually better to be self-motivated to tshuvah. For, "it would be known . . . that your tshuvah came from within if you're not impelled by one of these instances, but are drawn to it of your own volition." So, the purpose of this section is to provide us with the encouragement we'd need to do just that.

3. i.e., the admonishments offered in the six instances . . .

4. . . . soon . . .

5. But, what does the yetzer harah have to do with forgetting things? After all, forgetting is a natural phenomenon, and ostensibly has nothing to do with acting out of free will or not. Apparently, then, we're not talking about simply not "recollecting" something. What Rabbeinu Yonah means is that your yetzer harah convinces you to disregard these things, to "just forget about them," as the expression goes. Contrast that with the admonition in ¶1 to "remember your Creator" (see our comments there).

6. i.e., vaporous and short-lived.

admonishments that come from the righteous are pure and unadulterated, for their tongues are of choice quality. But a wrongdoer's heart only listens to their admonishments for a moment.[7,8]

So, you have to motivate yourself[9] when you hear words of admonishment, take them to heart, think about them all the time, expand upon them yourself, say things about them that come from your own heart, meditate upon them in the depths of your soul, continue to internalize the words of your critic, and not depend on his criticisms alone but criticize yourself every day and every moment until you take the admonishment to heart and are purified.[10]

"But even when I alone am for myself, what am I?"—for, even when I'm concerned enough to try to improve myself as much as I can, and delve into wisdom all the time, what am I, anyway? For, our grasp is limited and weak. And despite all our efforts and amends we actually only achieve limited spiritual advances. So, who am I and what is my life all about if I'm not even for myself enough to make the effort to improve myself?

As such, you're like a fallow field that can produce little, despite the effort to improve it and the work put into it. But which would produce nothing but thorns and grub if no effort went into improving it. For only a fertile field would produce crops even when unworked. As our sages said, "As to, 'He knows our urges' [Psalms

---

7. Rabbeinu Yonah writes in ¶18 that "all wrongdoers ever want . . . is to satisfy their bodily cravings" (see our comments there). Hence, they only listen to criticism for a short while because that's their pattern: they consume something with gusto until they tire of it and go on to the next. (See Supplementary Notes.)

8. The text continues with the following:

> As in, "I could bring their enemies to submission in short" (Psalms 81:15), meaning he can bring their enemies to submission *in a moment*. And the "heart" being referred to here is a ready and emended heart, as in, "One who takes criticism acquires a heart" (Proverbs 15:32) and "[How is the fool able] to acquire wisdom when he has no heart?" (Ibid. 17:16).

9. See Supplementary Notes.

10. According to Rabbeinu Yonah's understanding, "If I am not for myself, then who will be?" means to say that what you have to do is motivate *yourself* to grow and to do tshuvah. Since you can't depend on external motivation, because you're bound to forget what others say about your need to do tshuvah, and are only likely to listen to them for a moment or two, anyway.

Rabbeinu Yonah then goes on to explain the process of motivating yourself. But rather than utterly rejecting external motivation, his process involves *building upon* them. It includes, 1) taking the admonishments to heart, 2) "think(ing) about them all the time," 3) "expand(ing) upon them yourself," 4) "say(ing) things about them that come from your own heart," 5) "meditat(ing) upon them in the depths of your soul," 6) "continu(ing) to internalize the words of your critic," and, 7) "not depend(ing) on his criticisms alone but criticiz(ing) yourself every day and every moment until you take the admonishment to heart and are purified." Hence, we have a description of the sort of intense, inspired, and creative self-reflection and -motivation that will lead to tshuvah and metamorphosis.

103:14], it's like the story of the king who provided his subjects with a field, and warned them to work it and guard it, and have it produce thirty *kur*-measures of crop each year. The subjects made every effort and worked hard at it, but could only provide the king with five *kur*-measures. He said to them, 'What have you done?' And they replied, 'Your Majesty, the field you gave us was fallow. Yet, we worked it with all our might. And despite all our efforts we could not provide any more produce than this amount'" (*Avot D'Rebbe Natan* 16).[11]

"And if not now, when?"—It's not right for me to postpone for even a day or two my efforts to improve myself and allot time for Torah study.[12] Nor should I tell myself that I can't hope to have the time for it until I have enough money in my hands. Because there's no end to the world's demands,[13] as our sages said, "Never say, 'I'll study when I get the chance,' because you might never get the chance" (*Pirke Avot* 2:4).

27. Second,[14] you'd want to amass more[15] after earning and amassing.[16] As our sages said, "No one leaves this world with half his cravings fulfilled. If he has a hundred, he wants to make it two hundred. And if he has two hundred, he wants to make it four hundred" (*Kohelet Rabbah* 1:13). As it's written, "One who loves silver never has enough silver" (Ecclesiastes 5:9).[17]

28. Third, time is getting shorter, yet there's a lot of work to do—work on Torah, on self-improvement and on achieving spiritual qualities like love, fear and devotion to God.[18] As our sages said, "The day is short, there is a lot of work to do . . ." (*Pirke Avot* 2:15).[19]

---

11. It must be kept in mind that Rabbeinu Yonah isn't saying here that there's precious little hope. Just that, left to our own devices, we're all prone to allowing ourselves to lay "fallow," and need to be piqued and prodded—"pruned" and "shorn," so to speak. So, it behooves us to do as much as we can, while we can. In order to forestall the inertia that would overtake us if we'd allow it to.

The truth is if we too are able to say, "we worked it with all our might, and despite all our efforts we could not provide any more produce than this," the King will certainly have mercy on us as well. After all, "He knows our urges" and limitations only too well. (See Supplementary Notes.)

12. Note that Rabbeinu Yonah is underscoring the utmost importance of Torah study in both self-improvement and self-motivation to do tshuvah.

13. i.e., you'll seemingly "never have the time" . . .

14. . . . reason not to postpone motivating yourself to tshuvah is . . .

15. . . . wealth . . .

16. . . . it in the first place.

17. As to the layout of this section: we're now being offered nine reasons why it's unwise to forestall doing tshuvah and improving ourselves. First, above, because there are unending demands made upon us in life. Second, as put here, is because we'll never have enough money to put everything else aside and concentrate on tshuvah and self-improvement. And so on.

18. This is one of the most essential statements in *The Gates of Repentance*. Because

29.   Fourth, you come upon transgression and stumble upon sins all the time when you postpone self-improvement.[20]

30.   Fifth, your yetzer harah grows stronger and stronger, and your heart hardens when you postpone improving yourself, which then makes it more difficult to improve yourself later on. As it's written, "Behold, it was all grown over with thorns . . ." (Proverbs 24:31), about which our sages said, "When the yetzer harah is intertwined with sin it becomes somewhat like heresy,[21] and you do not have the chance to purify yourself" (*Avodah Zarah* 17A) And as it's put in Musar literature, "Routine rules over everything" (*Mibchar Hap'ninim*).[22]

31.   Sixth, you might not live long, and die before completing the tenets of tshuvah. That's why Solomon warned, "Let your garments always be white" (Ecclesiastes 9:8).[23]

32.   Seventh, your transgressions will age[24] if you postpone doing tshuvah,

---

while tshuvah is this book's primary concern, tshuvah is on one level just a stepping stone onto further growth. Because while I'd certainly need to undo any wrong I'd done to my Beloved if I'm to further and deepen my committment to Him. I nonetheless mustn't forget that *I have to actually further and deepen that committment!* In other words, it's not enough to undo and return to status quo. I'd need to grow and continue growing in that relationship.

For as Rabbeinu Yonah points out in 3:17, we were actually created to achieve very lofty and sublime qualities like holiness, the fear and love of God, etc. (See there; see 1:1, "God helps those who do tshuvah . . . by fostering a purity of spirit within them that allows them to love Him"; and see ¶'s 21–22.) We weren't created to merely undo any wrong we'd done. And further, as it's said at the end of 3:17, "what hope can there be for you if you don't put all your efforts and interests into the things you were created for?" As such, as it's said here, indeed, "there's a lot of work to do—work on Torah, on self-improvement, and on achieving qualities like love, fear, and devotion to God." (See 1:10 also.)

The astute reader might then point to our statement in note 9 to ¶1 above to the effect that tshuvah *itself* is the best way to draw closer to God and to transcend your corporeality (see there), and might then charge that that seems to contradict our point here. The response to that, though, is that there's tshuvah, and there's tshuvah. That is, on one level, tshuvah merely erases wrongs and allows for the necessary further advancement. But on another level, tshuvah–"High Tshuvah"—is itself a drawing closer to God, which is the loftiest and most sublime quality of all. As it's said, "Return, O Israel," i.e., realize High Tshuvah, and you will return "to God the Lord" Himself (Hosea 14:2).

19. See Supplementary Notes.

20. See Supplementary Notes.

21. i.e., your situation comes close to being that of a heretic . . .

22. That's both a warning and an offer of hope. It's a warning to remember not to slip into bad habits. And it's a reminder that you can always change for the good by habituating yourself to.

23. See Supplementary Notes.

24. i.e., will become *de rigeur* . . .

you'll quickly forget your sorrow about them, and wouldn't worry about them as much as you would have originally.[25]

33. Eighth, you wouldn't earn as much merit for doing tshuvah when you advance in age and your yetzer harah loses its strength as you'd have earned by improving yourself while you were young.[26] As our sages said, "Happy is the man who fears God (Psalms 112:1), that is, while he is yet a man"[27] (*Avodah Zarah* 19A). As well as, "When a thief has nothing to steal he considers himself honest"[28] (*Sanhedrin* 22A).

34. And ninth, you'll no longer have the same acumen once you become old, nor have the faculties needed to feel or think differently in order to fight off your yetzer harah, to achieve high spiritual levels, or to struggle and toil at Torah or good deeds. As it's said, "Remember your Creator in your youth, before the bad days come, and the years draw near when you will say, 'I have no desire for them'" (Ecclesiastes 12:1). So it's important to find refuge for yourself as hastily as possible.[29] As David said, "I made haste, and did not delay in observing your *mitzvot*" (Psalms 119:60).

---

25. See Supplementary Notes.
26. See Supplementary Notes.
27. i.e., still in his prime.
28. Literally, "to be a man of peace." That is, he forgets about all the damage he'd done, and all the havoc he'd wreaked in the past.
29. See Supplementary Notes.

Synopsis

There are six instances in which you're likely to be moved to do tshuvah. But do tshuvah every day, even if you don't encounter them, by remembering God (¶1).

The first instance: When afflictions strike, realize that your sins brought them on, and return to God. While people may deride your regret for what you did to them when you suffer as a result, God will not. But if you don't do tshuvah then or examine your ways and accept blame when that's called for, you'd be guiltier yet (¶2). Realize that God chastises you for two reasons: to forgive you and heal your soul (through bodily travail), and to move you to tshuvah. So, don't make matters worse by not doing tshuvah then (¶3). Rejoice in your afflictions when you improve yourself as a result, and thank God for them. For God is pleased when you take His chastisements to heart, and in fact only chastises those He favors and expects good things from (¶4). Trust God and hope that your affliction and darkness will be grounds for light. Fast, do tshuvah, and pray, as a congregation would when afflicted. And know that if you're pure and upright, and you suffer, your suffering will increase your reward, and that it's a product of God's love (¶5). The same goes for tshuvah and the wholehearted return to God on the day of death, as well. Though it's not as effective as other instances of tshuvah, it's nonetheless effective (¶6).

The second instance: Return to God and reflect on the approach of death, when you grow old, and He'll have mercy on you. But you'll only grow more and more guilty and loathsome to Him if you don't. And don't fail to recognize how much frailer and older you're becoming when you're middle-aged either (¶7). Tshuvah is dismissed by many because they consider themselves righteous and pure, when they're not. Such people have either taken their sins lightly, or forgotten them. Or else they've never inquired of God, or paid attention to scholars (¶8). The truly righteous always grieve over their sins, and bemoan their shortcomings in the active service of God, which is just as serious. How much more so should you, if you focus on your body and on the ephemeral rather than on the fear of God, Torah, and introspection. So, reflect on your destiny when you're young, abandon your cravings, and put your soul in order when you mature. And do that more and more the older you get, focusing less on the worldly, and more on the fear of God, self-examination and -improvement, Torah, and *mitzvot*. And by age ninety you should be completely occupied with prayer, praises to God, and with the recounting of His wonders (¶9).

The third instance: When you're admonished by a sage, take it upon yourself to do everything he says, do tshuvah, and you'll utterly transform yourself. You'll also instantly accrue upon yourself the merit associated with all the *mitzvot*, as long as you go back again and again to those who'd offer you criticism, to learn more (¶10). But you'd grow guiltier yet if you aren't moved by reproach, and you harden your heart in the face of it. For while there's always hope for those who fall sway to their impulses, there's none for those who can't take criticism (¶11). Hearing is even more valuable than seeing, because it can affect you more deeply. Hence, the ear is the most significant of the organs. So, if we're commanded to serve God with every element of our beings, aren't we all the more so expected to serve Him with our ears, by hearing out reproach? (¶12).

The fourth instance: When delving into Torah and you start to appreciate its admonishments, and to be intimidated by its warnings. And you determine to improve your ways. In fact, you'd only grow guiltier by studying it without being affected by it thusly (¶13).

The fifth instance: Realizing, during the Ten Days of Repentance, that your actions are being recorded and judged. Reacting as you would if you were being judged by a king, by doing whatever you could to be judged favorably, and avoiding everything that would distract you from accomplishing that. And by reflecting, scrutinnizing your deeds, pouring out your heart to God and doing tshuvah during this favorable period of time (to say nothing of Yom Kippur, when we're commanded to do tshuvah) (¶14).

The sixth instance: Recognizing that you should always be ready to greet God, because you never know when your end will come. As such, scrutinize your ways and consider them constantly; confess, and experience the fear of God all the time (¶15). Do new *mitzvot* every day in order not to be lacking in any one of them by the time you die, and to be considered as having fulfilled them all in your lifetime (¶16).

There are some who are as oblivious to the reality of death as animals, and do nothing to prepare for it. But, in truth, wrongdoers are tortured by death, because they'll no longer be able to satisfy their cravings then (¶17). The souls of those who lived to satisfy their earthly cravings rather than to serve God stay rooted to the earth after death (¶18). There are hidden sinners, who can't be perceived as such, who descend to the nether world after death. While there are secret righteous people, who can't be perceived as such, who join the angels above. So if you're wise, you'll see this world as a temporary dwelling-place—as short-lived as a bird's shadow flitting by. And only use it for the service of God and to stock up on supplies for your soul (¶19). In fact, the point of the Book of Ecclesiastes is to impress the fact upon you that the world is vacuous, and should only be used to serve God with (¶20).

Take to heart the fact that God sent you to this world to keep His watch and to observe His *mitzvot*. And that if you obey your charge, you'll return to Him as His faithful, happy servant (¶21). So remember the fact of death in order not to slacken off in your service to God, which includes Torah study, fearing God, correcting character flaws, and growing in fear and love, as well as glorifying and aggrandizing *mitzvot* and making yourself a repository of them (¶22). Forget the fact of death and you'll think you have a lot of time to accomplish things, when you don't (¶23). For as long as you're alive, you have a chance to do tshuvah and *mitzvot*, and to grow. But occupying yourself any other way is of no avail (¶24). Remember you're derived from a turgid drop, and you'll become humble. Remember where you're destined to go, and this world will mean little to you, and you'll use it to serve God, rather than see it as primary. And remember you'll be giving a reckoning to God someday, and you'll fear Him. Don't be like those who don't take time to consider their destiny (¶25).

It's important to realize, though, that reproach doesn't help unless you take what you hear to heart, reflect on it, and expand upon it on your own, day after day. But even if you do all of that, you can only hope to accomplish so much. So do as much as you can to improve yourself and to study Torah, as soon as you can. First, because you might not have the time later on (¶26). Second, because you'll seemingly never have enough (¶27). Third, because your time is limited and there's a lot to do in the way of Torah study, character improvement, and the attainment of greater degrees of love and fear of and devotion to God (¶28). Fourth, because you stumble upon sin all the time when you postpone self-improvement (¶29). Fifth, because your yetzer harah grows stronger the longer you vacillate about improving yourself. And that makes it harder yet to do it (¶30). Sixth, because you may die before fulfilling the tenets of tshuvah (¶31). Seventh, because when you vacillate about tshuvah, you become used to your sins. And you no longer worry about them (¶32). Eighth, because you wouldn't accrue the same merit doing tshuvah in old age as you would if you did it while you were young (¶33). And ninth, because you won't have the capacity to arrive at new ways to resist the yetzer harah or to acquire higher levels, to learn Torah, or to accomplish good things, when you're old (¶34).

Gate Three

AN EXPLANATION OF THE SIGNIFICANCE OF THE MITZVOT AND PROHIBITIONS, AND THEIR VARIOUS CONSEQUENCES

The multifarious *mitzvot* herein are arranged according to *halachic* category. They break down thusly, and are significant for various reasons.

Rabbinic decrees, which are the very pathway to the fear of God, which is itself the very basis of all *mitzvot* (¶'s 4–8).

Torah imperatives, which are just as much an expression of the fear of Heaven as avoiding prohibitions is, and their neglect brings on just as much personal ruin as the committing of prohibitions (¶'s 9–23).

Prohibitions connected to an imperative, including those against stealing, defrauding, abusing either physically or verbally, and against taking interest on loans (¶'s 24–25).

Prohibitions involving no (outward) action embracing the heart, including those against not remembering God, forgetting the Torah, assuming good fortune is a consequence of righteousness, testing God, getting discouraged, fearing harm in the carrying out of justice, being arrogant, being miserly, hardening your heart, taking revenge, hating, fantasizing lasciviously, plotting out sins, listening to heretics, accepting slander, and scheming to possess your neighbor's property (¶'s 26–43).

Prohibitions involving no (outward) action embracing speech, including those against studying or praying in immodest or unclean circumstances, swearing falsely or in vain, cursing with God's name, deciding *halacha* while intoxicated, verbally abusing, encouraging sinners, making rash and false decisions, offering improper or self-serving advice, tale-bearing, being inconsistent, mentioning an idol, complimenting idol-worshippers, provoking, exploiting, profaning God's name, not expressing respect for scholars, and cursing your parents (¶'s 44–63).

Prohibitions involving no (outward) action embracing your senses of hearing and seeing, including those against staring at anyone forbidden to you, being haughty-eyed, and listening to worthless or foul things (¶'s 64–66).

Prohibitions involving no (outward) action embracing withdrawing your hand and refraining from doing something, including those against not loaning to the poor, defrauding, delaying burials, being lax about protecting property, failing to criticize others, and delaying the fulfillment of vows (¶'s 67–74).

Prohibitions involving an action, including those against not salting meat, injuring others, wearing *shatnez*, touching extraneously, striking a grown child, offering wine to a Nazi, providing a limb torn off of an animal, selling materials or books of heresy, cutting down fruit trees, squandering money, exposing yourself to danger, committing suicide, benefiting from *orlah* or *revi'it*, benefiting from *gid hanashe*, stealing, practicing "divination" or "soothsaying," keeping dishonest weights and measures, dispiriting debtors, being part of an interest-bearing loan, blemishing a firstborn animal, plowing or threshing with different animals, breeding mixed animals, kneeling onto a stone floor, eating anything repulsive, inhibiting a bowel movement, handing over your daughter to anyone other than for marriage, keeping a concubine, having relations with an unmarried woman, encouraging your daughter to marry an old man, eating meat not slaughtered by a God-fearing *shochet*, taking payment to judge, carrying unnecessarily on a Festival, shaving off certain hairs, keeping a vicious dog or a defective ladder, working with firstborn oxen, shearing firstborn sheep, erasing God's name, using incantations or talismans, and eating chadash (¶'s 75–106).

Sins incurring death through the hands of Heaven, including eating *tevel*, oppressing widows and orphans, stealing from the poor, ruining reputations, exploiting minors, spilling seed, practicing onanism, not acting demurely, not speaking gently, not conducting business honestly, not attending a *beit midrash*, challenging authority, rendering decisions before teachers, stealing money meant for the poor, vowing to donate but not doing so, and not giving charity to poor relatives (¶'s 107–118).

The significance of excision, of which there are two types: those that cause you to lose life in this world; and those that cause you to lose life in this world, and to be excised from The World to Come (¶'s 119–125).

The four court-imposed death sentences, which are stoning, burning, impalement, and strangulation, are afflicted upon those who have incestuous relations, practice witchcraft, desecrate the Sabbath, curse parents, cohabit with the betrothed, incite idol worship, practice sorcery, are a *ben soreh u'moreh*, blaspheme God or worship idols, murder, live in an *eir hanidachas*, strike parents, kidnap a Jew, rebel against the court, prophecy falsely, prophecy in the name of idols, cohabit with a married woman, cohabit with a gentile maidservant, delay judgment and pervert justice, take false vows, and profane God's name (¶'s 126–135).

The significant sins you're to give your life for rather than commit include worshipping idols, committing adultery, or murdering. Even the slightest breach of them is forbidden (¶'s 136–142).

The significant sins whose violators have no place in The World to Come including profaning God's name and demeaning His Torah, committing well-known sins publicly and casting off the yoke of Heaven, despising the word of God, misinterpreting Torah, demeaning the Holy Days, demeaning Torah scholars, not believing that mention is made of the Resurrection of the Dead in the Torah, and not believing that the Torah is from Heaven. Others include heretics, "God's enemies," informers, and those who cause the multitude to sin, those who elicit fear, who "separate themselves from the community," and those who "abandon God" (¶'s 143–171).

An explanation of the sins of "The Four Types": Individuals in these four categories do not experience the Divine Presence. They include those who malign, lie, flatter, or slander (¶'s 172–173).

Maligners insult others cruelly without personally benefiting from it, belittle and scorn others who fall short in worldly accomplishments, mock things and accomplishments, engage in small talk and meaningless things, and malign others out of sheer lightheartedness (¶'s 174–177).

Liars falsely repudiate others' oaths, disclaim legitimate agreements, bear false witness, conduct business dishonestly, etc.; underhandedly gain the confidence of others; acquire things by lying or importuning; distort things; gratuitously tell others they'll do him a favor; disappoint others; delude others into believing they've done him a favor; take credit for qualities they don't have; and distort details (¶'s 178–186).

Flatterers tell sinners they've done nothing wrong; publicly praise sinners; complement wrongdoers; befriend wrongdoers; wrongly characterize someone as trustworthy; don't protest wrongdoing when they can; see others sinning and don't reproach; and show respect for wrongdoers (¶'s 187–199).

Slanderers seem to deny God's existence, and their sin is even more serious than idol worship, illicit relations, and murder. They're of six types: those who attribute imaginary faults in others; those who slander others without lying in the process; rumor-mongers and disclosers of secrets; those who encourage slander; those who speak obscenely, and those who find fault for no good reason (¶'s 200–231).

Chapter One

1. *The Rationale*[1]

You've already been alerted to scrutinize your ways and to note any transgressions and sins you've committed when you do tshuvah.[2] So, be sure to determine just how serious each and every sin is when you finish thoroughly scrutinizing them, as it's said, "Let us scrutinize and examine[3] our ways, and return to God" (Lamentations 3:40). And do that in order to know just how guilty you are in the case of each sin you committed. Because there are some instances of guilt that approach Heaven, they're so extreme, and some instances of wrongdoing so deplorable that they're equivalent to many great sins.[4]

For, the more earnestly you examine your sins, the greater will be your tshuvah.[5] Because you'll either have discovered just how numerous and serious they

---

1. This phrase isn't included in the text, and was inserted here for ease of reference.

2. See Supplementary Notes.

3. The word we translate as "examine" here, לחקר, is the same used for "determine" above (we translated the expression both ways for clarity's sake). That's to say, you're to both scrutinize your wrongful ways, and to determine just how serious they are when you do tshuvah.

4. That's to say, it's not enough to know you've offended or hurt your beloved. You'd also have to know how seriously she took it, and how significant what you did was to her. For while you might perceive some particular offense as minor, she might consider it major. And you'd need to know that to understand how to change and reconcile.

5. Rabbeinu Yonah already pointed out that God Himself "observes all your actions, examines your innermost being, and scrutinizes your thoughts" (1:22). And that your realizing that will bring you to humility and shame. Hence he's underscoring that point again here. And asserting that by realizing your faults and mistakes on your own (before God does, so to speak) you'd be achieving even greater tshuvah for them.

were and will grieve as a result. Or they'll cause you to humble yourself and thus make your transgression acceptable.[6] As it's said, "If their uncircumcised hearts are humbled then, and they make their transgression acceptable, then I will remember My covenant with Jacob, My covenant with Isaac, and My covenant with Abraham" (Leviticus 26:41–42).[7]

2. Another reason to determine just how serious your transgressions are, is in order to cover your face with humiliation when you ask for forgiveness.[8] As it's said, "O my God, I am too ashamed and humiliated to lift up my face to You, God" (Ezra 9:6). Also, in order to bear shame before God after He assures you He'll forgive you. As it's said, "That you may remember and be ashamed . . . when I will have forgiven you for all you did" (Ezekiel 16:63). And to see with your own eyes just how kind God is to forgive you, as it's said, "For Your kindness is before my eyes" (Psalms 26:3).[9]

For if a servant were to sin against his master, for example, and were to then humble himself before him, the master wouldn't favor him again until the servant realized just how defiant he'd been. And he'd become even angrier if he imagined the servant was taking his sin lightly. In just such a way, you're obliged to realize just how significant your sin was, and the consequences for it. As it's said, "Behold, I have been a fool, and been very, very wrong" (1 Samuel 26:21).

So we must teach the Jewish Nation the serious consequences for each

---

The point is also to be made that Rabbeinu Yonah said in 1:13 (and reiterated in ¶217), that "the bitterer and sadder you feel, the more effective and profound will be your tshuvah." Hence the underlying statement is that earnest and honest examination of your sins will invariably embitter and sadden you. That the effect of all that will be true tshuvah. And that the deeper that goes, the deeper your tshuvah.

6. . . . to God, after the fact. That's to say, your having done deep tshuvah for them will make you as pleasing to God as you'd been before you sinned.

7. What this refers to is a stunned revelation of truth based on honest instrospection, which utterly shocks, undoes, and moves you to true tshuvah. In fact, the more profound the reflection upon the number and depth of your sins, the more sincere your anguish and subsequent surrendering of your heart and tshuvah.

In terms of relationships that's to say, the more sensitively you scrutinize how much you offended your beloved (and come to understand her in the process), the truer your regret, the more honest your humility, and the greater your reconciliation as a consequence.

8. See Supplementary Notes.

9. First and foremost, we're presented here with a sure affirmation of the fact that God forgives! The other matter is more subtle. It's based on a fact that many are not aware of—that *gratitude* is a great delight for the soul, which it enjoys both in this world, and the next. And that it's even more robustly felt in the latter. Rabbeinu Yonah's point here is that you'd never enjoy the full degree of gratitude you'd otherwise enjoy in the next world unless you first come to know the depth of your guilt, and how meaningful your forgiveness therefore was. (See Supplementary Notes.)

transgression and sin, through instruction and confirmation, which is why we've included this introduction.[10]

But there's another eminently important reason to do this. For I see that most people take a lot of serious acts of defiance lightly. Or they consider warnings not to commit sins that incur the death penalty[11] or excision[12] as[13] extra righteousness, or only for the pious. And so they stumble in them without thinking, and aren't even criticized.[14] As it's said, "Was your ear not opened then?" (Isaiah 48:8).

So we have to alert them,[15] and to open their ears to how significant many sins are. As well as to the fact that there are many ways and instances in which a person can come to utter catastrophe and spiritual destruction by[16] minor *mitzvot*.[17] In fact, many wrongdoers changed their ways when they learned about the ruin and devastation brought on by them,[18] and when the seriousness of their sin as well as what was decreed[19] for committing them was shown them. And many who had stumbled[20] would gird their loins to prevail over their cravings. For after all—how could they ever stand to see their own destruction?

---

10. "This introduction" could either refer to ¶'s 1–3 of this gate, as we've laid them out to be. Or they could refer to all that preceded this in this book, so far.

If the latter is true, then what Rabbeinu Yonah would be saying all in all is that—yes—tshuvah exists and is available to you, God forgives when you do tshuvah, and the more deeply you do it, the more lovingly He'll take you back—which would be the gist of the first gate. That while—yes—there will always be things that will prod you into doing tshuvah, and it's nonetheless best to understand its importance and preciousness on your own—which would be the gist of the second gate. But nonetheless, it's essential that you know that sin is real, that it truly threatens the quality of your immortal relationship to God Almighty, and that you'd need to heed that warning—which is the gist of this gate. (And that the fourth gate, which addresses the varying degrees of forgiveness, follows all that necessarily.) (See Supplementary Notes.)

11. See Supplementary Notes.

12. *Karet* (כרת), which we refer to as "excision," is usually translated as "being cut off." And while both imply rejection, severance, and being cast asunder, we prefer excision because "being cut off" has financial connotations in our age (e.g., "He's being cut off from the inheritance").

The term is found in a number of places in the Torah, including Genesis 17:14, Exodus 12:15, etc. And Rabbeinu Yonah explains in ¶120 that there are two sorts, depending upon the offense committed. The "lighter" sort, as a result of which one dies before age fifty (see ¶124), is discussed in ¶'s 119–125; while the more serious sort, as a result of which one loses his place in The World to Come, is discussed in ¶'s 143–171.

13. . . . examples of . . .

14. . . . for having done them, so that they might do tshuvah.

15. . . . to the seriousness of those particular sins . . .

16. . . . committing certain . . .

17. i.e., prohibitions.

18. i.e., brought on by committing certain minor prohibitions.

19. . . . for them . . .

20. . . . in the past . . .

3. It's like the situation of the man who wanted to go to a certain city and was told that the road to it was strewn with thorns, traps, and snags, who went at first[21] because he needed to, then stopped short when he was told that there was a lion on that road, and a leopard ready to leap out.[22]

And so Solomon advised us, "To know wisdom and *Musar* . . ." (Proverbs 1:2), where "wisdom" refers to improving your ways and ridding yourself of your sins, as in, "It[23] is your wisdom" (Deuteronomy 4:6). But after learning and coming to know which[24] are *mitzvot* and which are sins, you'd need to learn just how reprehensible sins are, and how much devastation and ruin they bring,[25] in order to withdraw from them and criticize[26] yourself by keeping their consequences in mind, and in order to admonish others. That branch of knowledge is referred to here as *Musar*.[27] How gratifying it would be for those who publicly criticize[28] to impart this knowledge!

We'll now explain the degrees of significance of the *mitzvot* and prohibitions, and their various consequences.

---

21. . . . despite that . . .

22. That's to say, people might have been *hesitant* to commit those sins in the past, when they only expected to encounter "thorns, traps, and snags" in their pursuit of them. But when they learn that they'll actually confront a "lion" and a "leopard," they'll utterly refrain.

23. i.e., the Torah.

24. . . . deeds . . .

25. "Fair" or not, our actions invariably have consequences, whether we're aware of them or not, which are either subtle or blunt. That's simply an existential "given," no less real and no more forgiving sometimes than the "laws of nature."

26. Here's another instance of "criticism" as a warning. See our Supplementary Note to 2:11.

27. Literally, "admonishment," but understood to mean the formal art and science of betterment and devotion known as *Musar*, which Rabbeinu Yonah defines here as knowledge of "just how reprehensible sins are, and how much devastation and ruin they bring."

28. i.e., those who discourse upon and instruct in ethics.

Chapter Two

4. The First Level:
The Significance of the
Sages' Decrees

We're obliged by the Torah to accept the decrees of the prophets[1] and judges, and to obey the words of the sages[2] and heed their precautions.[3] As it's said, "Do not deviate from whatever they declare to you, to the right or the left" (Deuteronomy 17:11). As such, since the Torah itself warns us to observe everything they teach, we see that a Torah-based commandment is more significant than their[4] words. By virtue of the fact that the point[5] is explicitly stated in God's Torah and thus expressly demanded of us by God Himself.[6]

Yet there are instances in which the words of the sages are more significant than the Torah's own. As our sages[7] put it, "The words of the sages can be more significant than the Torah's. For if a scholar denies the mitzvah of *t'phillin* and a

---

1. Like Solomon's authorization of an *Eruv* to in order to carry on *Shabbat*, etc.
2. Like lighting Channukah candles and Shabbat candles, etc.
3. Like reciting the *Shma* before midnight (when it's technically all right to recite it at any point in the night), in order not to neglect it.
4. i.e., the prophets', judges', or sages'.
5. . . . about following their dictates . . .
6. The point is as follows: there are two sorts of *mitzvot*: Torah-based and Rabbinic-based. In one sense, Torah-based *mitzvot* are more weighty than Rabbinic-based ones, since the Torah itself commands us to obey Rabbinic-based *mitzvot* (thus evidencing more authority than they). In another sense, though, Rabbinic-based *mitzvot* are more weighty than Torah-based *mitzvot*—as we're about to see.
7. . . . themselves . . .

Torah law will be transgressed,[8] he's nonetheless exempt.[9] But if that scholar says that there are to be five *totaphot*[10] and thus adds on to what the sages decreed, he is liable"[11] (*Sanhedrin* 88B). And, "Whoever violates the words of the sages is culpable for death"[12] (*Berachot* 4B).[13]

5. Wouldn't you like to know why someone who violates the words of the sages is even more deserving of the death penalty than someone who violates Torah prohibitions and imperatives? The answer is as follows.

When you violate the words of the sages, you do so willingly, because their directives mean little to you, rather than because your impulses have overtaken you. Also because your eyes had become too feeble to behold the brilliance of their words,[14] you no longer pursue the glow of faith, you're no longer impelled by the yoke of their decrees, and you don't strive to fulfill what they say since it isn't written in the Torah. As a consequence, you don't act like those who transgress the Torah itself, who become bitter as a result, haunted by what they did, frightened, and then suffer the fact that they've been brought to sin by their impulses.[15]

That's why you'd be culpable for the death penalty—because you'd have rejected one of their goodly decrees, and as much as said, "Let us break their bonds!" (Psalms 2:3). In fact, you'd be in the same category as the elder sage who rebels against the sages,[16] about whom it's said, "The man who will act presumptuously and will not listen . . . to the *cohen* . . . will die" (Deuteronomy 17:12).

6. The second reason is because you'd be unlikely to do tshuvah, since you don't consider what you did to be serious, and you'd be repeating your sin all the time (when, in fact, the consequences of a minor sin committed many times are even greater than those for a single serious sin).[17]

---

8. . . . by someone, as a result of that scholar's ruling . . .

9. i.e., that scholar is not guilty of being a "rebellious elder" (see original citation).

10. i.e., five *t'phillin* sections, rather than the required four.

11. i.e., that scholar *is* guilty of being a "rebellious elder."

12. . . . by the hands of Heaven, though not in a court of law.

13. That is, since in certain instances someone who violates a Rabbinic-based mitzvah is culpable for a more serious penalty than one who violates a Torah-based mitzvah would be, we see that in another sense Rabbinic-based *mitzvot* are more weighty even than Torah-based ones.

14. Literally, "the light (emanating from) their words."

15. That's to say, you forsake the dictates of the sages after having made a conscious, deliberate decision to. On one level your decision could be said to have been based on the seemingly reasonable idea that what they said isn't written in the Torah, so you're not bound by it. But on a deeper level, it's actually rooted in spiritual ennui, apathy, and disenchantment, and your unwillingness to strive for betterment (which is the root of the fear of God, see ¶7; and of tshuvah, see ¶6). As such, you're too shallow to feel bitter, haunted, or frightened in relation to sins, anyway.

16. . . . spoken of above . . .

17. See Supplementary Notes.

7. Our sages also said, "The verse, 'Your love is better than wine' (Song of Songs 1:2), implies that the words of the sages are more beloved than the 'wine' of Torah" (*Shir Hashirim Rabbah* 1:2). We have to explain that, too.

It's well known that the fear of God is the basis of all *mitzvot*, for it's said, "And now, Israel, what does God your Lord ask of you,[18] but to fear God your Lord" (Deuteronomy 10:12). And that those of His creations who do fear Him, please God, as it's said, "God desires those who fear Him" (Psalms 147:11).

What the decrees and precautions of the sages are then, are the primary pathways to the fear of God,[19] since they act as fences and precautions against your participating in a Torah prohibition.[20] Just as a property owner would put a fence around his property which he values so, and which he fears other people might come onto, or that oxen might wander onto it and sheep tread upon it. As it's said, "Observe[21] My restrictions" (Leviticus 18:30), which the sages explain to mean, "Set up further restrictions to My restrictions" (*Yevamot* 21A). And, in fact, aren't most of the prohibitions, precautions, and restrictions against forbidden things rooted in the fear of God?

So, the more precautions you take, the greater will be your reward, as it's said, "Your servant is cautious in them, and there is a great reward for keeping them" (Psalms 19:12). And that's why, "The words of the sages are more beloved than the 'wine' of Torah"—because their precautions and decrees are rooted in the fear of God. And because the reward for fulfilling the one mitzvah of fearing God is greater than that for many others, since they're founded upon it.[22]

An exemplar of that would be the man who'd be sure not to be secluded with a woman, as our sages decreed (cf. *Sanhedrin* 21B), for fear that he might stumble and sin, who'd certainly do that because the light of the fear of God had shown upon him.

---

18. . . . all in all . . .

19. See Supplementary Notes.

20. As we've indicated in our notes, we're to foster a deep and fast relationship to God, which is the import of the requirement that *we* "fear" Him, which is to say, that we take His presence very, very seriously. Because when we do, He draws close to us as well, as is pointed out by the verse, "God desires those who fear Him" cited here. All other *mitzvot*, then, are offshoots of and means toward this one essential requirement on our part. But sometimes those other *mitzvot* aren't so clearly inclined in that direction. Since the decrees of the sages are clearly rooted in and intended to be means toward the fostering of that fear, though, they're of primary importance.

21. Literally, "restrict" . . .

22. Note that "many other" *mitzvot* are founded upon the fear of God, but not all. Those others are founded upon the *love* of God, which is the other side of the deep and fast relationship to Him required of us, just indicated. And while avoiding prohibitions is rooted in the fear of God, pursuing imperatives is rooted in the love of Him. That's based on the fact that I'd avoid what threatens my relationship to my beloved out of fear, but I'd be drawn toward things that deepen it out of love.

8. As we already mentioned in *The Gate of Fear*,[23] you're obliged to observe and appraise your children, and to differentiate between the more crooked and cunning, and the honest ones, for the very important reason we mentioned. For you yourself can see certain wretched people spurning the[24] washing of hands, and sitting down to eat bread without reciting a blessing before eating bread or after the meal. And doing the same when it comes to many Rabbinic decrees[25] whose precautions they trespass. That alone proves and shows you just how very wrong and sinful to God their ways are, and that they're headed toward ruin. For the maxim, "Whoever violates the words of the sages is culpable for death" (*Berachot* 4B)[26] applies to them.[27]

It's not the yetzer harah that forces them to do those things, nor does the repercussions of being physical[28] or of craving material things compel them to sin that way. They do what they do simply because they're villainous and have cast the yoke of Heaven off their shoulders.[29] As such, they're like all other evildoers who say to God, "Go away from us, for we do not care to know about Your ways!" (Job 21:14), and they're nearly heretics.

The same goes for those who aren't careful to avoid eating cheese made by gentiles or foods cooked by them, because they take the words of the sages lightly. For even though they're only sinning in order to fill their bellies, they nonetheless disparage the words of the sages, and break off the yoke of Torah and the fear of God.[30] The maxim, "Whoever violates the words of the sages is culpable for death," which we've explained, applies to them, too.

Second, because they know the Holy Nation observes these things, and they're completely segregating themselves from our people and separating themselves from

---

23. To our great regret, this work no longer exists.

24. . . . Rabbincally required . . .

25. . . . concerning food, which is the context of this ¶, as will be seen.

26. . . . which is cited in ¶4 . . .

27. Assumedly, the point Rabbeinu Yonah made in *The Gate of Fear* was that it's important to guide your children in *mitzvot* from the outset, so they'll never grow up disregarding a single one. And in order for them to learn how to be honest and devotional.

28. See Supplementary Notes.

29. That is, it's not that they're so ravenous that they have to eat as soon as possible, and haven't the time to recite a blessing before eating, or to wash their hands. Or, that they're so extraordinarily pressed that they haven't the time to recite a short blessing afterward. They've simply shucked any commitment to do that aside (and have apparently done that all their lives, based on our assumptions of what Rabbeinu Yonah said in *The Gate of Fear*).

30. That is, while the former clearly had no excuse not to do what's required of them before or after eating. These might be thought to have not resisted forbidden things because they were overtaken by cravings. But in fact they sinned because they took the prohibition against such things lightly. "Cheese is cheese!" they might have argued, or the like. When the sages instituted what they did as precautionary measures.

the ways of the community.[31] And our sages already said, "Those who separate themselves from the ways of the community descend into Gehenom, where they're judged for generation after generation" (*Rosh Hashanah* 17A).[32]

Know that whoever transgresses the words of the sages can be sentenced in court to disobedience-flogging,[33] if the court determines it's appropriate to sentence and admonish them that way then (whether with less than the usual forty stripes, or more).

---

31. See Supplementary Notes.

32. They're "judged for generation after generation" that they may be shown each generation of Jews and grow bitter for having separated themselves from each one, not just their own.

33. מכת מרדות—"Rabbinic flogging" as opposed to "Torah-based flogging."

Chapter Three

9. The Second Level: The Significance of Imperatives

All merits and rewards are founded upon and rooted in your transposing your Divine service into the fulfillment of Torah imperatives.[1] For it's said, "One who fears a mitzvah will be rewarded" (Proverbs 13:13) and, "You will return and distinguish between . . . those who serve God and those who do not" (Malachi 3:18).[2]

---

1. Imperatives are what are referred to as "positive *mitzvot*" — things you're to do (like eating matzoh on Passover, for example), rather than things you're to resist (like slandering). As such, we're being told that you're to concentrate upon fulfilling these positive *mitzvot* rather than focus upon shunning prohibitions. And that's because while you'd certainly avoid all sorts of unwanted developments by not committing sins against your Beloved and thus not threatening your relationship. You'd only truly enjoy the benefits to be had from a deep and fast relationship (its "rewards") if you actively pursue such a relationship.

This is clearly a very, very important point in the eyes of Rabbeinu Yonah, by virtue of the fact that he started it with the words, יסוד השבר ושרש הגמול, the initial letters of which spell out the four-letter name of God. That's invariably a key to utmost importance, and is often a device used to begin an entire book. See, for example, the beginning of *The Path of the Just* and of Maimonides' *Mishne Torah* (in the original).

2. The implication is that those who fulfill imperatives can truly be said to "serve God" rather than avoid offending Him. The text then continues with the following:

"Service" refers to action-based [rather than thought- or speech-based] *mitzvot*—regardless of whether they involve [fulfilling] imperatives alone, or [avoiding] prohibitions, too. As is the case of charity, about which it's said, "Do not harden your heart" (Deuteronomy 15:7). [That's to say, giving charity both fulfills the imperative to give it, and avoids the prohibition against *not* giving it. That's why it's used as an example of an action-based mitzvah that involves both an imperative and a prohibition.]

The mitzvah of "service" itself will be explained in *The Gate of Service*, God willing.[3]

When it comes to merits, you can be credited with having fulfilled an imperative by being careful not to commit a prohibition.[4] As would be the case if you were faced with a sin that you had a strong urge to succumb to, but you nonetheless prevailed over your impulse.[5] Because doing that[6] is one of the underpinnings of the fear of God.[7]

So, too, if you were faced with the chance to become rich by cheating or double-crossing someone, when there'd be no one around to see or know anything of it, and you'd nonetheless go about your business in all innocence and honesty. You'd be rewarded for doing that as much as you would for giving charity, or for being involved in a mitzvah.[8] As it's written, "They also do not transgress; they walk in His ways" (Psalms 119:3) which our sages explained means, "They 'walk in His ways' because they 'do not transgress,'" (J. T., *Kiddushin*, end of Ch. 1). But we've already explained the import of this verse.[9]

Our sages put it, "If one stayed in place rather than commit a sin—for example, if he was given the chance to sin, but he managed not to—he is to be rewarded as much as he would be for performing a mitzvah" (*Makkot* 23B). And they said, "The verse, 'Those who feared God, who took heed of His name' (Malachi 3:16) refers to someone faced with the chance to sin, who nonetheless manages not to" (Midrash *Tehillim* 30).

The reward granted here is also founded and based upon your fulfilling the

---

3. "Service" also denotes prayer, known as "The service of the heart" (*Ta'anit* 2A). And prayer is the subject of Rabbeinu Yonah's *The Gates of Service*.

4. That is, not only can you earn merit by fulfilling an imperative, but you can earn the same merit by simply not committing a prohibition.

5. See Supplementary Notes.

6. i.e., conquering your impulses.

7. See the following note.

8. i.e., any other mitzvah.

Two sorts of people would be honest in such risk-free circumstances: those acting out of a heartfelt or well-taught civic sense of duty and honesty; and those acting out of a fear of God. And while the former would likely glow with pride at first in the face of his own honesty; nonetheless, in the course of time, the idea that he was being a "chump" will overtake him. And he'll begin to "wisen up" and "not be such a fool" because, as it's said, "everyone else is doing it"—is stealing, etc. But the sort of person who'd be honest out of the fear of God would know full well that while no one else may be, God is aware of him then, He knows what he's thinking, and He's assessing his response to each situation. And while such a person may waiver in his fear of God, and be tempted as well, he'll nonetheless have the sort of perspective that would be far less influenced by social pressures and comparisons with others around him. And would likely be more honest in the long run.

9. . . . when we said in the previous paragraph that "you can be credited with having fulfilled an imperative by being careful not to commit a prohibition."

imperative of prevailing over your impulses out of the fear of God, and it's said, "Fear God your Lord"[10] (Deuteronomy 10:20).

Our sages also said, "Be as scrupulous to fulfil an insignificant mitzvah as you would be to fulfill a significant one, because you never know the reward for *mitzvot*" (*Pirke Avot* 2:1). For the Torah enunciates what will happen to anyone who transgresses a prohibition. And it offers rules about the consequences to be suffered and the verdicts to be carried out, including forty lashes,[11] capital punishment, excision carried out by Heavenly means, and the four court-imposed death penalties. Yet the reward the each mitzvah fulfilled isn't stated in the Torah, so that you don't bypass insignificant *mitzvot* in favor of significant ones.[12]

10. Our sages compared it to the situation of the king who told his subjects to plant all sorts of attractive trees in his garden, and that they'd be rewarded for doing that. But he never specified which tree planted would get which reward, because he didn't want his garden to be deprived of anything. And so, many very attractive sorts of trees were planted as a consequence. But if his subjects knew the particular reward for each tree planted, they'd concentrate more on the trees that promised larger rewards than on the others, in order to earn more (*Devarim Rabbah* 6:2).[13] So, too, when it comes to *mitzvot*. God wanted to give Israel the merit of fulfilling all of the *mitzvot* in order to enable us to inherit eternal life, and so that all the *mitzvot* together would be "an ornament of glory" (Proverbs 1:9) about our heads. And in order for us to be fully compensated by Him for our efforts[14] when we'd have completed all of them.

For, in fact, haven't our sages said, "One who only engages in Torah study is like a Godless man" (*Avodah Zarah* 17B) even though they also said that, "Torah study is equivalent to them all" (*Peah* 1:1)?[15]

In fact, the reward for an "insignificant" mitzvah is so great and astounding that it can't even be calculated. For, isn't it said about sending off a mother bird,[16]

---

10. That is, when you prevail over your impulses because you fear God, you're thus fulfilling an imperative as well as avoiding a particular prohibition.

11. i.e., flagellation.

12. That is, since there are such dire consequences to certain transgressions (flagellation, the death sentence, etc.), I might reason that it's actually more important to avoid transgressions than to fulfill any obligations (as Rabbeinu Yonah argues). But that's not necessarily so, "because you never know the reward for (positive) *mitzvot*."

13. See Supplementary Notes.

14. . . . which would only come about . . .

15. That is, even though the reward for Torah study is equivalent to all other *mitzvot* combined (so everyone would logically be inclined toward studying Torah and not fulfilling any other *mitzvot*), it's nevertheless essential that you fulfill other *mitzvot* as well.

16. . . . before sending off her chicks. That is, It's written, "If a bird's nest happens to be before you on the road, in a tree or on the ground, and there are chicks or eggs, with the mother sitting upon the chicks or eggs, you may not take the mother along with the

which involves so little and costs nothing to do, "So that all will be well with you,[17] and so that you may extend your days" (Deuteronomy 22:7)? And didn't our sages say that, "There is not a single 'simple' mitzvah in the Torah which the Resurrection of the Dead is not contingent upon?[18] For it is said about sending off a mother bird,[19] 'So that all will be well with you . . . ,' that is, so that all will be well with you in the world of all goodness; and, '. . . so that you extend your days' in the world of eternally long days" (*Chullin* 140B). So, if the Torah says that about an "insignificant" mitzvah that costs you nearly nothing to fulfill, it's all the more so true of significant *mitzvot!*[20]

    11. We'll now address the consequences of *not* fulfilling an imperative. As our sages said, "If you alert someone to build a *sukkah*[21] or use a *lulav*[22] and he does not, strike him to the point of death" (*Chullin* 132B).

    "Those who never placed *t'phillin*[23] on their heads are labeled the 'physically defiant'[24] of Israel, and the consequences they would have to suffer are more severe than those who incur either excision or a court-imposed death sentence would"[25] (*Rosh Hashanah* 17A).

    "Whoever has more transgressions than merits—including the physically defiant of Israel, like those who never wore *t'phillin* and those Gentiles who are physically defiant and sin by having illicit relations, for example—descend down to *Gehenom* on the day of judgment, where they are judged for twelve months, when (after the twelve months are over) their bodies will have decomposed, their souls would be consumed, and their spirit would be spewed about beneath the feet of the righteous. As it's said, 'You will trample down the wrongdoers, who will be ashes . . .' (Malachi 3:21)" (*Rosh Hashanah* 17A).

    And, "One who takes an imperative lightly, by defiling Chol Hamoed,[26] for

---

young. *You must let the mother go, then take the chicks with you; so that all will be well with you, and so that you extend your days"* (Deuteronomy 22:6–7).

    17. i.e., be sure to do that, "so that all will be well with you" as a consequence . . .

    18. See reference above to inheriting eternal life, and donning "an ornament of glory" about your head (see 2:17 as well).

    19. . . . before sending off her chicks . . .

    20. That's to say that if simply complying with the imperative to send off the mother bird before sending off the chicks—which demands so little of you, and costs you nothing—offers resurrection and a place in The World to Come as its reward, then imagine the reward for complying with more demanding *mitzvot!*

    21. i.e., a temporary hut one dwells in throughout the festival of Sukkot (see Leviticus 23:42).

    22. i.e., a combination of plants carried on Sukkot (see Leviticus 23:40).

    23. i.e., phylacteries (see Exodus 13:9).

    24. i.e., rather than just defiant in attitude.

    25. Those who may be taken aback by this statement should see our comments to 1:2, as well as the Supplementary Notes there, in regard to Torah perspectives on punishment.

    26. Chol Hamoed are the intermediate, non-sacred days between the first two sacred

example (which involves an imperative, as it's said, 'Observe the Festival of Matzot' [Exodus 23:15]), has no portion in The World to Come, even if he has learned Torah and done good things" (*Sanhedrin* 99A).[27]

Furthermore, each imperative also involves an overarching prohibition, as it's said, "Do not add to it or diminish from it" (Deuteronomy 13:1).[28]

12. Fulfilling an imperative is also referred to as "fearing God," just like avoiding a prohibition.[29] For it's said, "Rise up before the hoary head, honor the face of the old man, and[30] fear your Lord. I am God" (Leviticus 19:32). And, "I will teach you the fear of God" (Psalms 34:12), which is followed by, "Depart from evil, and do good; seek peace, and pursue it"[31] (v. 15).

That comes to teach you that if you don't actively do good and pursue peace, you undermine the fear of Heaven, and you'd be a wrongdoer for the fact that you didn't fear God. As it's said, "It will not go well for the wrongdoer, nor will his days that are like a shadow be extended. Since he does not fear God" (Ecclesiastes 8:13).

13. People are careless about some very significant imperatives,[32] like mentioning God's name in vain, when it's said, "Fear God your Lord" (Deuteronomy 10:20), and our sages said, "That comes to warn us not to mention God's name in vain" (*Temurah* 4A).[33]

And about benevolence, which is an[34] imperative. As it's said, "And He let you know the path you should follow" (Exodus 18:20), which "refers to benevolence"

---

days of Sukkot and Pesach (which are each eight days long), and their last two sacred days.

27. Notice that all these instances address the sort of audacious individual who'd have been, "alert(ed) to build a *sukkah* or use a *lulav*" and refused to, who "*never* wore *t'phillin*" and who makes light of Chol Hamoed." (See Supplementary Notes.)

28. So whoever doesn't fulfill an imperative automatically transgresses a prohibition.

29. It's said in ¶7 that "the fear of God is the basis of all *mitzvot*," and that "most of the prohibitions, precautions, and restrictions against forbidden things (are) rooted in the fear of God." So I might think that I could only be said to fear God when I steer clear of prohibitions. That's why Rabbeinu Yonah is sure to point out here that "fulfilling an imperative is also referred to as 'fearing God.'"

30. . . . thusby . . .

31. . . . all of which are imperatives.

32. It's a very human failing to be careless—often even reckless and rash about some very important things in life, including our own health, other people's feelings, bad habits we might have had our children fall into, etc. But that goes for our failings in regard to some very important *mitzvot* as well. For just as we would when it comes to all that, we also tend to lapse into reveries of "It'll all be okay, nothing will happen" when it comes to our spiritual life as well—when that just might not be true! For, like individuals who mutter for years, "If I'd only . . ." after failing in the material realm, there are also long-gone souls stunned even now with the haunting thought that if they'd only done thus or such . . .

33. That is, while there's a prohibition associated with mentioning God's name in vain as would be expected, there's also an imperative connected with it, "Fear God your Lord."

34. . . . obvious . . .

(*Babba Metziah* 30B). Our sages also said, "Benevolence is even greater than charity. Because charity goes to the poor, but you are to be benevolent to the poor *and* the rich" (*Sukkah* 49B).[35] That's why it's said, "The world is sustained by three things: by Torah, by service, and by benevolence" (*Pirke Avot* 1:2). Also because while you can be charitable with your money, you can be benevolent with your very being as well as with your money.[36] For you're obliged to try to do good for your people, and to make every effort personally for another's welfare, whether he's poor or rich.[37] In fact, it's one of the most significant and basic *mitzvot* asked of us. As it's said, "He has told you, O man, what is good; and what God requires of you, which is to act justly, and to love benevolence" (Micah 6:8).[38]

It's also a mitzvah to go beyond the requirements of the law.[39] As it's said, ". . . and the work they are to do" (Exodus 18:20),[40] which our sages said, "refers to going beyond the requirements of the law" (*Babba Metziah* 30B). There are, in fact, many instances in which this mitzvah becomes very significant, depending on circumstances. For as our sages said, "The only reason Jerusalem was destroyed was because the sages based their decisions on the strict requirements of the law, without going beyond it" (Ibid.).

14. Many people believe that personal devastation and spiritual ruin only really come about as a result of action-based sins, and that one who's free of such

---

35. Benevolence (also called "acts of loving-kindness") includes visiting the sick, burying the dead, taking in guests, doing personal favors, loaning money interest-free, giving advice, and the like. And it's applicable to the poor and the rich, while charity is limited to giving money, goods, food, etc., to the poor.

36. See Supplementary Notes.

37. This harkens back to the statement in ¶12 that, "if you don't actively do good and pursue peace, you undermine the fear of Heaven, and you'd be a wrongdoer." (See Supplementary Notes.)

38. The charge to act benevolently toward another is said so stunningly outright, so point-blank in the Torah. — "And He let you know the path you should follow" and, "He has told you, O man, what is good; and what God requires of you, which is to act justly, and to love benevolence" — that it's astoundingly crystal clear. And logic would only dictate that we're each to do all we can to "do good for (our) people, and to make every effort . . . for another's welfare" since benevolence is so clearly "one of the most significant and basic *mitzvot* asked of us." It, in fact, answers the very question so many desperate souls ask, which is, "What does God require of me?" so outright, that it would seem to be the answer to a prayerful search for meaning in life. So why don't we follow through on it? Simply because of the countervailing mortal craving for leisure and repose, license and abandon. And therein lies the great battle between high truth and ulterior motive.

39. Literally, "depending on the law."

40. The whole verse reads, "And you will teach them ordinances and laws, and will show them the way they are to go, and the work they are to do." Since the last expression seems superfluous, the Tradition explains it to refer to going beyond the requirements of the law.

sins, who doesn't go about transgressing, but who nonetheless doesn't fulfill *mitzvot* and good deeds, will never be devastated or die as a result.[41]

So, we're obliged to let these people know they're wrong. For as our sages said, "God overlooks idol worship, illicit relations and murder, but He never overlooks the sin of neglecting Torah study"[42] (J. T., *Chagigah* 1:7)[43] and, "Just as the reward for studying Torah is greater than that for all other *mitzvot*, so too the consequences for neglecting Torah study are greater than that for all other sins" (*Sifre, Eikev*). They also said, "'Because he despised God's word and broke His commandment, he will surely be excised' (Numbers 15:31) refers to someone who is able to study Torah but does not" (*Sanhedrin* 99A).[44] But we've already mentioned all this in *The Gate of Torah*.[45]

15. In fact, we find in the case of the people of Sodom, who were "very wicked and sinful to God" (Genesis 13:12) and committed many nefarious crimes including robbery, brutality, the miscarriage of justice, and having illicit relations (cf. *Sanhedrin* 109), that the[46] verse nonetheless cites the reason they were brought to ruin and devastation was because of the sin of not being charitable! As it's said, "Behold, this was the iniquity of your sister Sodom: arrogance, a glut of bread, and an abundance of idleness was in her and in her daughters, and she did not strengthen the hand of the poor and needy" (Ezekiel 16:49).

And it's said of people who don't focus their thoughts enough to concentrate upon the fear of God at all times, "Their fear of Me is a mitzvah of men learned by rote.[47] So, behold, I will do more marvelous things among this people, marvelous and wonderful" (Isaiah 29:13–14),[48] "Why does the way of wrongdoers suc-

---

41. That is, some are under the impression that if you merely avoid trouble and do nothing out of sorts, that your relationship will be secure and stable. The truth is, though, that if you merely avoid ruin, you'll slip naturally into decay and stagnation. So it's imperative to actively feed the relationship with fresh input and expressed longing. And one does that best when it comes to his relationship with God by studying Torah (as will soon be pointed out).

42. . . . which is an imperative. Hence we see that one need be as sure to fulfill an imperative as he is to avoid even serious transgressions (if not more so).

43. See Supplementary Notes.

44. For Torah isn't just the all-important mission statement we declared it to be in note 55 to 2:21. It's also the gist and chart of spiritual discovery, the soul's primal needs put flat out, and the insinuation God most insists we make of Him.

45. To our great regret, this work no longer exists.

46. . . . following . . .

47. See Supplementary Notes.

48. In the entirety these two verses read, "And God said, since this people draw near to Me and honor Me with their mouth and their lips, when they have removed their heart far from Me . . ." That is, since the people continue to make a show of things holy by following through on them externally and superficially, which is epitomized by the fact that, "their fear of Me is a mitzvah of men learned by rote" rather than a heartfelt fear. "Behold,

ceed? . . . You are close to their mouth, and far from their insides" (Jeremiah 12:1–2),[49] and, "For, behold, those who are far from You will perish" (Psalms 73:27).[50]

16. You should know that the greater the mitzvah, the greater the consequences for not observing it,[51] even when you do nothing to undermine it.[52] As in the case of the *mitzvot* of offering the Paschal Lamb and of being circumcised, which are imperatives, and nonetheless incur excision.

I will do more marvelous things among this people, marvelous and wonderful" as God does every single moment—which those who feel His presence therein know full well. And yet, "the wisdom of their sages will perish, and the understanding of their prudent will be hidden" because they're unaware of His presence, and oblivious to His wonders.

49. The point is that those frauds and hypocrites who keep God's name on their lips but not in their hearts are certainly wrongdoers rather than just misguided fools.

50. All in all, what this is referring to is the need to react earnestly to God's presence, rather than in the world-weary and routine way we often do. For many people engage in some very holy things so very casually that they astound the astute eye—as much as high government treasury officers would astound us with their blasé rearrangement of tons of gold bullion worth untold billions of dollars. And like the treasury officers, the casual "dabblers" in holiness would offer that what they do had become routine for them, and there was really nothing special about it, when there really was!

The other point, in terms of relationships, is that if I am elsewhere in my being and mind when I'm "with" my beloved, I insult her and can't be said to take her seriously. My priorities are elsewhere, and my being there with her is merely accommodating or meant to fulfill an obligation. While that's dutiful and self-abnegating, to be sure, and it attests to my feelings for my beloved on some level, it's nonetheless a sure sign of a less than binding, devoted tie to her. That's all the more so true of my relationship to God. While fulfilling *mitzvot* routinely without thought or intent still manages to accomplish good in the world and to resist the tide of unholiness, it's nonetheless a sign that the heart is elsewhere, and would rather be doing what it yearns for then and there—which apparently has nothing to do with the service of God.

But, how does one then fulfill *mitzvot* intently, as if enamored of God? As Moshe Chaim Luzzatto counsels, you're not to "suddenly and immediately rush into doing a mitzvah before having had time to reflect upon what you are about to do. Rather, you should ready yourself for it and compose yourself until you are properly focused, then consider what you are about to do and before Whom you are about to do it. As soon as you enter into this process of reflection you will find it easy to rid yourself of all external motivations and to set the proper and desirable intentions in your thoughts instead" (*The Path of the Just*, Ch. 17, p. 141).

51. See Supplementary Notes.

52. That is, the greater and more unique the opportunity to draw close to your beloved, the greater the loss and the consequences to your relationship if you do not. Compare this with Rabbeinu Yonah's statement in 1:2 about delaying tshuvah, along with our notes there.

17. You should also know that *the* noblest virtues are granted us through[53] imperatives. Like the virtues of[54] free choice,[55] as it's said, "Choose life" (Deuteronomy 30:19).[56] The virtue of Torah study, as it's said, "And you will speak of them" (Ibid. 6:7). The virtue of following God's ways, as it's written, "Go in His ways" (Ibid. 28:9). The virtue of complete trust,[57] as it's said, "Be pure and simple with God your Lord" (Ibid. 18:13). The virtue of reflecting upon God's greatness, as it's said, "Know today and set it in your heart that God is Lord" (Ibid. 4:39) and as David said, "God peers down from Heaven upon mankind to see if those who know are seeking God" (Psalms 14:2).

The virtue of recalling God's kindness and reflecting upon it, as it's said, "Remember the way God your Lord led you these forty years in the desert" (Deuteronomy 8:2), "Know in your heart that God chastises you the way a father chastises his son" (Ibid. v. 5), as David said, "Reflect upon God's kindness" (Psalms 107:43) and, "Your kindness is before my eyes" (Ibid. 26:3). The virtue of holiness, as it's said, "Sanctify yourselves, and you will be holy" (Leviticus 11:44). The virtue of service, as it's said, "Serve Him" (Deuteronomy 10:20). The virtue of fear, as it's said, "Fear God your Lord" (Ibid.). The virtue of love, as it's said, "Love God your Lord" (Ibid. 6:5). And the virtue of devotion,[58] as it's said, "Devote yourself to Him" (Ibid. 10:20). (And each one of these is comprised of many levels, as we'll explain, God willing.)

In fact, you were created to realize just these virtues, as it's said, "Everyone called by My name I have created for My honor" (Isaiah 43:7).[59] So what hope can there be for you if you don't direct all your efforts and interests toward the things you were created for?[60]

---

53. . . . the fulfillment of certain . . .

54. . . . acting out of . . .

55. See Supplementary Notes.

56. The point is that though we're certainly given free will by God, nonetheless we ourselves must activate the mechanism, so to speak. Or else we'd be acting perfunctorily and mutedly, as so many unfortunately do. (See our note to ¶15 above about fulfilling *mitzvot* by rote.)

57. . . . in God . . . (See note 55 to 2:21.)

58. This term (דבקות) is usually translated as "attaching yourself to Him," or "clinging onto Him." And it often refers to achieving a very, very high level of spiritual growth and to union with the Divine. Many would say that that is what's being required of us here. And that that would only be logical, in light of the fact that this virtue is mentioned right after the virtues of loving and fearing God, which are its basis. Nonetheless we've translated it as the more accessible and achievable quality of "devotion." However, we've made note of this other reading to alert the reader to the pure and holy implications of this quality as well.

59. See Supplementary Notes.

60. The astute reader will notice that these particular virtues—described as being the noblest of all, the very ones we were created to realize, and the only ones about which it's asked, "what hope can there be for you if you don't put all your efforts and interests into"

18. In fact, the consequences of not observing a mitzvah[61] are explained in the Torah, where it's said, "Cursed is he who does not fulfill the words of this Torah by doing them" (Deuteronomy 27:26). And we derive the fact that it's referring to not observing a mitzvah from the fact that it says "by doing them."[62]

19. You should also know that you're required to be a dependable emissary and an adroit servant in all that you do in your service to God.[63] Such a dependable worker would be swift in his own work, and he'd also monitor the job his co-workers were doing, see with his own eyes whether or not they were honest in their work, and he'd alert them about and let them know what they're supposed to be doing, because he'd only want his master's work done scrupulously. And he'd bolster those workers.[64]

As our sages put it, "The verse, 'Cursed is he who does not fulfill the words of this Torah'[65] (Ibid.) refers to the person who studies, reviews, teaches Torah to others and fulfills it, who also has the ability to bolster those who study Torah and do *mitzvot*, and does not. He is included among those about whom it's said, 'Cursed is he who does not fulfill the words of this Torah'" (J. T., *Sotah* 7:4).[66]

20. Another of the more significant *mitzvot* is not bringing a case before a gentile court.[67] As it's said, "These are the judgments that you are to bring before

---

realizing—all have to do with having a relationship with God, with your electing to have one (i.e., free will), with your learning how to (i.e., Torah study), and with your emulating Him (i.e., holiness and following in His ways), as would be expected of anyone in a profound relationship. Can there be a greater proof that *The Gates of Repentance* is addressing just such a relationship? (See Supplementary Notes.)

61. i.e., an imperative.

62. i.e., that one who doesn't fulfil an imperative is cursed, and rejected, by God (in keeping with ¶'s 15–17 above).

63. See Supplementary Notes.

64. A couple of points are being made here. First, that as "dependable emissaries" of God we're to perceive of ourselves as "vice presidents" of sorts, which is to say, as having a lot in our purview, and having to answer to only one person—who nonetheless happens to be the "President." As such, we're very authoritative and prominent, and very liable and accountable, too—as well as vulnerable. Indeed, that's the human situation. (See ¶'s 33–34 about being in such a position.)

Second, this comes to illustrate what's actually required of us as servants of God. For many mistakenly believe that serving God requires one to respond robotically and mindlessly to constant orders. But the best of servants work independently, creatively, and industriously, and are self-motivated enough to require clarification only from time to time. Such is the "adroit servant" spoken of by Rabbeinu Yonah here, who is "swift in his . . . work" and "alert," who cares that his master's orders are carried out scrupulously by others as well as himself.

65. . . . cited in the previous ¶ . . .

66. That is, he doesn't live up to or fulfill his mission of being an emissary to God.

67. . . . rather than a *beit din*, a *halacha*-based court (which adjudicates civil cases,

them" (Exodus 21:1), that is to say, before *them*, not before Gentiles (*Gittin* 88B). The defiant stumble in this one. And we've already spoken about the ways this sin brings about death.

21. It's said of those who neglect to fear[68] their father and mother, which is[69] an imperative, "Cursed is he who dishonors his father or mother" (Deuteronomy 27:16), where "dishonor" denotes denigrating their honor and undermining the fear of them. As our sages put it, "(It is written) 'A man should fear his mother and father' (Leviticus 19:3). How does one express such fear? By not sitting in a parent's seat, not contradicting what he says, and not disproving him" (*Kiddushin* 31B).[70]

The *mitzvot* of *t'phillin* and *mezuzah* are imperatives, and they're elements of taking the yoke of the Kingdom of Heaven upon yourself. That's why they were included in the *Shma Yisroel*.[71] And you can extrapolate out the consequences for not observing those *mitzvot* from that.[72] For you'd be like one who cast off the yoke[73] and undid the bonds.[74] But we've already spoken about the significance of these *mitzvot*.[75]

22. Our sages said about the mitzvah of *tzitzit*, "*Tzitzit* add holiness,[76] as it's written, 'That you might remember and observe all My *mitzvot*, and be holy to your God' (Numbers 15:40)" (*Sifre*, Bamidbar 115). And though you'd only have to observe the mitzvah of *tzitzit* if you had a four-cornered garment,[77] and if you

---

and whose decisions are accepted by civil law as having been arrived at by mutually-acceptable "private arbitrators").

68. . . . or, "revere" . . .

69. . . . also . . .

70. So sadly, many see revering and honoring their parents as much as an anachronism as presenting a case to a *beit din*, in our day and age (see previous ¶). As such, we in modernity alone can draw a lesson from the proximity of one to the other.

71. The recitation known as the *Shma Yisroel* ("Hear, O Israel") begins with, "Hear, Oh Israel, God our Lord is One God" and continues with, "And you will love God your Lord with all your heart, all your soul, and all your might. These words, which I am commanding you this day, should remain in your heart; and you should teach them diligently to your children, and speak of them when you sit in your house, when you walk upon the road, when you lie down, and when you rise up"—all of which refers to your taking the yoke of the Kingdom of Heaven upon yourself. And it continues with, "Bind them for a sign upon your hand and make them frontlets between your eyes"—which refers to *t'phillin*. Then it ends with, "And write them upon the doorposts of your house and on your gates"—which refers to *mezuzot* (Deuteronomy 4–9).

72. i.e., from the fact that they're elements of accepting the yoke of service, as well as from the fact that they're included in the cardinal declaration of *Shma Yisroel*.

73. . . . of the Kingdom of Heaven . . .

74. . . . that bind you to God, by not observing those *mitzvot*.

75. See Rabbeinu Yonah's *Igrot Hatshuvah* 3:5.

76. . . . which is one of the noble qualities we're to strive for, as indicated in ¶17.

77. . . . to attach them to, for it's written, "Speak to the people of Israel, and charge

haven't one you wouldn't have to buy one; nonetheless our sages said, "You would surely suffer in times of trouble in light of the fact that you didn't relish the beauty and reward of the mitzvah enough to oblige yourself in it by buying a four-cornered garment to place *tzitzit* on" (*Menachot* 41A).

23. Know that if you[78] feared God's word you'd be just as rigorous, exacting, and self-sacrificing for an "insignificant" mitzvah as you would be for a significant one.[79] For rather than concentrating on how "insignificant" one mitzvah is compared to others, concentrate instead on the greatness of He who cautions you in it.[80]

Open your eyes fully enough to see that this venerable principle is explained in the Torah itself, by virtue of the fact that the expression used in conjunction with the mitzvah of rising before the hoary head (Leviticus 19:32), of fearing your father and mother, and of observing the Shabbat is the same—"I am God" (Ibid. v. 3). Which means to say that you're to take to heart and know that it is I, God, who commands and cautions you.[81]

We've thus included many of the *mitzvot* that numerous people of our generation are negligent in, and cited the basis of each one of them in this work. Take them all to heart.

---

them to make fringes [*tzitzit*] on the borders of their (four-cornered) garments" (Numbers 15:38) . . .

78. . . . truly . . .

79. That is, concentrate upon *all* the *mitzvot* enunciated here, not just the noble ones enunciated in ¶17, which "you were created to realize," or the other significant ones mentioned here.

80. See Supplementary Notes.

81. . . . in *all* these things.

Chapter Four

24. *The Third Level:*
Prohibitions Connected
to an Imperative[1]

Our sages said, "A prohibition connected to an imperative does not incur flogging"[2] (*Chullin* 141A). An example would be the prohibition against taking the mother bird with her chick (Deuteronomy 22:6), which is connected to the imperative to "surely let the mother go" (Ibid. v. 7). Yet, even though you wouldn't be flogged[3] by the court, you'd nonetheless have to suffer significant consequences for some of them by the hands of Heaven, and your sentence would escalate ever upward.

For it's said of stealing, "Do not steal" (Leviticus 19:13), and that's connected to the imperative to "Return the stolen object" (Ibid. 5:23). And,[4] as our sages pointed out, "The judgment against the generation of the flood was based on[5] the offense of stealing alone. As it's said, 'The end of all flesh has come before Me, for the earth is full of robbery because of them' (Genesis 6:13)" (*Sanhedrin* 108A). And even though having illicit relations is more serious a sin than stealing, the

---

1. This is alternately explained as "a prohibition committed that can be remedied by fulfilling a subsequent imperative."
2. i.e., one who violates a prohibition connected to an imperative is not flogged for his offense.
3. . . . for what you did . . .
4. That is, one can rectify the sin connected with "Do not steal" by fulfilling "Return the stolen object," and would therefore avoid flogging, and yet . . .
5. Literally, "sealed on," or finally came to be based upon . . .

consequences for stealing encompass drawing closer and closer to calamity, and hastening toward what's due you.[6] They also said, "Despite a full quotient of transgressions, none is more impeaching than stealing" (*Vayikrah Rabbah* 3:10).

Solomon remarked about fortune gained through fraud and deceit, "Acquiring fortunes through a lying tongue is a fleeting vapor; they lead to death" (Proverbs 21:6). That is, fortunes acquired through fraud and deceit are a "fleeting vapor," since they're sure to be eradicated. And even when they're in the hands of their owners, they cause them trouble, demand their lives,[7] and bring about their deaths. As Habbakuk said, "Woe to him who gets dishonest gain for his house. . . . For the stone will cry out from the wall . . ." (2:9–11).

And one who steals from a poor person is culpable for death by the hands of Heaven.[8] As it's said, "Do not rob the poor because he is poor, nor abuse the impoverished in the gate. For God will plead their case, and rob the life of those who rob them" (Proverbs 22:22–23).

That's to say, "Do not rob the poor because they are poor" and have no one to help them, and don't "abuse the impoverished" by humiliating and shaming them "at the gates" meaning, in public. As it's said, "What do you mean by abusing My people, and crushing the faces of the poor?" (Isaiah 3:15). "For God will plead their case," since they have no one else to rely on or to plead their case. And He'll "rob the life of those who rob them" means to say that when the poor man's cries are brought before Him, God won't claim the same amount of money from the thief as that which the thief had taken from the poor man. Instead, He'd take the thief's life. As it's said, "For what hope is there for the flatterer, though he has gained, when God takes away his life?" (Job 27:8) and, "These are the ways of all who are greedy of gain; it takes the life of its owners" (Proverbs 1:19).

One who abuses and afflicts a widow or orphan—either by robbery, extortion, humiliation or any other means—is culpable for death by the hands of Heaven. And those judges who are able to have the money that had been extorted[9] returned,[10] who nonetheless don't judge favorably for the orphan, will themselves be sentenced to death. As it's said, "Do not afflict any widow or orphan. For if you afflict them in any way and they cry out bitterly to Me, I will certainly hear their cry. My anger will rage, and I will slay you with the sword. Your wives will be widows, and your children orphans" (Exodus 22:21–23). That is, "your wives will be

---

6. See Deuteronomy 32:35, "For the day of their calamity is at hand, and the things that will come upon them hasten." That is, their afflictions will materialize quickly because they tried to hasten the materialization of things they saw as "coming to them" in their greed.

7. . . . from them, i.e., they make impossible, life-threatening demands of them . . .

8. See Supplementary Notes.

9. . . . from an orphan . . .

10. . . . to him . . .

widows" because you afflicted the widow, and "your children (will be) orphans" because you afflicted the orphan,[11] measure for measure.[12]

In fact, any Jew who afflicts another Jew violates a prohibition, though the same consequences aren't cited in his case. For it's said, "Do not abuse one another" (Leviticus 25:17),[13] which our sages said refers to verbal abuse (*Babba Metziah* 58B), and which falls into the category of abuse and affliction, as in, "And I will feed those who abuse you with their own flesh" (Isaiah 49:26). The sages also informed us that, "All gates[14] are shut but the gate of the abused" (*Babba Metziah* 59A). And wherever the Torah mentions monetary abuse, it mentions business, too. As in, "And if you sell something to your neighbor, or buy something from your neighbor, do not abuse one another" (Leviticus 25:14).[15]

In fact, the sages revealed that verbal abuse is more serious than monetary abuse. Because while one[16] affects one's entire body, the other[17] affects one's money; and while[18] "Fear your God" (Leviticus 25:17) is said about the one,[19] it is not said in connection with the other"[20] (*Babba Metziah* 58B).[21]

25. Taking interest on or profiting from a loan also involve prohibitions.[22] As it's said, "Take no interest or profit from him" (Leviticus 25:36), which is then connected to the imperative, "that your brother may live with you" (Ibid.). That means to say, if you take interest or profit from him, return it to your brother so that he "may live with you."[23]

There are serious consequences for not righting that wrong—you'd never experience The Resurrection of the Dead. As it's said, "He has loaned money for interest, and taken profit. Will he live? No, he will not" (Ezekiel 18:13), which our sages explained refers to The Resurrection of the Dead (*Pirke D'Rebbe Eliezer* 33).

---

11. and you will thus be judged . . .

12. This refers to the principle of the punishment fitting the crime (see *Sanhedrin* 100A).

13. See Supplementary Notes.

14. . . . of appeal . . .

15. Hence, the implication is that you're not to abuse another through your business practices and mutter, "But business is business!" as an excuse.

16. i.e., verbal abuse . . .

17. i.e., monetary abuse, only . . .

18. . . . the admonition . . .

19. i.e., in the case of verbal abuse . . .

20. i.e., monetary abuse.

21. That's to say that you harm a person far more when you belittle and berate him than you do when you take his money—as any sensitive soul would know. The modern position seems to be the opposite, though, as is epitomized by the expression, "Sticks and stones may break my bones, but words will never harm me!" But the Torah emphasizes the greater harm done when feelings are hurt and egos are poisoned.

22. See Supplementary Notes.

23. i.e., on par with you; or, without embarrassment.

For, after all, loaning money on interest or for a profit doesn't incur the death penalty.[24] As our sages also said, "One who has sinned by taking interest on a loan does not have an advocating angel citing his merits"[25] (*Shemot Rabbah* 31:14), which is why "Will he live?" is written in question form, i.e., in order to ask, will an advocate argue for him to be judged for life? And they all respond, "No, he will not."

---

24. . . . so the expression, "Will he live? No, he will not" must refer to his not living after The Resurrection of the Dead.

25. . . . in Heaven.

Chapter Five

⭪⭫⭪⭫⭪⭫⭪⭫⭪⭫⭪⭫⭪⭫⭪⭫⭪⭫⭪⭫

26. The Fourth Level: Prohibitions Involving No[1] Action

While our sages said that, "A prohibition[2] that does not involve an activity does not incur flogging" (*Makkot* 16A), they also clearly said that, "A prohibition involving no activity is more significant than a prohibition connected to an imperative"[3] (Ibid.).

Some prohibitions involving no activity touch upon your heart,[4] others upon your tongue,[5] others upon withholding your hand, and yet others upon refraining from doing certain things.[6] There are also prohibitions that touch upon activities that affect your senses of hearing[7] and seeing.[8]

We notice that many people forget many of them. And that others know about them but aren't careful about them simply because those prohibitions don't involve actions.[9] Because those that do involve actions—like eating[10] fats, blood, and unkosher meats—are less likely to be stumbled in than ones having to do with your thoughts, your tongue, or with avoiding certain things.[11]

---

1. . . . outward . . .
2. i.e., one who violates a prohibition . . .
3. . . . which was just discussed in ¶'s 24–25.
4. ¶'s 27–43.
5. ¶'s 44–63.
6. ¶'s 67–74.
7. ¶66.
8. ¶'s 64–65.
9. See Supplementary Notes.
10. . . . particular sorts of forbidden . . .
11. That's to say, people are less likely to stumble in overt, tangible, and blunt sins

So we saw fit to mention some of the latter in order to remind and alert those who don't know[12] to be careful. But we didn't go into them at length, and only alluded to them, so that they may act as reminders for those who would do tshuvah for their violations.

27. Among the prohibitions embracing the heart are:

"Be sure not to forget God your Lord" (Deuteronomy 8:11).

Our sages said that, "Whenever the Torah says, 'Be sure,' 'For you might,' or 'Do not,' that implies a prohibition"[13] (*Menachot* 99B). So you're being alerted to remember God[14] at all times.[15]

You're thus obliged to always try to embrace the sorts of practices that would necessarily[16] have you remember God, like fearing Him, being demure, ennobling your thoughts, and putting your character in order.[17] For the Nation of Israel can achieve all sorts of lovely traits, which will then distinguish it, when it remembers God.[18] As it's said, "The Nation of Israel will become righteous and extolled through God" (Isaiah 45:25).

28. "Be sure and be very cautious, lest you forget the things your eyes have seen" (Deuteronomy 4:9).[19]

Our sages said, "Hence, whoever forgets anything he has learned transgresses against two prohibitions.[20] You might think, though, that that also has to do with

---

than they are in subtle, ephemeral, and nuanced ones. Because the former are more material, while the latter are more spiritlike. And most people are subject to material awareness alone.

12. . . . enough about them . . .

13. . . . involving no overt action, in this case.

14. i.e., keep God in mind.

15. See Supplementary Notes.

16. Or, "automatically."

17. How does one remember God, or keep Him in mind, all the time? After all, we eat and drink, interact with others, etc. Rabbeinu Yonah suggests that we remember Him by acting in unique, God-aware ways while doing those very things, by "fearing Him, being demure, ennobling your thoughts, and putting your character in order" at just such times. Hence, what we have here is a formula for living in the world and out of it at the same time—a veritable recipe for human holiness. That is, if we become so God-aware, so stunned with the reality of His presence throughout the world that we're moved to fear and awe, demureness and non-obtrusiveness, nobility of thought, and character improvement, then we're sure to be pleasing to God and humanity. And to thus fulfill our obligations to both.

18. See Supplementary Notes.

19. The warning is literally against forgetting "the day you stood before God your Lord at Horeb" (v. 10), that is, the day you received the Torah at Mount Sinai. And it isn't about forgetting your Torah studies. But the implication is that just as one can only recall God at all times by doing things in the spirit of one who senses God's presence at all times (see previous ¶), one can also only recall the giving of the Torah and Torah itself by studying it, and thus experiencing its revelation at all times.

20. i.e., "Be sure" and "lest you."

when you are overwhelmed by all your studies.[21] Hence that is followed by, '. . . for they may depart from your heart' (Ibid.). So the verse is only referring to one whose lessons depart from his heart because he forgoes Torah study and does not reflect on it all the time" (*Menachot* 99B).[22]

29. "Do not say to yourself when God your Lord casts them out before you, 'God has brought me in to possess this land because of my righteousness.' . . . Not for your righteousness or your virtue are you going up to possess their land" (Deuteronomy 9:4–5).

That comes to alert you never to imagine that your success stems from your righteousness or virtue. You're to believe and know in your heart instead that your success is a high favor from God, and a consequence of His great goodness. As Jacob said, "I am unworthy of any of the favors, and of all the truth" (Genesis 32:11).[23]

30. "Do not test God your Lord" (Deuteronomy 6:16).

This comes to alert you never to say, "I'm going to see now if my being charitable will have God make me successful. And I'm going to test whether being honest in what I do will bring me a lot of silver and gold." Because a good person would never stop acting out of wisdom, knowledge, and honesty or be discouraged if he's not successful at making money or satisfying his bodily needs.[24]

For as our sages said, "You are only allowed to test God when it comes to the

---

21. That is, you might think that simply by being tired after having studied a lot, or simply by not recalling every element of your studies that you'd be in violation. But, no, that's not so.

22. Thus Rabbeinu Yonah seems to indicate that you're not expected to remember everything you studied. Only that you're expected to remember to ruminate upon Torah all the time. (See Supplementary Notes.)

23. Assuming your success was a Divine reward for righteousness would actually seem to be a very devout response to it. And far more acceptable than, "My power and the might of my hand has gotten me this wealth" (Deuteronomy 8:17). But that only goes to underscore the fact that your assumption (no matter how lofty) is nonetheless rooted in a misunderstanding of a basic metaphysical truism—that God is beholden to nothing and no one. For He told Moses that He "will be gracious to whom I will be gracious, and will show mercy to whom I will show mercy" (Deuteronomy 33:19), which the Talmud explains to mean, "And I will be gracious to whom I will be gracious, *although he may not deserve it*, And I will show mercy to whom I will show mercy, *although he may not deserve it*" (*Berachot* 7A). For in truth, everything God grants us is "a high favor from God, and a consequence of His great goodness," rather than an imperative response to anything. But this is a very deep and recondite matter, not even fully explained to Moses, and far beyond the scope of this work. (See Luzzatto's *Da'at Tvunot*.)

24. Rabbeinu Yonah indicates here that a truly "good person"—not an especially righteous person, just good—wouldn't be so thwarted by his failures that he'd abandon wisdom, knowledge, and honesty. Yet, wouldn't many of us in modernity give up all hope at such a point, abandon many of our values to the wind, try desperately and even underhandedly to do all we could to recoup our losses? And wouldn't we allow ourselves to vent our

mitzvah of tithing. As it's said, 'Bring all the tithes to the storehouse, so that there may be food in My house, and test Me now with that, says the Lord of Hosts . . .' (Malachi 3:10)" (*Ta'anit* 9A).

As Solomon said, "Honor God with your possessions, and with the first fruits of all your produce. And your barns will be filled with plenty. . . . Do not resent God's admonishments, my son, nor be weary of His criticism" (Proverbs 3:9–11). That means to say, if you don't have enough to fill your barns with after giving away some of your things and some first fruits to charity, and you even become poor as a result, don't resent God's admonishments.[25] Realize instead that that, too, is for your good, "For God only admonishes one He loves" (Ibid. v. 12),[26] for his ultimate good. And in order to exchange the reward and honor granted in this world for the true, good reward that is hidden away[27] but endures forever.[28]

31. "Should you say in your heart, 'These nations are more numerous than I. How could I dispossess them?' Do not be afraid of them"[29] (Deuteronomy 7:17–18).

32. "When you go to battle against your enemies, and see horses, chariots, and a people more numerous than you, do not be afraid of them" (Ibid. 20:1).

This comes to alert you to sense God's salvation in your heart, and to trust in it when you see trouble looming.[30] As it's said, "Surely His salvation is near at hand

---

"outrage" at our fate, and hence at God? Especially after we'd congratulated ourselves for doing something "good" and then failed? The sensitive soul would take heed of this and be humbled.

25. See Supplementary Notes.

26. See Supplementary Notes.

27. . . . now . . .

28. This addresses the fact that we often make pacts with God. We may say in the midst of a crisis, "Please God, make me well, and I promise I'll . . . ," "Please God, let my business do well, and I promise I'll . . . ," or the like. Or in order to prevent crises we might suggest, "I'm going to . . . , and You then have to promise me that I'll always be well" or, ". . . that I'll always succeed." And we're dumbfounded when God doesn't keep "His side of the bargain." But, again, the point is that God is the Almighty Lord of the universe. And while He certainly, certainly does everything for our ultimate, sublime good (though not necessarily for our immediate good), He nonetheless has His own ways, and is beholden to nothing or no one.

29. ". . . remember what God your Lord did to Pharaoh, and to all Egypt," the verse continues, to underscore the fact that God has already come to our rescue despite all odds, and contrary to all logical expectations.

30. That is, faith in God's salvation is already implanted in our hearts as Jews. For we're referred to as "believers, and descendants of believers" (*Shabbat* 97A). The point is to have faith *in that faith itself*, (as is said in *Slonomer Chassidut*), and to not waiver or succumb to fear. (See Supplementary Notes.)

to those who fear Him" (Psalms 85:10) and, "Who are you, that you should fear a man who will die?"[31] (Isaiah 51:12).[32]

33. "Do not fear any man, for judgment is God's" (Deuteronomy 1:17).[33]

This comes to warn you to believe that no harm will come to you as a result of an honest decision you made,[34] in which you favored no one.

For as our sages said, "Mitzvah envoys[35] suffer no harm, either on their way there or back"[36] (*Pesachim* 8B). And that is the import of "Judgment is God's," which is to say, no harm will come to them as a result of such a judgment.[37]

34. ". . . that his heart not be lifted up above his brothers" (Deuteronomy 17:20).[38]

This comes to alert you to remove arrogance from your heart.[39] For one greater shouldn't be arrogant toward those lesser than he, and even a king shouldn't lift his head above others. For if he's to rule over them, he should also rule over his own character and be only humble.[40] In fact, arrogance is one of the most significant sins, and it ruins and destroys souls.[41] As it's said, "Whoever is proud-hearted is an abomination to God" (Proverbs 16:5).

For what good is having a lot of money, and wealth all "bound and made

---

31. . . . himself, anyway.

32. Both this and the previous ¶ go together. They come to underscore the need to foster a concrete and sure faith in God's presence, in His absolute capabilities, as well as in His promised salvation, despite all you see or anticipate seeing. For though fear serves to protect us against harm, it has its limitations and is harmful when left to abide in the soul. Like guilt, which is meant to encourage tshuvah, fear is meant to encourage trust in God.

33. The verse begins, "Do not favor people in judgment, but hear out the small as well as the great" and then continues with, "Do not fear any man, for judgment is God's." Hence the statement is being made to judges when they try cases.

34. . . . in adjudicating a case . . .

35. . . . including judges, who then represent God, and carry out His will . . .

36. i.e., neither while carrying their mission out or as a consequence of it.

37. . . . since they're envoys of God—as we all are in fact, in this world. Indeed, were we only to realize that, we'd also overcome all our fears and put our trust in God's decisions (see previous ¶).

38. The Hebrew reads, "לבלתי רום לבבו מזחיו," which can be translated as a warning not to "that his heart not be lifted off of" another's being, and as such serves as a warning against being emotionally removed and distant from another person. But to resonate and empathize with another, heart to heart, instead.

39. The context of this verse shows that this is a warning to kings, rather than to the rest of us (hence the reference to kings soon to follow). But Rabbeinu Yonah is universalizing it.

40. True conquest and control is self-control, and overcoming the inner inclinations that gnaw away at one's being, and weaken the soul's resolves. As a consequence, a leader who can't nurture enough self-discipline to be humble can't be said to be a true leader.

41. See Supplementary Notes.

secure" (Ezekiel 27:24), when all your revered splendor is abominable and foul,[42] and thus lower than the grave?

A sage would only compliment himself for his service to God and his fear of Him, for his trust and love of Him, and for his devotion to Him. As it's said, "He is your praise, and He is your God" (Deuteronomy 10:21) and, "Let not the sage glory in his wisdom, . . . But let him who glories glory in this: that he understands and knows Me" (Jeremiah 9:22–23).

35. "You will surely give to him, and your heart must not grieve when you give to him" (Deuteronomy 15:10).

That comes to alert you to uproot stinginess from within and to be generous instead. For as it's said, "The generous will be blessed" (Proverbs 22:9).

But it's not enough to just hand things over. You should cultivate beneficence within. That's why the verse warns you that "your heart must not grieve" after it says, "You will surely give him."[43]

36. "Do not harden your heart, or withdraw your hand from your poor brother" (Deuteronomy 15:7).

That comes to alert you to purge all cruelty from your heart and to cultivate pleasant traits[44] like compassion and unerring kindness.[45] As it's written, "Go in His ways" (Ibid. 28:9).[46] And since you might, in fact, refrain from withdrawing your hand from a poor person, or you might express good will to him other than out of compassion (as it's said, "The compassion of wrongdoers is[47] cruelty" [Proverbs 12:10][48]), it's thus written, "Do not harden your heart."[49]

---

42. . . . to God . . .

43. It's very easy for us, in modernity, to "hand things over" to others. We write checks for different causes all the time. But cultivating true beneficence is another matter, in that it means *wanting* to give. At one time being charitable meant doing without. If a poor person needed a chair, for example, and I had five, I'd give him one of mine, and would make do with four chairs myself from then on. The decision to give my chair away would affect my day-to-day life profoundly. But I'd accept that upon myself because I'd have *wanted* to give. By writing a check, as we do, I may sense a vague loss, and can read the numbers that prove it to be real, but I don't experience the loss on a daily basis. It's as if I'd given up a chess piece, but I know that I can always start a new game.

44. . . . instead . . .

45. Apparently the point is that these traits are to be reliable rather than occasional or erratic.

46. That's to say that God's ways are rooted in compassion and true kindness. We're to become aware of how true that is, and emulate Him.

47. . . . actually . . .

48. This refers to self-serving "compassion" that backfires, and destroys hope and trust in basic goodness.

49. That is, since you might appear to be generous for less than altruistic reasons — in order to impress others, to command respect, etc. — you're charged with being truly charitable. (See previous ¶.)

There's a very onerous and bitter consequence to being cruel, as we'll explain in *The Gate of Cruelty*, with God's help.[50] As our sages said, "The expression, 'He will show you mercy, have compassion on you, and multiply you' (Deuteronomy 13:18) indicates that whoever has compassion for others will be shown mercy by Heaven, and whoever does not have compassion for others will not be shown mercy by Heaven" (*Shabbat* 151B).

37. "Do not pity him, have compassion for him, or conceal him" (Deuteronomy 13:9).

That comes to alert you not to have compassion for or to pity those who cause others to sin or stumble. As our sages put it, "Whoever has compassion for the cruel will eventually be cruel to the compassionate" (*Yalkut Shmuel* 121).[51]

38. "Do not take revenge or bear a grudge against your people" (Leviticus 19:18).

Our sages said, "What is an instance of revenge? When one says to another, 'Loan me your axe' and the second says back to him, 'I will not loan it to you, just as you would not loan me yours!' And what is an instance of bearing a grudge? When the second person says, 'I am going to loan you mine, even though you would not loan me yours'" (*Yomah* 23A).

The consequences you'd have to suffer are not for what you said, but for the grudge you bore in your heart.[52] As our sages said, "The prohibition against bearing a grudge only has to do with money matters. But when it comes to[53] arrogance, shame, or harmful intentions, it is permissible to feel like that" (Ibid.).[54] They also said, "Any scholar that neither takes revenge nor bears a grudge like a snake[55] is not a scholar" (Ibid.).[56] But if he's apologized to, he should overlook the matter.[57]

39. "Do not hate your brother in your heart" (Leviticus 19:17).

That comes to alert you to purge yourself of the trait of hatred.[58] Because it fosters many acts of defiance and generates a lot of destructive deeds, including slandering (which is equivalent[59] to many sins that incur a court-imposed death

---

50. To our great regret, this work no longer exists.

51. Logic spurns compassion for the wicked and heartless (unless they do tshuvah), and abhors misplaced sympathies. And it declares that if you twist and bend your heart enough to pity the cruel, you'll manage to do the same to justify cruelty toward the kind.

52. That explains why this prohibition is included among those requiring no action.

53. . . . being a victim of . . .

54. i.e., vengeful or begrudging.

55. i.e., stealthily, rapidly, and consummately.

56. That is, any scholar who takes no revenge when someone else expresses arrogance, censure, or bad intentions against Torah or against himself hasn't the alacrity, dignity, or wherewithal to be a true scholar.

57. . . . and forgive.

58. See Supplementary Notes.

59. . . . in severity . . .

penalty, as we'll explain[60]), having harmful intentions, being pleased about others' misfortunes, causing harm to others, tale-bearing, taking revenge, and bearing a grudge.[61] And it undoes a lot of inner goodness,[62] as we'll explain in *The Gate of Hatred*.[63]

See how far-reaching the consequences for hatred are. As our sages put it, "The people studied a lot of Torah and did a lot of good things in the[64] Second Temple. So, why was it destroyed? Because of the needless hatred they expressed against each other" (*Yomah* 9B).[65]

40. "Keep yourself away from every bad thing" (Deuteronomy 23:10).

Our sages explained that to mean that you're not to fantasize during the day, so as not to come to impurity[66] at night (*Ketubot* 46A), even if you don't fantasize in order to act upon it.[67,68]

41. "Do not stray after your own hearts, or after your own eyes" (Numbers 15:39).

That comes to alert you not to muse about transgressing, or about being defiant and sinning in any way, or to be "one who muses about doing wrong"

---

60. See ¶'s 201–211.

61. The last two traits were just discussed in the previous ¶.

62. Not only does hate cause harm, it also eradicates goodness. So one who bears hate in his heart not only doesn't advance toward goodness; he regresses further toward evil.

63. To our great regret, this work no longer exists.

64. . . . times of the . . .

65. We see from the example Rabbeinu Yonah uses here that "the far-reaching consequences for hatred" he mentioned aren't *personal* consequences. Rather, they're consequences that affect the present and future physical and spiritual stature of the Jewish Nation itself. Hence, hatred should be seen as the dread and highly communicable disease with dire and wide consequences that it is.

The truth is we're all full of hate. We often take subtle, purposeless, or socially acceptable satisfaction when we see others in pain (by joking about it, for example, and excusing it with "I was only kidding! Don't be so serious!"). And our language and inference is often very, very violent. Haven't we the responsibility to accept our part in the world's violence and destruction and to own up to our own casualness about death and devastation in our age?

66. i.e., nocturnal emission.

67. That explains why this prohibition is included among those requiring no action (see notes 52 to ¶38).

68. The text continues with the following:

We infer that [. . . you're forbidden to fantasize even if you don't do so in order to act upon it] from what follows, which is, "If there is among you a man who is not clean because of uncleanness that comes upon him by chance at night" (Ibid. v. 11) [i.e., which focuses upon the nocturnal emission that might result, rather than upon any illicit relationship].

(Proverbs 24:8). And to not muse over the words of heretics, because you might stumble and be drawn toward them.[69]

Consider the fact that God is[70] peering into your heart and delving into your being. How could you be so rash as to sully and pour into your heart all sorts of unconscionable things?[71] As Solomon said, "Plotting out foolishness is a sin" (Ibid. v. 9) and as he said elsewhere, "There are six things God despises, seven which are an abomination to Him: . . . a heart that plots wicked plans" (Proverbs 6:16–18).

42. "Do not bear a false report" (Exodus 23:1).

That comes to alert you not to accept slander.[72] As the Targum puts it, "Do not accept a false report."

43. "Do not covet your neighbor's house" (Exodus 20:14) and "Do not crave your neighbor's house" (Deuteronomy 5:18).[73]

That comes to alert you not to devise an evil scheme to take over your neighbor's field or vineyard, or anything else of his—even if you'd pay him for it. In fact, you're actually being alerted against *thinking* of doing such a terrible thing itself, or of resolving to do it.[74] As it's said, "Do not covet."

If you'd like your neighbor to sell you his field or vineyard, or something else, but[75] he doesn't want to, but if you pressure him with all sorts of pleas that he'd be too embarrassed to refuse you, you're then forbidden to pressure him. Since doing that is[76] forcing him.

And if you're so well respected that any request you'd make would never be refused, then you're forbidden to ask your neighbor to buy or sell anything unless you know he'd do so willingly, and wouldn't bemoan having done it.

---

69. Whereas the previous ¶ only alerted us to physical mishaps, we're being alerted here to the possibility of attitudinal mishaps as well.

70. . . . always and presently . . .

71. . . . knowing that. That is, God Himself is there, in your heart. As is cited in ¶44, "God your Lord walks in the midst of your camp . . . Your camp should be holy, so that He see no unclean thing in you" (Deuteronomy 23:15). How repulsive it would be to allow untoward thoughts in there with Him.

72. That is, not to automatically accept negative statements about others simply because they were made outright. (See Supplementary Notes.)

73. See Supplementary Notes.

74. See note 67 above.

75. . . . you know that . . .

76. . . . tantamount to . . .

Chapter Six

CRITICAL DECORATIVE BORDER

44. Among the Prohibitions Involving Speech[1]

"For God your Lord walks in the midst of your camp to save you, and to give your enemies over to you. Your camp should be holy, so that He see no unclean thing in you" (Deuteronomy 23:15).[2]

Our sages said about this, "Included in this prohibition is[3] that our 'camp should be holy, so that He see no unclean thing' in us when we delve into God's Torah and express our prayers to Him" (*Berachot* 25B). We're thus commanded to only mention God's name in a state of holiness, and to only engage in Torah and to pray in a state of holiness. That is, not to mention God's name or to enunciate words of Torah while undressed, or in the presence of someone who's undressed. We're also alerted to keep the site[4] clean. As it's said, "You should dig with it[5] and turn back to cover over your excrement" (Deuteronomy 23:14).

You're all the more so being alerted not to mention God's name if your hands are unclean. And to wash them if they've touched anything repellent. As it says, "I

---

1. The overall seriousness of these sorts of sins is best expressed at the end of this section, where Rabbeinu Yonah states, "Know that the personal devastation and ruin most people suffer originates in the tips of their tongue" (¶61), "Whoever hears someone uttering God's name in vain should shun him. And if he does not, he himself should be shunned" (Ibid.), "The ruination of all of those in the 'four classes' [explained at the end of this gate] comes as a result of the sin of their mouth and the words of their lips" (¶62), and, "Reflect on and see how especially defiant transgressions of the tongue are" (¶63).

2. See note 71 to ¶41.

3. . . . the idea . . .

4. . . . of our study and prayer . . .

5. i.e., a spade

will wash my hands in cleanliness"[6] (Psalms 26:6). So, if you're traveling and unsure the road[7] is clean, don't mention God's name or utter words of Torah. If there's something unclean behind you like excrement, a carcass, or foul water, go a distance of four *amot*[8] from where the odor ends. If it's facing you, then distance yourself from it until you can't see it any longer. Caution in this is part of fearing God. As it's said, ". . . for those who feared God and took heed of His name" (Malachi 3:16).[9]

Our sages said, "The verse, 'He despised the word of God' (Numbers 15:31)[10] refers to one who utters words of Torah in alleyways and filthy places" (*Berachot* 24B). They also said, "'(God) gives wisdom to the wise' (Daniel 2:21) because the wise honor the Torah, and engage in it in a state of holiness. For had He given it to fools, they would have uttered words of Torah in alleyways and filthy places" (*Kohelet Rabbah* 1:7).[11]

45.   Some prohibitions involving speech[12] incur flogging. For as our sages said, "Prohibitions involving no action do not incur flogging—except for swearing falsely, substituting,[13] and cursing someone with God's name" (*Makkot* 16A).

And though swearing falsely doesn't incur a court-imposed death penalty, it nonetheless brings about more significant consequences from Heaven than many sins that do. Because one who swears falsely profanes God's name. As it's said, "Do not swear falsely by My name, nor profane the name of your God, for I am God" (Leviticus 19:12). And the consequences to suffer for profaning God's name are greater than for all other sins.[14]

In fact, that's only said in conjunction with the sins of swearing falsely and of worshipping idols.[15] For it's said, "Because he gave of his seed to Molech, to defile My sanctuary, and to profane My holy name" (Leviticus 20:3). And as it's said about the prohibition against worshipping idols, "Do not bow down to them and do not

---

6. The term (נקיון) is usually translated as "innocence," but it implies both innocence and cleanliness.

7. . . . you're on . . .

8. Approximately seven feet.

9. The entire verse reads, "Then those who feared God [and thus practiced cleanliness] spoke to one another [i.e., they studied Torah together]; and God listened and heard it [i.e., their Torah study and their prayers], and a book of remembrance was written before Him *for those who feared God, and who took heed of* [i.e., and thus respected] *His name.*"

10. The entire verse reads, "Because *he despised the word of God*, and has broken His commandment, that soul will be utterly excised. His iniquity will dwell upon him."

11. That's to say, one who'd discount odors as "nothing" simply because they can't be seen would discount anything non-visible. And though there's certainly, certainly no comparison, they'd discount the invisible presence of God as well.

12. . . . are so serious that they . . .

13. . . . one animal for another, consecrated one. See Leviticus 27:9–10.

14. See Supplementary Notes.

15. . . . which shows you how serious a sin swearing falsely actually is.

serve them, for I, God your Lord, am a jealous God" (Exodus 20:5). That means to say that God doesn't forgive idol worship the way He forgives other sins. As it's written, "How can I pardon you for this? Your children have forsaken Me, and sworn by false gods" (Jeremiah 5:7). And it's said about swearing falsely, "God will not cleanse one who takes His name in vain" (Exodus 20:7). In fact, the reason why the prohibition against swearing falsely follows the one against idol worship is simply because swearing falsely encompasses profaning God's name.

Our sages actually said the following about the verses, "Do not foist poverty or riches upon me . . . lest I become full and deny You, and say, 'Who is God?' Or lest I be poor and steal, and profane my God's name" (Proverbs 30:8–9)—that, "The latter is more formidable than the former, as it's said, 'As for you, O house of Israel, . . . let everyone serve his idols, and hereafter also, if you will not listen to Me. But do not profane My holy name any more' (Ezekiel 20:39)" (*Vayikrah Rabbah* 22:6).

That means to say that the consequences to be suffered for swearing falsely in court[16] are more significant than for worshiping idols in secret, because of the profanation of God's name.[17] And our sages said, "When it comes to all other sins in the Torah, the penalty is exacted from him[18] and his family. But here[19] it's exacted from him and from the whole world" (*Shavuot* 39A).

If a court impels you to take an oath, and you know that what you have to say is untrue, it's forbidden to accept the oath upon yourself and to say, "I'll take an oath on that!" in order to intimidate the other party, even when you don't actually intend to take the oath. As it's said, "Do not take the name of God your Lord in vain" (Exodus 20:7). Among the implications of that are that you're not even to resolve to take a vain oath, as our sages said (*Mechiltah, Yitro* 20:7). In fact, the *Targum* translates, "Do not take God's name in vain" (Exodus 23:1) as "Do not resolve to take God's name in vain."

It's also forbidden to take an oath for no reason, even when it's based on truth. For it's said, "Do not take the name of God your Lord in vain" (Exodus 20:7), which the *Targum* translates as "Do not take it upon yourself to take a false oath."

Whoever causes another to take an oath in vain commits a major sin. As would be the case if, for example, someone owes you $100, and you claim he owes more and thus force him to take a Torah-required oath on the part[20] he can't attest to. Or if you make a false claim against someone for something he knows nothing about, and thus force him to take an equity oath.[21]

---

16. i.e., in public.
17. . . . involved.
18. i.e., the guilty party.
19. i.e., in the case of swearing falsely.
20. . . . of your claim . . .
21. i.e., a Rabbinically ordained oath that one who denied a claim made against him may take. See *Kiddushin* 43B.

Our sages referred to someone who'd do that as a thief, because he "stole" someone's confidence (*Shavuot* 39A). It's said of him, "I will send it forth, said God . . . , and it will enter into the house of the thief, and into the house of him who swears falsely by My name. And it will remain in the midst of his house, and consume it along with its wood and stones" (Zechariah 5:4).

And if you know that people would doubt your word if you took an oath to something, because of the excuses you'd offer, you should refrain and not take the oath even if the truth is on your side, so as to give honor to God.

46. "Do not curse the judges nor curse the ruler of your people" (Exodus 22:27) and "Do not curse the deaf" (Leviticus 19:14).

These come to alert you never to curse another Jew[22] through the name of God,[23] or with any expression for Him. As to the Torah mentioning not cursing judges, the ruler, and the deaf, that comes to alert you not to curse a judge when he decides against you, or a ruler who penalizes you for being defiant. And the deaf are mentioned as well for otherwise you'd think there's nothing wrong with cursing them, since they can't hear, and wouldn't feel hurt by your curse.[24]

"Do not curse the judges" comes at the end of the "Judgments" section[25] to say you're not to curse a judge who arrives at the decisions[26] there. But a judge who makes an illegal judgment *is* to be cursed.

Our sages said, "Whoever curses either another person or himself with the name of God is to be flogged" (*Shavuot* 35A). And Heaven will exact even greater consequences for that. As it's said, "If you will not take care to observe all the words of this Torah . . . that you fear this glorious and awesome name, God your Lord, God will make your plagues remarkable . . ." (Deuteronomy 28:58–59), which our sages said refers to anyone who curses either another or himself through God's name (*Temurah* 3B).

47. It's forbidden to say, "This is true—God help me!" when it's not. Because you'd be drawing a curse upon yourself through the name of God, since the contrary is implied in your assertion.[27]

48. "Do not drink wine or strong drink . . . so that you may differentiate between the holy and profane . . . And so that you may teach the people of Israel" (Leviticus 10:9–11).

---

22. i.e., *any* other Jew.

23. The original reads, "Do not curse אֱלֹהִים," which can be translated either as "judges" or "God."

24. This underscores how inherently wrong it is to demean another (other than a reprobate judge, to be mentioned shortly), even when it seems to do no harm.

25. See Exodus 21.

26. . . . enunciated . . .

27. That is, for all intents and purposes you'd be saying, "May God *not* help me, since what I'm saying isn't true." And you're forbidden to condemn yourself.

Our sages said about this, "One who drinks an undiluted *rivi'it*[28] of wine must not decide a case. And he must not decide a case if he drinks more than a *rivi'it* of diluted wine" (*K'ritut* 13B).

49. "Do not abuse one another" (Leviticus 25:17).

This refers to verbal abuse, as we indicated above.[29] Our sages said, "If someone has done tshuvah, do not say to him, 'Remember what you used to do!' "[30] And if he is a descendant of converts, do not say to him, 'Remember what your ancestors did!' " (*Babba Metziah* 58B). That's why it's said, "Do not abuse a stranger[31] or pressure him" (Exodus 22:20), which is to say, don't abuse him verbally, and don't pressure him about money (*Mechiltah, Nezikin,* ch. 18).

The Torah often alerts you not to abuse the convert, since he forgot[32] his people and his family in order to take refuge under the wings of the Divine Presence. As it's said, "You have left your father and mother, and the land of your birth, and come to a people you did not know" (Ruth 2:11), which is then followed by, "A full reward will be given to you by God, the God of Israel, under whose wings you have come to take refuge" (Ibid. v. 12).

His situation would be like that of a deer who'd come upon a flock of sheep and settled in to graze there with them, whom the shepherd then had mercy on, because the deer had left his spacious pasture to settle into a narrow one.[33]

50. "Do not follow a majority to do wrong" (Exodus 23:2).

This comes to alert you not to verbally encourage sinners, and not to join in with those who advocate wrongdoing.[34] As it's said, "Do not say, 'It is a conspiracy!,' about whatever this people might call a conspiracy" (Isaiah 8:12).

---

28. Approximately 3 ½ liquid ounces.

29. See ¶24.

30. It's important to recall that this entire work is directed toward those who will or are in the process of doing tshuvah. So we're being warned not to harass those in that situation — ourselves included! Rabbeinu Yonah is also drawing an analogy between one who does tshuvah and a convert. Because like the convert (according to the parable cited shortly, see there), one who does tshuvah experiences alienation, displacement, and degradation. He becomes part of a minority in which he stands out. But he's also shown mercy by the "shepherd" who realizes his plight, as well as his preciousness.

31. The term (גר) either translates as either "foreigner," "alien immigrant," or "stranger"; or, alternately, as "convert."

32. Or, forsook. That's to say, "forgetting" can be an act of consciously and willfully turning your back on something or someone — as some may do when it comes to their relationship with God. See ¶27.

33. See our reference to this parable in note 30 above. Aside from that point, though, it could be said that Rabbeinu Yonah is suggesting that while a sinner might first seem to be like a deer who is lithe and pretty, free to roam, who then becomes part of a flock of dutiful sheep, it's also not to be denied that those sheep (and that deer) have a "shepherd" who's capable of expressing mercy, and of supplying all of the needs of His flock.

34. i.e., who agree that something wrong should be done, even though they themselves wouldn't do it. (See Supplementary Notes.)

51. It's forbidden to associate with wrongdoers in worldly matters.[35] As it's said, "God will destroy what you have made because you associated with Achazyahu" (2 Chronicles 20:37). It's even forbidden to associate with wrongdoers for the sake of a mitzvah.[36] As it's said, "Do not envy the brutal man, and choose none of his ways" (Proverbs 3:31). As our sages said, "Do not befriend a wrongdoer even for the sake of a mitzvah" (*Avot D'Rebbe Natan* 9).

In fact, many deadly things come from befriending wrongdoers. But we've already discussed this transgression, and its serious consequences.[37]

52. "Do not place an impediment before the blind" (Leviticus 19:14).[38]

This comes to alert you not to decide *halacha* for the Jewish Nation in a way that's not in accordance with the faith or the law. As our sages put it, "Be methodical when coming to judgment" (*Pirke Avot* 1:1).

Those who are in a hurry to understand, and to arrive at a decision can't help but place an impediment before the blind, and they sin very gravely.[39] As it's said, "They do not know, nor do they understand. They walk in darkness while the foundations of the earth shake" (Psalms 82:5). "Be careful in your instruction, because an accidental sin in instruction is tantamount to an intentional one" (*Pirke Avot* 4:12).[40] And, "'She has cast down many wounded . . .' (Proverbs 7:26), refers to a student who isn't qualified to judge, but does anyway. While, '. . . indeed, many strong men have been slain by her' (Ibid.) refers to a student who's qualified to judge, but doesn't" (*Sotah* 22A).

53. This verse also comes to alert you to offer good advice to whomever of our people you advise,[41] and to not cause them to stumble as a result of bad advice. Nor to counsel them to your own advantage.

---

35. See Supplementary Notes.

36. That is, I might rationalize associating with wrongdoers when it comes to doing good works. And convince myself that I'd be bettering them in the process, or at least having an impact upon them. But we're told otherwise here—that you're more likely to be sullied in the process than not, and that the threat to heart and soul is too great.

37. See ¶'s 59, 151, and 187–199.

38. As Rashi indicates in his commentary to this verse, we're being warned, "לֹא לִפְנֵי הַסּוּמָא בַּדָּבָר לֹא תִתֵּן עֵצָה שֶׁאֵינָהּ הוֹגֶנֶת"—not to place an obstacle before anyone who's blind—or susceptible—to one harmful thing or another, by suggesting he do something he'll regret later on. But Rabbeinu Yonah is particularizing the warning.

39. This not only serves as a warning to judges and rabbis, but to all of us, not to simply rattle off what we "feel" the *halacha* would be in a certain instance. But to either know in fact, or to ask. Too often individuals who haven't a true grasp of either the situation or the *halacha* will offer a quick suggestion based on nearly nothing. Or one that's extrapolated from an isolated incident in their own life. But if harm can result from inappropriate advice handed over with the best of intentions (see next ¶), that's all the more so true of advice touching upon the soul and its associations with God through *halacha*.

40. See Supplementary Notes.

41. See Supplementary Notes.

54. You're obliged to think a situation over and offer someone sound and cogent advice. In fact, this is one of the basic tenets of benevolence.[42] As it's said, "Salve and incense rejoice the heart, as does the sweetness of a friend's own counsel" (Proverbs 27:9).[43]

55. "Do not go about as a tale-bearer among your people" (Leviticus 19:16). As our sages said, "Included in this prohibition is that of not besmirching another person's good name from among your people" (*Ketubot* 46A). Heaven will exact a significant price for that, as we'll explain in the section on those who incur the death penalty.[44]

They also said, "'Do not go about as a tale-bearer among your people' is also a warning to judges not to be lenient to one,[45] and harsh toward another (*Ketubot* 46A).

56. "Do not mention the name of other gods" (Exodus 23:13).

That is, don't say to someone, "Meet me by so-and-so's idol" (*Sanhedrin* 63B).[46]

57. "Show them no mercy" (Deuteronomy 7:2).

Our sages explained it to mean, "Do not acknowledge their charm,[47] for it is forbidden to say, 'How attractive that Gentile is!'" (*Avodah Zarah* 20A). They also explained it to mean you're not to be so charmed by them that you give them gratuitous gifts.[48]

58. "Do not be like Korach and his contingent" (Numbers 17:5).[49]

As our sages said, "Whoever encourages conflict transgresses the prohibition, 'Do not be like Korach and his contingent'" (*Sanhedrin* 110A). Yet our sages said (J. T., *Peah* 1:1) that it's permitted to slander people who encourage conflict.[50] As

---

42. See Supplementary Notes.

43. We often offer advice very willingly and off the top of our heads. And we don't think of the consequences upon the lives of the people we advise when we do that. How many poor souls have been undone by bad advice—how many careers have been shattered, marriages destroyed, lives ruined by bad advice innocently offered in a moment of personal aggrandizement on the part of the thoughtless person offering it. Nonetheless, we're obliged to offer advice. As a consequence, we're to be slow, deliberate, and sensitive when doing that.

44. See ¶111.

45. . . . litigant . . .

46. We in modernity would tend to dismiss that as a simple reference to place. But the Torah indicates that it's also an acknowledging of the reality of the unreal.

47. The term for "mercy" (חן) can also mean "charm."

48. "Gratuitous" is חנם, which is again a cognate of חן (see previous note). That's to say, offering that an idol worshipper (who's actually the object of our concerns, not just any non-Jew) is attractive can bespeak a degree of jealousy about how his lifestyle contributes to his grace and good looks. And extending gratuitous gifts may seem to be an offering to a false God unto itself. (See Supplementary Notes.)

49. See number 16.

50. See reference to this in our note to the following ¶. (See Supplementary Notes.)

it's said, "But me, your servant, and Zadok the priest, Benaiah the son of Yehoyada, and your servant Solomon, he has not called" (1 Kings 1:26).

59. But if you don't encourage conflict with people who consistently[51] pursue the wrong path or draw others to sin, then you yourself will suffer the consequences of each one of their acts of defiance and sin. And you'd also be transgressing the prohibition, "Do not bear sin on his account" (Leviticus 19:17).[52]

As it's said, "O Israel, you have been sinning since the days of Gibah. For they stood, rather than wage war at Gibah against the children of iniquity" (Hosea 10:9). That means to say that if this generation had stood there, they wouldn't have fought to eradicate iniquity in Gibah, as the earlier generation did.[53] That is, they[54] have been sinning from that point onward. For the earlier ones were better than they, since they[55] united and faced death in order to eradicate wrongdoing.[56]

It's also said, "Curse Meroz, said the angel of God, curse its inhabitants bitterly. Because they did not come to help God, to help God battle the mighty men"[57] (Judges 5:23) as well as, "Do not fear any man"[58] (Deuteronomy 1:17).[59]

In fact, one who is for God would sacrifice his life to sanctify His name. As it's said, "'Whoever is for God, let him come to me!' And all the Levites gathered to him" (Exodus 32:26) and, "When Pinchas . . . saw it, he . . . took a spear in his hand" (Numbers 25:7).

Indeed, every God-fearing individual—even "one who loves purity of heart" (Proverbs 22:11)[60]—is obliged to become fervently opposed when he sees leaders and authorities practicing deceit.[61] As our sages said, "Any breach made by anyone other than a leader is not a breach, as it's said, 'For they have taken their daughters for themselves and for their sons, so that the holy seed have mixed with the people of those lands. And the hand of the princes and rulers has been foremost in this trespass' (Ezra 9:2)" (*Breishit Rabbah* 26:5).

---

51. i.e., firmly, fixedly, and intentionally.

52. See Supplementary Notes.

53. The text continues with the following:

. . . in which case, "For they stood" would read, "*If* they had stood there," just as "He would leave his father" (Genesis 44:22) could read, "*if* he would leave his father."

54. i.e., the people of this generation.

55. i.e., the earlier generation.

56. . . . while the people of this generation would not have.

57. i.e., the wrongdoers.

58. i.e., don't be intimidated by wrongdoers.

59. See Supplementary Notes.

60. i.e., even the most sensitive and caring . . .

61. That's to say, even if it goes against your grain, when you're in the presence of people who instigate disputes (see previous ¶), or who "consistently pursue the wrong path or draw others to sin" you must nonetheless become zealous, despite yourself. (See Supplementary Notes.)

60. "But over your brothers, the people of Israel, you may not rule one over another harshly" (Leviticus 25:46).

Don't exploit another person. If he's intimidated by you or embarrassed to contradict you, then don't order him to do anything, great or small, unless he either agrees to it, or it's for his own good. That includes asking him to warm up a pot of water[62] or to go on an errand to the city to buy a loaf of bread.[63] But you can order a dishonest man to do whatever you'd care for him to do (*Babba Metziah* 73B).[64]

61. "Do not profane My holy name" (Leviticus 22:32).

This is one of the prohibitions that incurs excision, as we'll explain.[65]

Know that the personal[66] devastation and ruin most people suffer originates in[67] the tips of their tongues. Because they utter the name of God for no reason, or irreverently.[68] In fact, our sages said, "The ox knows[69] his owner, and the donkey his master's crib; but Israel does not know"[70] (Isaiah 1:3) refers to just this (*Vayikrah Rabbah, Emor* 27). They're also not scrupulous about the cleanliness of their environment or their hands.[71]

In fact, our sages used to shun and banish anyone who'd mention God's name in vain, and would suspect[72] his oaths. They even said, "Whoever hears someone uttering God's name in vain should shun him. And if he does not, he himself should be shunned" (*Nedarim* 7B).[73]

62. As to people who aren't careful to speak about Torah scholars respectfully, whether in their presence or not—they're heretics, and they have no place in The World to Come (*Sanhedrin* 99B).

---

62. . . . for you . . .

63. We of modernity tend to derive a lot of satisfaction out of demanding just these very sorts of things. And to feel powerful and self-important along the way. But it's often cruel and certainly heartless.

64. See Supplementary Notes.

65. From ¶143 and onward.

66. Or, spiritual . . .

67. . . . the actions of . . .

68. It's stunning to notice how often the very least reverential of people "drop" God's name into the conversation, in our day and age. For no good reason, and sometimes as if to purposefully besmirch it. It's equally stunning to notice how rarely people of faith seem to mention His name—as if embarrassed to. Credit might be given to the latter, however, for they might be reticent to mention God's name in light of how often it's mentioned irreverently by the former.

69. . . . fears, and respects . . .

70. . . . fear or respect God, since they mention His name in vain and offhandedly.

71. . . . when they utter God's name. (See Supplementary Notes.)

72. i.e., question and tend to doubt . . .

73. That's to say, regardless of whether he's ostracized or you, the two of you must be separated, in light of the fact that he separated himself from God, and you beheld that.

Doesn't the ruination of all of those in the four classes[74] come as a result of "the sin of their mouth and the words of their lips" (Psalms 59:13) in fact, as will be explained in the course of this gate?[75] That's why it's written, "Death and life are in the power of the tongue" (Proverbs 18:21).[76]

63.   Just reflect on and see how especially defiant transgressions of the tongue are. For the consequences for cursing your father or mother are more significant than for striking them, since the judgment for one who curses them is stoning, which is the most serious court-imposed death sentence. While the judgment for one who strikes them is strangulation (*Tosefta, Aruchin*).

---

74. . . . of people who haven't a place in The World To Come (see ¶172 and onward) . . .

75. See ¶143 and onward.

76. See Supplementary Notes.

Chapter Seven

Among the Prohibitions
Involving Your Senses of
Seeing and Hearing[1]

64. Many go astray or become ensnared by profaning their so very important senses of seeing and hearing.[2]

It's said about seeing, "Do not stray after your own hearts, or after your own eyes" (Numbers 15:39), comes to alert you not to stare at a married woman, or at any other woman forbidden to you.[3] Because you might go astray as a result.

65. Included among the sins rooted in your sense of seeing is having upturned eyes, which stems from arrogance.[4] As it's said, "I will not suffer one with upraised eyes and an arrogant heart" (Psalms 101:5).

66. Our sages said about the sense of hearing, "A person should never allow his ears to listen to nonsense, because the ears are the first of the organs to be scorched" (*Ketubot* 5B).[5] And it's said about people who listen to profanity,[6] "Alien mouths are a deep pit" (Proverbs 22:14) (*Shabbat* 32A).

---

1. While this wording isn't found in the original, we've inserted it here to conform with previous entries in this category.

2. They "profane" their senses of seeing and hearing by using them for less than holy ends, when everything was created to be used in holiness and to thus honor God, as is indicated in ¶148. (See Supplementary Notes.)

3. See Supplementary Notes.

4. See Supplementary Notes.

5. i.e., deeply affected by whatever it comes in contact with.

6. See Supplementary Notes.

Take all this seriously if you fear God and want to do tshuvah. Because doing so will protect you from the flames.[7] But we've already said important things about this in *The Gates of the Restrictions Involved in Caution*.[8]

---

7. . . . of passion and self-deceit. (See Supplementary Notes.)
8. To our great dismay, this work no longer exists.

Chapter Eight

ᏇᎲᏇᎲᏇᎲᏇᎲᏇᎲᏇᎲᏇᎲᏇᎲᏇᎲᏇᎲᏇᎲ

Among the Prohibitions Involving Withdrawing Your Hand[1] and Refraining from Doing Something

67. "Do not withdraw your hand from your poor brother. . . . Beware lest there be an unconscionable thought in your heart, so as to say, 'The seventh year, the *Shmittah*, is close by,' and look wrongly against your poor brother, and you give him nothing" (Deuteronomy 15:7–9).[2]

We thus learn that if you refrain from loaning money[3] to a poor person, you transgress two prohibitions: "Beware" and "lest there be." So,[4] if you're warned not to refrain from loaning money when the seventh year approaches, despite your fear

---

1. . . . from a poor person . . . (See Supplementary Notes.)

2. The point must be made that the verse that goes between the two cited above reads, "But you will open your hand wide to him, and will surely loan him enough for his needs. . . ." As such the operative problem in this category of sins isn't just not fulfilling the imperative. It includes delaying and forestalling, and being insensitive to the acuity of the situation. For even if you avoid the prohibition against withdrawing your hand and you "fulfill your responsibility," you still breach your duty to sensitize your heart, and to respond warmly and openly to a need.

Nonetheless, the needs of the recipient himself must always be taken into account (see end of ¶69), as well as your own special abilities (hence the requirement to offer either advice *or* action, in ¶70).

3. . . . without interest (see Exodus 22:24) . . .

4. . . . it stands to reason that . . .

of[5] the *Shmittah* year, how great then is the sin of withholding a loan when you wouldn't lose your investment?[6]

In fact, the sin of withdrawing your hand from loaning[7] is so great that the verse calls[8] a stingy *thought* about a loan "unconscionable." And our sages said that, "Whoever averts his eyes from[9] charity is like an idol worshipper" (*Ketubot* 68A),[10] since in the first instance[11] it's written, ". . . that there be no *unconscionable* thoughts in your heart" and in the second[12] it's written, "Certain men, *unconscionable* people, have gone out from among you" (Deuteronomy 13:14).

Our sages said that, "Anyone who is stingy is called 'unconscionable.' As in, 'Observe this unconscionable man, Naval' (1 Samuel 25:25), who was a stingy man, for he asked David's servants, 'Should I take my bread, my water, and my fresh meat . . .' (Ibid. v. 11)" (*Yalkut Tehillim* 53).

They also added that "loaning money to a poor person is greater than offering charity" (*Shabbat* 63A).

68. "Do not defraud your neighbor" (Leviticus 19:13). Or as David put it, "Wrongdoers borrow and do not repay" (Psalms 37:21). "A hired worker's wages should not remain with you overnight until the morning" (Leviticus 19:13) and, "Give him his wages in the day, so that the sun will not set upon it" (Deuteronomy 24:15).

As our sages said, "A day worker is to collect his wages all day and all night, and a night worker is to collect his wages all night and all day" (*Babba Metziah* 110B), "Regardless of[13] payments for animals, people or utensils, you still trespass

---

5. . . . the monetary consequences of loaning before . . .

6. That's to say, if you're directed in Deuteronomy 15:2 to nullify all debts at the time of the *Shmittah* year and you're nonetheless warned in verses 7–9 not to refrain from loaning money from the outset despite that, it follows that withholding a loan when you *can* collect on it is all the more so forbidden.

7. i.e., refraining from loaning money . . .

8. . . . even . . .

9. . . . the need for . . .

10. The phrase, "Whoever averts his eyes from charity is like an idol worshipper" could more literally be translated as "Whoever *raises* his eyes from charity is like a *star* worshipper." And that would be because star worshippers raise their eyes toward "higher," albeit impotent, forces to do what they themselves should. As such we should keep our eyes focused on each other's needs, rather than wait for help to come for them from God's other messengers. In fact, the story is told that a holy man once said that *everything* can be used for good. "But, how can atheism be used for good?" he was asked. And he responded, "When you're confronted with a poor man who needs your help, be an 'atheist' and don't depend on God's help for him. Provide him with help then and there yourself!"

11. i.e., regarding not loaning money . . .

12. i.e., regarding idol worshipping . . .

13. . . . whether you're overdue for . . .

the prohibition against delaying payment" (Ibid. 111A), and ". . . you[14] trespass the prohibition against delaying payment for[15] contracted-for workers" (Ibid.).

69. "His body shall not remain all night upon the tree" (Deuteronomy 21:23).[16]

One who allows a dead relative to remain[17] overnight transgresses a prohibition—unless he does so out of respect for him (*Sanhedrin* 46A).[18]

70. "You may not hide yourself" (Deuteronomy 22:3).[19]

This comes to alert you not to be lax when it comes to saving another's money, whether[20] goods or property. As our sages said,[21] " 'And every lost thing of your brother's, which he lost and you found, do likewise' (Deuteronomy 22:3) includes loss of property. So if, for example, a flood was coming toward his property, you'd be obliged to set up barricades against it" (*Babba Metziah* 31A).

You're also being warned to try to rescue someone or offer him advice in times of trouble.[22] As it's written, "Do not stand by the blood of your neighbor" (Leviticus 19:16).[23]

---

14. . . . can also . . .

15. i.e., when it comes to . . .

16. The verse refers to the corpse of a criminal hanged by court order, but it's universalized here to refer to the respect due all corpses.

17. . . . unburied . . .

18. i.e., to allow for the arrival of an important member of the family at the funeral or the like. (See note 2 above at this point.)

19. Immediately preceding this (in vv. 1–3) is found the injunction, "You must not watch your brother's ox or sheep go astray and hide yourself from them. You must in each case return them to your brother. And if your brother is not near you, or if you do not know him, then you must bring it to your own house, and it will be with you until your brother searches it out, when you must restore it to him. You must do the same with his donkey, and you will do that with his garment, and every lost thing of your brother's, which he lost and you found, do likewise. *You may not hide yourself.*"

20. . . . in the form of . . .

21. . . . the expression . . .

22. That is, if we're obliged to use all available resources to rescue someone's cattle, we should all the more so use all our personal resources to rescue him himself—which is the thrust of the very next ¶. (See note 2 above about this point.)

23. The text continues with the following:

As Solomon put it, "If you faint in the day of adversity, your strength will be small" (Proverbs 24:10). That means to say, if you're able to help somebody by offering him advice, or by doing something for him, but you appear as if you haven't the ability or strength, your strength will [then] diminish [as a consequence, and you'll be compensated for that] measure for measure. For as it then says, "If you say, 'Behold, we did not know about it'—Does He who ponders the heart not understand? And does He who keeps your soul not know of it? Will He not respond to everyone according to his conduct?" (Ibid. v. 12). As such it follows that If you refrain from helping someone or from offering him practical advice, God will then consider that to be "your conduct" [and will respond to you accordingly].

71. It would be very good to have knowledgeable volunteers in each and every city ready and prepared to help any Jewish man or woman in trouble. Because if you're obliged to be involved with[24] your brother's ox or sheep when it goes astray, and to hold onto it until he comes to ask for it (Deuteronomy 22:1–2),[25] how much more so should you show their owners honor and respect.[26] As it's written, "Bring the outcast poor into your house" (Isaiah 58:7).

72. "Criticize your neighbor diligently, and do not bear sin on his account" (Leviticus 19:17).[27]

This comes to alert you not to incur sin because of your neighbor's sin[28] by not criticizing him. For if someone sins and his sin becomes known, the entire community will suffer the consequences of his sin if it doesn't criticize and admonish him. As such, it's written, "Did not Achan Ben Zerach trespass against the devoted thing, and did not wrath fell on all the community of Israel? That man did not perish alone in his iniquity" (Joshua 22:20) and, "The revealed[29] belongs to us and our children forever"[30] (Deuteronomy 29:28). And if Gentiles[31] said, ". . . that we may know who is to blame for this bad" (Jonah 1:7), how much more so must we Jews, who are responsible for each other[32] (*Sanhedrin* 27B).

73. In order to be spared such consequences, it's important to appoint honest individuals and to set courageous men over the people to act as overseers in the marketplaces and townships, in order to oversee their neighbors, and to criticize them for every act of defiance. And to thus eradicate wrongdoing.[33]

74. "When you make a vow to God your Lord, do not delay in implementing it" (Deuteronomy 23:22).

There are consequences to vacillating fulfilling vows and charity pledges, even when you fulfill them afterward. So if you vow to give charity to the poor, you're obliged to implement it right away. And if you delay because you forgot, you'd nonetheless certainly have to suffer the consequences for that. For you know people

---

24. . . . recapturing . . .
25. See note 19.
26. . . . by caring for them and maintaining their upkeep.
27. See Supplementary Notes.
28. . . . as you would . . .
29. i.e., revealed, exposed sins . . .
30. . . . and are our responsibility.
31. i.e., the sailors on the ship Jonah was on, on his way to Nineveh . . .
32. That's to say, if the sailors on that ship knew enough to find out who was to blame when the ship was about to capsize, and to then criticize him and have him do whatever he had to do so that they wouldn't suffer the consequences of his sin, shouldn't we do the same? For after all, as Jews we're all "in the same boat," as the expression goes. That thus proves to be the import of the verse, "Criticize your neighbor diligently, and do not bear sin on his account." Which is to say, we're to criticize our fellow Jew when he sins, or else we'll suffer the consequences of his actions, since our destiny is tied inexorably to his.
33. See Supplementary Notes.

forget things, so you should have kept your vows in mind all the time in order not to forget.[34] As it's said, "It is a snare for a man to declare rashly, 'This is sanctified!,' and to inquire only after making his vows" (Proverbs 20:25).

In fact, you'd have to suffer significant consequences for such acts of defiance, for it's said, "Do not let your mouth cause your flesh to sin, and do not say before the angel that it was a mistake. For why should God be angry at your voice, and destroy the work of your hands?" (Ecclesiastes 5:5). That's to say, "Do not let your mouth cause your flesh to sin"—by making a vow you're not going to be careful enough to fulfill, and thus bring guilt upon yourself? But we've already explained this verse in *The Gates of the Restrictions Involved in Caution.*[35]

As our sages said, "Children die as a consequence of the sin of[36] vows, as it's said, 'For why should God be angry at your voice, and destroy the work of your hands?'[37] (Ibid.)" (*Shabbat* 32B). This verse can also serve to explain[38] slander,[39] since you'd have to suffer the consequences of that act of defiance even when you didn't intend to insult the other person.

We're even commanded not to take vows. As it's said, "It will not be considered a sin if you withhold from vowing" (Deuteronomy 23:23), which our sages explained to mean that "if you vow, that *will* be considered a sin on your part, since vows are pitfalls for those who make them" (*Nedarim* 77B), because they might fail to fulfill them, or vacillate in them.

A righteous person who's[40] generous, gives without vowing, except when he's in danger and he has to (as in, "And Jacob vowed a vow, saying . . ." [Genesis 28:20]); and except when the leaders of Israel gather together to institute vows to bolster the weak-willed.

---

34. See Supplementary Notes.
35. To our great dismay, this work no longer exists (see ¶66).
36. . . . not implementing . . .
37. i.e., your children.
38. . . . the serious consequences for uttering . . .
39. See Supplementary Notes.
40. . . . always . . .

Chapter Nine

75. The Fifth Level: Prohibitions Involving an Action[1]

Our sages said, "A prohibition involving an action incurs flogging" (*Makkot* 16A) and that "flogging is[2] forty stripes minus one" (Ibid. 22A). They also said that, "Flogging stands in place of a death sentence" (*Sanhedrin* 10A) and that "One who is flogged and repeats his crime is to be jailed" (Ibid. 81B).[3]

It's incumbent upon all who criticize the people[4] to scrutinize their ways, to determine and know where they stumble, and to thus alert them.[5] Because people are sometimes careful about part of a prohibition and careless about the rest (as happens in the case of the prohibition against[6] *malachot*[7] on the Sabbath, which Sabbath observers sometimes transgress[8]).

But there are some *malachot* that some of the people aren't careful about at all, since they're unaware of them. And they thus continue to make mistakes as a consequence of not dwelling among scholars, and thus not asking to learn Torah

---

1. From ¶26 to now we'd been discussing prohibitions involving no action. We now begin to discuss those that do.
2. . . . the administration of . . .
3. See the very end of this section, at ¶106, where we harken back to this point in our note there. And notice there, too, the great reward for being cautious in these things: the numinous ability to "irradiate like the lights of the sky," even though many of these requirements may seem trivial or mundane to the modern mind.
4. i.e., all rabbis, teachers, pedants, and spiritual guides.
5. . . . when they err. (See Supplementary Notes.)
6. . . . certain . . .
7. i.e., forbidden actions.
8. . . . in part, as was just indicated.

from them. So they commit transgressions and suffer the consequences. As it's said, "Though a favor will be shown to a wrongdoer,[9] he will nonetheless not learn righteousness" (Isaiah 26:10). Thus, many defiant people stumble[10] because they weren't trained in childhood, in their father's house, to be careful in these things. They've thus inherited foolishness, don't listen to their teachers, and sin on purpose.[11]

76. And so while everyone is careful not to ingest animal blood (both the primary,[12] and secondary[13]), some are nonetheless careless about preparing meat with salt, in order to remove the blood left over in it,[14] as they must.

There are very many other instances of this[15] when there's neither knowledge nor criticism.[16] For, "When there is no overseeing, the people cast off all restraints" (Proverbs 29:18).

77. And there are prohibitions that some people transgress outright, like[17] injuring or striking someone. In fact, you transgress two prohibitions if you strike someone. As it's said, "Forty stripes he may give him but no more, lest . . . your brother seem vile to you" (Deuteronomy 25:3).[18] In fact, many men transgress against these prohibitions by striking their wives.[19]

Our sages also said, "Whoever raises a hand against another is called 'a wrongdoer' even if he does not strike. As it is said, 'And he said to *the wrongdoer,* "Why would you strike your neighbor?"' (Exodus 2:13). Notice, it does not say, "Why *did* you strike" but rather, "Why *would* you strike"[20] (*Sanhedrin* 58B). And Job said, "If I have lifted up my hand against an orphan . . . Let my arm fall from my shoulder blade, and my arm be broken from the bone" (31:21–22).

Our sages also said, "Rav Hunah would have the hand of someone who strikes

---

9. i.e., despite the fact that God Almighty has given us His Torah . . .

10. . . . only . . .

11. . . . as a tragic but natural consequence.

12. i.e., the blood that emits from the animal at slaughtering.

13. i.e., the blood that emits from the carcass after the slaughtering.

14. i.e., yet remaining in the pores of the flesh.

15. i.e., of a lack of the more subtle applications of the prohibitions.

16. i.e., of instruction.

17. . . . those against . . .

18. The two prohibitions are indicated by the terms "but no more" and "lest" (see ¶67). That's to say, though there are certainly to be court-imposed sentences of flogging, a single blow above the fixed number is forbidden in that instance. So it stands to reason that individuals are forbidden to strike each other for no good reason.

19. The *halacha* clearly forbids doing that. And warns against it in the strongest of terms, labeling such a practice utterly un-Jewish. See the *Haga'ah* in *Even HaEzer* 154:3 for the definitive statement about this; and *Hilchot Chovel* 5:1 for the warning against striking children.

20. Hence, he was called a wrongdoer despite the fact that he hadn't yet struck the other person.

another cut off. As it's said, 'The uplifted arm shall be broken' (Job 38:15)" (*Sanhedrin* 58B).

78. The same goes for shaving your beard, as it's said, "Do not shave the corners of your beard" (Leviticus 19:27).

Certain sinners leave behind only a wisp of hair. But since we don't know exactly where the corners of the beard lie, these individuals are acting like "ruthless children" (Isaiah 1:4) when it comes to those corners of the beard.

And trimming the corners of your scalp[21] with scissors is as forbidden as shaving.

79. Some people aren't careful about avoiding *shatnez* in their clothing,[22] and either sew linen threads into woolen garments, or they hem a woolen garment with linen.

80. "None of you may draw close to anyone who is near of kin to him" (Leviticus 18:6).

All[23] contact is forbidden, such as shaking[24] a married woman's hand.[25] And it's referred to as "uncovering nakedness"[26] because "drawing close" leads to promiscuity.

Should you interject, "But where in this verse do we find the Torah setting a limit that would lead us to say that hand-to-hand contact is forbidden as a defense against[27] sin?" We would answer that the prohibition is derived from the mitzvah of *Nazir.*[28] For the latter is essentially based upon[29] "Lest he drink, and forget the decree" (Proverbs 31:5) and that "the spirit of harlotry" will "have them make mistakes" (Hosea 4:12). Hence, the Torah[30] forbids anything "produced from the grape vine" (Numbers 6:4). And the other restrictions are intended to act as a

---

21. i.e., the *peyot* or "sidelock" area.

22. See Leviticus 19:19, "You will keep My statutes. You must not let your cattle breed with a different kind; you must not sow your field with mixed seed; *nor may a garment mixed of linen and wool come upon you.*" The latter refers to *shatnez.*

23. . . . forms of extraneous physical . . .

24. Literally, "touching."

25. See Supplementary Notes.

26. The very next verse reads, "None of you may approach any who is near of kin to him, *to uncover their nakedness.*"

27. . . . a greater . . .

28. See Numbers 6:2–4 (cited partially below), which says, "When a man or woman will separate themselves to take a Nazirite vow, in order to separate themselves for God, he should sever himself from wine and strong drink, and drink neither vinegar, wine, nor strong drink. Nor may he drink any liquor of grapes, or eat moist grapes, or dried. He must eat nothing that is produced from the grape vine, from the seeds to the grape skin all the days of his separation." (See Supplementary Notes.)

29. . . . the dual concerns . . .

30. . . . itself . . .

defense against and a deterrent to his drinking wine, as our sages pointed out in the Midrash (*Shemot Rabbah* 16:2).[31]

81. "Do not place an impediment[32] before a blind person" (Leviticus 19:14).

Our sages remarked (*Moed Kattan* 17A) that you're being alerted here not to strike your full-grown child, as that might cause him to falter and stumble as a result, and sin verbally by insulting you.[33]

You're also being alerted here not to set a sin-impediment before any Jew or Gentile. For example: to not offer a cup of wine to a *Nazir*,[34] a limb torn off of a live animal to a *Ben-Noach*,[35] or to hand him anything forbidden that already belongs to him (*Avodah Zarah* 6B). Similarly, if a Gentile comes to buy incense or candles from you to use as an offering to an idol, you may not sell it to him. Nor may you sell him heretical books, or cause him to stumble in any of the other areas *B'nei-Noach*[36] have been warned about.

82. "Do not destroy its trees by wielding an ax against them" (Deuteronomy 20:19).

You're being alerted here not to cut down fruit-bearing trees, even to build a fortress,[37] as long as there are enough bare trees.

You're also being alerted not to squander money—even a *prutah's* worth.[38] As our sages said, "One who rends more of his clothing than he must[39] for his dead relative incurs flagellation" (*Babba Kama* 91B). All the more so if you break things in anger. For you'd then be doing two bad things: wasting money, and giving your anger license to sin against the Torah.[40] Since you'd be thrust then into a battle with your impulse to be angry,[41] which would have you sin against the faith. As it's

---

31. That's to say, the fundamental prohibition against having illicit relations with someone is expanded to include not having extraneous contact with her, so as to prevent the former—just as the fundamental prohibition for a Nazir is against drinking wine, which is expanded to include not having extraneous contact with grape products, so as to prevent the former.

32. Literally, "A stumbling block."

33. . . . to say nothing of the fact that he may stumble by striking back at you.

34. . . . who may not drink it (see previous ¶) . . .

35. Literally, "A Child of Noah," which is to say, a Gentile who observes the seven Noachite Laws, which involve not eating a torn limb from a live animal (as indicated here), not blaspheming the name of God, not stealing, establishing a legal system, not worshipping idols, not murdering, and not having illicit relations.

36. Literally, "*Children* of Noah," referring to those Gentiles discussed in the previous note.

37. . . . in wartime . . .

38. A "prutah" is a coin of the smallest denomination, equivalent to a penny.

39. . . . in mourning . . .

40. See Supplementary Notes.

41. i.e., "with your temper."

written, "A furious person abounds in defiance" (Proverbs 29:22). We've already cited what our sages said about this,[42] that, "You are to consider anyone who breaks things when he is angry an idol worshiper. Because that is the way of the yetzer harah—today it tells you to do thus-and-such, and tomorrow it tells you to worship other gods!" (*Shabbat* 105B).

Our sages also said, "You may not pour the water out of your well when others need it" (*Yevamot* 44A). And we've been alerted not to expose our body to danger, or to pummel and waste it away for no reason, or endanger it, by fasting when you're troubled, angry, or mourning for your dead.[43] Nonetheless, if you fast or mourn[44] for your sins, it's then said of you, "I have seen his ways, and will heal him. I will lead him also, and comfort him and his mourners" (Isaiah 57:18).

It's also said, "I will surely require blood for your lives" (Genesis 9:5), which our sages explained to mean, "I will require your blood if it is shed by your own hands"[45] (*Babba Kama* 91B).[46]

83.   "It is *orlah* to you for three years, do not eat it" (Leviticus 19:23).[47]

The prohibitions against *orlah* are observed outside of Israel,[48] and you can't benefit from it.[49] And since something that a Jew can't benefit from, can't be given as a gift to a Gentile, the Torah had to[50] allow you to give unkosher-slaughtered meat to a Gentile, to let you know that the latter can be benefited from. Hence it says, "You must not eat any unkosher-slaughtered meat. Give it to the stranger in your gates, who may eat it . . ." (Deuteronomy 14:21). But if you give *orlah* to a Gentile, or *chometz*[51] on Passover, or meat cooked in milk,[52] you'd incur flagellation, just as you would if you'd given it to your dog to eat.[53]

The mitzvah to burn *orlah* or *kilei hakerem*[54] is observed in Israel as well as outside of Israel. Hence, if a Gentile has a tree with *orlah* fruits you can't take any of it off for him, even if you charge him nothing to, since you'd be benefiting from

---

42. See 1:38.

43. The point is that "wasting" also implies endangering something (your body, in this case) so much so that it can't be used to full advantage. (See Supplementary Notes.)

44. . . . in order to do tshuvah . . .

45. i.e., if you commit suicide.

46. We're being warned, over all, not to undervalue or take for granted anything bestowed upon you by God—from your clothing, utensils, food, and money, to your body, and your very life.

47. "Orlah" is fruit from a tree, which may not be eaten, sold, etc., for the tree's first three years.

48. . . . as well as in . . .

49. i.e., from the fruit.

50. . . . explicitly . . .

51. i.e., leavened bread.

52. . . . at any time . . .

53. Of course that's not to equate a Gentile to a dog, but only to underscore the fact that you can't derive benefit from it one way or the other.

54. "Kilei hakerem" are mixed fruits, and the prohibition against it is based on the

the fact that the Gentile would admire you for it.[55] You're also forbidden to offer a Gentile his very own[56] wine to drink, either for payment or gratuitously.

You also can't benefit from *kerem reva'i*[57] either, unless you redeem them[58] (*Babba Kama* 69A). And they can't be redeemed until they enter the tithing stage, which starts when their fruits have completely ripened. As our sages taught, "When are fruits required to be tithed? In the case of dates, . . ." (*Maaserot* 1:2).

84. "Therefore the people of Israel do not eat of the sinew of the vein which is in the hollow of the thigh" (Genesis 32:32).

It's forbidden to benefit from the sinew of the vein, and to give it to your Gentile servant, male or female. You also can't give a Gentile a thigh with the sinew in it, or feed the sinew or the fat surrounding it to your dog or cat.

85. "Do not steal, deal falsely, or lie" (Leviticus 19:11).

Our sages said, "Do not steal in order to disturb someone" (*Babba Metziah* 61B). That is, don't say, "I'll steal this thing in order to aggravate and disturb its owner, so that he'll[59] be careful with his things. Then I'll give it back to him." It's also forbidden to take something from someone's house underhandedly, use it, then return it to him.

And you must never steal back something that was stolen from you, in order not to appear to be a thief (*Babba Kama* 27B).

86. "Do not recite incantations, and do not observe times" (Leviticus 19:26).

"Do not recite incantations"—like those who recite them over weasels or birds, or say it's a sign of upcoming failure if a piece of bread falls from a person's mouth or a deer crosses his path (*Sanhedrin* 65B), etc., who then counsel a change of tack. That's to say, don't consult with those who practice incantation in order to decide whether or not to do something.

"Do not observe times"[60]—like those who say, "Such-and-such day would be good for starting that" or, "It's not good to go at such-and-such a time."[61]

---

verse, "You must not sow your vineyard with different seeds. For the fruit of your seed which you have sown and the fruit of your vineyard will be defiled" (Deuteronomy 22:9).

55. Hence we see that there is emotional as well as material benefit to be derived from certain things (which are both forbidden, in this case).

56. . . . forbidden . . .

57. Literally, "fruit of the vine of the fourth year," the prohibition against which is based on the verse, "But in the fourth year all its fruit shall be holy for praise-giving to God" (Leviticus 19:24).

58. That is, unless you set their cash value aside, and expend it in Jerusalem.

59. . . . learn to . . .

60. The text continues with the following:

. . . [The term "לא עונה"] derives from the term for periods of time or hours, "עונות."

61. We'd refer to such individuals as "soothsayers."

Don't listen to astrologers either, but trust wholeheartedly in God, the Lord of the Heavens and earth instead. That's why it's said about this, "Be guileless with God your Lord" (Deuteronomy 18:13), which comes to teach us that those who observe times and recite incantations lack trust.[62] Such perverse practices were pursued in Canaan, as it's said, "The nations whom you will overtake listen to those who observe times and who recite incantations. But as for you, God your Lord has not allowed you to do that" (Ibid. v. 14).

87. "Do not be unjust in judgment" (Leviticus 19:15), which is immediately followed by, "Do not respect the person of the poor, nor favor the person of the powerful; but judge your neighbor in righteousness" (Ibid.).[63]

What kind of "judgment" is being referred to at the beginning of the verse? Our sages said it refers to[64] dimensions, weights, and quantity (*Torat Cohanim, Kedoshim* 8:5–6). That comes to teach you that one who calculates dimensions is tantamount to a judge, and that when he falsifies dimensions, he debases judgment, and is to be referred to as "unjust," "appalling," "odious," and "despicable." In fact, he brings on the same five things one who's unjust in judgment does: he contaminates the land, profanes God's name, removes the Divine Presence, impales the people upon the sword, and expels them from their land.

"Dimensions" refers to the dimensions of the Land of Israel, "weights" is self-explanatory, and "quantity" refers to the quantity of both dry and perishable goods. "Just weights" refers to the weights used on a scale. An *ephah* is a dry weight, while a *hin* is the weight used for perishables.

"For I am God your Lord who brought you out from the land in Egypt" (Leviticus 19:35–36)[65]—in Egypt I differentiated between the seed of the firstborn and the others. So, I'm sure to demand payment from one who dips his weights in salt to defraud those who are unaware.[66]

88. "If you lend money . . . do not be[67] a creditor to him" (Exodus 22:24).

---

62. It's forbidden to pursue these practices both because you prove to be "dependent" on them rather than on God (as one meaning of "trust"—בטחון—can be "dependence"). And because you rely on extraneous "signs" for revelation of God's will, which have nothing to do with Torah, which *is* His revealed will. (See Supplementary Notes.)

63. That's to say, the end of the verse refers to obligations upon a judge, while the beginning seems to refer to obligations upon the individual. Rabbeinu Yonah is about to explain the connection between the two.

64. . . . the "judging" or calculating of . . .

65. The entire verse reads, "Do not be unjust in judgment, in dimensions, weights, or quantity. You must have just scales, just weights, a just *ephah*, and a just *hin*. For I am God your Lord who brought you out from the land of Egypt."

66. That's to say, if God could distinguish the subtle differences between one sperm and another, He can certainly sense the presence of salt on a scale.

67. i.e., do not *act* like . . .

You're being alerted here not to vex anyone who borrows from you, and not to approach him when you know he can't meet a payment. For you'd thus be oppressing and disheartening him. As our sages said, "It would be like sentencing him twice,[68] as in, 'You have caused men to ride over our heads; we went through fire and water' (Psalms 66:12)" (*Babba Metziah* 75B).

And it's important to incite fervent reactions to, and to criticize those scourges among our people in certain places who bind debtors in chains when they're in no position to make payment!

89. "Do not charge him interest" (Exodus 22:24).

This comes to alert witnesses that loaners, borrowers, guarantors, *and* witnesses[69] commit a prohibition[70] (*Babba Metziah* 75B). And so "Do not charge" is written in the plural[71] after the singular "Do not be a creditor to him"[72] in order to alert witnesses.

90. "There may be no blemish in it" (Leviticus 22:21).

You're being alerted here not to bring about a blemish in a firstborn animal, even in our days.[73]

91. "Do not plow with an ox and a donkey together" (Deuteronomy 22:10).

You're being alerted here not to plow or thresh with two different species joined together by a yoke or by rope. The same applies to moving them along while they're joined, but plowing is specified because that's the usual situation. It's even forbidden to move them along by voice alone[74] (*Babba Metziah* 90B). And two mules, one of whom was a product of a horse and the other whom was a product of a donkey, are also considered two different species (*Chullin* 79A), and can't be moved along together. It's also forbidden to move along a mule with either a horse or a donkey (*Kelaim* 1:6).

"Do not let your cattle breed with a different kind" (Leviticus 19:19).

A mule that's to be mated is not to be paired with either a horse or a donkey, but rather with a mule of its own kind (*Chullin* 79A). As, for example, when the she-mule's mother and the he-mule's mother are equivalent, and both come from either a horse or a donkey.

92. "Do not set up any image of stone in your land to bow down to" (Leviticus 26:1).

You're being alerted here not to bow down upon a stone floor either in a

---

68. i.e., first to repayment, and second to vexation.

69. . . . to a loan on interest. . . .

70. . . . by complying.

71. "לא תשימון."

72. "לא תהיה לו בנשה."

73. . . . when there's no longer a Holy Temple, and such a blemish will do nothing to affect the animal's status as a sacrifice.

74. i.e., by verbal command.

synagogue (*Megillah* 22B) or anywhere else outside of the Holy Temple (*Torat Cohanim* 9:5).

93. "Do not make yourselves despicable" (Leviticus 11:43).

You're being alerted here not to eat anything repulsive, and to thus not eat fish or grasshoppers until they're dead (*Shabbat* 90B). And that it's also forbidden to drink from a blood-letting beaker. One who inhibits his bowels[75] also transgresses the prohibition against making yourself despicable (*Makkot* 16B).

94. "Do not profane your daughter to be a harlot, so the land will not fall to harlotry, and thus become full of lewdness" (Leviticus 19:29).

Our sages explained that this verse comes to alert you not to hand your unmarried daughter over for intercourse for any reason other than marriage (*Torat Cohanim* 7:1–4). ". . . So the land will not fall to harlotry"—that's to say that if you do,[76] then the land itself will fall to harlotry and will bear its fruit elsewhere, rather than in your country.[77] As it's said, "And so the showers have been withheld and there has been no latter rain, yet you have a harlot's forehead . . ." (Jeremiah 3:3).

Only a king is permitted to keep a concubine without a marriage contract or betrothal, because people fear him. As a consequence, other women wouldn't succumb to harlotry along with her.[78] That's why a king's pairing with a concubine is like marriage. But since a king was allowed a concubine, our sages decreed that a woman who hasn't completed the marriage ceremony[79] is as forbidden to her husband[80] as a menstruant would be to her husband.

95. You can understand what serious consequences would result from designating an unmarried daughter for harlotry from the fact that it's said, "So the land will not fall to harlotry, and thus become full of lewdness" (Leviticus 19:29). That's why you'd incur flagellation if you have intercourse with an unmarried girl just one time (though by means of the "defiance" type[81] the sages instituted).

Nonetheless, that's aside from the great and terrible impediments that befall those who have intercourse with an unmarried girl, who's too embarrassed to immerse in a river or a *mikveh* to be purified of her impurity,[82] because word about her prostituting herself will get out to the public. And so she'll remain impure, for[83]

---

75. Or, refrains from moving his bowels.

76. . . . hand your unmarried daughter over for intercourse for any reason other than marriage . . .

77. . . . just as a harlot would bear your illegitimate children elsewhere, rather than in your home.

78. i.e., the king's concubine.

79. Literally, "without a blessing," which alludes to the marriage ceremony.

80. . . . to be . . .

81. . . . of flogging . . .

82. . . . as any woman would have to do before having intercourse . . .

83. . . . as it's said . . .

"Her impurity was in her skirts; she gave no thought to her fate" (Lamentations 1:9).

Our sages also said that, "'Do not profane your daughter to be a harlot' (Leviticus 19:29) is a warning not to marry your daughter to an old man" (*Sanhedrin* 76A).

96. "Do not eat from an animal carcass" (Deuteronomy 14:21).

Our sages said, "Any animal that becomes defective when slaughtered is a carcass" (*Chullin* 32A).[84]

How wonderful It would be if those who admonish the people would alert them to be scrupulous in the details of kosher slaughtering; to satisfy its requirements; and to select a God-fearing, knowledgeable *shochet*[85] for each community.

Because a great many Jews depend on him for their meat slaughtering and inspection. And though the sages said that, "Most *shochetim* are experts" (*Chullin* 3B), there are nonetheless places where there is neither serious enough concern, nor those to admonish.[86] So the many people there use *shochetim* who are consequently not expert.

We also see many experts who are nonetheless far from God-fearing, to our great dismay. And if one is not God-fearing, he won't be determined to be meticulous about inspecting the[87] knife, when he'd have to concentrate so very intently to do that. Haven't you yourself seen many instances where someone who'd inspected his knife[88] two and three times without sensing a subtle nick, suddenly sensed it only because he concentrated that last time? For the sense of touch is only as accurate as one's concentration.[89] And that's beside the fact that a non-devout individual would continue to act defiantly by refusing to inspect the animal for other signs and indications that all is in accordance with what's clearly required by all who know the law.

97. "Do not take a bribe" (Exodus 23:8)—even if you do so to free the innocent or indict the guilty (*Ketubot* 105A). And even if both parties to the case agree to pay you together.[90] For as our sages said, "The decision of anyone who takes payment to judge a case is null and void" (Ibid.).

---

84. That's to say, any animal that's incorrectly slaughtered is as forbidden to us as a carcass that wasn't at all slaughtered.

85. i.e., ritual slaughterer.

86. . . . wrongdoers.

87. . . . slaughtering . . .

88. . . . for disqualifying nicks . . .

89. The knife in this instance is symbolic of the individual himself, who passes swiftly and purposefully through time, being, and life itself. And charges forever forward as events, consequences, and all sorts of things pass him by, to his sides. Unless such a person concentrates upon his character and being, and remains introspective, he'll overlook the very "subtle nicks" and blemishes that would render him "unkosher."

90. i.e., equally.

Nonetheless litigants are allowed to reimburse judges for the money they lose by being taken away from their business, as long as the amount is clear, delineated, and known of by all. And as long as one party doesn't pay more of that fee than the other.

98. Our sages said, "'Do not take a bribe'—implies even a verbal bribe" (*Ketubot* 105B). So, for example, if one of the litigants tries to ingratiate himself to the judge, that judge should remove himself from the case.

If a litigant brings the judge a gift as he comes before him, the judge isn't to accept it. And if the gift was offered and he took it, that judge becomes disqualified to try the case.

99. "No sort of work should be done in them,[91] except for what everyone must eat" (Exodus 12:16).

Our sages said, "Since carrying was permitted for eating purposes on the Holy Day, it was also permitted for[92] other than eating purposes" (*Betzah* 12A). As long as it was done for the needs of the day. They also said you can take a Torah scroll out to the public domain on the Holy Day to read from there, and on that day. But you can't take it out for just any reason—only for the needs of the Holy Day.

Many people sin by taking their storehouse keys out with them to the public domain even when there's no food there to be eaten on the Holy Day.[93]

100. "A man should not wear woman's clothing" (Deuteronomy 22:5).

That's to alert you not to shave your underarm or pubic hair[94] (*Nazir* 59A).

101. "Do not bring any blood upon your house" (Deuteronomy 22:8).

That's to alert you not to keep either a vicious dog or a defective ladder into your house (*Ketubot* 41B).[95]

102. "Do no work with your firstborn bull, nor shear your firstborn sheep" (Deuteronomy 15:19).

The prohibition against working the firstborn is to be observed both in Israel and outside. A firstborn that intermingles with a hundred or[96] a thousand[97] makes it forbidden to benefit from the lot of them.

103. "Do not do so to God your Lord" (Deuteronomy 12:4).

This is to alert you against erasing God's name[98] (*Makkot* 22A).

---

91. i.e., in the course of the Holy Days.

92. . . . reasons . . .

93. . . . and thus their keys carry no functional Holy Day purpose.

94. . . . aside from the literal sense of the verse.

95. See Supplementary Notes.

96. . . . even . . .

97. . . . other animals . . .

98. i.e., one of the seven special, sanctified names. This is best understood in the context of the verse that immediately precedes it, which reads: "Overthrow their altars, and break their pillars, and burn their Ashera-trees with fire; cut down the carved images of their gods, and *destroy their names out of that place.*"

104. "Do not follow along in their ordinances" (Leviticus 18:3).

You're being alerted here to dissociate yourself from Amorite ways,[99] including reciting incantations, and using amulets whose healing capability hasn't been proved.

105. "You may eat neither bread, parched grain, nor green ears of corn until that very day" (Leviticus 23:14).

"New" grain[100] is forbidden by the Torah itself, even outside of Israel (*Kiddushin* 37A).

106. We've now listed some of the things that many inadvertently and unknowingly sin against. Either because it was never told to them, or because they were never aware of how significant a prohibition it entailed, though they knew it was prohibited.

We've also mentioned them so that people wouldn't persevere in their sins inadvertently. "A sage would hear and increase learning" (Proverbs 1:5), and will alert the people about other such things they might come across. And the knowing will be careful and will thus irradiate like the lights of the sky (cf. Daniel 12:3).

---

99. . . . of doing things . . .
100. i.e., the types of grain referred to in this verse . . .

Chapter Ten

ᘓᘔᘓᘔᘓᘔᘓᘔᘓᘔᘓᘔᘓᘔᘓᘔᘓᘔᘓᘔᘓᘔ

107. The Sixth Level: Sins Incurring Death Through the Hands of Heaven[1]

The difference between death[2] and excision is that if one is sentenced to death, only he rather than his descendants is so sentenced. Whereas if he's to suffer the consequences of excision, both he and they are excised.[3]

Nonetheless our sages said, "On one level and in a certain sense, death[4] is more serious than excision. For death comes up upon the windows[5] of one who's culpable for death at the hands of Heaven.[6] His animals and livestock die, his cow grazes in ash then dies, his chicken feeds on filth then dies, and death attaches itself onto him until it consumes him" (*Pesachim* 32B).[7]

108. Some of those culpable for death at the hands of Heaven are listed in

---

1. The gist of this section is as follows: There are instances in which someone deserves to die because of something onerous he's done, but for one reason or another an earthly court isn't empowered to carry out that sentence. Nonetheless, justice will be done, and Heaven will see to it that the guilty person dies one way or another, or is excised, for his crime.

2. i.e., by Heaven rather than by a court of law.

3. See notes 12 to 3:2 for an explanation of excision, and our use of the term. (See Supplementary Notes.)

4. See note 2 above.

5. Based on Jeremiah 9:20, "For death has come up into our windows, and has entered into our palaces..."

6. That is, it's to be found wherever he looks.

7. See Supplementary Notes.

the Mishna.[8] They include those who eat *tevel*, i.e., grain from which *trumah*[9] and *ma'aser*[10] haven't been removed, which is thus still deficient. The mitzvah[11] is observed in Israel, and affects impure *cohanim* who eat pure *trumah* and a non-*cohen* who eats[12] *trumah*.

109. Others of them were enunciated by our sages in the Talmud and Midrash.[13] Most, however, can be extracted directly from verses.

They include those who afflict widows and orphans.[14] As it's said, "Do not afflict any widow or orphan. For if you afflict them . . . My anger will rage and I will slay you with the sword . . ." (Exodus 22:21–23).

Our sages added that that holds regardless of whether they cry out or not (Mechiltah, Neziikin 8), which means to say that the consequences for afflicting widows and orphans will be the same regardless of whether your victim cries out as a result of what you did or doesn't. But, retribution will come more quickly when that orphan cries out to God.

110. It includes those who steal from the poor. As it's said, "Do not steal from the poor because he is poor . . . For God will plead their case, and steal the life of those who steal from them" (Proverbs 22:22–23). But we've already explained this above, in the third level.[15]

As our sages put it, "Stealing from the poor is tantamount to taking their very souls. For it is said, 'Such are the ways of all who are greedy of gain; it takes the soul of its owners' (Proverbs 1:19)" (*Babba Kama* 119A). For there are times when he's deprived of his entire source of income if you steal less than a *prutah's*-worth from him.[16] As a consequence, you'd be accredited with having spilled his blood by stealing a[17] *prutah's*-worth.

111. It includes those who ruin a reputation. As it's said, "The men who issued a bad report about the land died by plague before God" (Numbers 14:37). And as our sages said, "If those who gave the land[18] a bad reputation were sentenced to death, one who gives a Jew" who observes Torah and *mitzvot*—a bad name should all the more so be" (*Aruchin* 15A).

It's also said, "And they will fine him a hundred shekels of silver, and give them

---

8. See *Sanhedrin* 3:1, *Challah* 1:9, etc.

9. The *Cohen's* portion. See Deuteronomy 18:3–4.

10. The tithe. See Leviticus 27:32; Deuteronomy 14:22–29.

11. i.e., the prohibition against eating *tevel.*

12. . . . any sort of . . .

13. See *Berachot* 4B, *Eruvin* 21B, *Sotah* 4B, etc.

14. See Supplementary Notes.

15. See ¶24.

16. As we've already indicated, a *prutah* is the smallest denomination of coin, equivalent to a penny.

17. . . . mere . . .

18. . . . of Israel (see context) . . .

to the father of the girl,[19] because he ruined the reputation of a virgin of Israel" (Deuteronomy 22:19). Notice that the verse says nothing about the man's sinful desire to have the girl's life taken, or to have her sentenced to death in court through[20] his false witnesses to the fact that she prostituted herself to him. Only that he transgressed by ruining her reputation. That's because the latter is an even greater sin than wanting someone killed.[21] For the torment of humiliation is bitterer yet than death.[22] And so our sages pointed out, "The verse exacted a sentence of flogging and a fine for ruining her reputation, but not for wanting her killed" (*Ketubot* 46A).

Our sages also said, "One who ruins the reputation of an entire bloodline can never be atoned for. As it would not be enough for him to be forgiven by those[23] alive now, since he maligned and shamed all who are to follow" (J. T., *Babba Kama* 8:7). But we'll clarify that further when we explain the significance of the sins of the "four types."[24]

112. Those who exploit children[25] or titillate themselves one way or another[26] are also thus culpable for death.[27] And our sages said, "He suffers the same consequences those of the generation of the flood, who were depraved did" (*Niddah* 13B).

The same goes for one who does what Eir and Onan did, by "threshing" within and "winnowing" without, in order to waste seed.[28] They, too, are culpable for death.[29] As it's said, "And what he did displeased God, so He executed him also" (Genesis 38:10). And it's said that those who spill seed in vain, "Burn with lust among the terebinths, under every green tree, slaying the children . . ." (Isaiah 57:5).

---

19. . . . whose reputation was ruined . . .

20. . . . the testimony of . . .

21. That is, in verses 20–21 following the one cited above we're told that if the man who besmirched her reputation succeeded in his plans, the young woman falsely accused would have been sentenced to death by the court. As it's written, "But if this thing [i.e., his accusation] is true . . . they shall bring out the girl to the door of her father's house, and the men of her city shall stone her with stones until she dies." Rabbeinu Yonah's point is that despite the seriousness of that, the Torah nonetheless chooses to stress the fact that he besmirched her reputation, and is to be punished for that. And it thus clearly places a lot of weight on that.

22. See Supplementary Notes.

23. . . . in the family . . .

24. See ¶208.

25. . . . sexually . . .

26. Literally, "by hand or by foot."

27. . . . at the hands of Heaven.

28. i.e., who engage in *coitus interruptus*.

29. . . . at the hands of Heaven.

113. Torah scholars who don't act demurely[30] are also culpable for death,[31] because they alienate people from the Torah. Our sages said that the verse, "Those who hate Me, love death" (Proverbs 8:36) alludes to them (*Shabbat* 114A), in that "Those who hate Me" refers to "those who cause Me to be hated" by having people hate Torah.

Our sages also said, "What people say when a person who studies Torah in depth speaks gently with others, when he conducts business ethically in the marketplace and is honest in his business affairs is, 'How fortunate is this one who has studied Torah! How fortunate are his father and mother who taught him Torah! Woe to those who do not study Torah! For you see how pleasant the ways of this one who studied Torah are, and how well he acts! The verse, "And He said to me, You are My servant, O Israel, in whom I will be glorified" (Isaiah 49:3) applies to him.' But what people say when a person who studies Torah in depth does *not* speak gently with others, does *not* conduct business ethically in the marketplace, and is *not* honest in his business affairs is, 'Woe to this one who studies Torah! And woe to his teacher and father who taught him Torah! People who do not study Torah are so fortunate! For you see how despicably this one who learned Torah acts, and how horrible his ways are! The verse, "They profane My holy name, when men said of them, These are the people of God, who have come from His land" (Ezekiel 36:20) applies to him' (*Yomah* 86A).

114. Our sages said, "Anyone with a *bet midrash*[32] in his town who does not attend it is culpable for death"[33] (*Derech Eretz Rabbah* 11).

115. One who challenges the authority of his teacher is culpable for death[34] (*Kallah*).

116. One who decides the *halacha* in front of his teacher is culpable for death[35] (*Eruvin* 63A). As our sages said, "When Nadav and Avihu offered an aberrant fire on the altar, they did not die because of the sin of having brought the offering, since all their intentions were for the sake of Heaven. For they argued that since it's written in the Torah that, 'The sons of Aaron . . . should place fire upon the altar' (Leviticus 1:7), that meant that though fire would descend from Heaven,[36] it was still a mitzvah for an individual to present the fire himself. The reason they

---

30. The original (בצניעות) is usually translated as "secretly," "submissively," or the like. We've translated it throughout as "demurely" in keeping with Rabbeinu Yonah's soon-to-come characterization of the person who acts thusly as quiet, calm, honest, and trustworthy—as opposed to brash, braggadocious, and cunning.
31. . . . at the hands of Heaven . . .
32. A Torah study hall.
33. . . . at the hands of Heaven.
34. . . . at the hands of Heaven.
35. . . . at the hands of Heaven.
36. . . . upon the altar . . .

suffered the consequences they did was because they decided the *halacha* in front of Moses" (*Eruvin* 63A).

117. Our sages said, "Pestilence comes to the world[37] to fulfill the death sentencesprescribed in the Torah which were not referred to the court,[38] and because of[39] seventh-year fruit" (*Pirke Avot* 5:8).

They also said, "There are four times when pestilence increases: The fourth year,[40] the seventh, the end of the seventh, and the end of every *Sukkot*. On the fourth year, because of[41] tithes for the poor in the third year; on the seventh year, because of[42] tithes for the poor in the sixth year; at the end of the seventh year, because of[43] fruits of the seventh year; and at the end of every *Sukkot* because of the stealing of gifts due the poor" (*Pirke Avot* 5:9).[44]

We see from this that you're culpable for death through the hands of Heaven for stealing gifts due the poor. As such, you can now realize and deduce the seriousness of vowing to give charity and not fulfilling that vow.

118. The same goes for withholding charity from your poor brother, and shutting your eyes to your poor relatives. Since you're obliged to contribute to them, it's as if you've stolen gifts due them.[45]

---

37. See Leviticus 26:25, "I will bring a sword upon you that will avenge My covenant. And when you are gathered within your cities, I will send the pestilence among you." And Deuteronomy 28:21, "God will have the pestilence affix itself to you."

38. Either because the Torah itself excludes those particular cases from a human court, because the court wasn't aware of the sins, or because the sins were committed when the Jewish community isn't empowered by the civil authorities to enforce the death sentence.

Hence we see that "Justice will be done" in one form or another. And that there are always consequences to our actions, even when they seem to come from "out of nowhere." Because there is One Judge, and He has many means of carrying out His sentences. In fact, this is the underlying principle behind this entire section, as we indicated in our very first note to ¶107.

39. . . . trespasses involving . . .

40. . . . of a seven-year cycle . . .

41. . . . negligence in . . .

42. . . . negligence in . . .

43. . . . negligence in . . .

44. See Supplementary Notes.

45. . . . when you don't help them.

Chapter Eleven

෴෴෴෴෴෴෴෴෴෴෴෴෴

119. The Seventh Level: The Significance of Excision

The very same sins for which you'd be culpable for excision if they'd been done purposefully, would require a sin-offering if they'd been done inadvertently. And so our sages said, "A person is only obliged to bring a sin offering for those sins he would suffer excision for if they had been done on purpose" (*K'ritut* 2A).

When it comes to excision, both the one culpable for it and his descendants are excised.[1] As it's said, "They will bear their sin—they will die childless" (Leviticus 20:20).

120. There are, however, two forms of excision. The first pertains to those who are excised from the world, like those who cohabit with their sister, their father's sister, their mother's sister, their wife's sister while their wife is still alive, or their brother's wife after the brother had divorced her or died. Similarly, those who cohabit with their father's brother's wife or their mother's brother's wife, those who eat forbidden animal fats or blood, those who eat *chometz* on Passover, those who desecrate Yom Kippur, those who don't bring a Paschal offering, and those who cohabit with a menstruant.[2]

121. The second[3] pertains to those who are excised both from this world and The World to Come, like those who worship idols; those who sin brazenly; those who demean Torah by demeaning those who study it, for example; "enemies of

---

1. See Supplementary Notes.
2. See Supplementary Notes.
3. . . . form of excision . . .

God;" and those who undo their circumcision. We will explicate these categories in the tenth level.[4]

122. Sometimes the merits[5] of the person culpable for excision extend for two or three generations (*Shavuot* 39A). But their death is delayed in order to reward them[6] in this world, yet bring them to ruin in The World to Come.[7] As it's said, "(God) repays His enemies to their face to bring them to ruin. He will not reprieve His enemies. He will repay them to their face" (Deuteronomy 7:10).

As it's said outright in David's statement, "An ignoramus would not know, nor would a fool understand how wrongdoers can blossom like grass, and all the workers of iniquity can flourish. They will be brought to ruin forever"[8] (Psalms 92:7–8). And as Asaph put it, "I envied the haughty when I saw the peaceableness of the wrongdoers, for there is no anguish at their death . . . Until I entered God's Sanctuary, when I understood their end" (Ibid. 73:3–4,17). That means to say that retribution will eventually befall the guilty. As it's said, "There will be no reward for the guilty; the wrongdoers' candle will be put out" (Proverbs 24:20).

123. Our sages remarked, "Rabbi Yoshiyah said that God forestalls His wrath against wrongdoers in this world[9] either because they might do tshuvah,[10] or because they did *mitzvot*, which God is rewarding them for in this world, or because they may produce righteous children. In fact we find that God forestalled his wrath against Achaz, and Chizkiah[11] descended from him, just as Yoshiyah[12] descended from Amon, and Mordechai[13] descended from Shimi" (*Kohelet Rabbah* 7:32).

124. What excision amounts to is a shortening of one's life span. As it's said, "The years of wrongdoers will be shortened" (Proverbs 10:27). But there's a difference between death[14] and excision as far as a shortening of one's life span is

---

4. See ¶'s 143–171.

5. . . . earned for extraneous good deeds . . .

6. . . . for those extraneous good deeds . . .

7. This and the following ¶ come to explain why those guilty of sins that incur excision obviously do *not* die young oftentimes (as well as why the wicked sometimes prosper while the righteous suffer). And in essence the reply lies in the fact that things are not always as they appear to be—that there are calculations and arrangements being made in the distant background, out of our hearing range and beyond our ken. But that in the end, justice will be done, though we might not be able to follow its passage in our own lifetimes. Of course, the arrogant among the living would love the "story" to come to an end when they can yet appreciate it. But God's own timing is far different and more elongated than our own. And He hasn't a need to satisfy our sense of high drama. (See Supplementary Notes.)

8. i.e., the answer is that they will be brought to *ultimate* ruin.

9. . . . for three reasons. . . .

10. See Supplementary Notes.

11. See 2 Kings 16–21.

12. See 2 Kings 21–23.

13. See The Book of Esther.

14. i.e., through the hands of Heaven (see ¶'s 107–118) . . .

concerned. When it comes to excision, a person dies before the age of fifty. But when it comes to death,[15] the person dies before the age of sixty, like those who died in the desert (*Moed Kattan* 28A). That's to say that one who was[16] destined to live to seventy or eighty, would die before sixty if he was culpable for death.[17] Nonetheless, there are righteous people who live less than sixty years.[18] As our sages said, "Shimei the Haramite was to die at fifty-two" (J. T., *Bikkurim* 2:1).

It's said, "Do not cut off[19] the tribes of the family of Kehot from among the Levites" (Numbers 4:18). It's in fact from this verse that the sages taught that excision comes before age fifty. They explain the verse thusly: Do not be the cause of Kehot's being cut off[20] from the Levite service. Because if you don't make sure that they don't enter to see when the holy objects are being covered over, they'll be cut off from the Levite service, and will die before age fifty. As it's said, "They will return from the ranks of service at age fifty" . . . (Ibid. 8:25).

125. Among those culpable for excision are those who cohabit with menstruants, and inflict their descendants with terrible impediments and depravities, as well as eventual excision. They[21] are referred to as "descendants of wrongdoers" (Isaiah 1:4) since they bear the mark of brashness on their foreheads as long as they live (for as our sages said, "Is a brash person not the child of a menstruant woman?" [*Kallah Rabbati* 2]). In fact, the child's sins will settle upon the father's bones, since the father brought him to defiance from the womb. Woe to such a guilty wrongdoer![22] For he corrupted himself so, and both he and his wife will be excised, as well as all their unconscionable descendants.[23]

---

15. See previous note.

16. . . . originally . . .

17. i.e., through the hands of Heaven.

18. This once again addresses the issue raised in the previous two ¶'s about Divine justice. It also speaks to the fact that certain individuals are destined to live shorter lives for reasons beyond our ken, having nothing to do with their moral status.

19. Or, excise.

20. Or, being excised.

21. i.e., those descendants.

22. See Supplementary Note.

23. The text continues with the following:

A woman remains an impure menstruant even if she's been cleansed of her flow and has counted the required seven days [of continuous non-flow], as long as she hasn't yet immersed in a *mikveh* [a ritual immersion pool] or in either a stream or in a well with forty *se'ahs* of water in it. An allusion to that [based on *Gematria*, i.e, arithmetic congruity] is found in the expression, "The waters of Shiloach flow softly" (Isaiah 8:6) [where the numerical value of "softly" (לאט) is 40, in correspondence to the requisite 40 *se'ahs* of water in a *mikveh*].

Chapter Twelve

ॐॐॐॐॐॐॐॐॐॐॐ

126. The Eighth Level: The Four Court-Imposed Death Sentences

They are: stoning, burning, death by the sword, and strangulation. Stoning is more significant than burning; burning is more significant than death by the sword, and death by the sword is more significant than strangulation (*Sanhedrin* 49–50).

Among the sins culpable for stoning are: cohabiting with your father's wife, your daughter-in-law, or with another male; practicing sorcery; profaning the Sabbath; cursing your father or mother; cohabiting with a betrothed young woman; instigating others;[1] practicing magic; and being a "gluttonous rebellious" child.[2] The most significant of all is blaspheming[3] and worshipping idols (Ibid. 53A).[4]

127. Among the sins culpable for burning are: cohabiting with a woman along with her daughter; with your wife's daughter, her son's daughter, or her daughter's daughter; with your mother-in-law, your mother-in-law's mother, or your father-in-law's mother (*Sanhedrin* 75A).[5]

128. The two sins culpable for death by the sword are: murdering, or being a resident of a "captivated city" (*Sanhedrin* 76B).[6]

129. And among sins culpable for strangulation are: striking your father or mother, kidnapping a fellow Jew, being an elder[7] who rebels against the decree of the

---

1. . . . to worship idols . . .
2. See Deuteronomy 21:18–21.
3. . . . God's name . . .
4. See Supplementary Notes.
5. See Supplementary Notes.
6. See Deuteronomy 13:13–19.
7. . . . sage . . .

court,[8] being a false prophet, prophesying in the name of an idol, and cohabiting with a married woman (*Sanhedrin* 84B).[9]

130. Our sages said, "Even though the four court-imposed death sentences have not been carried out since the Holy Temple was destroyed, the law of the four death sentences has never been nullified. As a result, one culpable for stoning would either fall from a roof or be trampled by a wild animal; one culpable for burning would either fall into a fire or be bitten by a snake; one culpable for death by the sword would either be turned over to the authorities or be attacked by robbers; and one culpable for strangulation would either drown in a river or die of diphtheria" (*Sanhedrin* 37B).[10]

131. One who cohabits with a[11] maidservant is like those culpable for a court-imposed death sentence for two reasons.[12] First, as our sages put it, "One who cohabits with a Gentile woman should be struck by a fervent believer" (*Sanhedrin* 81B). As it's said, "He impaled them both" (Numbers 25:8).[13] That's to say, if you find such a person erring in full sight of others, and he won't stop, you're to kill him as soon as you come upon him.[14]

And thus, in a sense, this sin is more significant than all others culpable for a court-imposed death sentence. For those others are only sentenced to death after witnesses,[15] warning,[16] and judgment of the Sanhedrin. But this sinner[17] is to be killed by whoever comes upon him—without witnesses or warning.

---

8. See Deuteronomy 17:11–12.

9. See Supplementary Notes.

10. That's to say, God's purposes will always be carried through, one way or another. So, it's shortsighted to say that while there may have been repercussions to our wrongdoings in the distant past, there aren't any anymore. Because there are immutable ethical, cosmic laws. And while their applications will vary, their underpinnings won't.

Though the tradition that addresses these underpinnings don't speak about them in these terms, it's not hard to imagine that we suffer the *emotional* counterparts of their repercussions now. As such, we may suffer the angst, anxiety, terror, torture, or anguish that so many of us do as a consequence of these immutable laws.

See our note to ¶122 about why it is that many do not suffer these consequences—on a physical level—who apparently should (aside from the fact that they might have done tshuvah for their sins).

11. . . . Gentile . . .

12. The first reason follows immediately, while the second is stated in ¶133.

13. This verse and the ones preceding it read as follows: "And, behold, one of the people of Israel came and brought to his brothers a Midianite woman in the sight of Moses, and in the sight of all the congregation of the people of Israel . . . And when Pinchas, the son of Eliezer, the son of Aaron the priest, saw it, he arose from among the congregation, and took a spear in hand, and went after the man of Israel into the tent, and *he impaled them both*."

14. See Supplementary Notes.

15. . . . had testified against him . . .

16. i.e., after he'd been given prior warning.

17. i.e., the one who cohabits with a Gentile maidservant . . .

132. Aside from that, this wrongdoer "has profaned God's holiness by loving and marrying the daughter of a foreign god" (Malachi 2:11). Each Gentile child produced becomes a pitfall and a snare to him, as well as a reminder of his sin. And he, the father, will bear his child's sins because he betrayed God by having borne alien children.

133. Second, "Heaven[18] will reveal his transgression, and the earth will rise up against him" (Job 20:27). For his sin will quickly bring about his downfall, and he'll ultimately hang by his scalp from a tree. He'll thus be like one culpable for a court-imposed death sentence since the destruction of the Holy Temple by being sentenced by Heaven to death for his acts of rebellion in the unusual ways we indicated above.[19]

And so our sages said, "Whoever cohabits with a[20] maidservant is to be hung by his scalp. As it is said, 'God will smite the heads of His enemies, the hairy scalp of those who continue on in their guilt' (Psalms 68:22)" (*Bamidbar Rabbah* 10:4). That is, He'll smite their "hairy scalp" by hanging them by their hair. And as it's said, "God will excise whoever does that—who calls and responds from the Tents of Jacob" (Malachi 2:12). And our sages explained that one who "calls" refers to sages, and one who "responds" refers to their disciples (*Sanhedrin* 82A).[21]

134. Our sages said, "A sword comes upon the world as a result of tormenting[22] judgment, perversions of justice, and because of decisions made against *halacha*. Ferocious beasts come upon the world as a result of false oaths, and the profanation of God's name" (*Pirke Avot* 5:8–9).

135. How gratifying it would be if those who criticize the people would alert and point to the things that cause a breach in Sabbath observance, whether of the primary or the secondary *malachot*. Because many of them[23] have become concealed from the people. And if no one will tell,[24] no one will listen.

---

18. . . . itself . . .
19. See ¶130.
20. . . . Gentile . . .
21. That's to say, *whoever* is guilty of so great a sin—be he a sage or a disciple—will be struck.
22. . . . delays in . . .
23. i.e., many of the details of Sabbath observance.
24. . . . the people about them . . .

Chapter Thirteen

136. The Ninth Level: Those Significant Sins You're to Give Your Life for Rather Than Commit

Our sages said that when it comes to all[1] Torah transgressions, if someone says to you, "Transgress or you will be killed!," you're to transgress rather than give up your life. For it's said, "So, keep My statutes and My judgments . . . and live by them" (Leviticus 18:5)—which is to say,[2] live by the *mitzvot*, rather than die by them. With the exception of[3] idol worship, licentiousness, and murder.[4] So, if someone says to you, "Commit one of these three sins or you will be killed," you're to give up your life rather than commit it—even if you're told to commit the sin in private.

But if you're told to transgress against any of the *mitzvot* of the Torah in public—you're to give up your life rather than transgress it. As it's said, "And I will be sanctified among the Children of Israel" (Leviticus 22:32). And at a time of persecution you're to give up your life rather than sin,[5] even[6] in private (*Sanhedrin* 74A).

---

1. . . . other . . .
2. . . . you're to . . .
3. . . . the prohibitions against . . .
4. The point of fulfilling *mitzvot* is to live an exalted life of attachment to the very Source of life Himself. But one who'd be guilty of any one of these crimes could not. Because he's either attached to another (i.e., a false god, or another person) ignobly, or (in the case of murder) he's too attached to his own will.
5. . . . against any mitzvah . . .
6. . . . if only . . .

137.   And the consequences for the slightest breach of any of these three (which our sages referred to as the "dust" of these prohibitions[7]) is even more significant than for many other significant sins.

They said, for example that, "Anything could be used to cure someone of a life-threatening disease except wood from an *Ashera*[8] tree" (*Pesachim* 25A). So if someone tells you to bring *Ashera* wood so that another could be cured, that sick person must give up his life rather than be cured by it. And even though one who derives benefit from *Ashera* wood wouldn't be worshipping idols, nonetheless since it[9] is an instance of the "dust" of idol worship the sick person should give up his life rather than be healed through it. Because he'd be encouraging people who worship *Ashera*s to say that the *Ashera* saved him.

138.   The same goes for licentiousness—you're to give up your life rather than be cured by[10] the "dust" of licentiousness. So, for example, if you desired a married woman and you were told that you'd only be cured[11] if she stood undressed before you or if you were to speak to her,[12] you're to give up your life rather than breach the restrictions against sinning with a married woman (*Sanhedrin* 75A). Now you can understand the seriousness[13] of shaking hands with a married woman.[14]

139.   The "dust" of murder[15] involves making someone blanch[16] to the point where he turns pale and loses all the coloring in his face, and looks as if he'd been murdered,[17] as our sages pointed out (*Babba Metziah* 58B).

Secondly,[18] because the torment from blanching in shame is bitterer yet than death.[19] That's why our sages said, "A person should throw himself into a fiery furnace rather than make another blanch[20] in public" (Ibid. 59A), which they said about no other significant sin. They thus equated[21] the "dust" of murder to murder itself. And since, as we indicated, you're to give up your life rather than murder

---

7. For unlike something's "shadow," its "dust" is a bit of the thing itself, rather than just an offshoot or projection of it. Perhaps that's why the wood per se of an *Ashera* tree is mentioned shortly, rather than its perfume.

8. i.e., an idolatrous tree. See Deuteronomy 16:21.

9. i.e., the act of using wood from an *Ashera* tree.

10. . . . an instance of . . .

11. . . . of a life-threatening disease . . .

12. . . . that way, or in any lewd manner . . .

13. . . . of the prohibition against . . .

14. See Supplementary Notes.

15. i.e., an instance of the "dust" of murder . . .

16. . . . in shame . . .

17. i.e., as if you'd murdered him and caused the blood to exude from his face.

18. i.e., it's also like murder . . .

19. See Supplementary Notes.

20. . . . in shame . . .

21. . . . this instance of . . .

(*Sanhedrin* 74A), along the same lines they said that you should thrust yourself into a fiery furnace rather than cause another to blanch in public.[22]

We can also deduce this from the incident of Tamar. For it's said, "When she was brought forth she sent[23] to her father-in-law saying, 'I am with child by the man whom these belong to'" (Genesis 38:25). That is, even though she was being brought forward to be burned to death, she nonetheless didn't reveal the fact that Judah impregnated her, in order not to make him blanch.

140.   They also said, "Whoever descends into *Gehenom*[24] reascends except for three, who descend but never reascend: One who makes another blanch in public, one who calls another person by a nickname,[25] and one who cohabits with a married woman" (*Babba Metziah* 58B).

Notice how they equated making another blanch in public and calling another by a nickname—which also makes him blanch—with cohabiting with a married woman, which is one of the transgressions you're to give your life for rather than violate (*Sanhedrin* 74A).[26]

141.   They also said, "One who makes another blanch in public has no place in The World to Come" (*Babba Metziah* 59A). As to why they didn't also say that a murderer hasn't a place in The World to Come, that's because one who makes another blanch doesn't realize the seriousness of his sin and doesn't grow bitter in reaction to his sin the way a murderer would. He's thus too[27] removed to do tshuvah.

142.   Our sages said about the mitzvah of observing the Sabbath, "The Sabbath is equivalent to all the other *mitzvot*" (J. T., *Nedarim* 3:14),[28] which they explained by saying, "One who worships idols or publicly[29] desecrates the Sabbath is an apostate to all of Torah. Whatever meat he slaughters is unkosher, whatever wine he comes in contact with is forbidden" (*Chullin* 5A).

---

22. We in modernity should blanch in shame ourselves for how insensitive we are to this. Who among us wouldn't have even a dear friend blanch shamefacedly in public for the sake of a "good laugh"? Few of us care enough even to apologize for that.

23. . . . a message . . .

24. . . . eventually . . .

25. . . . he'd rather not be called by . . .

26. Hence, Rabbeinu Yonah is equating calling another by a nickname with making him blanch.

27. . . . emotionally . . .

28. Rabbeinu Yonah ends this section with a warning against Sabbath desecration as he did the previous one (see ¶135) to underscore the tragedy of it.

29. . . . and high-handedly . . .

Chapter Fourteen

⧼⧽⧼⧽⧼⧽⧼⧽⧼⧽⧼⧽⧼⧽⧼⧽⧼⧽⧼⧽⧼⧽

143. The Tenth Level: Those Significant Sins Whose Violators Have No Place in The World to Come[1]

We were created to bring honor to God,[2] as it's said, "Everyone called by My name I have created for My honor; I formed him, even made him" (Isaiah 43:7).[3] So it's

---

1. It's imperative to understand the character of The World to Come if we're to understand the woe and calamity inherent to being excluded from it. (See note 20 to 1:42 for something of an illustration.) And then, after coming to understand the richness of a place in The World to Come, it behooves us to do all we can to avoid losing the opportunity for so sublime an experience. That's what makes this section, which alerts us to the things that would deny us a place in The World to Come, so vital to our spiritual well-being.

In fact, the great and holy late champion of Musar, Rav Yechezkel Levenstein זצ״ל, counseled that if one hasn't the opportunity to review the whole *Gates of Repentance* in the days preceding Rosh Hashanah and Yom Kippur as he should, he'd do well to at least review the first gate (and minimally, ¶'s 1–11, at that), then skip to 3:4–23. And to most especially concentrate upon *this* section (Preface to *Ohr HaTshuvah*).

2. . . . and to sanctify His name, as will be pointed out shortly. (See Supplementary Notes.)

3. See ¶17, where this verse is first cited, in the context of our potentials for excellence. For in truth we're capable of spiritual excellence, high righteousness, and full devotion, as is indicated there. But we're also capable of the sort of deviance and defiance spoken of here shortly. The so very human contrast is stunning and daunting, should give us pause, and it should also impel us toward excellence.

only reasonable[4] that if you profane God's name or demean His words, you'd lose all hope.[5] For not only would you not have fulfilled what's required of you from the very start, which was to honor God and sanctify His name; but you'd have done all you could to do just the opposite by profaning His holy name instead.[6]

And so it's written, "The person who does so with a high hand . . . blasphemes God. That person will be excised from the midst of his people because he demeaned the word of God and undermined His mitzvah. He will be utterly excised, and will bear his transgression" (Numbers 15:30–31). That is, he "will[7] bear his transgression" despite his having been "utterly excised," since death won't atone for him, and he'll have no place in The World to Come.[8] And that's why "bearing" a transgression is mentioned in connection with this sin when it isn't mentioned in other instances of excision.

The expression, "The person who does so with a high hand" refers to one who[9] commits well-known[10] sins in public, as well as one who casts off the yoke of Heaven[11]—even in private—who's also considered to have acted with "a high hand." Examples of "casting off the yoke" include being heretical enough to eat unkosher meat, forbidden fats and blood, or to desecrate the Holy Days,[12] even if you violate no other *mitzvot*. Because by doing that you'd have already rebelled against God by casting off the yoke of a single prohibition.

In truth, even the righteous stumble from time to time and sin.[13] Yet only by accident, when their yetzer harah gets the best of them. But they're vexed bitterly by it, and are aware of it from then on. But if you convince yourself to cast off the yoke of a prohibition every time you want to violate it, you're referred to as an "apostate in one area,"[14] as we already explained in the first gate of this book.[15,16]

---

4. . . . to assume . . .

5. . . . of ever having a place in The World to Come.

But apparently there *is* hope, even if you go so far as to profane God's name, as Rabbeinu Yonah himself points out in 1:47 and 4:5. As long as you do tshuvah and sanctify God's name. See ¶171 in this gate, as well. So it seems the underlying, overall message is this: If you don't try to live up to your spiritual potential here, in life (see note 3), you won't reach your spiritual potential in The World to Come either. Unless you acknowledge your error and do tshuvah.

6. That is, not only would you not have honored God. And not only would you not have avoided dishonoring Him. You'd have gone so far as to earnestly dishonored Him.

7. . . . continue to . . .

8. i.e., otherwise, how could one be said to "bear his transgression" after having already been "utterly excised"?

9. . . . brazenly . . .

10. i.e., undeniable and incontestable.

11. . . . entirely . . .

12. . . . in a brazen, high-handed manner . . .

13. See Supplementary Notes.

14. . . . and you haven't a place in The World to Come.

144. We've thus explained the gist of, "The person who does so with a high hand." We're now about to explain how "He demeaned the word of God."[17]

As our sages put it, "He demeaned the word of God" refers to one who says the Torah isn't from Heaven,[18] who misinterprets Torah,[19] who demeans Torah scholars and the Holy Days.[20] For even if that person studied Torah and did a lot of good things, he nonetheless hasn't a place in The World to Come (*Sanhedrin* 99A).[21]

145. What "misinterpreting" Torah refers to is being audacious enough to say things about Torah that aren't so. Like, "These verses and stories in the Torah serve no purpose," simply because you're arrogant and proud, you can't decipher the point being made, and because[22] "There's nothing hidden there."[23] But as it's said, "It is not a meaningless thing for you" (Deuteronomy 32:47), about which our sages said, "If it is 'meaningless,' it is from you"[24] (J. T., *Ketubot*, end of Ch. 8), in that you don't know how to explain the point being made.

The same holds true if you abandon one aspect of Torah and do not acknowledge it. You'd also be misinterpreting Torah then. An example would be if you say, "What good does it do us to have Torah scholars?[25] For if they learn

---

15. See 1:6.

16. The text continues with the following:

As such, the sages spoke of "shepherds who are neither to be lifted up from the pit nor lowered into it" [i.e., transgressors who aren't to be aggressively punished, but whose actions are nonetheless unacceptable] (*Avodah Zarah* 26A). By [using] "shepherds" the sages were alluding to those who might herd their animals into others' fields, who thus cast off the yoke of the [responsibility not to violate the] prohibition against stealing, and are thus like anyone "heretical" enough to eat unkosher meat or commit any other sin only in order to satisfy a craving [rather than to rebel against God].

But heretics and renegades [who *do* go out of their way to do wrong] are to be lowered into the pit, like those heretical enough to adamantly eat unkosher meat, who *are* heretics. Because by sinning "adamantly" we don't mean eating something forbidden that you have a craving for. But rather, defiantly selecting unkosher meat even when kosher meat is right in front of you. And never taking it upon yourself to be careful not to violate the prohibition against eating unkosher meat.

17. . . . included in the verse cited in the previous ¶.

18. See Supplementary Notes.

19. Literally, "who uncovers facets of the Torah (that aren't there)."

20. These will be discussed in the ¶'s to follow.

21. See Supplementary Notes.

22. . . . you think . . .

23. Such a person believes that if he doesn't "get it," there's nothing to be "gotten" from it.

24. i.e., the meaningless is coming from you. That's to say, if you find something in the Torah to be one-dimensional, it only appears to be so because you're looking at it one-dimensionally.

25. See Supplementary Notes.

anything at all, they learn it all for themselves, and we gain nothing from the merit they amass!" You'd thus be rejecting the declaration in the Torah that "(God) will spare the place for their sake" (Genesis 18:26).[26]

146. What "demeaning the Holy Days" refers to is doing work on the intermediate days,[27] and demeaning the consequences[28] because the prohibition against doing work on the intermediate days isn't stated outright in the Torah. Doing that, you'd be like the adamant "apostate in one area" who, as we explained,[29] hasn't a place in The World to Come.

Our sages said, "One who comes to convert and says, 'I will accept all of Torah but this one Rabbinic decree' is not to be accepted"[30] (*Bechorot* 30B). They also said, "One who demeans the Holy Days is like an idol worshipper. For it is said, 'Keep the festival of unleavened bread' (Exodus 34:18), which is immediately preceded by 'Make no molten gods for yourself' (Ibid. v. 17)" (*Pesachim* 118A). Our sages explained, "'Keep the festival of unleavened bread' implies that you are to do no work throughout the festival." (*Chagigah* 18A). Thus you *are* alerted not to do work on the intermediate days.[31]

147. The sages' statement that one who demeans Torah scholars also demeans God's word and hasn't a place in The World to Come[32] can actually be arrived at logically and deductively. For we ourselves will now be presenting a reasoned and rational explanation.[33]

---

26. This refers to Sodom and Gemorrah, which wouldn't have been destroyed had there been a few righteous individuals there (see Genesis 18:23–33). Hence we find that the presence and practices of the righteous are for everyone's benefit, regardless of what practical applications result.

27. Referred to as "Chol Hamoed," i.e., the intermediate, non-sacred days between the first two sacred days of *Sukkot* and Passover (which are each eight days long), and the last two. (See Supplementary Notes.)

28. . . . of doing that . . .

29. See ¶143 (as well as the citations noted in the Supplementary Notes there).

30. Hence we find the Torah requiring Jews to carry out the whole of it.

31. The text continues with the following:

As to the fact that it's written, "The first day will be a Sabbath, and the eighth day will be a Sabbath" (Leviticus 23:39) [which seems to imply that the intermediate days *aren't* sacred], that's because there are many tasks that *can* be done on the intermediate days, as our sages indicated.

32. Cited in ¶144 (see ¶121 also).

33. The text continues with the following:

As Solomon said, "The wise will inherit honor, and fools will be acclaimed by baseness" (Proverbs 3:35) where "baseness" means "a base *person*" — just as "I am prayer" (Psalms 109:4) means "I am a *man* of prayer," and "Your dwelling-place is in the midst of deceit" (Jeremiah 9:5) means "Your dwelling-place is in the midst of *men* of deceit." So ["The wise will inherit honor; and fools will be acclaimed by baseness"] means that [only] a base and degenerate person would acclaim, honor, or praise a fool.

In fact, there are several great benefits to be had from honoring wise and honest people,[34] and many and powerful pitfalls involved in honoring fools and wrongdoers.[35] First, when you glorify scholars and grant them prestige, others listen to them, and the people follow and heed their advice.

Second, people learn to strive for and acquire honor for themselves when they see all the honor being given them, and knowledge will flourish as a consequence. As our sages said, "One should even study Torah and do *mitzvot* for less than altruistic reasons. For by doing that,[36] he will eventually do it altruistically" (*Pesachim* 50B).[37]

Third, many sleeping hearts will awaken when they see the Torah's resplendent honor.[38] And they'll come to realize its greatness. They'll yearn for it, they'll delve into it for God's own sake, and they'll come to serve Him wholeheartedly.[39]

148. Though these reasons are so terribly important and compelling, there's yet another one that's of primary importance. We alluded to it already at the beginning of our discussion of these types of wrongdoers.[40]

As is known, among the ways to sanctify God's name is to show with everything you say, every blink of your eye, and every action and movement of your hand that what underlies man's existence, where his prominence lies, and what is so becoming, important, exalted and valuable about him is his service to and fear of God and His Torah.[41] As it's written, "For this is the whole of man" (Ecclesiastes 12:13).[42] For that is what brings honor upon God.[43]

But when you demean scholars and those who fear God,[44] you undermine this

---

34. To be discussed in this and the following ¶.

35. See ¶'s 149 (at end) through 152.

36. . . . initially . . .

37. That is, while satisfying the quest for honor isn't the best reason to study Torah, nonetheless you should start off with that inducement, and you'll eventually study for the best of reasons.

38. See Supplementary Notes.

39. All in all what Rabbeinu Yonah is saying is that when you honor Torah scholars you not only honor them. You also elevate and thus bring honor upon others in the process, and thus do everyone good. (See next ¶ as well.)

40. See ¶143.

41. Or, ". . . is his ability to serve and fear God and His Torah."

42. In its entirety the verse reads, "The end of the matter, all having been heard (is this): Fear God, and keep His commandments. For this is the whole of man."

43. That is, despite all our grand delusions and fancies about ourselves and our place in the universe, the only reason we're at all prominent, "becoming, important, exalted and valuable," is because we're able to honor God by fearing Him and His Torah. As such, we're like a king's intimate and confidant, who enjoys respect and fame as long as he enjoys proximity to the king, and honors him. But who loses it all—utterly and abysmally—when he's no longer associated with the king.

44. See Supplementary Notes.

whole idea, and express its opposite in everything you do. It's as if you were saying that Divine service isn't primary, but that all honor and glory is based on worldly achievements, and that something other than serving God is essential.[45]

You'd thus be profaning the Torah if you did that, you'd be lost and no longer a part of the community, and all hope[46] would be lost. For while those who don't know[47] claim to serve God without delving into Torah, it's nonetheless understood that the only way Divine service is preserved is when scholars delve into Torah day and night. For they impart knowledge, and "understand the times, so as to know what Israel ought to do" (1 Chronicles 12:33). They preserve the Torah within the Jewish Nation so that it will never be forgotten. For in places where no one delves into Torah, all sorts of pitfalls come about, and there aren't honest people.[48]

So, honor those who serve God—the Torah scholars—in order to honor God. And in order to let it be known that serving Him is the most important thing we can do.

Once it becomes clear to you that God created everything for His honor, you're obliged to think of ways to constantly honor God; to sanctify Him with everything you say; and to constantly aggrandize, praise, and bless Him. As it's said, "I will bless God at all times; His praise will always be in my mouth" (Psalms 34:2). When you're with others or speaking to a friend, think about and carefully mull over everything that comes out of your mouth, in order to sanctify God by what you say.[49] Make sure you praise service to Him and laud the fear of Him, and

---

45. Ever so sadly, many of us have lapsed blindly into this. And are prepared and convinced enough to say that it's eminently logical to believe that a person's status depends on his worldly achievements. "After all," we might say, "if it weren't for so-and-so's input, the world wouldn't enjoy thus-and-such," etc. And so we honor the people who've accomplished rare feats. Rabbeinu Yonah isn't denigrating the accomplishments of such individuals, though. Only their status—only their import vis à vis eternity and "the big picture." Because in the process of time, all will wither and flitter away—including all *record* of everything that had so flittered. And all that will remain will be what is now invisible, rarefied, and recondite—God Almighty, the spirit of things (our's included), and one other thing—our relationship to God. Personal status at that time will depend on the latter alone. Those fortunate and wise enough to realize that now, and to thus dedicate themselves to God and His Torah in this life, are to be honored. Dishonoring them we dishonor God Himself, and eschew the fundamental reality of life's impermanence.

46. . . . of your ever attaining a place in The World to Come . . .

47. . . . any better . . .

48. . . . according to God's revelations of what honest and dishonest is—which isn't always so apparent. Because while there may seem to be honest people about us in society, our concepts of honesty are often askew and based on selfish needs rationalized.

49. For as we suggested earlier on in this ¶, we're like intimates and confidantes of God who represent Him at every turn. Thus we need to be on guard not to belittle Him or demean His image in the eyes of others. (See 3:19, which speaks of being God's emissary in this world.)

compliment everyone who serves and fears Him. You'll thus earn the sort of great merit that approaches the Heavens by means of your thoughts and words alone, without[50] effort or strain. Since that's one of the main reasons man was created.

For it's said, "The refining pot is for silver, the furnace for gold; but man[51] by what he praises" (Proverbs 27:21). That means to say that a person's status is determined by what he praises. For if he praises good deeds, sages, and the righteous, you'd know and could determine for yourself that he himself is good and basically righteous.[52] Simply because nothing but praise for goodness and good people comes from his mouth, along with hate for sin, and a belittling of those who sin, who aren't repelled by wrongdoing and don't choose to do good.

And while such a person may have committed some secret sins himself, he's nonetheless a lover of righteousness and is rooted in what's right. And he's thus a member of the community of those who honor God.

But one who praises terrible deeds or compliments wrongdoers is himself an out-and-out wrongdoer who profanes the service of God.[53]

149.   Solomon also said, "A righteous man who falls down before the wicked is like a muddied fountain and a polluted spring. It is not good to eat a lot of honey; but honor is due those who search out honor" (Proverbs 25:26–27).

That means to say, when someone sets a fountain in disarray with his feet, he muddies its waters for a while. But as soon as the water settles down, it becomes as clear as before. The same goes for a righteous person. If he ever "falls down before"[54] a wrongdoer, he nonetheless doesn't descend or diminish himself. And even if he befouls himself for a while, "A righteous man will fall seven times then rise up" (Proverbs 24:16), and he'll be just as strong and as venerable as before. And while "It is not good to eat a lot of honey," nonetheless, "honor is due those" who do a lot to "search out honor" in the righteous.[55,56]

But honoring wrongdoers carries a lot of well-known pitfalls along with it. For

---

50. . . . having to expend physical . . .

51. . . . is to be judged . . .

52. See Supplementary Notes.

53. Much like what's said above in this ¶, this, too, is a major statement about what truly matters and what doesn't. For in fact, we are each the product of our dreams and realizations. They define us and motivate us to act as we do. As such, if your dreams are grounded in goodness, and your realizations are rooted in Torah ideals, you're essentially right, though you may lapse ever so humanly. But if your dreams are grounded instead in wrong, and your realizations are rooted in extraneous self-serving ideals — then *despite whatever good you might happen to do*, you're essentially wrong. Pity the poor soul who has no sense of what moves him and drives him onward in his life! (See Supplementary Notes.)

54. i.e., succumbs to.

55. This harkens back to the statement in the previous ¶ that a person is to be judged by what he honors.

56. The text continues with the following:

doing so profanes Torah and Divine service, and it's[57] a transgression that destroys body and soul.

150.   Second,[58] because many are drawn to them and copy their actions.

151.   Third, because people who associate with wrongdoers experience the same retribution they do, even when they don't do what they do (*Avot D'Rebbe Natan*, Ch. 30), as we've already mentioned.[59]

152.   And fourth, because they lower the esteem due men of truth, and undermine the service of God.[60] For the only way the righteous will assume the honor due them is if the honor shown those wrongdoers is dashed.[61] As it's written, "The house of wrongdoers will be overthrown and the tent of the upright will flourish" (Proverbs 14:11), and, "The city is exalted by the blessing of the honest, but destroyed by the mouth of the guilty" (Ibid. 11:11).

153.   Our sages also said, "Included among those who 'demean God's word'[62] are those who discuss Torah in dirty alleyways" (*Berachot* 24B),[63] those who are able to study Torah but don't (J. T., *Sanhedrin* 10:1),[64] and whoever reads heretical books (*Sanhedrin* 99A). And as to the statement, "undermined His mitzvah,"[65] that refers to someone who "undermines" his circumcision[66] (Ibid.).

That is, since "a righteous man" is mentioned at the beginning of the phrase [we can thus infer that] the term "a lot" [from the phrase, "It is not good to eat *a lot* of honey"] has to do with those who search out the honor due the righteous. That pattern is followed in many instances. [And the import of the verse is thus, while it's usually not good to overindulge in things (like honey), it's nevertheless good to "overindulge" in praise of the righteous.]

57. . . . consequently . . .

58. i.e., honoring wrongdoers also does harm . . .

59. In Rabbeinu Yonah's *Iggeret Hatshuvah* ¶22. (See Supplementary Notes.)

60. That is, because service to God is based upon the revelation of truth that is Torah; consequently, if men of Torah are demeaned, Divine service is demeaned as well. And falsehood is given credence instead.

61. See Supplementary Notes.

62. See ¶143 and what follows.

63. See Supplementary Notes.

64. See Supplementary Notes.

65. See ¶143.

66. i.e., who extends the flesh covering the site of his circumcision in order to appear uncircumcised.

Chapter Fifteen

಄಄಄಄಄಄಄಄಄಄಄಄

Other Significant Sins Whose Violators Have No Place in The World to Come[1]

154. We've also learned that, "All of Israel has a place in The World to Come, as it's said, 'All of Your people are righteous; they will inherit the land forever' (Isaiah 60:21)" (*Sanhedrin* 90A). But the following do not have a place in The World to Come: those who say that there's no mention of The Resurrection of the Dead in the Torah,[2] that Torah isn't from Heaven, and heretics. With this statement our sages alert us to trust that the tenet of The Resurrection of the Dead is written in the Torah, and that it's one of its principles.

One of the places in the Torah where The Resurrection of the Dead is cited is the verse, "I bring to death and I bring to life; I wound and I heal" (Deuteronomy 32:39). Our sages remarked, "Might I not think that He has one die and brings another to life? But the verse continues with 'I wound and I heal,' which is to say, 'Just as I wound and heal the same person, so too do I bring death and life to the same person'" (*Pesachim* 68A).[3]

---

1. This is not included in the text.

2. It's written in Ezekiel 37:12–14, "Thus says God the Lord: Behold, My people, I will open your graves and have you come up out of your graves, and bring you into the land of Israel. And you will know that I am God when I will have opened your graves, My people, and brought you up from your graves. I will place My spirit within you and you will live, and I will set you in your own land." Obviously, then, The Resurrection of the Dead is cited among the prophecies. The point being made is that it's alluded to in the Torah as well. (See Supplementary Notes.)

3. I might then argue that the verse is merely saying that God brings a person to life

155. A "heretic" was explained by our sages (*Sanhedrin* 99B) to be one who doesn't exhibit fear and respect for Torah scholars, even though he may not demean them.[4] He might, for example, demean *another* person in front of a Torah scholar, and thus not show respect for the scholar's learning. And since he didn't have enough respect for the Torah to exhibit fear, he hasn't a place in The World to Come.[5] For that too is considered[6] profaning the Torah.[7] As our sages said, the verse, " 'Fear God your Lord' (Deuteronomy 6:13) comes to include[8] Torah scholars as well" (*Pesachim* 22B).

156. Second,[9] fearing them leads to the fear of Heaven.[10] Because when their words are listened to in fear, they're able to instruct and guide people in the fear of the glorious and awesome name of God. As it's said, "All the people greatly feared God and Samuel" (1 Samuel 12:18).

Included among heretics are those who say, "What do we get out of all the studying the scholars do? Do they ever say anything new? They've never[11] made raven permissible to eat, or forbade us from eating dove!" (*Sanhedrin* 99B-100A).[12]

Such people don't understand, listen, or so much as open their ears to the benefits there are to delving into Torah.[13] Torah study is thus menial in their eyes, hence they join the ranks of those who rebel against its great illumination and have no place in The World to Come.

As such, we're obliged to teach the Jewish Nation the benefits there are, in fact,

---

and then has him die, in the natural course of things, and that nothing more than that was being said. But the word order is exact: just as God wounds then heals, He first has one die, then He resurrects him.

4. See Supplementary Notes.

5. See Supplementary Notes.

6. . . . an instance of . . .

7. A "heretic" is usually taken to be an adamant non-believer who undermines and denigrates Torah and observance. But this statement asserts that heresy is far more ingrained and subtle than that, and evidences itself indirectly in how one acts in the presence of Torah, and feels about those who embody it.

8. . . . fearing . . .

9. i.e., the second reason why one who demeans Torah scholars hasn't a place in The World to Come is based on the fact that . . .

10. See Supplementary Notes.

11. . . . suddenly . . .

12. In other words, of what practical use is all their studying? But, as we've already pointed out in our last comment to ¶145, this attitude itself is un-Godly.

13. . . . altruistically and with no practical end in sight. For though practical applications may be derived from their studies, the very fact of selfless, ideal study is of benefit to the world. (And while the analogy fails fairly shortly on, it's somewhat like the study of "pure" vs. "applied" science or mathematics. In that, like concentration upon pure science and mathematics, pure Torah study may indeed lead to practical applications; nonetheless, pure and pristine study itself contributes both to our knowledge and our beings.)

to delving into Torah. With God's help we've been able to cite some of them in *The Gate of Torah* and to thus incite hearts toward Torah study.[14]

As for those who aren't able to study Torah,[15] they should[16] know about the respect and honor inherent to studying Torah. They'll earn merit just knowing that, and won't lose a place in The World to Come.[17]

157. Included as well among heretics is one who calls his teacher by his name[18] (*Sanhedrin* 100A). In fact, it was said that Gach'zi suffered the consequences he did[19] because he called his teacher by his name. As it's said, "This is the woman, and this is her son, whom Elisha[20] restored to life" (2 Kings 8:5).

158. The consequences spoken of on this level[21] come about essentially as a result of profaning the Torah.[22] And as our sages said, "Profaning God's name[23] is the most profound sin of all. And it is not possible to be atoned for it through tshuvah or suffering"[24] (*Yomah* 86A), which we'll explain in the gate that discusses the types of atonement.[25] Our sages also said, "Retribution for profaning God's name will not be withheld, regardless of whether the act was done inadvertently or intentionally" (*Kiddushin* 40A).

Now, reflect a moment on our great obligation to sanctify God's name.[26] The primary reason God sanctified us through His Torah and *mitzvot*, and selected us to be His people was so that we'd sanctify and fear Him. So it's important for those who sanctify Him to be holy themselves, just as the utensils used in God's service[27] were holy. For it's said, "Do not profane My holy name; for I will be sanctified among the people of Israel. I am God, who sanctifies you" (Leviticus 22:32). Notice how what we just said is reflected in this verse, in fact.

It's also said, "He has commanded His covenant forever; holy and awesome is

---

14. To our great regret, *The Gate of Torah* no longer exists.

15. . . . and would thus not likely be drawn to the closeness to God that is the essential experience of The World to Come . . .

16. . . . at least come to . . .

17. Because as has been pointed out in ¶148, one is defined by what he praises. So if such an individual can be taught to praise Torah study, he'll be considered among those who are well-nigh involved in it, though he wasn't literally so.

18. . . . alone, and without title . . .

19. i.e., leprosy, see 2 Kings 5:27.

20. . . . his teacher (whom he was thus referring to familiarly and without due honor) . . .

21. . . . involving the loss of one's place in The World to Come . . .

22. See the very beginning of this section (¶143), which states outright, "Everyone was created to bring honor to God" and precedes onward in that vein (see ¶148 as well).

23. Rabbeinu Yonah is thus equating profaning Torah with profaning God's name.

24. . . . alone . . .

25. See 4:6.

26. See Supplementary Notes.

27. . . . in the Holy Temple . . .

His name" (Psalms 111:9), which means to say that because His name is "holy and awesome" He "commanded His covenant[28] for ever," and sanctified us with His *mitzvot* so that we might sanctify and fear Him. And that's why that's followed by, "The fear of God is the beginning of wisdom . . ." (Ibid. v. 10).

Thus, thanks to the holiness of the *mitzvot*, when we sanctify God, we're as esteemed as the celestial holy ones who sanctify and fear Him. As it's said, "God is greatly feared in the assembly of the holy ones" (Psalms 89:8).[29]

159. There are other types of sinners who haven't a place in The World to Come either, including: "God's enemies," those who "destroy God's vineyard," and those who "strike terror in the land of the living." We'll now explain their situations, and present evidence of the consequences they'll suffer.

It's stated outright in the Torah that "God's enemies"[30] lose their place in The World to Come. As it's written, "He repays those who hate Him to their face in order to destroy them. He will not delay when it comes to one who hates Him, He will repay him to his face" (Deuteronomy 7:10). That means to say that God repays His enemies for the *mitzvot* they did while in this world in order to have them perish in The World to Come.[31] As *Targum Onkelos* translates it, "He repays His enemies for the good they did in His presence in their lifetimes, so that they might perish" (Ibid.).[32]

But as David said, "Wrongdoers will perish, but God's enemies will be like the fat of lambs who will be consumed; consumed like smoke" (Psalms 37:20). Notice that he speaks of wrongdoers "perishing," and uses the same term used in connection with suffering and exile.[33] That's so because wrongdoers[34] will endure suffering,

---

28. . . . with us . . .

29. This calls for some explanation. The term for "sanctify" is מקדש. Aside from referring to either declaring something holy or making it so, it also refers to dedicating or reserving something for a unique role (e.g., something of value is מקדש, "sanctified" or reserved, for use in the Holy Temple; a woman is מקדש, "sanctified" or "reserved" for her husband-to-be when they're engaged, etc.). So, the issue this ¶ is addressing is the one we've focused on throughout this work: Fostering and enriching a relationship with God. That's to say, when we "sanctify God's name," we both declare and acknowledge His holiness, and we "engage" and commit ourselves to Him (as opposed to when we profane His name and thus betray Him — see 3:132). We thus become "sanctified" ourselves, and earn (rather than lose) our place in The World to Come, which alludes to the greatest degree of intimacy we could possibly experience with God Almighty.

30. To be defined in the following ¶. (See Supplementary Notes.)

31. See Supplementary Notes.

32. That is, good will *always* be rewarded, regardless of the actual character of the one who does good. Nonetheless, justice will always prevail in the end, and wrongdoing will always be recompensed — even if we don't see it. For it's only the existence of both life as we know it, and The World to Come, that allows for the "time" for full reward and punishment to come to fruition.

33. The text continues with the following:

tribulation, or[35] death. And they'll[36] suffer the judgments meted out for their actions[37] in The World to Come for some limited amount of time.[38]

But notice as well that "God's enemies" are likened to the fat of lambs— which melts away in fire and goes up in smoke—rather than to the *flesh* of lambs, which burns to a crisp but nonetheless leaves ash behind. That's why it's said that God's enemies "will be consumed, consumed like smoke"—because they'll be utterly destroyed, like the fat of lambs, which goes up in smoke. That is, their spirit will be destroyed, and they'll lose their place in The World to Come.[39]

It's also said, "I, God your Lord, am a jealous God, visiting the iniquities of the fathers upon the children to the third and fourth generation of those who hate Me" (Exodus 20:5). That's to say that He visits "the iniquities of the fathers upon the children . . . of those who hate" Him as much as their fathers hated Him.[40]

160. "God's enemies" are sometimes even found among those who observe *mitzvot* and are careful to avoid all physical and verbal sins.[41] That is, when such individuals are troubled by and can't bear[42] other people studying Torah. Or they can't stand seeing others serving and fearing God, like people who hate a certain king

---

As in, "And it shall come to pass in that day, that the great shofar shall be blown, and those who were lost [אבד], in the land of Assyria will come . . ." (Isaiah 27:13), "My people has been lost [אבד] sheep; their shepherds have caused them to go astray" (Jeremiah 50:6), and "I have strayed like a lost [אבד] sheep" (Psalms 119:176). It's also the term used in connection with death. As in, "I would have perished [אבד] in my affliction" (Ibid. v. 92), "the destruction [אבד] of my kindred" (Esther 8:6), "I will destroy [אבד] that soul" (Leviticus 23:30), which refers to being excised from this world.

34. . . . as opposed to "God's enemies" . . .

35. . . . premature . . .

36. . . . also . . .

37. i.e., their sinful actions while in this world.

38. . . . but they'll eventually inherit a full, secure, and blissful place in The World to Come.

39. That is to say, while "mere" wrongdoers always maintain *some* tenuous connection to the Source of life and thus remain, "God's enemies" do not, and are thus destroyed.

40. The text continues with the following:

That's, in fact, how our sages (*Sotah* 31A) explained, "'And show mercy to thousands of those who love Me and keep my *mitzvot*' (v. 6)—that is, when the fathers love Me I act kindly to their offspring for thousands of generations." And it's said of those who observe *mitzvot*, "Know therefore that God your Lord, is God, the faithful God who keeps His covenant and mercy to a thousand generations with those who love Him and observe His *mitzvot*" (Deuteronomy 7:9).

Notice that it says, "of those who hate Me" after it says, "visiting the iniquities of the fathers." That's because while the consequences of some transgressions are only suffered by the sinner himself and not his offspring, those of the enemies of God are visited upon their children, grandchildren, and great-grandchildren.

41. See Supplementary Notes.

42. . . . the thought of . . .

couldn't endure seeing others honoring or serving that king. They're all the more so His enemies if they put those thoughts into action and actually discourage others from studying Torah or doing *mitzvot*, out of their hate for God.

The same goes for those who belittle the honor accorded honest and righteous Torah scholars, and despise their crown of honor. Or who can't bear[43] those scholars being elevated into positions of power and leadership in their generation. As it's written, "They have not rejected you, they have rejected Me, that I should not reign over them" (1 Samuel 8:7).[44]

And all the more so if they want the honor accorded those scholars to[45] humiliate them, or for them to be belittled. Or if they admire the honor accorded wrongdoers who[46] rule over mere dust.[47]

Such individuals are truly God's enemies. They don't want Him to be served, and they're displeased with the emphasis placed on how holy it is to fear God, and on more and more people serving and fearing Him.

161. That's true as well of those who "destroy God's vineyard,"[48] like informers and those who cause the multitude to sin. They're also enemies of God, just as people who destroy a king's cities, vineyards, and gardens would be considered the king's enemies. And it's said, "For the house of Israel is the vineyard of the God of Hosts, and the men of Judah are His pleasant plant" (Isaiah 5:7).

It's also said, "They have conspired against Your people, and consulted against Your hidden ones" (Psalms 83:4); "For they conspire together harmoniously; they make an alliance against You" (Ibid. v. 6); "The rulers take counsel together against God, and against His anointed" (Ibid. 2:2). And so our sages said, "Informers and those who sin and cause the multitude to sin descend into *Gehenom*, where they are judged for ever and ever"[49] (*Rosh Hashanah* 17A).

162. It's true of those who "strike terror in the land of the living," about whom Ezekiel said, "(The transgressions of) those who struck terror in the land of the living . . . will be upon their bones" (Ezekiel 32:24–27). That comes to teach us that death will not atone for them, but that their transgressions will forever remain on their bones.[50]

---

43. . . . seeing . . .

44. The context of this verse indicates that when people reject a scholar's ideas they don't reject the scholar himself, so much as God, who is the catalyst of those ideas.

45. . . . somehow . . .

46. . . . actually . . .

47. That's to say, wrongdoers may seem to have power, but they actually only reign over the mortal and fallible. While the wise who appear to be powerless in fact reign over what's immortal and infallible. (See Supplementary Notes.)

48. i.e., the Jewish Nation, as will soon be explained. They, too, haven't a place in The World to Come, and are considered "God's enemies."

49. . . . and thus have no place in The World to Come.

50. . . . and they will not have a place in The World to Come.

Our sages said, "Renegades; apostates, heretics, informers, those who deny Torah and The Resurrection of the Dead, those who separate themselves from the ways of the community; and *those who strike terror in the land of the living* (like community leaders who evoke excessive fear for unholy reasons;[51] and those who sin and cause the multitude to sin, like Jeroboam ben Navat and his compatriots[52]) descend into *Gehenom* and are judged there for ever and ever"[53] (*Rosh Hashanah* 17A). As it's said, "They will go forth and look upon the carcasses of the men who have transgressed against Me; their worm will not die, nor will their fire be quenched" (Isaiah 66:24).

163.   The consequences for those who "strike terror in the land of the living"[54] come about for five reasons, two of which touch upon the perpetrator himself, and three of which touch upon his victims.[55]

Of the two that touch upon the perpetrator himself, the first comes because man is a worm and a maggot, and is even called that while he's alive.[56] Not only does this person not cower and humble himself,[57] he actually governs over others—and does so for unholy reasons! When even the *thought* of pre-eminence—without actually governing others—causes great harm. As it's said, "The haughty are an abomination to God" (Proverbs 16:5).[58]

164.   Second, because we're obliged to always be prepared to express the dread and fear of God in our hearts.[59] In fact, it's said of wrongdoers that, "They never say in their hearts, Let us now fear God" (Jeremiah 5:24). Yet one who "strikes terror in the land of the living" for unholy reasons has no fear in his heart for God, and wants to provoke fear for himself among others instead. So rather than concentrate on ways to express the fear of God in his own heart, he concentrates on

---

51. i.e., for reasons other than for the spiritual and ethical well-being of the community (See Supplementary Notes.)

52. See 1 Kings 11–16.

53. Both this citation and the one to follow indicate that such individuals will not have a place in The World to Come.

54. i.e., exclusion from The World to Come.

55. See our overall analysis of this trait in our comment to ¶167.

56. See Job 25:5–6 where man isn't seen as food for worms and maggots, as we might think, but as a veritable worm and maggot himself. As it's said, "Behold, even the moon is not bright and the stars are not pure in His sight. How much less so is man, who is a worm? And the son of man, who is a maggot?" This would thus be referring to man's coarse physicality and mundanity.

57. . . . as a worm or maggot would be expected to do, but . . .

58. That is, not only is he insensitive to his inborn coarseness, he's even audacious enough to exert power over others, when even the thought of that is reprehensible. (See Supplementary Notes.)

59. See Supplementary Notes.

ways to provoke fear for himself in God's people.[60] As it's said, "One who rules over others must be righteous, and must rule with the fear of God" (2 Samuel 23:3). That means to say that it's important for someone who rules over others to be righteous, and to rule[61] with the fear of God. For people should only fear him if he fears God.

165. Now, the first of the three reasons[62] that touch upon the victims. Because he[63] oppresses the community when he strikes terror upon them. And it's said, "You must not abuse one another" (Leviticus 25:17), which refers to verbal abuse, as we've already explained.[64]

166. Second, because many impediments come about as a result of striking terror in others. As our sages said, "A person should never strike unnecessary fear in his household. For the husband of the concubine of Gibah struck unnecessary fear in her, and she overthrew tens of thousands of Jews as a result" (*Gittin* 7A).

167. And third, because the people of the holy nation, who serve God, should never have to subjugate themselves to any human being. In fact, the only reason why anyone should allow himself to be feared is for the sake of Heaven. For it's said, "For the people of Israel are to be My servants" (Leviticus 25:55), rather than servants of[65] servants (*Babba Metziah* 10A). As it's said, "You are to be a kingdom of *Cohanim*,[66] a holy nation unto Me" (Exodus 19:6). ("*Cohanim*" implies lords and masters,[67] as in, "David's sons were *Cohanim*"[68] [2 Samuel 8:18]. And a "kingdom" implies the whole nation, as in, "There is no nation or kingdom . . ." [1 Kings 18:10] and, "For the nation and kingdom . . ." [Isaiah 60:12]).[69]

What that means to say is, you are to be a nation of lords unto Me, and are to serve[70] no human being. As it's said, "Who are you that you should fear mortal man?" (Isaiah 51:12) and, "Do not fear the taunts of men" (Ibid. v. 7).

As our sages said, "When many arose who called bad 'good,' and good 'bad,' they cast off the yoke of Heaven, and accepted the yoke of human rule" (*Sotah* 47B). And as David said, "Arise, God! Do not let man prevail; let the nations be judged before You. Implant fear in them, God; and let the nations know that they are only human" (Psalms 9:20–21). That comes to teach us that it's when people become

---

60. . . . . as if taking God's place in the lives of those others as well as in his own heart, so to speak.

61. . . . over them . . .

62. . . . why such a person loses his place in The World to Come . . .

63. i.e., the perpetrator.

64. See ¶'s 24 and 49.

65. . . . My . . .

66. Literally, "priests."

67. . . . in this instance . . .

68. Literally, "lords and masters."

69. While I might think that a "kingdom" implies a "government" or a "governing body" and an elite, Rabbeinu Yonah's point is that the Torah is referring to *all* of Israel.

70. Literally, "bear the yoke of."

insolent that they forget that they're only human, and that it's not right for anyone to rule over others, other than for the sake of Heaven.[71]

168. We'll now explain the reason for the consequences suffered by those who separate themselves from the community, which are like those suffered by the types[72] discussed so far.[73]

When the leaders of the nation[74] or of communities gather to serve God by agreeing to institute *mitzvot* for the people, they sanctify His name.[75] As it's said, "And there was a King in Jeshurun when the heads of the people and the tribes of Israel were gathered" (Deuteronomy 33:5)[76] and, "The nobles of the nations are gathered, the nation of the God of Abraham. For the shields of the earth belong to God, and He is greatly exalted" (Psalms 47:10).[77]

One who separates himself from the ways of the community is something of a prosecutor against their decision to serve God. And by excluding himself from those who sanctify God's name and demonstrating that he doesn't want to be their confidant,[78] or to be included in their proceedings, he profanes Divine service. So he's thus included among those we mentioned who demean the word of God and haven't a place in The World to Come.

---

71. All in all, the mistake those who strike terror in the hearts of others make is that they forget that God alone deserves our fear and obedience. And that believing otherwise is fraught with danger and serious consequence. But the happy outcome of realizing that you should really fear no mere mortal is that you come to fear no mere mortal, in fact. And you thus rise above all petty and mundane fears.

72. . . . of sinners . . .

73. . . . in that they also haven't a place in The World to Come. (See Supplementary Notes.)

74. . . . in general . . .

75. This refers to instances that require communal and national leaders to meet and set up measures (i.e., to "institute *mitzvot*") that address specific problems at hand.

76. The "King" refers to God (see Rashi), underscoring Rabbeinu Yonah's point that God is sanctified and glorified when the leaders of the Jewish Nation gather to serve Him.

77. The text continues with the following:

The Jewish people are referred to as "nations" [i.e., plural] here because they're comprised of twelve tribes, as in, "They will call the nations to the mountain" (Deuteronomy 33:19), though they're one nation when it comes to serving God, which is why it's said, ". . . the nation of the God of Abraham." And their kings and rulers are called "shields," as in, "Anoint a shield" (Isaiah 21:5).

What that means to say is that when the nobles of "the nations," whose kings and rulers are God's servants and loyal subjects—as in, "For our shield belongs to God; and our king [is dedicated] to the Holy One of Israel" (Psalms 89:19)—gather together in the service of God, "He is greatly exalted" (Psalms 47:10). That is, God is exalted and praised in His world by their gathering together and their service.

78. See Supplementary Notes.

Secondarily, by separating himself from the community he discourages the hesitant, and causes the multitude to sin.[79]

169.   We'll now explain the situation of those who "abandon God." They're people who don't bear the yoke of the fear of Heaven, and they perform *mitzvot* by rote.[80] And when the yetzer harah overtakes them to the point where they turnabout and sin intentionally, they neither sigh nor worry about their sin. Instead, they eat and dab their mouths, and think they've done nothing wrong.[81] As it's said, "Defiance speaks to the wrongdoer in his heart, and there is no fear of God before his eyes" (Psalms 36:2).

170.   Some of these wrongdoers have not only divested themselves of all fear.[82] They've actually overturned all decrees and judgments by bragging about and complimenting themselves for having indulged their cravings.[83] They're among those who anger and antagonize God. As it's said, "For the wrongdoer boasts about his cravings, and the greedy man curses and renounces God" (Psalms 10:3).

Isaiah spoke of the utter destruction of this type of sinner when he said, "While the defiant and sinners will both be broken, those who abandon God will be demolished" (Isaiah 1:28). He thus likened the defiant and sinful to broken utensils with pieces left intact,[84] but declared that "those who abandon God will be utterly demolished" and will have no place in The World to Come.[85] As it's said, "The day that comes will burn them up . . . and will leave them neither root or branch" (Malachi 3:19).

171.   But, the aforementioned types of sinners will only be destroyed[86] if

---

79. They're thus included among those who "destroy God's vineyard" (see ¶161), and lose their place in The World to Come as a consequence of that. All in all, though, those who separate themselves from the community also separate themselves from God, and would have others do the same. As a consequence, they're isolated from God and the Jewish Nation by being denied a place in The World to Come, measure for measure.

80. That is, they *do* observe God's *mitzvot*, but they "abandon" Him emotionally by doing so superficially and indifferently. They're thus like the spouse who might very well do what what's asked of him, but without any inner determination, and obviously not out of love. (See Supplementary Notes.)

81. . . . since they're so emotionally removed from what they're doing. That's to say that while they perform *mitzvot* mindlessly and listlessly, when it comes to sinning, they "lick their fingers" with alacrity, so to speak, in order to derive the last drop of satisfaction. (The expression itself is based on Proverbs 30:20, ". . . she eats, dabs her mouth, and says, I have done nothing wrong.")

82. . . . of God.

83. These individuals not only "lick their fingers" (see last ¶), they actually gloat over it and take pride in their taste. As such, they're like adulterers who tout their conquests and are callously removed from their spouses.

84. . . . when he said they'd merely be "broken" . . .

85. See Supplementary Notes.

86. . . . and lose their place in The World to Come . . .

they don't do tshuvah. For if they turn from their wrongful ways, they'll escape destruction.[87] As it's said, "Return, you faithless children, and I will heal your faithlessness.[88] Behold, we come to You, for You are God our Lord" (Jeremiah 3:22), "Return, O Israel, to God your Lord; for you have stumbled in your iniquity" (Hosea 14:2), and, "You will be saved in ease[89] and rest" (Isaiah 30:15).

---

87. See Supplementary Notes.
88. See Supplementary Notes.
89. i.e., in "שובה," which is a cognate of תשובה, tshuvah.

Chapter Sixteen

ଽଡ଼ଽ୧ଽଡ଼ଽ୧ଽଡ଼ଽ୧ଽଡ଼ଽ୧ଽଡ଼ଽ୧ଽଡ଼ଽ୧ଽଡ଼ଽ୧ଽଡ଼ଽ୧ଽଡ଼ଽ୧ଽଡ଼ଽ

172. An Explanation of the Sins of "The Four Types"

Our sages said, "Four types[1] never encounter the Divine Presence: maligners, liars, flatterers,[2] and slanderers.[3]

Maligners because it's written, 'He withdraws His hand from maligners' (Hosea 7:5).[4] Liars because it's written, 'A liar will not remain in My sight' (Psalms 101:7). Flatterers because it's written, 'A flatterer will not come before Him' (Job 13:16). And slanderers because it's written, 'For you are not a God who takes pleasure in wrongdoing; nor will evil dwell with You' (Psalms 5:5)" (*Sotah* 42A).

173. We'll now consider the make-up and character of each.[5] And in order to have you understand each in depth, we'll sort them by category, in order to show just what significant consequences would result from[6] such awful things.

In fact, a lot of good will come from sorting them that way. You might not

---

1. . . . of sinners . . .

2. Or, either "hypocrites" or "ingratiators" (those who try to find favor in others whom they believe can benefit them). We'll use any or all of these choices of translation as the context dictates.

3. Both the four types, who don't encounter the Divine Presence, and those in the previous section who haven't a place in The World to Come, are separated, perhaps even "divorced" from God. But while the latter ruptured that relationship with their attitudes and decisions, those mentioned here are spurned by God Himself, because of the hateful sorts of people they are. For as Moshe Chaim Luzzatto put it, "God only loves those who love the Jewish Nation" (*The Path of the Just*, Ch. 19, p. 171). (See Supplementary Notes.)

4. i.e., We know maligners never encounter the Divine Presence because it's written (and the same wording-pattern is used in the three other instances) . . .

5. . . . of the "four types."

6. . . . being guilty of . . .

come to a complete understanding of just how significant each one's act of defiance is if we didn't; you might not see how harsh and significant the consequences of each are; or you might see some, but not all.

We've also arranged them so that the first category is more significant than the next.[7] That way, from our discussion of the more lenient sections alone you'd be able to fathom just how dreadful and lethal these traits are, and you'd know that they all ultimately lead to death.[8]

Your ears might never have been open before, or you might have thought you were on the right path.[9] But now, thanks to our explication of the bitterness of these sins, you'll start to have anxious thoughts about them. You'll also begin to accept the appropriate admonishment, once you see that I'll be providing you with such impeccable witnesses[10] as logical arguments, Torah verses, as well as the sayings and wondrous parables of our sages to testify and offer proof.[11] And you'll be able to choose the truth.[12]

A certain favor from on high will then be stirred within you, which will extinguish your bad traits. And your heart will be uplifted as a result by words of purity.

---

7. . . . and the second is more significant than the third, etc. Which is to say, they've been set out in descending order of significance.

8. That is, you'd come to say, "If those are the consequences for just that, imagine the consequences for . . ."

9. . . . all along.

10. . . . for my side of the argument . . .

11. . . . of the heinous nature of these sins.

12. . . . and change your ways. In short, Rabbeinu Yonah is about to analyze these wrongful traits step by step, so that we might be convinced of just how bad they are. And of how cruel, small, and base we'd be to express them.

which refers to one who has the chance to study Torah and does not (*Sanhedrin* 99A), as we already indicated.[27]

Our sages said, "Whoever goes where people gather for amusement is within 'a gathering of maligners.' And by virtue of the fact that it's said, 'Do not sit among a gathering of maligners' (Psalms 1:1) which is followed by, 'Let your preferences lie in God's Torah, and dwell upon His Torah day and night' (Ibid. v. 2), we learn that[28] 'a gathering of maligners' leads to not studying Torah" (*Avodah Zarah* 18B).

In fact, if you haven't already resolved to study Torah whenever you're free to, you should, in order to not come to ruin. Use those moments to be alone, to consider and reflect upon your ultimate destiny, to scrutinize your ways, to foster outstanding personal qualities, and to draw close to God.[29]

And the fifth category consists of those who verbally malign actions taken, and things. But not in a heartfelt way—rather the way people who are jolly and laugh for no reason would.[30] That's sometimes a result of drinking and intoxication.[31] As it's said, "Wine is a maligner, strong drink is rowdy; and whoever is deceived by either will never be wise" (Proverbs 20:1). Meaning that "one who drinks wine is a maligner," and "one who drinks strong drink is rowdy."[32]

For, in fact, drinking leads to three bad things:[33] First, it causes you to malign. Second, it makes you rowdy and talkative, and as our sages said, "Speaking a lot encourages sin" (*Pirke Avot* 1:17)[34] and it's written, "A fool's voice is distinguished by a lot of words" (Ecclesiastes 5:2). And third, "Whoever is deceived by either will never be wise" (Proverbs 20:1).[35]

But know that the habit of maligning only becomes ingrained once one casts off the yoke of Heaven, as a consequence of which he's made to bear the yoke of misfortune[36] measure for measure.[37] As it's said, "Do not malign now, lest your

---

27. See ¶153.

28. . . . being among . . .

29. Rabbeinu Yonah provides us here with a very precious legacy, and tells us how to expend our energies. By using our spare time to study Torah, and to thusly arrive at the meaning of our lives, improve ourselves, and "to draw close to God!"

30. Small, feckless people tend to lapse into this. They intoxicate themselves (see the following), feel good and maybe important for a while, and then they disparage others' accomplishments for no good reason other than ego gratification. How small, and how mean! (And how commonplace!)

31. See Supplementary Notes.

32. The text continues with the following:

. . . as when "I am prayer" (Psalms 109:4) means, "I am a man of prayer" [i.e., one who prays].

33. . . . alluded to in the verse from Proverbs just cited.

34. Cited above in this ¶ in relation to speaking about nonsense.

35. That is, drinking makes one a maligner, rowdy, and hence unwise.

36. . . . thus paying the debt for his actions . . .

37. See Supplementary Notes.

binds be made strong" (Isaiah 28:22) and as our sages put it, "Rabbi Elazar said, 'Misfortune comes to those who malign, as it's said, "lest your binds be made strong" (Ibid.)'" (*Avodah Zarah* 18B).

Our sages would even alert their disciples not to malign others casually or occasionally.[38] And, in fact, it's important to alert against even that degree of it, since many stumble when it comes to casual maligning.

---

38. See Supplementary Notes.

Chapter Eighteen

ᏊᎧᏐᏊᎧᏐᏊᎧᏐᏊᎧᏐᏊᎧᏐᏊᎧᏐᏊᎧᏐᏊᎧᏐᏊᎧᏐᏊᎧᏐᏊᎧᏐ

178. As to the Liars, Whom We'll Classify into Nine Categories[1]

The first category consists of frauds who have forsaken Torah, and do harm and destroy things by what they say.[2] Like those who falsely repudiate others'[3] pledges, deposits, or salary claims. As it's said, "You must not steal, deal falsely, nor lie to one another" (Leviticus 19:11). And those who testify falsely against another. As it's said, "Do not bear false witness against your neighbor" (Exodus 20:13).

This category also includes those who carry out underhanded or onerous business deals and agreements. As it's said, "Do not abuse one another" (Leviticus 25:17) and, "Abuse and deceit never depart from her streets" (Psalms 55:12). They[4] are called "abusive" and "unconscionable." And theirs are among the most significant sins of any committed by the "four types," as we already stated in *The Gates of the Fear of Sin*.[5]

These are the ways of the "man of deceit" who expresses deceit by winking his eyes or pointing at something with his fingers.[6] As it's said, "An unconscionable

---

1. Lying is so, so pervasive in modernity, and so acceptable that it hardly seems prudent to mention it and thus indict so very many otherwise good people. But the wise will take Rabbeinu Yonah's revelations to heart, and be moved to do tshuvah.

2. This refers to out-and-out heinous liars who can't be trusted for anything.

3. . . . legitimate . . .

4. i.e., Those who practice that.

5. To our great regret, this work no longer exists.

6. That is, by making innuendoes without ever saying anything that could be proved to be out-and-out deceit.

person, a man of deceit . . . winks with his eyes, taps with his feet, points with his fingers" (Proverbs 6:12–13).

179. The second category consists of those whose lies cause no direct harm or damage to others, but who mean to bring about harm or do wrong. Like the liar who coaxes someone into believing he's his friend and confidant, and has him trust him and not be wary of him, which then makes it easy for the liar to do him harm.[7] As it's said, "He speaks peaceably with his neighbor with his mouth, but lies in ambush for him within" (Jeremiah 9:7) which is immediately followed by, "Should I not punish them for these things? says God. Should My Spirit not take revenge on a nation like this?" (Ibid. v. 8).

These two categories of liars suffer the consequences they do for two reasons: for their lies, and for the damage that results from them.[8] Because lying itself—aside from the damage it causes—is an abomination to God. As it's said, "There are six things God hates: . . . an arrogant look, a lying tongue, a heart that plots deceitful plans" (Proverbs 6:16–18), "I hate a ruthless mouth" (Ibid. 8:13) and "Who[9] is abominable and filthy? A man who drinks down deceit like water" (Job 15:16).

People themselves also find lying abominable. As it's said, "Lying tongues are an abomination to kings."[10]

180. The third category consists of people who disallow others to enjoy some good, or undermine it through some ruse or deception. They don't actually rob anything from their victim or assault him. What they do is set their sights on whatever good he's about to enjoy, hunt it down, and take it for themselves by lying. Or else they convince him to hand it over to them through their lies.[11]

The consequences these liars have to suffer are primarily based on their lying, but they suffer more when their victims suffer a loss (though they aren't primarily judged because of the loss, since their victim hasn't actually lost anything he'd already owned[12]).

As our sages said, "A swindler is like an idol worshipper" (*Sanhedrin* 92A). For

---

7. We'd refer to such a person as a "con artist."
8. See Supplementary Notes.
9. . . . does God trust less than one who . . .
10. There is no actual verse that says that. But it's the import of "It is an abomination to kings to commit wickedness; for the throne is established by righteousness. Righteous lips are the delight of kings; and they love him who speaks right" (Proverbs 16:12–13).
11. . . . to him. We'd describe people who'd do this as cruel and underhanded. Because while they don't technically do very much wrong, and they take nothing from anyone in fact, they're nonetheless so very mean, and nasty.
12. That is, the fact that this wrongdoer doesn't experience the Divine Presence is essentially due to his lying—not because of stealing. Because he didn't actually take anything from his victim. He'd nonetheless have to suffer further consequences of a different sort for the fact that his victim incurred a loss. But that's "besides the point," so to speak.

it's said, "Perhaps my father will touch me, and I will seem a deceiver[13] to him" (Genesis 27:12), and it's said about instances of idolatry, "They are nonsense, acts of deceivers" (Jeremiah 10:15).[14]

The sages said a swindler is "like an idol worshipper," and thus carried the analogy to its extreme, because swindlers are obscured by lies and helped by sham.[15]

181. The fourth category consists of those who lie when they relate things they've heard, and purposefully change things around. They don't benefit from their lies and their victims suffer no loss, but they do what they do because they prefer lying to being honest. They sometimes even make things up entirely.[16]

The consequences they're to suffer are minor in one respect, because no one loses anything as a result of their lies and nonsense. But they're very serious[17] because of the liar's audacity and love of lies, and their guilt is intensified because they love committing the sin even though they don't benefit from it. As Solomon said, "A false witness exhales lies" (Proverbs 6:19), which means to say that if you see a man "exhaling"[18] lies while speaking and relating things, know that such a trait would predispose him to testifying falsely against another, and to "bearing false witness against him" (Deuteronomy 19:16) because he loves telling lies.[19]

We're permitted to tell such lies, however, in order to fulfill *mitzvot*,[20] or to encourage goodness or peace. Our sages thus said it's permissible to praise a bride in the presence of her groom and to say that she's pretty and comely, even when she isn't (*Ketubot* 17A). And they said, "It is permissible to fabricate things for the sake of peace. For it's said, 'Before he died, your father commanded us, saying, "Tell Joseph the following: Please forgive your brothers' sins'[21]" (Genesis 50:16–17)" (*Yebamot* 65B).

Some people change part of what they hear without even knowing, by not bothering to listen closely. But this too is a bad trait.[22] For as Solomon said, "The

---

13. . . . or a "swindler" . . .

14. Thus equating deceivers (or "swindlers") with idol worshippers.

15. . . . just as idol worship is. There are two other points to be made here, though, about the correspondence between lying and idolatry. First, they are alike because liars try to act as gods by manipulating and manufacturing reality with their words. And second because idolatry is the ultimate lie, in that it falsifies the Ultimate Truth, which is God. And all other instances of lies are offshoots of that most fundamental one.

16. These are people who just *love* to lie, and are utterly inspired by the infinite creative possibilities of untruth. (See Supplementary Notes.)

17. . . . in another respect . . .

18. i.e., "exhuding" or "spewing forth" . . .

19. See Supplementary Notes.

20. i.e., specific and particular *mitzvot* unique to the moment that would require that for the good of all concerned. (See Supplemental Notes.)

21. . . . when it's never actually recorded that he said that.

22. That is, though it's not an unconscionable dependence on untruth, it still fosters that.

man who listens will speak forever" (Proverbs 21:28). That is, one who concentrates intently and listens for the point being made to him well enough to repeat it accurately without distorting anything, "will speak forever." Since people will always love to listen to what he has to say, and would never say to him, "Why are you still talking?"

182.   The fifth category consists of those who tell someone they're going to do him a favor or give him something, as they reiterate to themselves that they're not going to. As it's said, "Protect your tongue from wrongdoing, and your lips from distortion" (Psalms 34:14), which our sages said means that you're not to say one thing and mean another (*Babba Metziah* 49A).

They also declared that you can't be said to be unreliable or to be reneging on your word as long as you affirm what you actually say in your own mind (J. T., *Babba Metziah* 4:2).[23]

183.   The sixth category consists of those who promise to do someone a favor, then falsify their word by not doing it.[24] One should never break a promise once he's assured someone he'd do him a favor and gained his trust. For that would be lying, and would be breaking something of a covenant. And it's said, "The remnant of Israel will not act iniquitously, they will not speak lies, and a deceitful tongue will not be found in their mouths" (Zephaniah 3:13).

The same goes for mentioning to someone that you're going to give him a small gift.[25] Even though you wouldn't have promised it to him, our sages said that that would nonetheless deem you unreliable (*Babba Metziah* 49). Because the other person depended on what you said and trusted you,[26] since the gift is only a small one, and you'd certainly[27] give it to him. If the other person is poor, you'd be very wrong to go back on your word even if you'd promised him a very large gift.[28] Because you'd have made a vow to him, and it's said, "He must not break his word" (Numbers 30:3).

Similarly, if you bragged in public about a gift you were about to offer someone and thus lauded your own generosity, you'd have also made something of a promise. And it wouldn't be right for you to go back on your word then, after having glorified and lauded yourself that way.[29] For it's written, "One who lauds himself for a false gift is like mist, and wind without rain" (Proverbs 25:14). Which

---

23. See Supplementary Notes.

24. The ¶ above speaks of people who "tell someone they're going to do him a favor or give him something" when they know they'll never follow through. While this one speaks of those who promise to do someone a favor, and mean to follow through, but don't.

25. . . . and you don't.

26. i.e., he trusted you'd follow through on your word.

27. . . . be expected to . . .

28. . . . which he'd be more likely to doubt.

29. . . . since most people would assume you're bound to live by your word in that instance.

means to say that just as people are disappointed when signs of rain appear, and rain itself doesn't; so too do they become disappointed with "someone who lauds himself about a false gift." For his having lauded himself would[30] be a sign that he'd keep his word. And so the person promised the gift would become disappointed, since his expectations would have been dashed.[31]

184. The seventh category consists of those who mislead someone into believing they'd done him a favor or complimented him, when they hadn't. Our sages said, "It is prohibited to delude anyone, Jew or Gentile" (*Chullin* 94A). In fact, the sages consider that sin even more serious than robbing a[32] Gentile. Both because you'd be very guilty just being a liar, and also because we're obliged to be honest, since honesty is an instinct of the human spirit.[33]

185. The eighth category consists of those who extol themselves for qualities they don't have. Solomon said, "Exaggeration is no more appropriate for a fool than lying is for a prince" (Proverbs 17:7). That means to say that just as a fool hasn't a right to take pride in or credit for his ancestors' qualities,[34] a charitable person hasn't the right to laud himself by lying and saying, "I did this, I bestowed that, I gave there . . ." when he never did.[35]

Because while that would be a disgrace for anyone,[36] it would all the more so be disgraceful for a charitable person. For by praising himself for what he hadn't done, he'd be disgracing the charity he *had* given. Since that would indicate that all he ever wanted was a name for himself and praise when he gave charity in the past.

Also, if our sages said that one who has mastered one Tractate and is respected as much as one who's mastered *two* is obliged to say, "I only know one" (J. T., end

---

30. . . . seem to . . .

31. Literally, "proven a lie."

The operative terms in this ¶ are trust and disappointment. And the point of the matter is that we do so depend upon one another in society, and we're so very disappointed in life and in mankind when we fail each other, that we detract from the trust of God when we fail to accommodate each other. Another point to be made is that such instances of breaking promises, snatching things from beneath another's eyes, belying others' hopes and dreams, and destroying confidence are the very essence of cruelty.

32. . . . Jew or . . .

33. See Supplementary Notes.

34. The text continues with the following:

. . . even though it's said in the verse just before, "The glory of children are their fathers" [which would seem to indicate that *everyone* has a right to take credit for his ancestors' qualities] . . .

35. That is, just as a fool disgraces his ancestors when he takes credit for what they accomplished, a generous person disgraces his "ancestors," (i.e., his past deeds) when he takes credit for things he never did.

36. i.e., extolling themselves for qualities they don't have.

of *Shivi'it*), it's certainly forbidden to take false credit and to say, "I have heard many such things" (Job 16:2).[37]

186. And the ninth category consists of those who don't actually lie when relating what they'd heard or when reporting things.[38] But who'd nonetheless change things around at will—things that do no one any harm.[39] Simply because[40] lying brings them some satisfaction, even though they don't profit from it monetarily.

Our sages pointed out that this too is forbidden (*Yebamot* 63A). For it's said, "They have taught their tongue to speak lies" (Jeremiah 9:4).[41] Nonetheless, the consequences they'd have to suffer don't compare to the ones those who lie for no reason would, whom we mentioned in our discussion of the fourth category of liars, above.[42]

These, then, are the various categories of liars. We've thus also introduced rules about how to be an honest person,[43] which is an instinct of the human spirit.

---

37. In an attempt to fuse the two halves of this ¶ we'd offer that it's just as wrong to take credit for knowledge you don't have as it is to take credit for good you haven't done. Because you'd then be discrediting the knowledge you had the same way you discredited your past goodness.

38. That is, their testimony can be trusted.

(The literal translation of the beginning of this sentence reads, "And the ninth category consists of *children* who wouldn't lie when . . ." It alludes to Isaiah 63:8's, "Surely they are My people, *children who would not lie*")

39. That is, they'd innocently "add color" and elaborate upon things, and thus still participate in untruth.

40. . . . the very act of . . .

41. . . . with the clear implication that that is bad.

42. In ¶181.

43. See Supplementary Notes.

Chapter Nineteen

187. As to the Flatterers,[1] Whom We'll Classify into Nine Categories

The first category of flatterer either discerns, sees, or knows that someone is guilty of something[2] or is deceiving someone, or is sinning against someone by slandering or verbally abusing him, but tries to ingratiate himself onto him by saying, "You've done nothing wrong!"

At the very least, he's sinning by not criticizing him. For it's said, "Criticize your neighbor diligently, and do not incur sin on his account" (Leviticus 19:17). But he's also sinning by telling the other person that *he* isn't sinning. As it's said, "They empower wrongdoers" (Jeremiah 23:14).

This foolish flatterer has committed a grave sin. For, rather than being fervent about truth, he advances untruth; he calls bad, good; and he favors darkness over light. He also places two impediments before the sinner: First,[3] he'll never regret his mistake. And second,[4] he'll repeat his sin the very next day, now that the loathsome flatterer commended him for his cravings.[5]

---

1. See our note to 3:172 where we point out that the term used here, החנפים, can be translated alternately as "flatterers," "hypocrites," or the unwieldy but accurate "those who try to ingratiate themselves upon others (in order to curry favor with them)". We'll use the term most appropriate to the context. The astute reader will be embarrassed to find him- or herself and others so aptly singled out here!

2. . . . heinous . . .

3. . . . by making it likely that . . .

4. . . . by making it likely that . . .

5. That's to say, not only does this ingratiator lie and countenance sin, he also

And all that's aside from the consequences the flatterer would have to suffer for any damage the sinner's victim endured when he[6] justified the sinner's deed. And aside from the consequences he'd suffer for having lied. For it's said, "You destroy those who lie" (Psalms 5:7) and, "Both those who validate wrongdoers, and those who indict the righteous are an abomination to God" (Proverbs 17:15).

This is all the more true when the sin the other person committed is public knowledge. Because when the flatterer says to him, "You're innocent and guiltless" in front of everyone, he profanes and demeans both the faith and the law.

188.   In fact, you're obliged to expose yourself to danger rather than incur so wrong a sin. For our sages said that Aggripus was once reading from a Torah scroll when he came to the verse that reads, "You may not set a foreigner over you" (Deuteronomy 17:15) and he started to shed tears. They said to him, "But, you are our brother!" And right then and there the Jews were sentenced to annihilation (God forbid!) for trying to ingratiate themselves to Aggripus (*Sotah* 41A).[7] As such, one sitting in judgment must never be afraid of any mortal man.[8] For it's said. "You must not fear anyone"[9] (Deuteronomy 1:17).

While this particular category of flatterer and wrongdoer should be included among two different types of wrongdoers since he's a combination of liar and flatterer, nonetheless there are some flatterers who are destroyed for their hypocrisy alone, as we'll explain.

189.   The second category of flatterer publicly praises a wrongdoer, either to his face or not.[10] And while he doesn't justify the wrongdoer's offense or lie about his crime, he nonetheless describes him as a "good man."[11]

It's said about this, "Those who abandon Torah praise wrongdoers" (Proverbs 28:4), which implies that a person wouldn't praise anyone who violates words of Torah or nullifies its *mitzvot* unless he himself had abandoned Torah.

Even if he'd only praise the wrongdoer for what's actually good about him and

---

reinforces wrong by confounding the difference between good and evil, and by not discouraging wrongdoing.

6. i.e., the flatterer.

7. That is, had the leaders of the nation bravely and firmly stood their ground and not tried to ingratiate themselves to Aggripus (who was in fact not a Jew, and didn't belong on the throne), a lot of pain and ruin could have been avoided.

Parenthetically, we've tried to mitigate the daunting statement that "the Jews were sentenced to annihilation" by our exclamation, "God forbid!" The original does that by wording it euphemistically, "*Israel's enemies* were sentenced to annihilation." But we've presented it as we have in order not to confuse the English-language reader who wouldn't be familiar with this common rhetorical device.

8. See Supplementary Notes.

9. . . . or try to ingratiate yourself to him in order to curry favor with him.

10. See Supplementary Notes.

11. . . . despite his serious flaws.

intercede on his behalf to point out to others how honest he is,[12] that in itself is an unhealthy wrongdoing. For as a result of his mentioning what's good about the wrongdoer without mentioning what's bad, and as a result of his covering over his acts of defiance, those listening will consider the wrongdoer innocent, and they'll show him respect and encourage him. (But we've already mentioned the pitfalls and ruin that come about from showing respect for wrongdoers.[13])

So, it's wrong to mention wrongdoers' virtues without mentioning their vices and foibles.[14] For it's said, "The names of wrongdoers will[15] rot" (Proverbs 10:7). And it's also said, "I will cite your righteousness and your deeds, but they will not help" (Isaiah 57:12), which means to say that any good a wrongdoer has done won't help to protect him from the bad[16] when God comes to judge him and his many acts of defiance and deception are contrasted with the good.[17] For his sins will dominate.[18]

For our sages pointed out that, "One whose transgressions outnumber his merits is recorded and sealed for death" (*Rosh Hashanah* 16B);[19] and that wrongdoers can be recognized by their speech and their conduct,[20] as we mentioned in *The Gates of the Fear of Sin.*[21]

190. In fact, the righteous despise wrongdoers. As it's said, "A dishonest man is an abomination to the righteous" (Proverbs 29:27). But if you aren't a confidant of the righteous,[22] and you don't despise or curse wrongdoers, at least don't bless them.[23]

191. You might happen to praise a wrongdoer in all innocence, out of a naive belief that it's always good to offer praise, whether it's warranted or not. But you'd unwittingly be praising the dead. For our sages said that wrongdoers "are dead while they are alive, as it is said, 'The dead know nothing' (Ecclesiastes 9:5)"[24] (*Berachot* 18B).

---

12. . . . overall, despite his instances of wrongdoing . . .

13. See ¶'s 149–152.

14. Apparently, then, it's all right to mention bad people's virtues in the context of their faults. Just not apart from them.

15. Or, "should be allowed to . . ."

16. . . . he'd done . . .

17. . . . he's happened to have done.

18. That is, overall this person is bad. Any good he might have done in passing can't compare with the wrong. And that must be kept in mind.

19. That is, "One whose transgressions outnumber his merits has that recorded and sealed, and is immediately sentenced to death," despite any good he otherwise did.

20. Which is to say that some people are clearly evil, despite any good they might have done. (See Supplementary Notes.)

21. As was already indicated, this work no longer exists, to our great regret.

22. This is a polite way of saying, "If you yourself aren't quite righteous . . ."

23. See Supplementary Notes.

24. The full verse reads, "For the living know that they will die; but the dead know nothing, nor do they have a reward any more; for their memory is forgotten." And that's to

And what had[25] been an unintentional sin is then[26] intentional.[27] For no servant who loved his master's enemies and befriended those who distanced themselves from him could ever[28] love the master himself. And wouldn't they know that?[29] For it's said, "Fools will be acclaimed by the base" (Proverbs 3:35), as we've already explained.[30]

192.   The third category of flatterer praises the wrongdoer—but only to his face. Because he's[31] wise enough to realize that he shouldn't praise him in public, as that would set a trap for others. But you'd still be committing a serious sin if you did that,[32] because you'd be validating a wrongdoer in his own eyes. And he'd never do tshuvah for his bad ways nor worry about his sins, because he'd think he's righteous.[33] For only one outside the community of the righteous would say to himself, "I always knew it!" when he's flattered.[34]

For it's said, "A flatterer destroys another with his mouth, but the righteous is delivered through knowledge" (Proverbs 11:9), which means to say that a flatterer destroys another with his mouth when he praises him, and when the latter believes what he says, becomes fixed in his ways, starts to see himself as "special,"[35] and hasn't a sense of the darkness and pit he's plunged himself into. His heart begins to swell, and he starts falling into the trap of arrogance. The flatterer would have thus utterly destroyed him with his flattery.

"But the righteous is delivered through knowledge," that is, the righteous are delivered thanks to their knowledge of the harm flatterers do. For if those flatterers were to praise the righteous, their hearts wouldn't swell as a result. As our sages said,

---

say that while the "living" (i.e., the righteous) know they are mortal, and do as much good as they can in life, their opposite, "the dead" (i.e., wrongdoers) don't give a thought to their mortality, and become undone. The import of the statement is that when you praise wrongdoers you praise individuals destined for destruction, and hence "dead" for all intents and purposes. So, "save your breath," as we might say.

25. . . . originally . . .

26. . . . proven to have been . . .

27. . . . all along. That is, the compliment that seemed to be offered in all innocence is actually rooted in bad intentions.

28. . . . really be said to . . .

29. i.e., isn't that just logical? And doesn't that prove that they did it intentionally all along?

30. See ¶147.

31. . . . at least . . .

32. . . . despite the privacy of your act.

33. See Supplementary Notes.

34. While the righteous take no credit for the good they do. (See Supplementary Notes.)

35. Or, "privileged." In fact, the wicked always look for confirmation of their long-held feelings of superiority when others flatter them. And they actually believe what they hear.

"Even if the whole world says you are righteous, consider yourself a wrongdoer" (*Niddah* 30B) and, "If some friends praise you and others criticize you, love the ones who criticize you, and reject the ones who praise. For they[36] bring you to eternal life, while the others make you feel good about your wrongdoings with their praise" (*Avot D'Rebbe Natan* 29).

The verse could also be understood to mean that the righteous deliver others with their knowledge by not flattering them, and by criticizing them instead. As well as by guiding them onto the path when they roam about in aimless oblivion.[37]

Some flatterers purposely ingratiate themselves to powerful people in order to be admired and advanced by them. But our sages warned that whoever flatters others in order to be admired will ultimately withdraw from them in shame (*Avot D'Rebbe Natan* 29).

193. The fourth category associates with wrongdoers, and not only do they not criticize them roundly and separate themselves from them — they actually befriend them, when it's said, "God severed your works because you befriended Achazyahu" (2 Chronicles 20:37).[38] But the righteous utterly despise wrongdoers, as it's said, "(A righteous person is one) in whose eyes a vile person is despised" (Psalms 15:4).

As our sages said, "It is not for no reason that the starling went with the raven — they are of the same sort" (*Babba Kama* 92B) and, "Birds dwell with their kind, and people dwell with others like themselves" (Ibid.).[39]

They also said, "It is forbidden to stare at an evildoer,[40] as it is said, 'Were it not for the fact that I am beholding the face of Jehosephat the king of Judah, I would not look at you, nor see you' (2 Kings 3:14)" (*Megillah* 28A). And, "The eyes of the person who stares at an evildoer dim in old age, as it is said. 'And it was that when Isaac was old, his eyes became too dim to see' (Genesis 27:1)," because he stared at Esau (though he wasn't aware of what Esau was doing since Esau was hiding his actions, as in, "Their deeds are done in the dark" [Isaiah 29:15]).

---

36. i.e., your critics.

37. The text continues with the following:

It's also said, "A smooth [i.e., flattering] mouth brings on ruin" (Proverbs 26:28), where a smooth [חלק] mouth is likened to a slippery [חלקלקות, a cognate of חלק] road, to point out that just as a person can [easily] fall and stumble on a slippery road — as it's said, "Let their way be dark and slippery" (Psalms 35:6) — so, too, can one fall and stumble as a consequence of a "smooth," flattering tongue, as we explained.

And David said, "God will excise all smooth lips, all tongues that speak arrogantly" (Ibid. 12:4), and thus cursed smooth lips because they destroy people, as well as the opposite of "smooth lips," "rough" tongues, which express slander.

38. That is, they flatter wrongdoers by not only not avoiding them, but by actually befriending them.

39. As the expression goes, "Birds of a feather flock together." Which is to say that only those who are themselves actually bad would befriend bad people.

40. . . . so it's even more so forbidden to befriend them. (See Supplementary Notes.)

But we've already explained well enough how life-threatening it is to befriend wrongdoers.[41]

194. The fifth category is the sort of person who's word is trusted, who's depended upon by whoever hears him, who then sets out to promote an individual or a relative he's close to by declaring him a sage when he's not. He[42] will become a snare and a stumbling block to others, because they'll depend on his decisions, and on his resolutions of their disputes. As a result, he'll pervert justice and destroy the world.[43]

The same would apply if the flatterer declared someone trustworthy whom no one knew well enough to say whether he was or not. And, based on his word, someone then gives him a position in his household and puts everything within his reach,[44] at which point the flatterer denies it,[45] saying, "I never saw him!"

For as our sages put it, "Whoever appoints an unqualified judge is like one who plants an *Ashera* tree.[46] If he does so when a true scholar is available, it is as if he planted the *Ashera* next to the altar" (*Sanhedrin* 7B).[47] In fact, it was once the case that anyone who appointed someone unqualified to make decisions would be quoted the verse, "Woe to him who says to wood, 'Awake!'; who says to the dumb stone, 'Arise!' Does he teach it? Behold, it is overlaid with gold and silver, and there is no breath at all in it" (*Habbakuk* 2:19).

In the end, God will exact retribution from all who appoint such individuals. As it's said, "God is in His holy sanctuary; let all the world be silent before Him" (Ibid. v. 20).

195. The sixth category of flatterer has the opportunity to protest[48] and neither protests nor criticizes. He also doesn't stare incredulously at what wrongdoers do, scrutinize them, or criticize them at all, even though we're commanded to purge wrongdoing from our midst.[49] As it's said, "Purge wrongdoing from your midst" (Deuteronomy 13:6).

As our sages said, "Whoever can protest in his household and does not, is held responsible for it; whoever can protest in his city and does not, is held responsible

---

41. See 3:50–51,59,151 as well as ¶'s 197–198. (See Supplementary Notes.)

42. i.e., the person declared a sage.

43. i.e., he'll thus undermine society, which depends on justice, and on the trustworthiness of those who commend others for responsible positions.

44. . . . who was then robbed.

45. i.e., that he'd recommended the person.

46. A tree that was worshipped idolatrously. See Deuteronomy 16:21, which reads, "Do not plant you an *Ashera* tree near the altar of God your Lord."

47. i.e., he has had the audacity to erect an idol near the Holy Temple itself, for all intents and purposes.

48. . . . against something wrong or heinous . . .

49. . . . rather than accept it passively (or with a wink of an eye) as such hypocrites do, in an effort to ingratiate themselves to the wrongdoers.

for it; and whoever can protest in the world and does not, is held responsible for it" (*Shabbat* 54B). And it's said, "They will trip over each other" (Leviticus 26:37), which our sages explained to mean, "They will trip[50] over each other's sins" (*Sanhedrin* 27B). As well as, "Each Jew is responsible for every other Jew" (Ibid.).[51]

196. The seventh category of flatterer sees people around him being stubborn,[52] and tells himself that since they're not likely to listen to him if he speaks honestly to them and criticizes them harshly, he won't.[53] But he'd be sinning by not trying to criticize and alert them. For he might have awoken them from their foolish slumber by rousing their spirits, rather than been a party to their error.

For our sages said about the verse, "Go through the city, through Jerusalem, and put a mark upon the foreheads of the men who sigh and who cry for all the abominations that are done in its midst"[54] (Ezekiel 9:4), that God's Attribute of Justice declared, 'Even though they are perfectly righteous and observe the Torah, they should have protested, but they did not.' God Himself then said, 'But it is perfectly clear to Me that if they had protested, they would not have been listened to.' The Attribute of Justice then implored, 'Master of the Universe! Even if it was perfectly clear to You, *they* had no idea whether the people would listen to them or not.' So God commanded them to 'Slay old men and young men . . . And begin at My Sanctuary' (Ibid., v. 6), referring to the sanctified and righteous ones, who were then made to suffer the consequences of not protesting (*Shabbat* 55A).[55] And it is said, "Criticize your neighbor diligently, and do not bear sin on his account" (Leviticus 19:17).

Nonetheless, if it's clear to everybody, well known, proven, and determined that a particular sinner hates admonishment, and wouldn't listen to his teachers or pay heed to anyone who'd instruct him, then it's said of him, "Do not criticize a maligner, for he may hate you" (Proverbs 9:8). And as our sages said, "Just as it is a mitzvah to say something that will be listened to, so too is it a mitzvah to not say something that will not be listened to" (*Yebamot* 65B)[56] and, "It is better that they sin unintentionally than presumptuously" (*Beitzah* 30A).[57]

---

50. . . . and stumble . . .

51. Hence, it's important for us to interfere with the immoral plans of others.

52. i.e., stubbornly defiant and sinful.

53. And he thus tries to ingratiate himself to them by seeming to accept them.

54. . . . rather than do something about it . . .

55. The sages were illustrating an "argument" God was having with His own Attribute of Justice, so to speak. The latter argued that the righteous should have criticized wrongdoers rather than just cried and sighed about their misdeeds—even if they wouldn't have been listened to. And God agreed, and punished them for not trying.

56. See Supplementary Notes.

57. That is, while as a rule it's irrelevant whether a maligner hates you for criticizing him or not, in this case it's very relevant. Because his hating you would cause him to sin presumptuously rather than unintentionally.

197.   The eighth category[58] would hear about people slandering others or speaking profanely, or would commune with people who deride and demean Torah and *mitzvot*, and would keep his mouth closed, because he knows what "briars and thorns" (Ezekiel 2:6)[59] they are, and that they wouldn't listen to him if he criticized them.[60]

But he, too, would[61] suffer the consequences of not responding to fools in their folly. Because others would say he's just like those wrongdoers and agrees with them. He's obliged to respond to them and to scold them, to exalt the Torah and *mitzvot* they'd demeaned and taunted, and to be zealous about the honor due the innocent and righteous they'd spoken against.

198.   This is one of the situations in which you're obliged to stop associating with wrongdoers.[62] Because[63] you'd have to suffer the consequences of always hearing their evil words and being reticent about responding to them.[64]

This is the gist of Solomon's statement, "Do not be jealous of wrongdoers or desire to be with them. For their hearts dwell on destruction, and their lips speak of troublemaking" (Proverbs 24:1–2). Which is to say, you yourself will incur a sin as a result of their sins, by constantly listening to their evil words and remaining silent.

199.   And the ninth category shows wrongdoers respect in order to preserve the peace.[65] In truth, he doesn't say anything good about them, and doesn't show them the kind of respect that would lead others to think he's doing that because he believes they deserve it. And he only shows them the kind of respect one would show the wealthy (i.e., with ruffles and flourishes, and expectations of return[66]) who happen to be successful rather than deserving. But he'd be guilty of sinning then, nonetheless. Because while it's permissible to show respect for the wealthy, it's not permissible to do so for wrongdoers. As it's said, "Look upon the arrogant and debase him . . . And crush wrongdoers beneath them" (Job 40:11–12).

---

58. . . . is the sort of person who . . .

59. i.e., how adamant and antagonistic . . .

60. Rather than seeing people doing harm and not saying anything (which was true of the previous type), this sort of hypocrite hears about harmful things being said and doesn't respond, because he hopes to maintain a relationship with the wrongdoers. (See the next ¶'s insinuation of that last point when it says, "This is one of the situations in which you're obliged to stop associating with wrongdoers.")

61. . . . have to . . .

62. See Supplementary Notes.

63. . . . otherwise . . .

64. That is, you're sure to be exposed to evil words when you associate with evildoers. But because you're the sort of person who'd want to ingratiate yourself to others as much as possible, you wouldn't respond to them. And you're bound to suffer as a result.

65. i.e., in order to be on good terms with them, rather than to fend off harm (as will be discussed).

66. . . . from it in the future.

The only time it's permissible to do that[67] is when you're worried they might harm you or cause you monetary loss.[68] That is, when they're in control, or the times are brazen, when we're unable to force them to comply and are powerless to restrain them.[69]

Only then is it permissible to show them the kind of respect you'd show a powerful and menacing person you'd fear and anguish over—including standing up,[70] showing them honor, and the like. But you're never to praise them, or speak well of them to others. As our sages said,[71] "It is permissible to flatter the world's wicked" (*Sotah* 41B).

---

67. i.e., to show respect for government or other such officials who are wrongdoers.
68. . . . if you don't.
69. Which is to say, as long as we're in exile.
70. . . . in their presence, as a sign of respect . . .
71. . . . about such instances . . .

Chapter Twenty

𐰈☄𐰈☄𐰈☄𐰈☄𐰈☄𐰈☄𐰈☄𐰈☄𐰈☄𐰈☄𐰈

200. As to the Slanderers[1]

Our sages said, "One who slanders seems to deny the existence of God.[2] As it's said, '. . . who have said,[3] We will prevail with our tongue; and our lips are our own. Who is our master?' (Psalms 12:5)" (*Aruchin* 15B).

They're seen as denying God's existence because their slander does so much damage and brings about so much harm to the people whose reputations they've besmirched or whom they've harmed in other ways.[4] And a person wouldn't possibly inflict others with the kinds of weapons and means of doing the sort of harm that's

---

1. This section serves as an introduction to the subject of slanderers. The pattern established with our discussion of maligners, liars, and flatterers of classifying them by categories will be continued with ¶'s 211–231.

2. Literally, he "negates the most important thing"—that is, he acts as if God doesn't exist.

3. i.e., It is slanderers who have said . . .

4. That is, slanderers can be said to seem like non-believers because they think they're Godlike themselves. Since they're apparently able to affect others' lives with words alone. But they're sorely mistaken and terribly one-dimensional in their perceptions.

Another point needs to be made here. And that is that we run into trouble throughout this section if we think of "מספרי לשון הרע" (the expression used here) as "slanderers" only. For slanderers do others harm by besmirching their reputations. And while מספרי לשון הרע may do that, they may also express things that have nothing to do with others' reputations, which nonetheless harm them (like obscenities, and fault-finding sharp criticisms, as found in ¶'s 229–231). As such, מספרי לשון הרע should be understood to be people who do verbal rather than physical harm. But we'll continue using the term "slanderers" because, while limited, it's still the only English term available other than "bad-mouthers" or "speakers of bad things," which, while more technically correct, are nonetheless untenable.

It's also vital to point out how very widespread this trait is, in modernity. And how minor a character flaw it's considered to be in society, when it's anything but minor, in fact. And, sad to report, it can't be denied that whole lives and whole professional careers are

bitterer yet than death[5]—which the slanderer himself neither benefits nor profits from—had the yetzer harah not caught him in its snare, and had he not cast off the yoke of Heaven from himself and removed its reins.[6]

As David said,[7] "Strangers have risen against me, oppressors have threatened my life. They have not set God before them" (Psalms 54:5). Our sages explained that to mean that "'they have not set God before them' because they wanted Saul's blessing. Since he said to them, 'You are blessed by God for having had pity on me!' (1 Samuel 23:21).[8] And 'they have not set God before them' despite the fact that it's written in His Torah, 'Cursed be whoever strikes another in secret' (Deuteronomy 27:24)" (Midrash *Tehillim* 54).[9]

It's said, "There is no advantage in being a slanderer" (Ecclesiastes 10:11), and it's said of Doeg, "Your tongue plots destruction . . . You love evil more than good, and speaking falsely more than righteously" (Psalms 52:4–5). Our sages explained those verses as follows: "What advantage did you[10] enjoy, and how did you profit by slandering? You needed no money, for you were rich. (As it is said, 'Doeg was one of Saul's chief herdsmen' [1 Samuel 21:8].) It could only be that you 'love evil more than good, and speaking falsely more than righteously' because you have cast off the yoke"[11] (Midrash *Tehillim* 52).

It's also said, "Do people not despise a thief even if he steals . . . when he is hungry?" (Proverbs 6:30), which is followed by, "One who commits adultery is heartless . . ." (Ibid. v. 32). What that means to say[12] is that an adulterer is worse than one who steals when he's hungry. But a slanderer is worse yet than both,[13] our sages said, for he commits a great sin which he derives no benefit from.[14] As it's said,

---

founded upon just such traits and nothing is thought of it. If we'd only sensitize ourselves to the great hurt and harm we cause others when we exhibit this trait!

5. i.e., the besmirching of a reputation, or the like. (See Supplementary Notes.)

6. That's to say, only a Godless, essentially evil individual would besmirch another's reputation and do him so much harm for no rational, or even self-serving, reason.

7. The text continues with the following:

in the Psalm beginning, "When the Ziphites came and said to Saul, Does David not hide himself among us?" (Psalm 54)

8. That is, we're told both in Psalm 54:2 and in 1 Samuel 23:19 that the Ziphites did an un-Godly, evil thing and endangered David's life when—for no other reason than to get Saul's blessing—they informed him that David was hiding among them and waiting to depose him.

9. That is, they obviously haven't set God before them, since they openly rejected the dictum against "striking in secret" (i.e., slandering).

10. i.e., Doeg.

11. . . . of Heaven.

12. i.e., what that juxtaposition seems to suggest is that . . .

13. See Supplementary Notes.

14. That is, a slanderer is worse yet than an adulterer or a hungry thief. For while they

"How would a false tongue benefit or profit you? (Psalms 120:3)" (Midrash *Tehillim* 120:3).

201. The second reason why slanderers seem to deny God's existence is because they believe they can do whatever they care to do with their lips, since lips don't actually do anything,[15] and that they themselves are in charge of their tongues.[16] So they conclude that they don't have to refrain from saying whatever occurs to them, since a person is only forbidden to sin with his[17] limbs. As in, "Our lips are our own. Who is our master?" (Psalms 12:5).[18]

They'd never say,[19] "Where is God, my Maker, who controls the movements of each of His creations,[20] without exception; whose will all are bidden to carry out?"[21] Instead, they claim to have dominion over whatever comes from their lips.[22]

But that's not true of those wrongdoers who sin in other ways. For *they* know that forsaking God[23] is a bad and bitter thing to do. It's just that their cravings get the best of them, and their impulses overcome them, which then causes them grief.[24]

But our sages said, "Slander is more serious than three sins: idol worship, illicit relations, and murder. For it's said about idol worship, 'Please, God, these people have sinned a great sin' (Exodus 32:31). It's said about illicit relations, 'How can I

---

can be "excused" in light of the fact that their crimes can be seen to be the consequence of great cravings, slandering could never be condoned that way.

15. i.e., because while lips may instigate action, they themselves do nothing overt.

16. . . . anyway. (See Supplementary Notes.)

17. . . . outer . . .

18. In truth, this flies in the face of the American notion of the inviolable "freedom of speech." But while that freedom is certainly meaningful when it comes to fighting evil and injustice, it's sometimes over-cited, and used as a rank excuse to slander, demean, and defame others.

19. . . . anything like . . .

20. i.e., each component of His creations, which is to say, each body part. And not just the external organs.

21. See Supplemental Notes.

22. That's to say, slanderers are under the mistaken belief that a person is only forbidden to *do* harm. That our words and (by extension) our thoughts and motivations are "nobody's business" but our own, so they needn't conform to God's will. But the truth is that God's will infuses the whole of us, to the deepest levels. So our lips, as well as our thoughts, motivations, etc., should all serve Him. To think and say otherwise is atheistic.

The other point to be made is that speech and its ability to encapsulate the abstract is a uniquely human gift. So, if you assume your speech is under your control, you assume something so unique and precious isn't under God's authority, which is also atheistic.

23. . . . by sinning . . .

24. That is, other sinners don't rationalize their misdeeds with overblown philosophical claims to dominion over their own inner being. Those other sinners know in their hearts that it's mistaken to forsake God, for all intents and purposes, by sinning. They merely lapse as a natural consequence of their impulses, and then regret it sorely.

do something so wrong?' (Genesis 39:9). And it's said about murder, 'My sin is too great to bear' (Genesis 4:13). While it's said of slander, 'God will excise all smooth lips, all tongues that speak arrogantly' (Psalms 12:4)" (*Aruchin* 15B).[25]

202. But now we have to explain how the sin of slander could possibly be worse than those other three sins, when our sages said about each that, "You're to give up your life rather than commit it" (*Sanhedrin* 74A).[26] And when they said that, "The sin of idol worship is so severe that whoever concedes to it denies the whole Torah" (*Chullin* 5A); and that, "Being an apostate about idol worship is being an apostate about the entire Torah" (*Chullin* 4B)!

But when you reflect upon their words, you come to discover many essential principles[27] and many off-shoots of them.

203. First, the slanderer reiterates his foolishness again and again. He may humiliate, besmirch, disgrace, say too much, and "strike in secret"[28] ten times a day. And since he places no limit on what he has to say, there'd never be an end to the consequences he'd have to suffer. For if, as we indicated,[29] a minor sin repeated over and over again becomes very serious, that's certainly true of so major, wicked, and noxious a sin.[30]

So when our sages said that, "Slander is more serious than three sins . . . ," they were referring to someone who committed them as a result of being overcome by his impulses, rather than to the rare apostate who constantly commits them.[31]

204. Second, it's very hard for a slanderer to do tshuvah.[32] For after having trained his tongue to speak lies, consigned his lips to evil, and been in the habit[33] for so long, he can no longer control himself.[34] And it's as if his tongue were overtaking[35] his thoughts.

As it's said, "Your tongue[36] plots destruction" (Psalms 52:4), "A fool's lips will

---

25. That is, while idol worship can be prayed for, illicit relations can be mourned over and regretted, and murder may be a great personal burden for its perpetrators but nonetheless atoned for, it seems slander is utterly and eternally inexcusable. But see note 31 below. (See Supplementary Notes.)

26. See Supplementary Notes.

27. i.e., many fundamental truths.

28. i.e., slander others.

29. See 1:4–7,38.

30. . . . as this.

31. That is, slander is worse than accidental and impulsive instances of idol worship, illicit relations, and murder. But persistent idol worship, etc., is nonetheless more serious than slander.

32. See Supplementary Notes.

33. . . . of doing that . . .

34. See Supplementary Notes.

35. Literally, "causing" or "bringing about."

36. . . . rather than your mind . . .

consume him" (Ecclesiastes 10:12) and, "The fool's mouth is his ruination"[37] (Proverbs 18:7), where the term for "ruination" also denotes fear and fright. What that means to say, then, is that the fool is as afraid and frightened of being victimized by his raging tongue as he would be of an enemy, because[38] he hasn't any control over his lips.

205.   Third, a slanderer takes his sin lightly and says, "It's only talk."[39] So he never confronts all the damage he's done, and doesn't do tshuvah for his wrongful ways. Yet even if he'd do tshuvah, it wouldn't be a complete tshuvah, since he never recognizes the magnitude of his sin.[40] For[41] complete tshuvah that would cleanse a person of many acts of defiance only comes about when a firelike sorrow burns within the one doing it.[42]

206.   Solomon said, "A proud and haughty man, 'maligner' is his name, acts in arrogant wrath" (Proverbs 21:24).[43] That means to say, don't assume that a maligner whose arrogance moved him to strike with his tongue in pride and haughtiness, in wrath and in fury, would only strike by mouth, and not physically. Know that he "*acts* in arrogant wrath." Which means to say that if he cannot strike his enemies verbally, but is able to actually strike them, that he will—wrathfully and mercilessly.[44]

For as our sages pointed out in regard to Doeg, "when Saul ordered that the priests be struck and his men refused to, Saul said to Doeg, 'You've[45] struck them with your tongue—go strike them[46] with your sword.' As it's said, 'Turn around and fall upon the priests' (1 Samuel 22:18)" (J. T., *Sanhedrin* 10:2).

207.   Fourth, even if the slanderer were to do tshuvah, he'd have to ask forgiveness from everyone ever struck by his ferocious tongue.[47] But he wouldn't be able to remember them all, since he'd hurt and grieved so many. There may also be many he might remember having tarnished, who are nonetheless not aware of his

---

37. מחתה
38. i.e., knowing that . . .
39. There's a popular saying that "Sticks and stones may break my bones, but words will never harm me." But that sentiment runs contrary to the deeper truth that we're often far more deeply and permanently, emotionally and physically, hurt by words than we are by mere wounds. (See note 21 to ¶24.)
40. . . . and thus is never aghast by his own meanness.
41. . . . the sort of . . .
42. See Supplementary Notes.
43. See Supplementary Notes.
44. That is, if he's heartless and cruel enough to demean and besmirch, he certainly wouldn't be hesitant to maim and wound.
45. . . . already . . .
46. . . . now . . .
47. See Supplementary Notes.

having wronged them. And he'd be too embarrassed to let them know of the harm he'd caused (for his attacks[48] go unnoticed when he strikes).

As it's said, "How could a deceitful tongue benefit or profit you? Sharp arrows of the mighty . . ." (Psalms 120:3–4), where slander is compared to an arrow, since people often draw their bow and shoot arrows without the person they've hit ever knowing who struck them.[49]

208. Slander is like an arrow yet another way. For if you're drawing a sword and you take pity on the person pleading with you,[50] you could always return your sword to its holder. But that wouldn't be so if you were shooting an arrow, since you could never take it back. And that's true of a slanderer as well, since he could never take back[51] anything that's left his mouth.

Sometimes slanderers cite family blemishes, and thus do harm to all future generations.[52] He could never be forgiven for that. That's why our sages said, "One who mentions family blemishes will never be atoned for" (J. T., *Babba Kama*, Ch. 8).[53]

And the[54] person who'd speak with abandon[55] would[56] come to speak against the holy ones, too. For is there anyone over whom his wrongdoing wouldn't pass? And our sages said that a heretic[57] hasn't a share in The World to Come (*Sanhedrin* 90A).[58]

209. And fifth, the practice of slander even has those guilty of it speak mistakenly[59] of God.[60] As it's said, "They have aimed their mouth toward Heaven, while their tongue goes about[61] the earth" (Psalms 73:9).

As such, no other sin brings on the consequences the person who spews forth[62] words would have to suffer. In fact, our sages said that, "While our

---

48. . . . often . . .
49. . . . much like slanderers often harm others who "never know what hit them."
50. . . . not to stab him . . .
51. Literally, "rectify."
52. . . . of that family, by having besmirched the family name.
53. See Supplementary Notes.
54. . . . sort of . . .
55. . . . like that . . .
56. . . . eventually . . .
57. i.e., one who defames the righteous.
58. See Supplementary Notes.
59. i.e., slanderously, and falsely accusingly.
60. The tragic sequence is as followers: Slanderers start off speaking against others, and may even strike them (¶206). And they eventually come to speak against the righteous, and against God Himself. All because the slanderer "can no longer control himself" and "hasn't any control over his lips" (¶204).
61. . . . slandering Him from . . .
62. . . . heinous and denigrating . . .

forefathers were tested[63] ten times, they were incriminated for slander.[64] As it is said, 'I will do to you as you have spoken in My ears' (Numbers 14:28)" (*Aruchin* 15A).[65] And as it's also said, "And God heard the voice of your words[66] and was angry" (Deuteronomy 1:34), as well as, "You have wearied God with your words" (Malachi 2:17).[67]

David said, "God says to the wrongdoers, What right have you to declare My statutes, or take My covenant in your mouth? . . . If you see a thief, you go about with him . . . You allow your mouth free rein for evil, and your tongue devises deceit. You sit and speak against your brother, and slander the son of your own mother" (Psalms 50:16–20). And so we learn that Torah[68] doesn't protect slanderers, or inveterate thieves and adulterers, because they're unfit to engage in it. As our sages said, "Doeg's wisdom was of no help to him, and his Torah study couldn't protect him when he spoke slander" (*Sotah* 21A).

As to our sages' statement that, "A sin can extinguish a mitzvah, but it could never extinguish Torah. For it is said, 'A mitzvah is a lamp, but Torah is light'[69] (Proverbs 6:23)" (Ibid.)—that refers to someone who sins by accident, rather than one who casts off the yoke of the warning against sin.[70]

210. So, reflect on how pernicious a sin slander is. For not only do those guilty of it commit the serious sin of preventing their lips and mouths from discussing Torah, they completely corrupt themselves by slandering as well.[71] As David said, "Princes also sat and spoke against me, but Your servant ruminated upon Your statutes" (Psalms 119:23), which is to say that even though they didn't ruminate upon Your statues, and slandered me and spoke against me instead, I nonetheless ruminated upon Your statutes.

For, as our sages said, "The only cure for and protection against slander is the study of Torah. As it is said, 'The Tree of Life[72] cures the tongue' (*Aruchin* 15B)." That's also the implication of, "I will set a curb on my mouth" (Psalms 39:2), which our sages say refers to delving into Torah (Midrash *Tehillim* 39).

---

63. . . . and proven guilty . . .

64. . . . alone.

65. This verse is preceded by the one in which God says, "How long will I bear with this evil congregation, which murmurs against Me?" Hence, we find that Israel was slandering God at that point, and that He was incriminating them on the basis of that.

66. . . . of complaint against Him . . .

67. Which is followed by ". . . when you say, everyone who does evil is good in the sight of God, and He delights in them; or, Where is the God of justice?" Indicating again that Israel was slandering God.

68. . . . which is alluded to by the terms "My statutes" and "My covenant" . . .

69. . . . itself, rather than just a light-bearer, so it can never be extinguished . . .

70. See Supplementary Notes.

71. That is, not only do they not spend their spare time on Torah, reflection, and thought (see the end of this ¶). These perverse souls go further yet, and do harm.

72. (which is a metaphor for Torah)

They also said, "The Congregation of Israel is both beloved and despised for its voice. Beloved for it, as in, 'Let Me hear your voice, for your voice is sweet' (Song of Songs 2:14). And despised for it, as in, 'She has set her voice against Me, so I hated her' (Jeremiah 12:8)" (*Yalkut Tehillim* 721). And it's said, "Death and life are in the hands of the tongue, and those who love it[73] will partake of its fruit" (Proverbs 18:21). What "those who love it will partake of its fruit" means is that the only answer for those who love their tongue (meaning, people who love to speak all the time) is to "partake of its fruits." That is, to not talk about nonsensical things, but to talk about Torah, wisdom, and ethics; about peace between people; about presupposing the best about people; and about the value of good and the loathesomeness of evil. As well as to use speech in the fervent search for truth. For indeed, you can earn unlimited merit for yourself by means of your tongue, for "life is in the hands of the tongue," as was said.[74]

---

73. i.e., their tongue.

74. That's to say, the ability to speak is both a great favor and a scourge. Waste it on blather and nonsense, and you disgrace yourself. Use it, instead, for the discussion of noble and lofty things like Torah, wisdom, ethics, etc,. and you "earn unlimited merit." (See Supplementary Notes.)

Chapter Twenty-one

211. As to the Slanderers,
Whom We'll Classify into
Six Categories¹

The first category finds faults in people where there aren't any, and may even insult them for no good reason.² This type of slanderer embodies two of the four types of wrongdoers: liar³ and slanderer.

In fact, the Torah alerted us to not even accept slander⁴ because it might be unfounded and untrue.⁵ As it's said, "Do not bear a false report" (Exodus 23:1).⁶ Solomon said, "An evildoer listens to vicious lips, and falsehood hears out a mischievous tongue" (Proverbs 17:4). Which means to say that there are two types of people who accept slander. First, evil, malicious people (as in ". . . everyone is a hypocrite and an evildoer, and every mouth speaks maliciously" [Isaiah 9:16]), who suspect innocent people and love finding fault, laying blame, and denigrating

---

1. Rabbeinu Yonah now returns to the pattern he established with the three earlier sinner types. (See our note at the beginning of ¶200.)

2. The original is a clever play on words, and reads, ". . . and even replaces something lovely (יופי, pronounced 'yofie') with something invidious (דופי, pronounced 'dofie')." The gist of the matter is that slanderers may even turn laudable traits into faults.

3. See ¶'s 178–186.

4. i.e., not only to avoid *offering* it.

5. See Supplementary Notes.

6. See Supplementary Notes.

others.[7] Their brazen hearts tend to believe everything they hear from someone slandering another.[8]

And second, liars. They listen to and believe mischievous speech because they've never dissociated themselves from falsehood, and don't care if they accept lies or "bear a false report." As such, they're quick to accept slander.[9,10]

212. Know, that when you accept slander, you become a partner in crime with, and share the fate of, the person who offered it.[11] Because people will invariably say, "Since he accepted what he heard, then it's clearly true and accurate." Even only inclining your ear and seeming to listen to and believe what you're hearing promotes wrongdoing, denigrates the person being spoken about, and encourages people to speak against others.[12]

Solomon said, "A northerly wind withholds rain, and an angry look[13] a backbiting tongue" (Proverbs 25:23).[14] That means to say that an angry look withholds slander the way a northerly wind scatters clouds and holds back the rain. Because if someone about to slander would see his listener looking angry, he'd stop "raining down" words. But when he sees people being amused by what he has to say, he drinks down wrongdoing like water, and does nothing to hold back his lies. In fact, he'd do the same day after day, repeating his wrongdoing and continuing to slander, his tongue simply following along in the downpour of lies.[15,16]

---

7. See Supplementary Notes.

8. That is, evil and malicious people are always open to criticism of others. So they believe everything bad said.

9. And liars are apt to accept lies anyway, either from others or themselves. So they're quick to believe slander.

10. The text continues with the following:

"Falsehood hears out a mischievous tongue" [from the above-cited verse from Proverbs] connotes "*men* of falsehood hear out a mischievous tongue," just as "Your dwelling-place is in the midst of deceit" (Jeremiah 9:5) connotes "Your dwelling-place is in the midst of *men* of deceit," and "I am prayer" (Psalms 109:4) connotes "I am a *man* of prayer."

11. As we might put it, "you and he are in the same boat."

12. That's to say, not only is accepting slander onerous, even listening when it's spoken is wrong, too. Since it encourages it. (See Supplementary Notes.)

13. . . . withholds . . .

14. This is usually translated, "A northerly wind brings on rain; and a backbiting (i.e., slanderous) tongue (brings on) angry looks." Rabbeinu Yonah will explain how he reads it this way and thus derives the lesson he does.

15. That's to say, the best way to discourage slander is to show displeasure at the prospect of hearing it. For acting otherwise only encourages it.

16. The text continues with the following:

The word for "withholds" [תחולל], as in, "A northerly wind *withholds* rain" is derived from the word for "nullifies" [חליליה], as in, "He must not nullify his word" (Numbers 30:3)—that is, he must not undo it. And, "People were held back [הוחל] from calling . . ." (Genesis 4:26)—(i.e.,

213. Solomon also said, "A humble person[17] would hate a lying tongue" (Proverbs 26:28),[18] which is to say that a humble, "crushed,"[19] and meek person would hate a lying tongue, and would neither crave it or listen to it. For humble people want others to be respected, and they're troubled when others are disparaged or shamed.[20,21] Others interpret it to mean that a person with a lying tongue would hate to have others crush[22] or criticize him, and would never slander others again.[23]

In fact, we've already been alerted not to "bear a false report" (Exodus 23:1), that is, to never accept slander, convince yourself that what you heard was true, or think disparagingly of the person being spoken of.

214. The second category[24] slander, but avoid telling lies. They're what our sages referred to as slanderers who nonetheless don't fall into the category of liar (*Sotah* 42A).[25]

If, for example, you were to remind someone in private of some wrong his ancestors committed, you'd be transgressing against the verse, "Do not abuse one another" (Leviticus 25:17), which refers to verbal abuse, as we explained before.[26] It's also said, "The son is not to bear the iniquity of his father" (Ezekiel 18:20).

If you *publicly* humiliated him[27] with what his ancestors did, you'd be included among those who embarrass others in public whom our sages said, "descend to *Gehenom* and never reascend" (*Babba Metziah* 58B).[28]

---

their [desires to] call were nullified. [Which explains how it can be said that an angry look nullifies slander, despite the difficulty indicated in note 14.])

17. דביו

18. This is usually translated, "A lying tongue hates its victims."

19. דבא

20. The text continues with the following:

The ו in דביו replaces its root א just as the ו in עניו replaces *its* root א.

21. That is, you'd have to be arrogant and self-centered to accept slander about others. Otherwise you wouldn't dare wish others harm for no reason like that. For humble, good people prefer to see the good in others, rather than the ignoble or shameful. It's the arrogant who dwell on the negative in others, search it out, and spread it. The realization of this alone should give us pause, and make us consider how self-centered we are so often, in fact. For there are few among us who don't enjoy what's indelicately and shamefully referred to as, "juicy tidbits of gossip."

22. דביו

23. This goes along the same lines as the suggestion in the previous ¶ that you show disfavor toward slanderers. And it indicates that you are to criticize or embarrass them, and thus give them a "taste of their own medicine," in order to prevent slander in the future.

24. . . . of slanderer . . .

25. As opposed to the first category, who slander *and* lie (¶211).

26. See ¶'s 24 and 49.

27. . . . in his presence . . .

28. See Supplementary Notes.

If you publicly discuss and relate the terrible things a person's ancestors did out of his presence[29] in order to discredit and demean him in the eyes of others, you'd be the type of slanderer our sages said do not experience the Divine Presence (*Sotah* 42A).[30] The same holds true if you cite the sins a person committed before he did tshuvah[31,32] (*Babba Metziah* 58B).

215. But know, that if you see someone secretly transgressing the Torah and you reveal that in public, you'd be very wrong.[33] Because the sinner may have done tshuvah for his wrongful ways and be aggrieved by it (for, indeed, the heart alone realizes its own bitterness[34]). The right thing to do is to report it to a discreet scholar who wouldn't mention it to others.[35]

Nonetheless, keep yourself far away from the sinner until you know he's done tshuvah for his wrongful ways. But if he's a Torah scholar and God-fearing, then presume that, in fact, he'd already done tshuvah. And that while his impulses got the better of him then, he's been bitter about it ever since (*Berachot* 19A).[36]

216. Two[37] things happen when you slander: You harm and shame your victim. And you indict him, render him guilty, and delight in his misfortune.[38]

If you tell the truth when you slander, you commit a greater sin than you would by lying while slandering, on one level. Because people will believe you, since what you said appears to be true. As a consequence, your victim's reputation will be ruined in their eyes, and they'll despise him even after he'd have regretted his wrongdoing and been forgiven for his sin.[39]

217. Solomon said, "Fools malign the guilty; but there is favor among the

---

29. See Supplementary Notes.

30. See Supplementary Notes.

31. . . . when he was his own "ancestor" who'd done wrong, so to speak.

32. That is, you'd be slandering even if you honestly and accurately reminded a person of his ancestors' mistakes. And all the more so if you did that publicly—even though it was in his presence. And you'd be slandering him even more so if you did the latter (or belittled the person's own past) behind his back.

33. . . . and you'd be guilty of slander, when you thought you were doing something good. (See Supplementary Notes.)

34. . . . so you wouldn't know that. (See Supplementary Notes.)

35. . . . but would criticize the sinner privately and try to convince him to do tshuvah. (See Supplementary Notes.)

36. See Supplementary Notes.

37. . . . detrimental . . .

38. That is, not only do you "convict" and "sentence" him. You also take perverse and unfair relish in his pain.

39. The usual excuse for speaking maliciously and slanderously against others is, "But, it's the truth!" But, as Rabbeinu Yonah is pointing out here, that's exactly the problem. For while it's certainly commendable to warn others against wrongdoers in order to protect good people from bad ones, there's no reason to speak against wrongdoers gratuitously—just to denigrate them, rather than to do good for others. Especially since those wrongdoers may no

upright. The heart knows its own bitterness, no stranger can share in its joy" (Proverbs 14:9–10). That is, a fool would always malign the guilty, since he's always looking for faults and blame in others to insult them with. And he'd never praise others or find good in them.[40] Because, like flies, fools always head for and come to rest upon sordid places.[41] As our sages put it, "One who declares others unfit is unfit[42] and never praises anyone.[43] And he deems others unfit with his very own blemish" (*Kiddushin* 70B).[44]

"But there is favor among the upright,"[45] because it's the way of the upright to cover over others' acts of defiance, and to praise people for the good things about them. In fact, it's cited in books of ethics[46] that a certain individual and a sage passed by a carcass, when the individual remarked, "How putrid this carcass is!" to which the sage said, "How white its teeth are!"

The verse then continues with, "The heart knows its own bitterness." As every sage knows, Solomon didn't include meaningless phrases in his choice words of ethics.[47] What this idea does, then, is address the previous verse, and informs us of just how bad the fool who maligns the guilty really is. For the sinner might have done tshuvah for his wrongful ways, and his heart may be bitter. And no one could know another's bitterness or happiness but he himself.

So the sinner would have borne his guilt by then,[48] since tshuvah is essentially effected by heartfelt bitterness.[49] And the fool who'd be mentioning his transgression would be sinning himself, and wrong.

---

longer be wrongdoers. And you'd be criticizing newly righteous and innocent souls! This is a major point the reader would do well to recognize.

40. We're told in ¶213 that "humble people want others to be respected, and they're troubled when others are disparaged or shamed." And we're told here that "a fool would always malign the guilty, since he's always looking for faults and blame in others." Apparently, then, the opposite of a humble person isn't simply an arrogant one, but a fool. Because, in truth, it's utterly foolish to take yourself so very seriously that you overlook the good in others.

41. The text continues as follows:

"Malign" [יליץ] is in the singular here [even though the subject, "fools" (אולים), is in the plural], because it refers to [the actions of] fools in general, as in the verse, "The branch ['בנות — in the plural] runs ['צאדה — in the singular] over the wall" (Genesis 49:22).

42. . . . himself . . .

43. See Supplementary Notes.

44. That is, we often project our failings onto others, and are quick to recognize those failings in them. Yet we don't see them in ourselves.

45. That is, the upright always find favor in others.

46. See Supplementary Notes.

47. . . . so, what's the significance of this statement?

48. . . . and been forgiven . . .

49. See Supplementary Notes.

218. But you have to know that you'd only suffer consequences for "maligning the guilty" if you demean a God-fearing person—one who'd sinned and incurred guilt as a result of being[50] overpowered by his impulses, who'd ordinarily have remorse for his[51] deeds. Certainly all the more so if you knew he did tshuvah.

But if you've come to know someone and to have determined that he's not God-fearing and is always on the wrong path, then it's a mitzvah to degrade him and expose his sins, in order to shame sinners in the eyes of others, and to convince those listening to you to despise wrongful deeds.[52] As it's said, "A dishonest man is an abomination to the righteous" (Proverbs 29:27)[53] and, "Hating wrongdoing is fearing God" (Ibid. 8:13).

In fact, our sages said that it's permissible to refer to a wrongdoer who's the son of a righteous man as a "wrongdoer, son of a wrongdoer," and a righteous man who's the son of a wrongdoer as a "righteous man, son of a righteous man" (*Sanhedrin* 52A).

So, if you see someone saying or doing something that can either be deemed wrong or right, then if he's a God-fearing person, you're obliged to judge him to be truly innocent, even when what he did seems more likely to have been wrong.

If he's an intermediate[54] who's usually cautious enough not to sin but occasionally succumbs, then discount the doubt and incline in his favor. As our sages said, "One who judges in another's favor will be judged favorably by God" (*Shabbat* 127B). In fact, you're obliged from the Torah to do that,[55] as it's said, "Judge your neighbor in righteousness" (Leviticus 19:15). But if what he did seems to be wrong, consider it questionable, but don't assume it to be wrong.[56]

But if most of what that person does is wrong or you've determined that he isn't God-fearing, then assume he's wrong in what he did or said.[57] For as it's said,

---

50. . . . suddenly . . .
51. . . . untoward . . .
52. See Supplementary Notes.
53. See Supplementary Notes.
54. i.e., an ethically "run-of-the-mill," "average" sort of person . . .
55. i.e., it is a Torah imperative to do that.
56. . . . in fact.
57. That is, it's certainly true that the righteous "cover over others' acts of defiance, and . . . praise people for the good things about them." And that only "a fool would always malign the guilty," as was said in ¶218, above. Nonetheless, one needs to be astute and discriminating in his assumptions about others.
As Rabbeinu Yonah points out, clearly, the worst mistake would be to demean an otherwise God-fearing individual who obviously happened to have lapsed and sinned. And it's surely right and commendable to criticize a Godless individual who surely and spitefully sinned. As for other, less certain instances: If you see an otherwise truly God-fearing individual who *may* have purposefully sinned, assume he's innocent. If you see someone not quite righteous, but usually careful enough not to sin possibly sinning, give him the benefit of the

"The righteous man who considers the house of the wrongdoer leads the wicked astray to greater evil" (Proverbs 21:12). But we've already interpreted this verse.[58]

219. Solomon said as well, "Do not bear witness against your neighbor for no reason, and do not crush with your lips. Do not say, I will do to him what he did to me, and I will reciprocate according to what he has done" (Proverbs 24:28–29). Now, there was no reason to warn you not to bear false witness.[59] What's being said is, "Do not bear witness *for no reason*." That is, don't act as a witness against a person you[60] catch sinning, and needlessly publicize his sin, without[61] criticizing him.

Because even if he'd actually robbed or exploited someone, you'd only be obliged to testify against him in order for the stolen object to be returned[62] if there were a second witness (while if there wasn't another witness, the two parties would have to take vows[63]).

But if you see someone about to have illicit relations or about to sin some other way, it wouldn't be right of you to testify for "no reason," that is, without[64] criticizing him, even if there were another witness beside you to establish the fact.

Nonetheless, if the sinner is God-fearing,[65] then assure yourself that he has certainly done tshuvah.[66] Step back and say to yourself, "He probably has more merits than faults, since he's God-fearing. And our sages included a person with more merits than faults among the community of the righteous"[67] (*Kiddushin* 39B).

If the sinner is foolish enough to keep transgressing, then it's best to inform the judges,[68] so that they might admonish him and prevent him from wrongdoing. Nonetheless, if you're the only witness, then it's meaningless to bear witness against him, since your testimony would be of no use, and couldn't be relied on. For it's said, "One witness may not rise up against a man for any transgression or sin" (Deuteronomy 19:15). And you'd be considered someone who besmirches another's good name.[69]

But if the sinner is not God-fearing, and is for example someone who has cast

---

doubt. But if you see an ordinarily sinful person possibly sinning again, assume that he's in fact sinning.

58. See Rabbeinu Yonah's commentary to Proverbs, as well as his comments on *Pirke Avot* 1:6.

59. Because that's already warned against in Exodus 20:13.

60. . . . alone . . .

61. . . . first . . .

62. . . . to its rightful owner . . .

63. . . . in court to their claims.

64. . . . first . . .

65. . . . as a rule . . .

66. . . . already. (See Supplementary Notes.)

67. . . . overall, despite his lapses.

68. . . . "out of court," so to speak . . .

69. The text continues with the following:

off the yoke,[70] and he's careless about a particular sin that everyone knows is a sin,[71] then it's permissible to humiliate and demean him.[72] For our sages said, "'Do not abuse each other' (Leviticus 25:17) which means, do not verbally abuse someone who is with you in Torah and *mitzvot*" (*Babba Metziah* 59A). So, it's permissible to degrade the actions of one who doesn't follow the word of God, in order to let others know what abominable things he does, and to inundate him with contempt.[73] As our sages also said, "Hypocrites should be exposed because of[74] the profanation of God's Name" (*Yomah* 86B). But if that individual stumbles into sin by chance, and is ordinarily careful not to transgress, then his sin shouldn't be exposed, as we explained.[75]

You could also interpret "Do not bear witness against your neighbor for no reason" to mean don't testify against another about transgressions that you yourself are guilty of (which is why he'd be called "your neighbor"[76]). In fact, this is corroborated by what's said immediately afterward—"Do not say, I will do to him what he did to me."[77] Because though it's a mitzvah to expose inveterate sinners and hypocrites, nonetheless, if you sin as much as they, and you too sin against others, then don't publicize what they do. Because you won't have the right intentions when you set out to expose their secret, since you'd be taking comfort in their misfortune.[78]

Secondarily, how could you possibly not be ashamed to attribute the same invidious deed you yourself committed to someone else? As it's said, "And I will visit the blood of Yizre'el upon the house of Yehu" (Hosea 1:4). For even though Yehu fulfilled a mitzvah when he obliterated the house of Ahab, he nonetheless bore a sin because he was just as defiant.[79]

220. Our sages said that anyone who testifies alone about another's sin is to

---

The word "crush" [והמחה], in the above-cited verse, "do not crush with your lips"] is used in the active tense here [as if written "והמחה"]and implies that what you do is "grind" his face with your lips, as a result of all the humiliation he feels when you expose his secret transgressions. It's followed by, "Do not say, I will do to him what he did to me" because you're nonetheless not to take revenge or bear a grudge against him by doing to him what he did to you, if he exposed your sin. This is, in fact, a venerable moral principle, and an aspect of fearing Heaven [because revenge and grudge-bearing show an unacceptance of Divine justice on your part].

70. . . . of Divine service . . .
71. See Supplementary Notes.
72. See Supplementary Notes.
73. See Supplementary Notes.
74. i.e., to counteract.
75. . . . above in this ¶, as well as in ¶'s 116–118.
76. or, "you comrade."
77. i.e., ". . . what he did *like* me."
78. That is, you'd be glad *they* were being caught rather than yourself, as well as for the fact that the glare of public attention would be off of you.
79. See Supplementary Notes.

be flogged[80] (*Pesachim* 113B). What you could do is reveal what you saw privately to the sinner's teacher or to a confidant of his. But only if you know that they'd accept your word as much as they'd accept the testimony of two witnesses.[81]

If there's a second witness, then the judges should hear them both out in order to admonish the sinner in private, rather than publicly embarrass him. As it's said, "Criticize your neighbor diligently, but do not incur sin on his account"[82] (Leviticus 19:17).

221.   But know that when it comes to person-to-person offenses like theft, exploitation, personal damages, aggravation, embarrassment, and verbal abuse, you can tell what you've seen. In fact, you should even talk about it if you're the only one to have seen it, in order to help the victim, and to be fervent about the truth. For the Torah said that a single witness should testify in court when it comes to monetary claims, in order to force the accused to take a vow.[83] But you should criticize the offender first.[84]

222.   The third category[85] spread rumors, which we're warned against by the Torah. As it's said, "Do not go about as a rumor-monger among your people" (Leviticus 19:16).[86] Spreading rumors is also a form of slander; hence it's[87] included among the class of slanderers. For our sages described Doeg the Edomite as a slanderer for warning Saul and saying,[88] "David has come to the house of Achimelech" (Psalms 52:2) (Midrash *Tehillim* 52).

It's just not possible to estimate the damage done by spreading rumors, for it's boundless. It increases hatred in the world. And it has people transgress against the injunction, "Do not hate your brother in your heart" (Ibid. v. 17), when the world only goes on thanks to peace (*Pirke Avot* 1:18). And "the earth and all its inhabitants are dissolved" (Psalms 75:4) as a result of hatred, as we've explained.[89]

A rumor-monger often places a sword in another's hand with which to kill. As it's written, "There have been rumor-mongers among you who shed blood" (Ezekiel 22:9) and, "They are all terrible anarchists, going about spreading rumors—brass and iron all, dealing corruptly" (Jeremiah 6:28). And the sages referred to

---

80. Literally, with "rebellion-type flogging" (which is Rabbinically enacted, and more lenient than Biblically-ordained flogging).

81. i.e., if they'd give it as much authority as the account of two witnesses.

82. . . . by embarrassing him publicly.

83. . . . of innocence.

84. See Supplementary Notes.

85. . . . of slanderers . . .

86. Spreading rumors involves going from place to place, saying, "So and so says thus and such about you," or "I heard that so and so did thus and such to you" (*Hilchot De'ot* 7:2).

87. i.e., its practitioners are . . .

88. i.e., for promoting the rumor that . . .

89. See ¶39.

rumor-mongering as "Three[90] speech" (J. T., *Peah* 1:1) because it kills three: those who practice it, those who listen to it, and those spoken about. We know that from Doeg, who was driven out because he spread rumors, he brought about the death of the priests, and caused Saul (the recipient) to be punished.

223. Our sages said that though it's forbidden to accept rumors and to hate someone because of them, you shouldn't reject them[91] nonetheless. What you should do is protect yourself and be suspicious (*Niddah* 61A).[92]

The sages said that there were informers[93] in Saul's generation — Doeg and the Ziphites — whom the people went to war because of, which they lost. While there were no informers in Ahab's generation.[94] And the people won that war, even though Ahab was an idol-worshipper (J. T., *Peah* 1:1).

224. Instigating strife between relatives and friends, and stirring up animosity between them is the most serious form of slander.[95] As it's said, "There are six things which God hates, seven which are an abomination to Him . . . and one who sows discord among brothers" (Proverbs 6:6–19). Our sages said that this, the seventh trait, is the most serious one of all (*Vayikrah Rabbah* 15:1),[96] as we already explained in *The Gates of the Fear of Sin*.

225. You're obliged to keep a secret that someone divulged to you in private, even when disclosing it doesn't involve rumor-mongering.[97] Because disclosing a secret does harm to the person the secret is about, and frustrates his intentions. As it's said, "Intentions[98] are frustrated by of a lack of secrecy" (Proverbs 15:22).

---

90. . . . victim . . .

91. i.e., you shouldn't necessarily discount what's said outright, and reject them out-of-hand.

92. That is, though you shouldn't suspect or think less of the person the rumor is about, you should nonetheless take the necessary precautions to protect yourself against all harmful possibilities. What this comes to is a belief in the reality of evil in the world, and a concurrent uncertainty that the individual spoken of himself is evil.

93. i.e., rumor-mongers. Hence we see that spreading rumors isn't just innocent babbling away about what others do. It's revealing things about them that threaten their safety and well-being.

94. The text continues with the following:

> As we know from the incident of the prophets who were hidden from Izebel. For it's written, "I am the only remaining prophet of God" (1 Kings 18:22). That is, though Obadiah hid a hundred prophets then, no one disclosed that there were any there, other than Elijah. [i.e., a hundred prophets were hidden, and only Elijah was not, giving the impression that he alone remained. Yet no one disclosed that.]

95. And it's most often brought on by rumor-mongering, hence its inclusion here.

96. See Supplementary Notes.

97. See Supplementary Notes.

98. Literally, "thoughts."

Second, because you'd no longer be demure[99] once you'd disclose a secret, and you'd be undermining the secret-holder's wishes.

Solomon said, "One who discloses secrets is a rumor-monger" (Ibid. 20:19). That is to say, if you see someone not disciplined enough to refrain himself from disclosing a secret,[100] that trait will lead him to rumor-mongering (which is one of the four types of evil, even when it has nothing to do with spreading rumors about others) since he isn't in control of his tongue.

He also said, "A rumor-monger discloses secrets" (Ibid. 11:13), which is to say, don't entrust your secret to a rumor-monger. For since he can't keep his lips from spreading rumors, you can't depend on him to keep your secret, even if you divulge it to him privately and in confidence.[101]

The Torah warned us never to accept slander.[102] As it's said, "Do not bear a false report" (Exodus 23:1), and "When a leader listens to lies, his servants become wrongdoers" (Proverbs 29:12), which our sages explained to mean that when a leader accepts slander and rumors, his servants become wrongdoers and rumor-mongers as well, in order to find favor in their master's eyes (Midrash *Tehillim* 54).[103]

These, then, are the three sinner types our sages referred to as slanderers (*Sotah* 42A).[104]

---

99. That is, you'd no longer be as trustworthy as a demure person would be.

100. . . . you should know that . . .

101. That is, don't trust anyone who's careless about what he says. For he's sure to be careless in all such instances. (See Supplementary Notes.)

102. . . . which includes not accepting rumors, or hearing out secrets that are disclosed to you. (See Supplementary Notes.)

103. See Supplementary Notes.

104. i.e., those who attribute imaginary faults in others (¶211), those who slander but don't lie in the process (¶214), and rumor-mongers (¶222). The three instances of slander to follow are offshoots of these.

Chapter Twenty-two

As to Other Forms
of Disparaging Language[1]

226. The fourth category involves the "dust of slander." For, as our sages said, "Most people stumble when it comes to theft, a few do when it comes to illicit relations. But all do when it comes to the dust of slander" (*Babba Battra* 165A).[2] And they portrayed the "dust of slander" as things said that cause others to slander.[3] So they said, "One should never speak[4] well of another, because insult will result from the good spoken" (*Aruchin* 16A).

But let's explain that statement. For it's well known that praising sages and righteous people is a lovely trait to have, as it's said, "Honor is due those who search out honor" (Proverbs 25:27).[5] And it's said that fools never praise anything. Hence, this is the gist of what's being said: Only speak[6] well of someone in private—that is, when you're speaking to a friend of his rather than to the community, or in a crowd. Unless you know for a fact that no one there is his enemy, or jealous of him.

But if you want to praise someone already assumed by all and known to be an ethical person who has done no wrong and is guilty of nothing, then you can even praise him in front of his enemies and people jealous of him, simply because they couldn't insult him. Because if they did, everyone would know that they were uttering nonsense, and that their tongues were tripping them up.

---

1. This phrase isn't included in the original, and was inserted here for ease of reference.
2. See Supplementary Notes.
3. That is, anything you say that causes others to slander is considered "dust," a sprinkling about of slander.
4. . . . especially . . .
5. See Supplementary Notes.
6. . . . especially . . .

227. When our sages discussed slander they also said, "If one woman were to ask another to prepare a fire for her, and the other were to then say, 'Do you know where you can always find charcoal? In so-and-so's house. He is always roasting meat to eat,' that such a statement or its equivalent is[7] the dust of slander" (*Aruchin* 15B).[8]

It's said, "One who blesses his friend in a loud voice while rising up early in the morning will have a curse attributed to him" (Proverbs 27:14). As our sages explained, this verse refers to someone who praises another in a way that causes him harm (*Aruchin* 16A).[9] An example would be a houseguest who goes into town, speaks in a loud voice,[10] and tells all about how generous his host had been to him by preparing meat meals for him. For dishonest people will all gather at the host's house when they hear that.[11]

228. It's imperative for you to keep watch over your mouth and tongue so that your words are never held in suspicion, and you're never taken as a slanderer. For if you're ever suspected of that, any admonishment you'd offer would be undermined and considered the dust of slander.[12]

Now, reflect upon the following deeply in order to assimilate this axiom.

As we already indicated,[13] it's permissible to expose a sinner for the stolen goods in his hand[14] if you know he hasn't changed his ways — as in the case of a thief or robber; criminal or violent person; one who embarrasses, humiliates, and shames others; or a slanderer who either hasn't returned what he'd stolen, compensated for damages, or asked the individual he sinned against to forgive him. But you must first speak to him directly if you intend to reform him, since you just might divert him

---

7. . . . an instance of . . .

8. That is, it's unclear whether she was praising him for being generous, prepared, organized, forethinking, etc. Or insulting him for being gluttonous, carnal, excessive, etc. As such, even if she meant it as a compliment, others might take the ambiguity as an opportunity to slander him. So her statement would have proven to be slander-provoking, and an example of the "dust of slander."

9. See Supplementary Notes.

10. . . . first thing in the morning . . .

11. And so the grateful guest's innocent statement of appreciation would have cost his host a lot, and thus done him harm. And doing harm to another by what you say is an aspect of slander. As Rabbeinu Yonah said in ¶200, slanderers do "a lot of damage . . . to those whose reputations they've besmirched, or *whom they've harmed in other ways*" as in this case. See our note there, too, which underscores the point that the term for "slander" doesn't only mean besmirching one's reputation, but causing him any form of harm verbally.

12. That is, if you can't be trusted to give others the benefit of the doubt, and you're quick to come to judgment and to condemn, then any legitimate criticism you might offer would be held in suspicion. It would be taken as rank slander even when it's not, and would lead others to truly slander. (See our reference to this statement later on in the ¶, as well.)

13. See ¶221.

14. i.e., if you "catch him red-handed."

from his wrongful ways by criticizing him.[15] And then, if he utterly refuses,[16] you're to let others know of his ways and of what he's done.

But as it stands now, if you catch someone doing harm to another, and you tell others what he did and about how guilty he is, and you demean his actions on several grounds—you'd be discredited for doing that and branded a slanderer. People would say, "Even if it's true, he should have admonished him first." That is, those listening to you would hold you in suspicion for not criticizing him first. And they'd claim that you didn't say anything to him yourself because you were trying to ingratiate yourself to him, as in, "No one argues, and no one criticizes . . ." (Hosea 4:4). Or because you just like mentioning others' faults, that you're happy when others sin, or that you take advantage of others' misfortune behind their backs. And you'd be like a slanderer, since its dust will have attached itself to you.

People would also say, "There's no truth to what he's saying, and he's making it all up. If not, then why didn't he confront the sinner with his transgression first, rather than hide it from him?" And so our sages said, "When you say something about a person[17] that you would say to his face, then you are not slandering" (*Aruchin* 15A). What that means to say is, if you start off criticizing someone openly for what he did and he doesn't listen to you, then you can let others know how guilty and immoral he is. And you won't be suspected of just wanting to belittle the other person.[18]

The same holds true if you're already considered to be a person who doesn't play favorites or tries to get the best of people, but rather one who'd say to a person's face exactly what he'd say behind his back because he's not afraid of anyone, or as one who only speaks the truth. For then you wouldn't be held suspect for speaking to someone about another's guilt behind his back.[19]

Our sages spoke of the matter this way, "Rabbi Yossi said, 'I never said anything which I had to retract later on'" (Ibid.). That is to say, he never said anything about anyone behind his back that he'd have to contradict if he were to face him.

---

15. . . . first. (See Supplementary Notes.)

16. . . . to listen, or do tshuvah . . .

17. . . . behind his back . . .

18. Rabbeinu Yonah understands the dictum, "When you say something about a person (behind his back) that you would say to his face, then you are not slandering" to mean this: "If you criticize a sinner to his face and he nonetheless doesn't change his ways, you won't be held suspect whatsoever when you then go behind his back and tell others what he did."

19. This is an expansion and explanation of Rabbeinu Yonah's remarks at the beginning of this ¶ about how important it is to "keep watch over your mouth and tongue so that your words are never held in suspicion, and you're never taken as a slanderer." What you should instead be taken to be is someone who doesn't play favorites, or tries to get the best of others, but is instead "assumed by others to speak nothing but the truth" (as he says here). Otherwise, "any admonishment you'd offer would be undermined and considered an instance of the dust of slander," as he said above.

They also said, "Anything said before three[20] is not considered slander" (Ibid.), which means to say that since the person you spoke about will eventually come to know what you said because others were with you when you said it,[21] then it's as if you said it to his face.[22]

229. The fifth category[23] involves uttering profanity. Our sages said, "When a person utters profanity, even if seventy good years were[24] decreed for him, they will be overturned to bad ones" (*Shabbat* 33A). And Isaiah said, "This is why God is displeased with His young men, and why He shows no mercy for His orphans and widows—because they are all hypocrites and wrongdoers, and each mouth utters profanity. So, His anger is not rescinded, and His arm is still outstretched" (Isaiah 9:16).

You commit a serious sin and become loathsome and tainted by uttering profanity. You will have lost all sense of shame and demureness, which are two traits the Holy Nation is known by. And will have tread upon the path of brashness, which is the way of wicked speakers of profanity.[25]

Second, you will have profaned the holiness of Israel, about which it's said, "Surely this great nation is a wise and knowing people" (Deuteronomy 4:6). You will have followed the path of those reprehensible fools who remove themselves from the ways of reason, which are always attractive and pleasant. And would have emitted a foul odor and stench instead which any sage or knowing person would utterly despise and detest. You'd also have polluted[26] your mind, which is more precious than anything of value. As it's said, "The lips of knowledge are a precious jewel" (Proverbs 20:15)

You'd[27] have to suffer terrible consequences for listening to profanity. Because

---

20. . . . others . . .

21. . . . and when there are three or more people present, someone is bound to talk . . .

22. . . . because you'd know your words would get out, so you're unlikely to say anything that would endanger your own reputation when word gets back to the person you were talking about.

23. . . . of "slanderers" (see our third comment to ¶200, which discusses our use of the term "slanders" throughout this section) . . .

24. . . . originally . . .

25. Many of us cannot quite understand the seriousness with which Rabbeinu Yonah addresses what appears to be a rather innocent dalliance. But the truth of the matter is that many of us of modernity *have* lost all sense of shame and decency, and *have* become brash and brazen. By virtue of the fact that many of us are positively blasé about profanity, unabashed about all sorts of base obscenity, and think ourselves rather sophisticated and worldly to boot while engaged in it. When all we are often enough, are small and sordid juveniles licking at putrefaction, beaming.

26. Literally, "profaned."

27. . . . even . . .

you didn't close your ears to, or draw yourself away from people uttering it.[28] And the verse, "The mouth that utters alien things is a deep pit which those who are cursed by God fall into" (Proverbs 22:14), would apply to you (*Shabbat* 33A).

230. Our sages said, "A person should never utter anything indecent. In fact, the Torah itself contorted[29] eight of its letters in order not to say something indecent. For it is said, 'And from the animal that is not pure . . .' (Genesis 7:8)" (*Pesachim* 3A).[30] Because though impure animals were permitted to be eaten at the time, they nonetheless weren't pure enough to offer.[31] And it's considered indecent of a person to disgrace[32] things that people eat. Thus, you're obliged to be careful not to say anything indecent, even if you'd be drawing out your words and saying more[33] by avoiding indecency.[34]

This[35] acts as a fence of caution against profanity, which is such a serious sin. And it acts as a fence of caution against slander and insult.[36] For as our sages pointed out about keeping away from indecent speech, "The Torah would not even speak indecently about an impure animal" (*Babba Battra* 123A)[37] and, "A *cohen* once said to Rabban Yochanan Ben Zakkai, 'My portion of the showbread comes to the size of a lizard's rump.' He[38] investigated his background and found it to contain a disqualifying element" (*Pesachim* 3B).[39]

Our sages also said that you're obliged to choose refined rather than unrefined language, even if it's not indecent, regardless of whether you're discussing Torah or

---

28. See Supplementary Notes.

29. Or, rearranged, reordered, shuffled around, twisted about, etc.

30. The point is, the Torah is known for its pith and concision. And, in fact, it would have been far more concise for it to have said, ". . . and from the impure animal." So why didn't it? Because calling something "impure" would have been indecent and inelegant, for the reason to follow.

31. . . . as a sacrifice.

32. . . . or speak indecently about . . .

33. . . . than necessary . . .

34. That is, not only aren't you to speak profanely or even listen to profanity, as Rabbeinu Yonah indicated above. You're not even to speak less than delicately.

35. i.e., following this suggestion.

36. This, then, is the key: Train yourself to avoid indelicate language, and you'll automatically avoid profanity, slander, and insult.

37. See the previous paragraph.

38. i.e., Rabban Yochanan Ben Zakkai.

39. That is to say, since this individual spoke indecently, it seemed clear to Rabban Yochanan Ben Zakkai that he must not have been a *cohen* after all. For as Rabbeinu Yonah said in the previous ¶, when a person speaks profanely he loses "all sense of shame and demureness, which are two traits the Holy Nation is known by." And he'd have "profaned the holiness of Israel"—putting his ancestry into question. In fact, that suspicion proved to be deserved in this case.

worldly matters. As long as you don't come to draw out your remarks[40] as a consequence when you discuss Torah. Because you're obliged to teach students succinctly (*Pesachim* 3B).

As to what "refined language" is, it's the language and terminology that cultured and eloquent people—those who'd weigh and consider each word to determine what's refined and what's not—would use. As it's said, "Choose the language of the clever" (Job 15:5), "My lips will express knowledge clearly" (Ibid. 33:3), and, "The tongue of the righteous is like choice silver" (Proverbs 10:20).

231. And the sixth category[41] is the faultfinder.[42] Solomon said, "A faultfinder's words are like blows to the pit of the stomach" (Proverbs 18:8). That's to say, it's the way of faultfinders to always complain, grumble about, and find fault in others' deeds and words, even when that other person is perfectly innocent, and does him no harm.

Faultfinders see everything as wrong rather than right, and all mistakes as intentional sins.[43] And they see themselves as victims who've been terribly wronged by others, when *they* are the aggressors. For, like a storm driven into one's heart and arrows shot into the pit of the stomach, their words "are like blows to the pit of the stomach." Because they complain about people who haven't even touched them and have only been good to them.[44]

Solomon also said, "A faultfinder alienates a close friend" (Proverbs 16:28), which is to say, he alienates all friends and intimates, since they can't bear being friends with him.

Our sages said, "Do not be disgruntled too often, lest you come to sin" (*Derech Eretz Zutah* 9). For a faultfinder will often scoff at favors done him, consider them disfavors, and do harm in exchange for good.[45] When it's said that, "Evil will never depart from the house of one who does harm in return for good" (Proverbs 17:13). And he'll sometimes even consider favors from God to be acts of revenge and

---

40. . . . unnecessarily . . .

41. . . . of "slanderers" (see our first note to ¶229) . . .

42. See our comments about this point in our introduction to this gate.

43. See Supplementary Notes.

44. The text continues with the following:

The word for "blows" [מתלהמים] can be (inverted and) read as "beaters" [מתהלמים]—much as the word for "garment" [שמלה] in Deuteronomy (22:17) can be read "שלמה" in Exodus (22:8)—as in, "They have beaten me and did not know me" (Ibid. 23:35). And it could be read as if written, "The words of the faultfinder are like beaters."

The reason the plural form for "beaters" is used is because the term, "faultfinder" is generic for all faultfinders, as in ". . . sanctified flesh [i.e., singular] has passed [i.e., plural] from you" [Jeremiah 11:15], and ". . . that they may bring on [i.e., plural] salvation [i.e., singular]" (Isaiah 45:8).

45. See Supplementary Notes.

recompense. As it's said, "You found fault while in your tents and said, 'God took us out because He hated us'" (Deuteronomy 1:27).

So, avoid the ways of faultfinders. "For they have perverted their paths, and whoever follows their ways will never know peace" (Isaiah 59:8). Train your tongue to judge on the side of merit, and let fairness gird your loins.

Synopsis

It's important to know just how serious each sin you committed is. For the depth of your tshuvah is determined by how earnestly you scrutinize your sins, and by how humbly and dispiritedly you react to them (¶1). Doing that also enables you to feel more abashed before God, who promised to forgive you, and has been so good to you all along. For otherwise, you'd take your sins lightly. Besides, many people inadvertently commit very serious sins, and thus make themselves liable for terrible consequences. So it's incumbent upon us to make them aware of that, so they can correct their ways (¶2). And it's important to learn how reprehensible sins are and the harm they do, after learning what to do and what not to do. For then you can avoid them and warn yourself and others about them (¶3).

First Level: The Significance of the Sages' Decrees. Though the opposite is usually the case, there are nonetheless instances in which the decrees of the sages are more significant than the Torah's own, and when one who violates their decrees would incur the death penalty, while those who'd violate Torah injunctions wouldn't (¶4). That's because when you violate the words of the sages you don't do so because you've been overtaken by your impulses, which you'd then bitterly regret. But because of your lack of faith in their authority (¶5). It's also true because you're unlikely to do tshuvah and are likely to commit the same sin again and again (¶6). The words of the sages are the primary pathways to the fear of God, which is itself the basis of all *mitzvot*. Because their decrees act as protective fences around the Torah (¶7). Some people disregard specific decrees of the sages out of an outright casting off of the yoke of Heaven, rather than a need to satisfy their cravings. Or they do it to separate themselves from the Jewish Nation (¶8).

Second Level: The Significance of Imperatives. All reward and merit is rooted in actively fulfilling Torah imperatives. But reward and merit also ironically involve refraining from sin. And while the consequences of sins are enunciated, rewards for *mitzvot* aren't, in order for us to be sure to do what has to be done (¶9). For God wants us to do all the *mitzvot*. Hence, He rewards us greatly for even what appears to be the least significant and least demanding of them (¶10). Furthermore, outright and stubborn avoidance of an imperative is a serious matter, and carries very serious consequences (¶11). And fulfilling a positive mitzvah is just as much an expression of the fear of Heaven as avoiding sins (¶12). Yet there are some very serious imperatives that people are negligent about, including being sure not to mention

God's name in vain, and being benevolent (which we're very obliged in). It also includes going beyond the requirements of the law when that's called for (¶13). Many believe that personal and spiritual ruin only comes about by actively committing serious sins. And that those who don't, but who nonetheless overlook imperatives can avoid it. But that's not so (¶14). In fact, the people of Sodom were known to have committed many heinous crimes, but they were only brought to ruin for not being charitable. And many otherwise devout people are guilty of acting by rote in their service to God (¶15). The greater the mitzvah, the greater the consequences for not observing it. Even if you do nothing to undermine it (¶16). The attainment of *the* noblest qualities were all placed in the domain of imperatives, including: free will, Torah study, going in God's ways, trusting God, reflecting upon God's greatness, recalling His generosity, holiness, Divine service, fear, love, and devoting yourself to Him. For it's always been God's intention that you achieve these qualities (¶17). One who avoids fulfilling an imperative is referred to as "cursed" (¶18). So, you're advised to act as a faithful emissary to your Master and to not only be skilled in your work, but to oversee the work of others as well. And to encourage them in their service of God (¶19). Among the other such important *mitzvot*, are not having civil cases tried in Gentile courts (¶20), fearing and honoring your parents (¶21), and utilizing *tefillin* and *mezuzot*, which embrace accepting the yoke of the kingdom of Heaven, as well as *tzitzit*, which add holiness (¶22). A God-fearing individual would fulfil both "insignificant" and significant *mitzvot* as exactingly and selflessly as possible, in cognizance of the greatness of the One charging him with it (¶23).

Third Level: A Prohibition Connected to an Imperative. Avoid all acts of theft, fraud, and physical or verbal abuse (¶24). Don't take interest on, or profit from, loans. For if you do, you won't experience The Resurrection of the Dead, and won't have an advocating angel to cite your merits (¶25).

Fourth Level: Prohibitions Involving No Action. Sins in this category touch upon the heart, the tongue, withholding your hand, and refraining from things, as well as the senses of hearing and seeing. And they present more traps than sins involving action (¶26). Among those involving the heart: Remembering God all the time by demonstrating fear of Him, acting demurely, ennobling your thoughts, and putting your character in order (¶27). Not forgetting what you learned, by constantly studying Torah and reflecting on it (¶28). Not assuming that your good fortune comes as a product of your righteousness, but rather as a consequence of God's kindness alone (¶29). Not testing God by determining whether your charity or righteousness leads to success or prosperity (except in the case of tithing) (¶30). Don't say to yourself, "There are more of them than I! How can I dispose of them?" when faced with danger (¶31). Instead, believe and trust in God's salvation (¶32). Don't fear that harm will befall you when you administer justice fairly (¶33). Don't exhibit arrogance, which is one of the most serious sins. Take pride only in your service to God; in your fear, trust, and love of Him; and in your devotion to Him (¶34). Not only mustn't you be miserly, but you must cultivate inner generosity

(¶35). Don't harden your heart or shut your hand from others. Be compassionate and kind, just as God is, and you'll be shown compassion and kindness by Him (¶36). But show no mercy or compassion toward those who cause others to sin and stumble (¶37). Don't take revenge or bear a grudge against anyone in your heart. But you can bear a grudge against someone who's exhibited arrogance against you, shamed you, or meant you harm (¶38). Don't hate others in your heart, because that leads to many harmful things including slander, having harmful intentions, being pleased by others' misfortunes, causing harm, tale-bearing, revenge and grudge-bearing. And it undoes a lot of inner goodness (¶39). Don't fantasize lasciviously even without intent to carry your fantasies out (¶40). Don't think of committing a sin, and don't reflect on what heretics say (¶41). Don't accept slander as truth (¶42). Don't devise a plan to possess your neighbor's property, or even think of it. And don't pressure him to sell it to you, either verbally or by dint of your stature (¶43).

Among the prohibitions involving speech: Don't study Torah, pray, or mention the name of God if you're undressed or facing someone undressed, if you're in an unclean area, or if your hands are unclean (¶44). Don't swear falsely or even intend to; and neither swear in vain, nor cause others to, nor swear in instances where your oath will be doubted (¶45). Don't curse anyone (other than a reprobate judge) using God's name or any expression used for Him (¶46). Don't say, "This is true—God help me!" about something untrue (¶47). Don't decide *halacha* if you've drunk a *rivi'it* of undiluted wine, or more than a *rivi'it* of diluted wine (¶48). Don't verbally abuse anyone—especially one who's done tshuvah or a convert (¶49). Don't encourage sinners, and don't associate with those who sanction wrongdoing (¶50). Don't associate with the wicked for secular purposes, or even for a mitzvah (¶51). Don't make false *halachic* decisions, and be sure to be slow and deliberate in your conclusions (¶52). Don't give improper or self-serving advice (¶53). Don't give advice that's not grounded in reflection, because giving proper, appropriate advice is an act of benevolence (¶54). Don't be a tale-bearer, don't besmirch reputations, and don't be inconsistent with litigants if you're a judge (¶55). Don't mention the name of an idol, even if only just to say, "Meet me by so-and-so's statue" (¶56). Don't compliment a Gentile, look at him fondly, or give him gifts gratuitously (¶57). Don't provoke conflict—it's even valid to slander those who do (¶58). But don't avoid conflicting with wrongdoers—especially those in power (¶59). Don't exploit others, or order them to do something for your benefit alone. Unless they're dishonest people themselves (¶60). Don't profane God's name by mentioning it for no reason, without fear, or in unclean circumstances, like so many do (¶61). Don't be negligent about expressing respect for scholars (¶62). Don't curse your parents, which would be even more serious than striking them (¶63).

Among the prohibitions involving your senses of seeing and hearing: Don't stare at a woman forbidden to you (¶64). Don't be haughty-eyed (¶65). Don't listen to worthless or foul things (¶66).

Among the prohibitions involving withdrawing your hand and refraining from doing something: Don't refuse to loan money to a poor person (¶67). Don't defraud another by not repaying your debt, and by not paying your workers on time (¶68). Don't delay burial (unless it's for the benefit of the dead) (¶69). Don't be lax about protecting your neighbor's property, to say nothing of protecting him himself, either by offering him advice or by doing something yourself (¶70). It's important to have trained volunteers set up in every city to help those in trouble (¶71). Don't fail to criticize others, for their sins will affect you adversely if you don't (¶72). Select men of truth and fortitude to criticize members of the community, and to thus eradicate evil from their midst (¶73). Don't delay in fulfilling your vows to charity, and don't make vows in general (¶74).

Fifth Level: Prohibitions Involving Action. There are *mitzvot* that people observe only partially, and others that some transgress altogether, either because they don't associate with scholars, or because they were raised without having learned about them (¶75). So while all are careful not to eat primary and secondary animal blood, some are careless about salting (¶76). Others are negligent about not injuring or striking, as when they strike their wives or others (¶77). Some shave their beards and *peyot* (¶78). Some are careless about *shatnez* (¶79). Don't touch a married woman extraneously (¶80). Don't place a stumbling block before anyone. As such, don't strike your grown child; don't offer wine to a *Nazir*; don't provide a limb torn off of an animal to one observing the seven Noachite Laws; don't sell idol-worship materials or books of heresy to gentiles, etc. (¶81). Don't cut down fruit trees unnecessarily, don't squander money or things, don't expose yourself to danger, and don't commit suicide (¶82). Don't benefit from (or allow others to benefit from) the first three years' produce of trees, or the vineyard's fourth-year's fruit unless they're redeemed. Otherwise they must be burned (¶83). Don't benefit from the thigh-bone sinew (¶84). Don't steal from someone with the intention of returning it to him, in order to "teach him a lesson"; don't "borrow" something with the intention of returning it later on; and don't "steal back" what was stolen from you (¶85). Don't practice "divination" or "soothsaying." Trust in God instead (¶86). Keep honest weights and measures (¶87). Don't oppress or dispirit debtors (¶88). Don't be a party to anyone's taking interest on loans (¶89). Don't blemish a firstborn animal (¶90). Don't plow or thresh with different animals together, or even lead them together. And don't breed mixed kinds of animals (¶91). Don't kneel onto a stone floor outside of the Holy Temple (¶92). Don't eat anything repulsive, and don't inhibit a bowel movement (¶93). Don't hand over your daughter to anyone other than for marriage, and do not keep a concubine (¶94). Don't have relations with an unmarried woman. And don't have your daughter marry an old man (¶95). Don't eat unkosher meat, and select learned, God-fearing *shochetim* (¶96). Judges aren't to be paid to render judgment (though they can be fairly and equally reimbursed for their time) (¶97). A judge must disqualify himself if he's flattered by a litigant, or given a gift by him (¶98). One can only carry on a Festival for Festival needs (¶99). A man may not shave off his armpit hair or pubic hair (¶100). Don't keep a vicious dog or a defective ladder in your house (¶101). Don't work with the firstborn of your oxen, or shear the firstborn of your sheep (¶102). Don't erase God's name (¶103).

Don't use incantations and talismans (other than of proven medical value) (¶104). Don't eat "new" grain (*chodosh*) (¶105). These are some of the things that people neglect unknowingly, or because they don't recognize their seriousness. The learned should remind others of them (¶106).

Sixth Level: Sins Incurring Death Through the Hands of Heaven. In one sense, a sentence of death by the hands of Heaven is less serious than a sentence of excision. But in another, it's more serious (¶107). Among those who incur death through the hands of Heaven are those who eat *tevel* (¶108), who oppress widows and orphans (¶109), who steal from the poor (¶110), who ruin the reputation of individuals or families (¶111), who sexually exploit minors, spill seed in vain, and practice onanism (¶112), those scholars who don't act demurely, don't speak gently to others, and don't conduct their business admirably and honestly (¶113), who don't attend a *beit midrash* in their city (¶114), who challenge the authority of their teachers (¶115), who render *halachic* decisions before their teachers (¶116), who steal from money designated to the poor, who vow to donate to the poor but don't (¶117), and those who don't give charity to their poor relatives (¶118).

Seventh Level: The Significance of Excision. Excision affects both the one culpable for it and his descendants (¶119). But there are two categories of it: excision from this world (¶120), and excision both from this world, and The World to Come (¶121). Some who are to suffer excision have it forestalled for generations in order to be rewarded in the world for some good they did, yet be undone in The World to Come (¶122). The reason why God bears with sinners is either to give them a chance to do tshuvah, to reward them for specific *mitzvot*, or because of a righteous child they may bear (¶123). As a result of excision one dies before he's 50; as a result of death through the hands of Heaven one dies before 60 (¶124). Those who incur excision by cohabiting with a menstruant bring corruption as well as eventual excision upon their children (¶125).

The Eighth Level: The Four Court-Imposed Death Sentences. Culpable for stoning are those who cohabit with their father's wife, their daughter-in-law, another male; those who practice witchcraft, who desecrate the Sabbath, who curse their parents, who cohabit with a betrothed woman, who incite others to worship idols, who practice sorcery, who are "rebellious sons"; and most especially those who blaspheme God or worship idols (¶126). Culpable for burning are those who cohabit with a woman and her daughter; with his wife's son's or daughter's daughter; with his mother-in-law or her mother, or his father-in-law's mother (¶127). Culpable for death by the sword are those who murder, and those who live in a "captivated city" (¶128). Culpable for strangulation are those who strike their parents, who kidnap a Jew, those elders who rebel against the court's decision, false prophets, those who prophecy in the name of idols, and one who cohabits with a married woman (¶129). Though the death sentence is no longer enacted, nonetheless when someone is culpable for stoning, he might fall from a roof or be trampled by an animal; one who's culpable for burning might either fall into a fire or be bitten by a snake; one who's culpable for death by sword might either be turned over to the authorities or be attacked by robbers; and one culpable for strangulation might either drown or die of diphtheria (¶130). One who cohabits with a Gentile maidservant need not have the required witnesses, warning, and sentencing by Sanhedrin to be killed for his crime (¶131). For he has also profaned God's name by cohabiting with an idol worshipper, and will bear the sins of any offspring (¶132). Such a person dies in an unusual manner, such as by hanging by his hair (¶133). Other prohibitions in this category include delaying judgment, perverting justice, making decisions against *halacha*, taking false vows, and profaning God's name (¶134). Those who criticize the people should warn them about the particulars of Sabbath observance, which many are lax in (¶135).

Ninth Level: The Significant Sins You're to Give Your Life for Rather Than Commit. You must be prepared to give up your life rather than worship idols, commit adultery, or murder—but for nothing else. Nonetheless, if you're forced to commit any sin *publicly*, you must give up your life then, too. But at a time of persecution you'd have to give up your life if you're told to transgress a mitzvah even if only in private (¶136). The consequences for committing those three cardinal sins are the most serious of all. Even the slightest breach of them is forbidden. As such, it's forbidden to use part of an *Ashera* tree as a remedy (¶137). One may not engage in licentiousness even for therapeutic purposes (¶138). One may not publicly shame another, because that's tantamount to murder (¶139). One may not call someone by an unwanted nickname, because that's like shaming him publicly (¶140). In fact, one who shames someone publicly hasn't a share in The World to Come (¶141). And one who publicly desecrates the Sabbath denies the entire Torah. His *shechita* can't be trusted, and any wine he touches can't be drunken from (¶142).

The Tenth Level: Those Significant Sins Whose Violators Have No Place in The World to Come. One who profanes God's name and demeans His Torah doesn't have a place in The World to Come. Nor do those who commit well known sins publicly, and those who spitefully cast off the yoke of Divine service from themselves even in private, and even in regard to one thing alone (¶143). Though he might have done a lot of good and learned a lot of Torah, one who "despises the word of God" by denying Torah's Divine origin, misinterpreting Torah, or demeaning Torah scholars or the Holy Days has no place in The World to Come (¶144). One "misinterprets Torah" by saying impudently that certain things in Torah are there for no reason, simply because he doesn't understand them. Or he abandons or denies one aspect of Torah's demands, like the need for Torah scholars (¶145). One "demeans the Holy Days" by working on the intermediate days because the prohibition against doing that isn't enunciated in the Torah (¶146). When one "demeans Torah scholars" he causes their words to be overlooked, and prevents people from associating with them and asking their advice. He also prevents people from pursuing that kind of respect for themselves, and from awakening and coming to long for altruistic Torah study themselves (¶147). Those who humiliate Torah scholars disallow for the realization that Divine service is the very foundation of our lives. They encourage the idea that respect should be based on success in worldly affairs, and that something other than Divine service is fundamentally important in life. As such, upon realizing that we were all created to honor God, you should sanctify Him in all ways, as well as extol, thank, and bless Him at all times. Be sure to sanctify Him when you associate with others, as well as speak about the value of serving and fearing Him, and praise those who do. And since a person is defined by what he praises, when you praise goodness and righteousness, you yourself prove to be good and essentially righteous, even if you harbor hidden sins (¶148). Honor the righteous and you bring honor upon yourself as well. But never honor wrongdoers. First, because you'd be profaning Torah and Divine service (¶149). Second, because you'd be encouraging others to associate with wrongdoers and emulate them (¶150). Third, because you'd share in their punishment even if you don't do what they do when you associate with them (¶151). And fourth, you'd lower the esteem of men of truth and undermine Divine service (¶152). Those who "despise the word of God" discuss Torah in unclean places, they don't study Torah when they have a chance to, or they read heretical works. And those who "undermined His commandment" are those who have undone their circumcision (¶153).

Others who don't have a place in The World to Come include: those who don't believe that mention is made of The Resurrection of the Dead in the Torah, or those who don't believe that the Torah is from Heaven (¶154). Heretics, that is, people who don't act respectfully toward Torah scholars. In fact, one would be considered a heretic if he'd only humiliated another in a scholar's presence (¶155). While fearing Torah scholars fosters the fear of Heaven because it encourages those scholars to teach the fear of Heaven, heretics question the need for scholars and demean Torah study itself (¶156). One who'd call his teacher by his name alone is also a heretic (¶157). The essential wrong behind all that is profaning God's Torah, which we must never do. For God created us to sanctify and fear Him, and those who *do* will be sanctified as well (¶158). "God's enemies" haven't a place in The World to Come. And whatever good they do is rewarded in this world alone (unlike mere wrongdoers who'll suffer trials, tribulations, and death, and some measure of judgment after death for their misdeeds, but *will* have a share in The World to Come) (¶159). Sometimes even those who observe *mitzvot* are "God's enemies"— when they can't bear others learning Torah and serving God; when they belittle the honor shown to, and the achievements made by, scholars; and especially when they humiliate scholars, or they admire the honor shown to the evil (¶160). Informers and those who cause the multitude to sin also have no place in The World to Come (¶161). Those who elicit undue fear, like community leaders who assert their control for other than Godly reasons, have no place in The World to Come (¶162). They're wrong for a number of reasons: first, because rather than humbling themselves as we all should, they assert themselves for other than Godly reasons, when even haughty *thoughts* are anathema (¶163). Second, because a person should always condition his heart to fear God. But such individuals not only don't do that, but they'd even have others fear them instead of God (¶164). Third, because they verbally abuse others, when that's forbidden (¶165). Fourth, because they place many stumbling blocks before others (¶166). And fifth, because the Jewish Nation shouldn't subjugate itself to anyone but God (¶167). Those who exclude themselves from their decisions when leaders enact specific *mitzvot* for the people "separate themselves from the community," and have no place in The World to Come. They also weaken the determination of the others to join in, and cause the multitude to sin as well (¶168). Those who "abandon God" have no fear of God, they perform *mitzvot* by rote, and neither sigh nor worry when they sin, because they're convinced they've done nothing wrong. They also haven't a place in The World to Come (¶169). Some of them even brag about having indulged their cravings, and thus especially anger God (¶170). Nonetheless when any of these sorts of wrongdoers do tshuvah, they avoid destruction (¶171).

An Explanation of the Sins of "The Four Types." Individuals in these four categories do not experience the Divine Presence. They include those who malign, lie, flatter, or slander (¶172). We'll now enter into an analysis of the various categories of them (in descending order of seriousness) so that you can understand how serious these sins are, and surmount them (¶173).

The five categories of maligners: First are those who insult others cruelly without personally benefiting from it. Such a person is arrogant and a slanderer (¶174). Second are those who belittle and scorn others who fall short in worldly accomplishments or in power. Only arrogance, leisure, or overindulgence would have a person do that. Such an individual feels that a person's accomplishments are in his own hands, rather than in God's (¶175). Third are those who mock things and accomplishments themselves, without mocking the individuals behind them. Such individuals withhold any good that can come from those things, and may come to scorn *mitzvot* as well. They may reject admonishment because they consider themselves beyond the reproach of others, and then there's no hope for them (¶176). Fourth are those who engage in small talk and meaningless things, which leads to the avoidance of Torah, and indicates what little respect that person has for *mitzvot* or for the reward of The World to Come. And fifth are those who malign others not out of meanness, but out of sheer lightheartedness. This sometimes comes as a result of being intoxicated, but always as a result of casting aside the yoke of Heaven (¶177).

The nine categories of liars. First are those who falsely repudiate others' oaths, disclaim legitimate agreements, bear false witness, conduct business dishonestly, and the like (¶178). Second are those who underhandedly gain the confidence of others in order to cause them harm later on (¶179). Third are those who acquire things from others either by lying, or by importuning them into giving it to them as a gift (¶180). Fourth are those who deliberately distort what they've heard because they love to lie, or who inadvertently distort things others tell them by not listening to them attentively (¶181). Fifth are those who tell someone they'll do him a favor when they never intend to (¶182). Sixth are those who disappoint others by promising to do them a favor and not doing it, or by offering to give a gift and not giving it (¶183). Seventh are those who delude others into believing they've already done them a favor or said something favorable about them when they hadn't (¶184). Eighth are those who take credit for qualities or knowledge they don't have (¶185). And ninth are those who don't boldly lie, but who distort details (which cause no one any harm) because they simply like to lie (¶186).

The nine categories of flatterers. First are those who see or know about another's sins, but tell him he did nothing wrong (¶187). A person should sooner subject himself to danger than do that. For he'd be both a liar and a flatterer (¶188). Second are those who publicly praise sinners for one good point or another of theirs (though without justifying their sins, or covering them over) (¶189). But if you're not quite righteous and you don't despise wrongdoers, at least don't bless them (¶190). For only a fool would compliment a wrongdoer, in the mistaken belief that it's always good to compliment others (¶191). Third are those who compliment wrongdoers to their face, and thus encourage them in their deeds. Or they try to ingratiate themselves to powerful individuals (¶192). Fourth are those who befriend wrongdoers, when it's even forbidden to look at them full face (¶193). Fifth are those whose words are trusted by others who then commend someone to act as a judge who's undeserving, or characterize someone as trustworthy who isn't (¶194). Sixth are those who are in a position to protest or rebuke wrongdoing, but don't (¶195). Seventh are those who see others sinning, who don't believe they'd be listened to, so they don't reproach them. It should be noted, though, that people who are known not to take rebuke, should not be confronted (¶196). Eighth are those who hear about slander, profanity, or the derision of Torah, and don't respond (¶197). That's why it's important not to associate with wrongdoers—in order not to hear about what they say, and incur sins as a result of their sins (¶198). And ninth are those who show respect for wrongdoers in order to maintain peace, even though they don't speak well of them or indicate to others that the wrongdoers are good (¶199).

Slanderers: They're tantamount to deniers of God's existence for several reasons: First, because they cause great harm to others without gaining personally by what they say. And one could only love evil so purely if he has thrown off the yoke of Heaven (¶200). Second, because they believe that while one can't *do* whatever he'd like, he can nonetheless *say* anything, because he alone has jurisdiction over his mouth, not even God. In fact, though, our sages said that slander is more serious than idol-worship, illicit relations, and murder (¶201). But how could slander be more serious than such grave sins? (¶202) First, because the slanderer repeats his sin again and again. And if a minor sin becomes serious with repetition, that's all the more true of so serious a sin as slander (¶203). Second, because tshuvah is hard for the slanderer, since he's so trained his tongue to speak that way that it's no longer under his control (¶204). Third, because the slanderer takes his sin lightly, since he perceives it as being mere speech and harmless. So he either doesn't repent, or only barely so (¶205). It's also important to realize that if a slanderer can't harm someone verbally, he'll inevitably come to harm him physically, and mercilessly at that (¶206). Fourth, because even if he wanted to do tshuvah, the slanderer would have to ask everyone he's hurt for forgiveness. But since he'd hurt so many, he'd forget whom to ask. Or there'd be some he'd be hesitant to ask forgiveness from (¶207). And once words leave a slanderer's mouth, they can't be called back. As such, he might cast aspersions on someone's family and do damage for generations, and might even come to slander the righteous (¶208). And fifth, because slanderers even speak against God Himself. Even his Torah study will not shield him from punishment then (¶209). Not only do slanderers speak slander, they also don't speak about edifying things at the time, like Torah, wisdom, ethics, about whatever might foster peace between people and better them, about the good in good things or the bad in bad things, or about truth (¶210).

The six categories of slanderers: First are those who attribute imaginary faults in others. In fact, only evil, malicious people and liars would even accept slander. The former because they suspect innocent people and love finding fault in others. And the latter because they're quick to accept lies as well as offer them (¶211). In truth, you'd be just as guilty as the slanderer himself if you accept what he said. What you should do is show displeasure when faced with slander (¶212). A humble person wouldn't listen to slander, because he'd be pained to know that others were being shamed (¶213).

Second are those who slander others, but don't lie in the process. You're never to mention a person's ancestors' sins either in public or in private; or that person's own past sins, if he's done tshuvah for them (¶214). If you see someone sinning privately, relate that to a discreet scholar only. Because the individual might have done tshuvah for it. Nonetheless, avoid him until you know he has (¶215). Slander harms and shames its victim, and it has the slanderer rejoice over the victim's misfortune. And it does even more harm when it's based on truth (¶216). So, only a fool would readily find fault in others, who may not even deserve it. While the righteous would not (¶217). Nonetheless when it comes to known sinners who don't fear God, it's imperative to speak against them. But if you see a God-fearing man possibly sinning, give him the benefit of the doubt. If the sinner is an intermediate, be suspicious, but give him the benefit of the doubt, nonetheless. But if he doesn't fear God, consider him guilty (¶218). If you alone witnessed a sin, then don't testify to it, but do criticize the person. If the sinner is God-fearing, you're to assume he did tshuvah. But if he's someone who has cast off the yoke of Heaven, you may humiliate him, though you may not testify against him on your own. Also avoid exposing a sin you're guilty of as well (¶219). You can, however, tell the sinner's teacher or a confidant, if they'd believe you as much as if you'd been two witnesses to the sin, in effect. But if two witnesses report to the court, it should hear out their testimony privately (¶220). As a single witness, though, you can relate a person-to-person sin to its victim (¶221).

Third are rumor-mongers. Practice that, and you increase hatred in the world, and bring death upon yourself, upon the subject of your rumors, and upon those listening to them (¶222). While you shouldn't accept what rumor-mongers say or hate the subjects of their statements, you should nonetheless be leery, and on guard (¶223). The most serious form of slander is the stirring up of animosity between relatives and friends (¶224). It's imperative to keep a secret entrusted to you. In fact, never trust anyone who'd disclose your secrets, because he'd invariably lapse into slander as well (¶225).

Fourth are those who speak "the dust of slander" and say things that encourage others to slander. So, only praise somebody in private, for praising him in public may encourage others to denigrate him—unless you're addressing people who love him, or the individual is known to be righteous (¶226). You also speak "the dust of slander" when you praise somebody who then suffers a loss as a consequence (¶227). Take care never to be suspected of being a slanderer, for your words of reproach won't be taken to heart if you are. Hence, if you see someone sinning against another, reproach the sinner himself before disclosing his sin to others (¶228).

Fifth are those who speak obscenely, who've thusly abandoned shame and decency, as well as the path of wisdom. It's also forbidden to listen to profanity (¶229). All in all, you should never speak indecently, in order to avoid profanity, slander, and insult. Always speak in a refined manner instead (¶230).

And sixth are those who find fault in others, for no good reason. They perceive the best of intentions as bad, and unintentional errors as intentional. And they take themselves to be victims. Avoid all that, and judge others favorably instead (¶231).

Gate Four

THE VARIOUS MEANS OF ATONEMENT

This gate breaks down thusly:

The rationale: The first few sections serve to illustrate the idea that you sometimes have to "take bitter medicine" (i.e., experience tribulation, pain, or suffering) as a consequence of committing serious sins that tshuvah alone won't completely absolve you of. They nonetheless also underscore the idea that, just as you'd ordinarily only be absolved for profaning God's name with your death, yet you can accomplish a lot by sanctifying His name—so, too, can you rectify and be absolved of other serious sins by other means (¶'s 1–5).

The various means of atonement: While in the days of the Holy Temple you could offer a sacrifice and be atoned for not fulfilling an imperative or for having untoward thoughts (among other things) and now you can't; you can nonetheless achieve much the same in our days by studying the sacrificial orders in depth. And while Yom Kippur itself atones for transgressions, you can nonetheless accomplish a lot before Yom Kippur by longing for its arrival, and participating in the festive meal the night before it in the right spirit (¶'s 6–10)

You can avoid tribulations by giving charity, being benevolent, visiting the sick, burying the dead, consoling mourners, gladdening brides and grooms, studying Torah for the sake of Heaven, fasting, weeping, practicing self-denial, sighing, being apprehensive, and by accepting other afflictions for tribulations due you (¶'s 11–13).

You can avoid excision or capital punishment by confessing, asking for forgiveness, sighing, expressing apprehension and fear, and by studying the sin-offering orders in depth (¶14).

And you can rectify your accidental or careless sins by being preoccupied with what you did, as well as worrying about and fearing its consequences. But if you profaned God's name, not only would you do well to sanctify His name (see above)—you'd be wise to also study and dwell upon Torah (¶'s 15–16).

The last few sections present us with the ideas that we're especially charged to do tshuvah on Yom Kippur. But because the onset of Yom Kippur itself will not atone for interpersonal sins, you'd have to first appease anyone you sinned against, then confess to God for that sin, in order to be atoned for it (¶'s 17–22).

Chapter One

༺❀༻༺❀༻༺❀༻༺❀༻༺❀༻༺❀༻༺❀༻༺❀༻༺❀༻༺❀༻

The Rationale[1]

1. Just as the body experiences illness and disease, so too does the soul, whose illnesses and diseases are its bad traits and sins.[2] But God heals your soul's disease when you do tshuvah for your wrongful ways.[3] As it's written, "Have mercy on me, God! Heal my soul, for I have sinned against You!" (Psalms 41:5) as well as, ". . . and do tshuvah and become healed" (Isaiah 6:10).[4]

But just as you sometimes find a body starting to heal, then nearly fully healing, but still not entirely free of disease until the patient ingests a bitter tonic and endures the deprivation of having to do without food he craves—that's also true of

---

1. This phrase isn't included in the text, and was inserted here for ease of reference.

2. The point can either be made that bad traits and sins *trigger* disease in a soul, or that they *are* the disease. But, in fact, both are true. For bad traits and sins are both noxious flaws of the soul, as well as infectious precursors of further disease. It might also be said that sins and bad traits are signs of how severe a disease is, as well as symptoms of it. And that the disease itself is the willingness to expose yourself to sins and bad traits, and thus separate yourself from God and your own intrinsic well-being. (See Supplementary Notes.)

3. . . . though not entirely in some instances, and not at once, as is about to be explained. The analogy to healing also underscores the point that tshuvah can either be partial or full. For just as you can be cured of an acute pain or disease and nonetheless still suffer from an older, chronic disease, so too can you do tshuvah for one particular sin or character flaw and nonetheless still be guilty of past errors.

4. In its entirety this verse reads, "Make the heart of this people fat, make their ears heavy, and shut their eyes. Lest they see with their eyes, hear with their ears, and understand with their heart, do tshuvah, and become healed." This verse is an ironic way of laying out the essential elements of tshuvah, which include sensitizing your heart, as well as hearing, seeing, and fully grasping the truth of your ways. (It's ironic in that it's a backward prescription that tells what to avoid if you're not about to do tshuvah. See the commentators there for an explanation.)

a soul infected with serious sin. For even after most of the illness had dissipated, after some of the consequences you'd have to suffer would be spared you thanks to your tshuvah, and after God would have withdrawn His wrath—your soul wouldn't have been[5] cleansed of its disease nonetheless, and your sin wouldn't have been completely absolved until you'd been admonished with tribulation, criticized with pain, or made to experience suffering or troubles.[6]

As it's said, "My sin is too great to bear! You have indeed cast me out today from the face of the earth, and concealed me from Your face. I will be a fugitive and a wanderer about the land, and whoever finds me would kill me" (Genesis 4:13–14). That is, though most of Cain's sin was atoned for by his tshuvah, though he'd been spared most of the consequences,[7] and though he escaped death, as it's said, "And God placed a sign on Cain so that whoever would find him would not strike him" (Ibid. v. 15), he still had to endure exile. As it's said, "He dwelt in the land of Nod, to the east of Eden" (Ibid. v. 16).

Nonetheless, as our sages pointed out, the decree of having to wander about was also reduced after he did tshuvah. For, the original sentence had been for a double degree of wandering, as it's said, "I will be a fugitive and a wanderer in the land," which alludes to a double degree of wandering. But it's said, "He dwelt in the land of Nod," after he did tshuvah (*Vayikrah Rabbah* 10).[8]

2.   This idea[9] is further illustrated by the Torah's statement that, "Should an individual[10] from among the people of the land sin accidentally . . . he must bring as his offering a kid of the goats, a female without blemish, for his sin which he has sinned" (Leviticus 4:27–28). For, as our sages explained, a sin offering is required for any sin committed accidentally that would incur excision if it were committed purposefully (*K'ritot* 2A).[11]

---

5. . . . thoroughly . . .

6. Rabbeinu Yonah is about to cite Cain's experience of sin, decree, retribution, and eventual "reduction of sentence" as the exemplar of each soul's experience when a person does tshuvah for a serious sin. As he lays it out here, when you do tshuvah for such a sin, you *begin* to be cleansed of your disease, and you're spared the more serious consequences of that sin. But you nonetheless have to endure swallowing the "bitter tonic" of some retribution until you're fully cleansed, atoned for, and drawn close again to your Beloved (whom you'd been "isolated," i.e., estranged, from). (See Supplementary Notes.)

7. . . . of his sin . . .

8. This ¶ sets the theme for the rest of this gate. It offers that while tshuvah is indeed a "cure" for many, many sins and bad character traits, it's nonetheless not the cure per se for some of them. For the latter type would only be cured through more dire means (in the natural order of thing). Nonetheless, as Rabbeinu Yonah will indicate in the course of the gate, other, less dire means can be substituted.

9. i.e., that tshuvah alone cannot completely cleanse in certain instances.

10. Literally, "a soul," in keeping with the reference in the previous ¶ to the soul's need to be healed.

11. The Mishna cited here lists thirty-six instances in which this would be the case, all

That is, since a sin that incurs excision is so serious, you aren't completely atoned for it despite your having committed it accidentally until you'd bring a sin-offering—even after you'd have confessed to it. And your sin wouldn't be atoned for by the sin-offering[12] if you don't confess and do tshuvah—for it's said, "The sacrifice of wrongdoers[13] is an abomination" (Proverbs 21:27)—though it would be[14] atoned for with confession and an offering. As it's said, "The priest will atone for him,[15] and he will be forgiven" (Leviticus 4:31).

So, if you're[16] impure[17] for having sinned by accident despite your tshuvah until you present an offering, then consider how great the consequences you'd have to suffer[18] if you sinned on purpose! That's why the purposeful sinner's sin would[19] be[20] atoned for with tribulation. As it's said, "He is criticized in bed with pain . . . (So) he pleads with God, who is pleased with him" (Job 33:19, 26) and, "God criticizes those He loves the way a father criticizes a son he is pleased with" (Proverbs 3:12).

But as we'll explain,[21] there's a solution and an antidote for you[22]—good deeds, which will shield you from pain.

3. It's further illustrated[23] by the Torah's statement that "For on that day[24] the *cohen* will make an atonement for you to cleanse you, so that you may be cleansed of all your sins before God" (Leviticus 16:30). Which is to say that you'd need to experience the atonement of Yom Kippur after having done tshuvah, since the actual atonement that comes with Yom Kippur[25] comes after you've done

---

of which are heinous, perverse, or blasphemous. See ¶15 for a discussion of a remedy for having sinned accidentally, now that we can't offer sacrifices. And see ¶'s 6, and 11–14 for a discussion of sins that incur excision or capital punishment, and which incur tribulation. (See Supplementary Notes.)

12. . . . whatsoever . . .

13. i.e., those who are still wrongdoers, because they hadn't yet confessed and done tshuvah.

14. . . . partially . . .

15. . . . in the course of the sacrifice process . . .

16. . . . still . . .

17. i.e., unacceptable and as-of-yet unforgiven.

18. . . . for your sin . . .

19. . . . only . . .

20. . . . fully . . .

21. See ¶11.

22. That is, there's a way to prevent tribulation, if you'd ordinarily need to suffer it because of your sins. It's the practice of . . .

23. i.e., the idea that tshuvah alone cannot completely cleanse in certain instances is further illustrated . . .

24. i.e., Yom Kippur.

25. . . . only . . .

tshuvah.[26] As our sages said, "Death and Yom Kippur[27] atone along with tshuvah" (*Yomah* 86B).[28]

4. But there's one sin that—like a disease that the body can't be purged of its whole life—the soul isn't cleansed of, which it remains impure and unacceptable as a result of, until death comes to separate it from the body it sinned through. And that's the sin of profaning God's name.[29] As it's said, "Behold—glee and gladness, the slaughtering of oxen and sheep . . ."[30] (Isaiah 22:10). That is, instead of paying attention to the words of the prophet and trembling as a result of them, these individuals pillaged in public,[31] and met with friends for all sorts of festivities. And as was said, "This sin will not be atoned for you until you die" (Ibid. v. 14) and, "They mocked God's messengers . . . and disparaged His prophets, so God's scorn arose against His people until there was no cure"[32] (2 Chronicles 36:16).

5. Nonetheless, though this disease won't be cured[33] the way other sins would, there is a cure for it, with God's help—your sanctifying God's Torah in the presence of others, and your letting people know about God's might, as well as the glory and majesty of His rule.[34] Your sin will depart from you then, since you'd thus acted so uprightly, as opposed to how foolishly you'd acted when you'd sinned.[35]

---

26. See Supplementary Notes.

27. . . . only . . .

28. This, too, proves that tshuvah alone cannot completely cleanse in certain instances. See ¶'s 17–22 for a discussion of Yom Kippur.

29. That is, profaning God's name is so grave and serious a sin, that not only will doing tshuvah, offering sacrifices, suffering, or experiencing the atonement of Yom Kippur not expiate it. You'd have to die of it to be said to be "cured" of it. (Though see the next ¶.) (See Supplementary Notes.)

30. i.e., the people were publicly carousing and reveling, saying, "let us eat and drink, for tomorrow we will die."

31. It's the public and exhibitionistic aspect of such sins that define them as the profanation of God's name.

32. . . . other than their death. For as the next verse says, "And he set the king of the Chaldeans upon them, who slew their young men with the sword in the house of their sanctuary, and had no compassion upon young men or virgins, old men, or the feeble."

33. i.e., forgiven.

34. Rabbeinu Yonah is quick to insert the phrase "with God's help" here to underscore the point that you can't always be sure you'll have the chance to sanctify "God's Torah in the presence of others," or to let others "know about God's might, as well as the glory and majesty of His rule." For a person can never be sure he'll ever be given the time or chance to do tshuvah. It all depends on God's willingness to allow him that opportunity. That point is made here most especially, rather than elsewhere, because of the severity of this sin.

35. We thus return here to the principle of improving yourself through the very agent you used to sin. (See Supplementary Notes.)

For as doctors say, an illness will be cured by its opposite[36] and healed by its counterpart.[37]

Solomon said that, "Sin is atoned for through kindness and truth" (Proverbs 16:6), as we explained in the first gate.[38] The "truth" mentioned here refers to your preparing yourself to uphold truth, to help those searching for faith, and to dispose of untruth and injustice. Because spreading truth and restoring it to its full strength brings honor to God.[39] For it's said, "He judged the cause of the poor and needy, and it was for his good. Did he not do this to know Me? says God" (Jeremiah 22:16), while it's said about those who pursue untruth, "Through their deceit they refuse to know Me" (Ibid. 9:5). As our sages put it, "After Herod killed the sages, he asked Bava Ben Buta if he would cure him and treat his wound. But Bava Ben Buta said, 'You extinguished the lamp of the world. Now go and occupy yourself with the light of the world, and strive to build the Holy Temple'" (*Babba Battra* 4A).[40]

---

36. As when heat is applied to cold, and cold to heat.

37. As the expression goes, take "the hair of the dog that bit you" if you're to be healed. That is, the very thing that causes the malady is its own best cure. This notion is classical in nature (referred to as *similar similibus curantur*), and it's the basis of Homeopathy.

38. See 1:47, as well as 3:143, and ¶16.

39. In contrast to the dishonor you brought upon Him in the past.

40. See ¶16 for further discussion about a remedy for profaning God's name.

Chapter Two

᭢᭢᭢᭢᭢᭢᭢᭢᭢᭢᭢

6. *The Various Means of Atonement[1]*

Our sages said, "Rabbi Mattia Ben Cherash asked Rabbi Elazar Ben Azaria in Rome, 'I heard there are four types of atonement, according to Rabbi Yishamael.' Rabbi Elazar Ben Azaria explained, 'There are[2] three, with tshuvah a part of each. As such, if a person does not fulfill an imperative and does tshuvah,[3] he is forgiven immediately, before he even makes another move. As it is written, "Return, disloyal children, and I will cure your disloyalties" (Jeremiah 3:22). If he transgresses a prohibition and does tshuvah, his tshuvah is held in abeyance, and Yom Kippur atones for him.[4] As it's said, "For on that day you will be atoned for, and be cleansed . . ." (Leviticus 16:30). If he commits sins that incur excision or a court-inflicted death penalty and he does tshuvah, both tshuvah and Yom Kippur are held in abeyance, and tribulations purge him.[5] As it is said, "And I will visit their acts of defiance with a rod, and their sins with strokes" (Psalms 89:33). But when it comes to profaning God's name, tshuvah does not have the capacity to be held in abeyance,[6] Yom Kippur cannot atone, nor will tribulations purge. They are all held

---

1. Rabbeinu Yonah is about to expand upon the themes he introduced in the ¶'s just preceding.

2. . . . actually . . .

3. . . . right there and then . . .

4. i.e., he must wait for Yom Kippur to atone for him even though he would have done tshuvah right there and then.

5. i.e., he's not atoned for despite his tshuvah and despite his having experienced Yom Kippur, until he'll have experienced tribulations.

6. . . . until the sinner would have experienced Yom Kippur or tribulations. And when it will finally come into effect . . .

in abeyance instead, and death alone purges. As it is said, " 'This sin will not be atoned for until you die' (Isaiah 22:14)" (*Yomah* 86a).[7]

They also said, "A burnt-offering will only atone for one who transgresses an imperative after he does tshuvah" (*Zevachim* 7B). For though your sin will be atoned for with tshuvah, what the burnt-offering does is compound your atonement, and makes you more acceptable to God.[8]

7. They also said, "A burnt-offering atones for fantasies that arise in the mind,[9] and for thoughts of sinning" (J. T., *Yomah* 8:7).[10] As such it's written, "When the festive days came to an end, Job sent them out and sanctified them. And he arose early in the morning and offered burnt-offerings for each, 'For maybe my sons sinned,' Job said, 'and cursed God in their hearts' " (Job 1:5).[11]

8. Now that we can't offer sacrifices, due to our sins and the sins of our ancestors, what you should do if you sin in thought or fail to fulfill an imperative is recite the verses having to do with burnt-offerings, found at the beginning of *Vayikrah* and *Tzav* (Leviticus 1:1–17, 6:1–6). Reciting the verses having to do with it will then substitute for offering one, regardless of whether you read them from the Torah, or study[12] them from the Talmud.

As our sages said, "Whoever occupies himself with the verses having to do with burnt-offerings is considered to have offered a burnt-offering; . . . with the verses having to do with sin-offerings is considered to have offered a sin-offering; and . . . with the verses having to do with guilt-offerings is considered to have offered a guilt-offering" (*Menachot* 110A).

If you transgress a prohibition[13] and do tshuvah, then worry about your sin,

---

7. Nonetheless, note the recommendation offered at the end of the previous ¶.

8. To return to our theme of tshuvah being a reconciliation with one's beloved (Divine or human), if you've offended your beloved by not doing something she asked you to, you need only sincerely apologize, regret your oversight, feel bad about it, etc., (see the first gate's requirements) and you'll be forgiven. Though you'd be wise to give your beloved a gift, to draw yourself closer yet after the fact (analogous to the burnt-offering). But, if you've done something you should never have done, not only must you do the above. You must also experience a period of private reconciliation with your beloved (see comments to 2:14), which may even embrace anguish and dismay (depending upon how much you'd offended your beloved), if you're to be forgiven. If you'd utterly insulted and belittled your beloved, however, you'd never truly be forgiven, nor would your sin be overlooked, until many years later, after your death. When all will be forgiven, in retrospect.

9. This represents a play on words, in that the original says, "An עולה ("burnt-offering") atones for fantasies that עולה ("arise") in the mind . . ."

10. See Supplementary Notes.

11. So, not only does a burnt-offering (a "gift," see our note above) endear you to your beloved even more so. It also rescinds your misguided intentions after the fact.

12. . . . the explanation of . . .

13. . . . which cannot be expiated by reciting appropriate verses from the Torah . . .

and long for and anticipate the coming of Yom Kippur, when you'll be made acceptable to God.[14] For, in fact, He cares for every single body and soul, and wants each created being to live. As it's said, "He wants life" (Psalms 30:6).[15] And so our sages said, "Whoever prepares a meal for the eve of Yom Kippur is considered to have fasted on both the ninth of Tishrei[16] and the tenth[17] in compliance with a mitzvah" (*Rosh Hashanah* 9A). Firstly, because you'd show how happy[18] you are to have reached the moment of your atonement, which would then attest to your having worried about your guilt, and been sorrowful about your sin.[19]

9.   Second,[20] because we dedicate a festive meal on all the other Holy Days for the joy of the mitzvah,[21] since being happy about a mitzvah greatly increases and elevates its merits. As it's said, "I saw Your people there happy and offering willingly to You" (1 Chronicles 29:17) and, "Because you did not serve God your Lord joyfully and glad-heartedly" (Deuteronomy 28:47).[22] And yet we fast on Yom Kippur. So we dedicate a festive meal for the joy of the mitzvah[23] on the eve of Yom Kippur.

10.   And third,[24] in order to fortify ourselves for the extra prayers and entreaties we offer on Yom Kippur, and take counsel with ourselves about tshuvah and its principles.[25]

---

14. See Supplementary Notes.

15. Many approach Yom Kippur with the attitude that they're fasting and wracking their bodies to meet the demands of a stern and cruel Taskmaster. But the truth of the matter is that we're to greet Yom Kippur as the great rapprochement between us and our Beloved we've indicated it is. For who among us but the very crude would think of eating and drinking when he's so preoccupied, and so close to the One he loves.

16. . . . which is the eve of Yom Kippur . . .

17. . . . which is Yom Kippur itself . . .

18. i.e., relieved.

19. . . . all along.

Rabbeinu Yonah's suggestion that you worry about a prohibition you committed, and long for Yom Kippur's atonement of it, goes far to explain how reading verses about burnt-offerings can be a substitute for actually offering them. Apparently the point of reading those verses is to come to worry about the fact that "we can't offer sacrifices (now), due to our sins and the sins of our ancestors." And to have us long *and* prepare for the happy time when we'll all be able to. Doing that will likewise attest to our having regretted and been sad about our sins, which forestall the rebuilding of the Holy Temple in our own days.

20. i.e., the second reason why we eat a festive meal on the eve of Yom Kippur.

21. . . . particular to that day . . .

22. Verses 45 through 47 (here) read, "All these curses will come upon you, pursue you, and overtake you till you are destroyed; because you did not . . . serve God your Lord joyfully and glad-heartedly."

23. . . . particular to Yom Kippur . . .

24. i.e., the third reason why we eat a festive meal on the eve of Yom Kippur.

25. So, apparently we're to eat a festive meal on the eve of Yom Kippur to celebrate our impending atonement, to experience the joy of the festival beforehand, and to bolster our

11. Since any sin you committed that incurs excision or a court-imposed death sentence wouldn't be forgiven despite your tshuvah until you'd have experienced tribulations[26] (since the tshuvah would be held in abeyance and tribulations alone would purge[27]), resolve to fulfill the sorts of *mitzvot* that protect against tribulations, like charity. For charity even delivers from death, as it's said, "Charity will deliver from death" (Proverbs 10:2).

If you haven't enough money to give, then speak kindly to the poor and act as their delegate for help from others. In fact, our sages said that, "One who has others act, is even greater than those who act" (*Babba Battra* 9A).

Involve yourself in the mitzvah of benevolence, as well.[28] And help others by advising them, or doing something for them. As our sages said, "Benevolence is even greater than charity. Because while one can only give charity with money, he can be benevolent either personally or with money; and because charity can only be given to the poor, while benevolence can be shown either to the poor or the wealthy" (*Sukkah* 49B).

Or sympathize with the poor, show them respect, and comfort them when they're in trouble. For it's said, "Draw out your soul to the starving" (Isaiah 58:10), and our sages said, "The one who appeases someone is greater than one who would give him charity" (*Babba Battra* 9B). Or fulfill the *mitzvot* of visiting the sick, burying the dead, comforting mourners, and gladdening brides and grooms. Because those are also acts of benevolence.[29] Most importantly, fulfill the mitzvah of studying Torah for the sake of Heaven.[30]

Everything we've suggested here is included in Solomon's statement that "Sins are atoned for by kindness and truth" (Proverbs 16:6).[31] For when you acquire Torah[32] you acquire truth. As it's said, "Acquire truth, and never sell it, as well as wisdom, instruction, and understanding" (Proverbs 23:23) and, "Your Torah is

---

strength for all the prayer and reflection we're about to take part in. But how alien that all is to us! For *we* eat a meal before Yom Kippur because we dread the thought of doing without food for a day, and sense a need to store it up within for the long, cold, hungry "winter" of a day ahead, when we won't be able to satisfy every whim. It would obviously do us well to reflect upon Rabbeinu Yonah's words here at the approach of each Yom Kippur Eve.

26. See Supplementary Notes.

27. . . . you of the sin . . .

28. See Supplementary Notes.

29. Like tshuvah that does so much to purge you of sin, acts of charity and benevolence go far to undo tribulation, if that's due you. But most importantly . . .

30. . . . .for doing that is a favor for everyone—both those who directly benefit from your wisdom, and those who benefit indirectly from more wisdom and subsequent goodness in the world.

31. See Supplementary Notes.

32. . . . knowledge . . .

truth" (Psalms 119:142). And as our sages said in connection with the verse, "It[33] is a tree of life to those who grasp onto it" (Proverbs 3:18), "A person who commits a sin that incurs excision or a court-imposed death sentence should recite two chapters[34] a day if he is accustomed to reciting one. Or two[35] portions a day if he is accustomed to reciting one" (*Vayikrah Rabbah* 25:1).

Torah will protect you from tribulations for two reasons. First, as our sages said, because "Torah is equivalent to them all" (*Peah* 1:1).[36] And second, because your laboring in Torah, working hard at it, and losing sleep over it will take the place of tribulation. As our sages put it, "Everyone was born to toil. But one whose toil centers upon Torah is fortunate" (*Sanhedrin* 99B) and, "Why is Torah called 'wisdom'[37] (Isaiah 28:29)? Because it wears a person down"[38] (*Sanhedrin* 26B).[39]

12.   Also take fasts upon yourself, shed tears, and deny yourself pleasures in place of tribulations.[40] As it's said, "My knees have given way from fasting" (Psalms 109:24) and, "Return to Me wholeheartedly by fasting, weeping, and mourning" (Joel 2:12). Constantly sigh bitterly, as we indicated in the first gate,[41] and thus substitute a lot of bitterness for tribulations.

For it's said, "A man's spirit will endure his illness, but who can bear a broken spirit?" (Proverbs 18:14). For when one's body becomes ill, his spirit can[42] bear the illness.[43] It can help the body and shore it up by speaking to it, and consoling it so that it can accept and endure its illness. But when the spirit itself becomes ill and broken by sorrow and worry, who could ever console it, or sustain it and shore it up?

---

33. i.e., Torah.

34. . . . of Mishna . . .

35. . . . Torah . . .

36. i.e., it's worth as much as all of them together. So if charity and benevolence bestowed upon others will save you from tribulation, Torah study will all the more so.

37. תושיה

38. חשש

39. That is, it's the lot of each one of us to work hard, and experience some tribulation (God protect us all!). Fortunate is he who manages to fulfill his tally of hard work and tribulation, though, with Torah study. Fortunate is anyone, in fact, who manages to channel his so-human need to eat and drink, rest and relax, earn a living, occupy his mind, live a family life, etc., through the ways of holiness!

40. While the preceding ¶ provided more sociable, and outgoing means of avoiding tribulation, this one provides more passive, private, spiritual means, if you're so inclined. (See Supplementary Notes.)

41. See 1:12–14.

42. . . . usually . . .

43. The text continues with the following:

. . . where the term "endure" [יבלבל, often translated "maintain" or "support"] is used in the sense of "Who can endure [מבלבל] the day of his coming?" (Malachi 3:2)

For worry and bitterness is worse than bodily illness, since the spirit can shore up the body when it's ill, yet when the spirit is ill and broken by worries, the body cannot shore it up.[44]

If you're vexed and troubled when you're yet sinning, try to see the justice in the judgment brought against you,[45] and accept those admonishments lovingly.[46] Doing that will shield you from the many tribulations you actually deserve. As it's said, "When a man's own wrath will praise You, You will gird Yourself with the remainder of wrath" (Psalms 76:11).[47] That's to say, when the person himself thanks God as he suffers,[48] then "the remainder of (the) wrath" that was to be released upon him[49] will be girded by You, held back, and not allowed to come upon him, the way a sword would be drawn, then returned to its sheath.

It's also said, "I thank You, God, because You were angry with me, but You took back Your anger and consoled me" (Isaiah 12:1). That's to say, I thank you for Your chastisements, and I accept them lovingly. In fact, it was because I thanked you for Your anger that "You took back Your anger and consoled me."

The same can be said about being grateful for the kindness shown you.[50] As it's said, "I will forever thank You for what You did; I await[51] Your name which is good before Your pious ones" (Psalms 52:11). That's to say, I thank You for all the

---

44. That's to say, if you bring grief upon yourself by weeping, sighing, fasting, denying yourself pleasures, worrying, and the like, that will serve you far better than any tribulations you might otherwise have to endure. Because inner anguish like that affects you far more deeply than any tribulation could. As Rabbeinu Yonah put it in 1:13, "The bitterer and sadder you feel (about your sins), the more effective and profound will be your tshuvah. Because your tshuvah would be the result of the refinement of your soul, and the purifying of your mind." And "the harder you work at sighing about it, the less significant your sin then becomes. Because sorrow originates in a refined, sublime soul, which makes itself more favorable with sighing than with a lot of physical torment and pain."

45. . . . by your current vexations and troubles . . .

46. See Supplementary Notes.

47. Rabbeinu Yonah understands the verse to read, "When a man's own *vexation* will praise You . . ." as he's about to explain, rather than the more literal "When a man's own wrath will praise You" as we have it here.

48. The text continues with the following:

. . . as in, "If only my torments [בעשי, a cognate of בעס ("my anger"), which is then a synonym for the original חמתי, translated as "my vexation" in the verse from Psalms] were weighed" (Job 6:2), which refers to troubles.

49. The text continues with the following:

. . . as in, "One who girds his armor should not praise himself as much as one who *releases* it" (1 Kings 20:11).

50. . . . when you were chastised only somewhat, though you deserved to be chastised much more so.

51. . . . the revelation of Your . . .

favors You've done for me, and I await Your unending favor[52] as a consequence.

It's also said, "I will raise the cup of salvation and call out in the name of God" (Psalms 116:13) and, "I have found troubles and sorrows, yet I call out in the name of God" (Ibid. vv. 3–4). For as our sages said about[53] "A Psalm of David as he fled . . ." (Psalms 3:1)[54] and, "Justice carried out is a joy to the righteous" (Proverbs 21:15), it's the way of the righteous to pay their debts, then sing out to God. As such, they're like a tenant farmer who gathered the grain to be threshed and put it in a pile for the landlord to take as payment, and went home empty-handed but happy. And when asked how he could just leave the threshing floor empty-handed and be happy said, "But, the bill was paid and my account is squared!" (Midrash *Tehillim* 19:2).[55]

13. In fact, you're obliged to reflect[56] and realize that troubles and tribulations haven't come upon you because of the seriousness or number of your sins. Rather, because God has been admonishing you the way a father admonishes his son—mercifully.[57] As it's said, "Know in your heart that God admonishes you the way a father admonishes his son" (Deuteronomy 8:5). As our sages put it: "You know what you did, and what tribulations I brought upon you—and that I have not chastised you as much as you deserved to be" (*Yalkut, Shemot* 303).[58] And it's written, "Know that God exacts less from you than your sins"[59] (Job 11:6) and, "For You, God, have punished us less than our sins"[60] (Ezra 9:13).

For when God admonishes His enemies, they're destroyed for a single sin, and retribution comes upon them in one fell swoop.[61] As it's said, "The wicked will die because of their wickedness" (Psalms 34:22). And their other sins linger in their souls,[62] as it's said, "Their transgressions were in their essences"[63] (Ezekiel 32:27).

---

52. . . . which is exemplified by the revelation of Your name . . .

53. . . . the thrust of the Psalm beginning . . .

54. . . . which continues, ". . . from Absalom his son. How many are my enemies, God! So many rise up against me!"

55. That is, though he was left empty-handed, he was also thus free of all debt, had left his good name intact, and was able to start afresh from there. In fact, this is a metaphor for tshuvah itself.

56. . . . upon the fact . . .

57. See Supplementary Notes.

58. That's to say, in your heart of hearts you know only too well how surreptitiously heinous, nasty, thoughtless, and grandiose we all are from time to time. And you also know in your heart of hearts that if your case were brought in its entirety before a human court capable of reading your heart, that you'd be chastised far more than you've been chastised by God.

59. . . . deserve.

60. . . . deserve.

61. See Supplementary Notes.

62. That is, they'll nonetheless be made to suffer the consequences of their other sins in the afterlife.

63. The original reads עצמותם, which can either translate as their "bones" (as it usually is), or their "essences" (as Rabbeinu Yonah understands it here).

But when God admonishes the righteous,[64] retribution comes to them a little at a time, until their sin is undone.[65] As it's said, "You alone have I known of all the families of the earth, so I will punish you for all your sins" (Amos 3:2), which our sages likened to the situation of the man who loaned money to two people, one of whom he loved and the other of whom he hated. And while he asked the one he loved to repay in installments, he demanded immediate repayment from the one he hated (*Avodah Zarah* 4A). As it's said, "The righteous will fall seven times and rise up, but the guilty will stumble in their wrongdoings" (Proverbs 24:16). That is, they will stumble and be undone with just one act of wrongdoing.[66]

In fact, our sages drew another analogy when they said, "One who does not know how to strike, strikes his son across his eyes and face. But one who knows how to strike, strikes his son in a way that does him no harm" (Midrash *Tehillim* 38).[67] And so it's written, "God has certainly admonished me, but He has not let me die" (Psalms 118:8) and . . . "but spare his life" (Job 2:6).

In fact, the tribulations the guilty[68] suffer come specifically as retribution, while the kind the righteous[69] suffer are actually tests.[70] They accept those tribulations in love, and even take it upon themselves to improve their ways[71] as well, so that the tribulations come to be for their benefit and to their advantage, and serve to reward them greatly. As it's said, "God tests the righteous" (Psalms 11:5). Our sages likened that to the situation of the man who only struck at his flax when he knew it was strong enough for him to strike it hard enough to soften and improve it" (*Breishit Rabbah* 32).[72]

---

64. i.e., those who have done tshuvah for their sins.

65. . . . in their lifetime.

66. The text continues with the following:

It's also said, "Admonish me, God, justly only (אך במשפט), and not according to Your anger, lest You diminish me" (Jeremiah 10:24), where "אך במשפט" means "in keeping with Your ordained mercy and lovingkindness." As in, ". . . according to number, according to משפט" (Numbers 29:21), i.e., "according to Your ordinance." And as in, "He conducts his business justly" (במשפט) (Psalms 112:5), i.e., "as ordained by law."

67. This is like the artful and studied administration of a stun rather than a blow, in order to forestall the need for blows, that police sometimes use.

68. . . . including God's enemies, as enunciated a few paragraphs back . . .

69. i.e., those who have done tshuvah for their sins (see above).

70. . . . of their mettle, to determine if they'd learned the lessons they're supposed to.

71. . . . as a consequence of the lessons they will have learned . . .

72. That is, we all suffer in life (God protect us all!). But, we'll have suffered for perhaps no reason if we learn nothing from it. The righteous *do* learn from their pain, however. And they come to love it in retrospect, or even while it's happening (though they certainly don't yearn for it) as a consequence.

Chapter Three

⊗⊗⊗⊗⊗⊗⊗⊗⊗⊗⊗⊗⊗⊗⊗⊗⊗⊗⊗⊗

The Various Means of Atonement (Continued)

14. We'll now return to our discussion of specific means of atonement.

If you accidentally commit a sin that incurs excision or a court-imposed death sentence, you're obliged to confess to it and to plead for forgiveness. As well as to sigh bitterly, worry, and be afraid, since all are essential for atonement. You should also constantly occupy yourself with[1] the Torah portion of the sin-offering.[2] And you'll thus be credited with having brought one. Which is to say, it will help a lot, and atone for you much as the offering would have.

15. Know, however, that even if you sinned accidentally you'd certainly have to suffer consequences for that, as we explained.[3] Just as you would if you'd committed an "offense"[4]—which is to say, if you accidentally sinned in an area in which people are careful not to sin. Because you should have worried about and feared committing that sin.

But as our sages said about the verse, "A beautiful landscape, the joy of all the land, is Mount Zion; on the north sides, city of a great king" (Psalms 48:3)—when a person would sin accidentally,[5] he'd worry about it, shiver and dread his sin, until he'd[6] go to Jerusalem and bring a sin-offering, and be joyful.[7] That's what's meant

---

1. . . . study of . . .
2. . . . which you would have been obliged to offer (as is found in Leviticus 4:27–35).
3. See ¶2 above.
4. See Supplementary Notes.
5. . . . in the past . . .
6. . . . finally . . .
7. i.e., relieved.

by "(Mount Zion[8] is a) beautiful landscape, the joy of all the land." When the verse mentions "the north sides" it refers to the Altar, whose "north sides" were indeed "the joy of all the land." Since the sin-offering was slaughtered on the north side of the Altar (Midrash *Tehillim* 48).

Our sages were thus saying that if you sin, but you're then haunted by what you did, and you're frightened and consumed by dread, God will forgive you for it.[9] But if you dismiss your sin, belittle it, and consider it insignificant, you'd be like the man who was stung by a scorpion, who thought little of it and only pressed his foot to the ground to draw out the venom, to whom people who saw him said, "Don't you realize the venom will go from the sole of your foot to the top of your head!" (Midrash *Tehillim* 51).[10]

---

8. i.e., the site of the Holy Temple.

9. See Supplementary Notes.

10. What Rabbeinu Yonah is apparently saying in this seemingly disjointed ¶ is the following: It's important to realize that even sinning accidentally or carelessly has its consequences. When the Holy Temple yet stood, however, one could expiate those sins by bringing a sin-offering. And all his worries, fears, and trepidations would dissipate. Now that we can't bring a sin-offering (though we can study the pertinent sections of the Torah, which will help, as was said), you can nonetheless experience the same fear and trepidation about the consequences of those sins, and thus take it just as seriously as those in the past would have taken theirs. And that itself will lead to forgiveness.

Chapter Four

The Various Means of Atonement
(Continued)

16. We'll now discuss your profaning God's name, which can't be atoned for by tribulations.[1] As we explained,[2] you can be cured of it by constantly sanctifying God's name. But you could also be atoned for it through constant reflection upon and toiling in Torah.

For as our sages said about the verse, "The sin of the House of Eli will never be atoned for with sacrifices and offerings" (1 Samuel 3:14) — that is, while they wouldn't be atoned for with sacrifices and offerings, they *would* be atoned for with words of Torah (*Rosh Hashanah* 18A), despite the fact that the House of Eli desecrated the sacrificial order. As it's said, "I will judge his house forever for the iniquity he knows of; because his sons made themselves vile"[3] (1 Samuel 3:13).

That's because Torah is a cure for every grave affliction; as it's written, "The Tree of Life is a cure for the tongue" (Proverbs 15:4).[4]

17. As to the sages statement that, "When it comes to[5] excision and a court-imposed death penalty, tshuvah and Yom Kippur stand in abeyance, and tribulations purge" (*Yomah* 86A), it could be asked, isn't it also written, "You will be cleansed of all your sins before God" (Leviticus 16:30)?[6]

The answer is that the statement that you're to be cleansed before God is a

---

1. . . . alone. (See Supplementary Notes.)
2. See ¶5 (as well as 1:47).
3. . . . publicly, and thus profaned God's name.
4. That is, the "Tree of Life," which is a term for the Torah, is the cure for anything said that would profane God's name. (See Supplementary Notes.)
5. . . . sins that incur . . .
6. . . . which would seem to indicate that *all* sins will be purged with the advent of

declaration of the imperative to do tshuvah[7] by scrutinizing and examining your ways, and returning to God on Yom Kippur.[8] For though you're always obliged to do that, your obligation is compounded on Yom Kippur. And the "cleansing" on our part involves doing tshuvah and improving our ways.

As to the implication that we'll be atoned for and cleansed on that day,[9] that refers to God's cleansing us of our sins and His forgiving us entirely on Yom Kippur without[10] tribulations for transgressing prohibitions.[11] But when it comes to[12] excision or a court-imposed death sentence, tshuvah and Yom Kippur are held in abeyance, and tribulations purge.[13]

18. Our sages said, "(The expression) 'You will be cleansed of all your sins before God' also means that while sins committed against[14] God will be atoned for by Yom Kippur, those committed against another person will only be atoned for by Yom Kippur when the other person is appeased"[15] (*Yomah* 85B).

So, if you stole something from someone, you must first return the stolen object,[16] then confess.[17] But if you confess first, your confession is useless. For our sages said that if you steal something and take a false oath,[18] you're obliged to repay the original value[19] plus a fifth, and to bring a guilt-offering. But if you return the stolen object before bringing the guilt-offering, you'd have met your responsibility, which you would not have if you'd only brought the guilt-offering and not returned the stolen object.

And it's said of one who stole from a convert who hasn't a next-of-kin, that he's to bring a "guilt-payment" to the *cohen*,[20] . . . "aside from the atonement ram, by means of which an atonement will be made for him" (Numbers 5:8), where the "guilt-payment" refers to restitution, as in, "He will give it as guilt-payment to whomever he must" (Ibid. v. 7). As such, the thief would have to make restitution

---

Yom Kippur (which is the subject of this verse)—even those that incur abolishment and a death sentence.

7. See Supplementary Notes.

8. That is, the statement "You will be cleansed of all your sins before God" is not a pledge to that effect. But rather, an injunction that you see to it that you're cleansed before God on Yom Kippur by doing tshuvah.

9. i.e., as to God's part in that process.

10. . . . our having to go through . . .

11. . . . which nonetheless don't incur abolishment or a death sentence.

12. . . . sins that incur . . .

13. . . . as was said at the beginning of the ¶.

14. i.e., "before."

15. . . . and forgives you himself.

16. . . . to your victim . . .

17. . . . to God. (See Supplementary Notes.)

18. . . . of innocence . . .

19. . . . of the stolen object . . .

20. i.e., to the Holy Temple, in lieu of a next-of-kin.

as well as offer an atonement ram.[21] For only then would he be atoned for (*Babba Kama* 110A).[22]

19. Our sages said you'd have to appease anyone you'd vexed[23] (*Yomah* 87A), and needless to say, anyone you'd slandered, since the latter's one of the most serious of sins. If he doesn't forgive you,[24] then you must go to him along with three others.[25] If he still doesn't forgive you, go to him a second time with three others, and even a third time.[26]

Our sages pointed out that there's no remedy, however, for insulting a scholar, since you would have profaned the Torah.[27] As it's said, "But they mocked God's messengers, and . . . there was no remedy" (2 Chronicles 36:16).[28]

20. As to our sages' statement that if you profaned the name of God, then tshuvah, Yom Kippur, and tribulations are held in abeyance, and death purges (*Yomah* 86A), that's so because death purges any sin that tshuvah is done for.[29] And so, if you were to be executed and you confessed before you died, you'd be atoned for as soon as the fear of death overcame you.[30] And the executioner would be considered to have murdered an innocent, pious person.[31]

For it's said, "The flesh of Your pious ones[32] to the beasts of the earth" (Psalms

---

21. . . . for stealing from the convert.

22. The ¶'s proofs can be explained thusly: We can derive the fact that a person must make restitution to whomever he sinned against in order to be atoned for from the fact that he'd have to return a stolen object before bringing a guilt-offering to be forgiven. And from the fact that he'd have to make restitution for a theft as well as offer an atonement ram.

23. Literally, "offended verbally." (See Supplementary Notes.)

24. . . . right then and there for your insensitivity . . .

25. . . . and ask for his forgiveness in their presence.

26. The text continues with the following:

As Elihu put it, "He should assemble [ישׁר] a row of men and say: I have sinned and debased what was right [חם], and it did not profit [שׁוה] me" (Job 33:27). That's to say, I wronged someone honest, as in "honest [ישׁר] and upright [חם]" (Job 1:1) by not seeing this honest man's merits, and taking him to be base and dishonest. And that neither profited me, nor was it fair, where "profit" [שׁוה] is used in the same sense as "An even [שׁוה] surface" (Isaiah 28:25) and "The even [שׁוה] valley" (Genesis 14:17), thus implying fair and even [i.e., *evenhanded*].

In fact, it's because you demeaned an honest [ישׁר] person that you must subjugate yourself to him, and confess in public. That's why it says, "He should then assemble [ישׁר] a row of men." And the reason why Elihu singled out this sin is because it's one of the most significant and personally ruinous of all [i.e., ruinous for you, as well as for your victim].

27. See Supplementary Notes.

28. See Supplementary Notes.

29. . . . even the profanation of God's name.

30. Hence, not only is death itself an atonement—the fear of impending death is an atonement as well. (See Supplementary Notes.)

31. . . . for all intents and purposes, as a consequence of your tshuvah.

32. . . . were given . . .

79:2), which our sages explained even applies to the wrongdoers among them[33] (Midrash *Tehillim* 79), about whom it's said, "They were like well-fed horses . . . each neighing for his neighbor's wife"[34] (Jeremiah 5:8), who were nonetheless considered pious once their sentence was carried out.[35] As in, "Your brother will be demeaned before your eyes" (Deuteronomy 25:3), which is to say that he becomes "your brother"[36] once he's flogged.

21. Our sages said, "The sins you confess to this Yom Kippur should be confessed to again the following Yom Kippur. As it is said, 'My sin is always before me' (Psalms 51:5). But Rabbi Eliezer Ben Yaakov said you should not confess to them again the following Yom Kippur" (*Yomah* 86B).

In fact, the Midrash strongly warns you *not* to confess to them again the following Yom Kippur (Midrash *Tehillim* 32), for three reasons. First, because you'd prove to have little trust,[37] and to have little confidence in God's great forgiveness, or in His bearing sins and overlooking acts of defiance.[38] And they cite[39] "Keep your lying lips still" (Psalms 31:19).[40]

Second, because if you only cite your earlier sins, it seems as if you're only worried about *them*, because you haven't sinned since. And that would seem to show that you hadn't scrutinized or examined your ways, which is a terrible malady.[41] For those who are self-aware always catch sight of sins or[42] personal traits on their part, of how negligent they'd been about growing in the fear of God, and of how negligent they'd been in service to God and in Torah study, which bear such serious

---

33. . . . who'd done tshuvah, and thus entered into the category of "pious" as well . . .

34. i.e., at one point, but . . .

35. i.e., once they were executed as a result of a court-imposed death sentence.

36. . . . in piety . . .

37. . . . all in all . . .

38. . . . in particular. Because many people simply do not believe that God forgives sins they've done tshuvah for. But the *halacha* is clear when it comes to our need to forgive others who've sinned against us. As Rambam put it (H. T. 2:10), "It is forbidden to be cruel and unappeasable (when being asked for forgiveness). You should instead be quick to accept, and slow to anger. When a sinner comes before you to ask for forgiveness, offer it to him wholeheartedly and willingly. And even if he caused you a lot of trouble and sinned against you again and again, you should nonetheless not be vengeful or spiteful." And obviously, that's how God reacts to our sins, too — being "quick to accept, and slow to anger"; forgiving "wholeheartedly and willingly." And despite our having caused Him "a lot of trouble, and sinned against (Him) again and again."

39. . . . the following verse as proof . . .

40. That's to say, if you'd sinned in the past, but done tshuvah. And you now claim to have sinned in the past despite your tshuvah, you'd be "lying." Because your sins had been eradicated.

41. . . . onto itself, aside from your sins.

42. . . . untoward . . .

consequences. And of having offended verbally,[43] in reference to which our sages said, "There are three things a person can never escape from: thoughts of sin, the 'dust' of slander, and very often not praying from the heart" (*Babba Battra* 164B).[44]

And third, you'd seem to be boasting about not sinning consequently by[45] confessing to earlier sins. For as the Midrash put it, "Are you confessing to those early sins because you haven't committed any new ones?" (Midrash *Tehillim* 32).[46]

The Midrash explains "My sin is always before me" (Psalms 51:5)[47] to mean that your sins should indeed always be before you, and you should always remember them. But you nonetheless shouldn't enunciate them. The Jerusalem Talmud (*Yomah* 8:7) also explained[48] that you shouldn't think you'd never committed them, but rather that you did commit them, but that they've been forgiven, as we indicated in the gate explaining the principles of tshuvah.[49]

What you should do is ask your whole life long for both your earlier and later transgressions to be forgiven in all mercy. And be frightened for the fact that you might not have fulfilled the principles of tshuvah, and for the fact that only tribulations purge sins that incur excision, as we said.[50] For as David also said, "Do not recall the sins and acts of defiance of my youth"[51] (Psalms 25:7).

But don't enunciate your earlier sins, since you've already done tshuvah and confessed to them the previous Yom Kippur, when you fulfilled the mitzvah of confessing to them. And trust that your earlier confessions were accepted, and atoned for those sins that confession atones for. Pray the rest of the year that your sins be forgiven,[52] as we indicated. But you needn't enunciate those sins when you pray. Only when you confess.

There's another reason to pray about your earlier sins, however. Because there

---

43. See Supplementary Notes.

44. Again, as was said before, sin is a sad and tragic but all-too-human "given." And to think otherwise is itself a sin. At the very least we're all negligent in the quality of service we offer God in relation to the great good He does for us at all times.

45. . . . only . . .

46. That is, are you so brash to think that you need only confess for earlier sins, and that you've committed none since?

How appropriate these three points are to the entire book (coming as they do nearly at its very end). Rabbeinu Yonah's intent here is to underscore one last time the power and splendor of tshuvah. Hence, he reminds us how fallible we all are. And how arrogant we'd have to be to claim otherwise. Yet he's sure to remind us of God's great forgiveness. As well as His willingness to bear with our sins, and overlook our acts of defiance—as long as we do tshuvah for our aberrations. Is that not the point of the entire work?

47. Which is cited above to prove you should repeat your confessions every year.

48. . . . the verse to mean . . .

49. See 1:48.

50. See ¶'s 6 and 11.

51. . . . , God.

52. . . . in all mercy . . .

might be some you either hadn't thought of or remembered, and hence hadn't confessed to.[53] As it's said, "Cleanse me of hidden faults"[54] (Psalms 19:13).

22. The order of confession is as follows: "We have sinned, transgressed and been defiant."

"Sins" are accidental sins and "offenses." And the latter, according to our sages, refer to instances in which you're careless[55] when others are usually careful, as we already indicated.[56] "Transgressions" are deliberate sins.[57] And "being defiant" means rebelling, as in "The King of Moab defied me" (2 Kings 3:7).

Ever so kind, God even forgives those who rebel against Him[58]—when they return to Him wholeheartedly.[59] As it's said, "God our Lord is compassionate and forgiving, though we have rebelled against Him" (Daniel 9:9), "For Your name's sake, God, pardon my transgression, though it is great" (Psalms 25:11), and, "Transgressions overcome me, yet You forgive our acts of defiance" (Ibid. 65:4).

---

53. So, pray for help in doing just that.

54. i.e., those that are hidden from me, because I've overlooked them.

55. . . . about avoiding a sin . . .

56. See ¶15.

57. i.e., sins committed in order to satisfy personal cravings, rather than to rebel or otherwise defy.

58. . . . and, needless to say, those who only sin accidentally, carelessly, or purposefully though not spitefully . . .

59. And it is here that Rabbeinu Yonah returns to the theme he introduced in the book's very first ¶, that God "never closes the doors to tshuvah to us, even when we're very defiant and rebellious, and utterly unfaithful."

Synopsis

Sin and character flaws are diseases of the soul, and tshuvah is their cure. But often the soul has to "take bitter medicine," in instances where tshuvah alone won't completely heal, such as the experience of tribulation, pain, or suffering (¶1). That explains why a sin-offering was required for certain accidental sins even after the sinner did tshuvah. And why one who committed them purposefully would have to suffer tribulation (¶2). And it explains why Yom Kippur comes to cleanse and atone after tshuvah, also (¶3). But the profanation of God's name is a "fatal disease," and it can ordinarily only be "cured" through death. (¶4). Nonetheless, a remedy does exist for the profanation of God's name—sanctifying God and His Torah in public, in contradistinction to what you did before (¶5).

The various types of atonement: If you do tshuvah for not having fulfilled an imperative, you're forgiven immediately. If you do tshuvah for committing a prohibition, Yom Kippur atones. If you committed a prohibition that incurs excision or capital punishment, you must endure tribulation to be atoned for. But if you profaned God's name, you can only be atoned for by your death.

A burnt-offering brought for not fulfilling an imperative atoned more deeply than tshuvah alone can (¶6). Burnt-offerings also atoned for untoward thoughts, and for thoughts of sin (¶7). But now that we can't offer sacrifices, you can accomplish much the same by studying those sections of the Torah that speak of the different offerings. And if you transgressed a prohibition, then show you long for Yom Kippur by dedicating a festive meal the night before (¶8). For while we eat a festive meal in the course of other Holy Days to show how happy we are, we eat a festive meal on the eve of Yom Kippur to show how happy we are for the approach of that Holy Day (¶9). We also eat a festive meal then to fortify us for the following day's prayers and supplications, and to concentrate upon tshuvah (¶10).

You can give charity to avoid tribulation; do favors for others; visit the sick, bury the dead, console mourners, make brides and grooms happy; and study Torah for the sake of Heaven (¶11). You can substitute fasting, weeping, self-denial, bitter sighing, being apprehensive about your sins, and accepting other afflictions for tribulations due you (¶12). Nonetheless, realize that any tribulations that come to you aren't at all proportional to the number and depth of your sins. And that while God's enemies are punished in one fell swoop and in vengeance, the tribulations the righteous suffer are meant to test them and help them grow (¶13).

Returning to our discussion, if you accidentally committed a sin that incurs excision or capital punishment you should confess, ask for forgiveness, sigh, be apprehensive and afraid, and occupy yourself with the readings about sin-offerings (¶14). If you sin accidentally or carelessly, then be preoccupied with what you did, worry about and fear it's consequences. And God will forgive you (¶15). But if you profaned God's name, you should not only sanctify His name. You should also study and dwell upon Torah. Because Torah is a cure for every grave affliction (¶16).

We're especially commanded to do tshuvah on Yom Kippur, when we're cleansed of all sins other than those that incur excision or capital punishment (¶17). Because Yom Kippur will not atone for interpersonal transgressions, you must first appease one you sinned against, and then confess to God for the sin (¶18). You must appease anyone you vexed, to say nothing of someone you slandered. If he won't forgive you, you should go before him again with three others, and again and again if you must. But there's no remedy for demeaning a Torah scholar (¶19). Death purges every sin for which tshuvah was done. As such, if you're sentenced to capital punishment, you'd be atoned for from the moment the fear of death overtook you (¶20).

Don't confess to the same sins every Yom Kippur. Just remember your old sins, without enunciating them. Nonetheless, always be afraid that you haven't fulfilled all the requirements for tshuvah. Be concerned for the sins that are only forgiven by tribulation, and pray to be forgiven for sins you've forgotten and not confessed to (¶21). Finally, the order of confession is, "We've sinned, transgressed, and acted defiantly." "Sinned" refers to error and to sins committed in areas where others are careful not to sin; "transgressed" refers to deliberate sins; and "acted defiantly" refers to acts of rebellion, which God forgives as well, if you return to Him wholeheartedly (¶22).

Supplementary Notes

Gate One

꧁꧂꧁꧂꧁꧂꧁꧂꧁꧂꧁꧂꧁꧂꧁꧂꧁꧂꧁꧂꧁꧂

1. "Our impulses": We've translated the term "*yetzer*" here as "impulses" rather than as the "yetzer harah," commonly translated as the "evil inclination." Rabbeinu Yonah uses two terms throughout the book: *yetzer*, and *ha'yetzer*, with the definite article, as if to say, *the* impulse *par excellence*. But we hold that "*the* yetzer" stands for the yetzer harah (see our note to ¶4), and "yetzer" stands for impulses in general. (After all, if that were not the case, ¶10's statement, ". . . *v'halachti acharei yitzri k'sus*" would translate as, "following my yetzer harah like a horse . . ." when animals haven't yetzer harahs, only impulses.)

We've always been troubled by the translation "evil inclination" (see our comments to our translation of *The Path of the Just*, p. 15, note 9; and to our translation of *The Duties of the Heart*, pp. 230–232). As we indicated then, while all of us have a yetzer harah, few of us are "inclined toward evil," with obvious exception. And the yetzer harah would be best understood as the pull toward earthiness, and a very bad idea (spiritually speaking). As such, we don't even translate the term.

But in short what the yetzer harah is, is a spiritual "mechanism" of sorts implanted by God into our being that would have us avoid holiness and pure goodness, and would instead encourage us to satisfy our selfish cravings (see *The Duties of the Heart*, p. 240, where it's characterized as the antithesis of reason). It must be recalled that the yetzer harah isn't a *mistake* on God's part. Something He "let slip by," so to speak. Its existence is purposeful and necessary, both for the maintenance of reality as we know it, and for the exigencies of free moral choice. The reader is encouraged to delve into the sources cited for more about this.

Impulses can be said to be material, biological reactions to the inner rousings of the yetzer harah. Interestingly, we often believe those impulses are driven by personal temperament or constitution. But the latter are only one level deeper than the impulses themselves. While the yetzer harah is far deeper, and rooted in spirituality, not physicality.

"He never closes the doors to tshuvah to us": See *Hilchot Tshuvah* (to be abbreviated "*H. T.*"), where Rambam enunciates the twenty-four impediments to tshuvah, but ends with, "And while all these and other such things may hinder tshuvah, they cannot prevent it." Contrast that, however, with Rambam's statement in 6:3 about instances in which tshuvah is withheld. And see 1:51–52 below.

"And utterly unfaithful": See 3:171. See *H. T.* 7:7, where Rambam contrasts the "before" and "after" of tshuvah.

"To a lot of suffering": See 2:2. See *Birchat Peretz*, which explains why it would help to do tshuvah because of suffering, when there'd seem to be no regret involved (a fundamental requirement of tshuvah, see 1:19). As he explains there, the poor victim of suffering would be humbled by his sorrows, and would lose the arrogance that separates us all from God in the first place. His tshuvah would therefore be genuine.

2. ". . . the consequences to be suffered for your sins": Some additional remarks about "punishment." Rabbi Aryeh Kaplan *zatz'al* said, "Just as God created a self-sustaining system of physical law, so He created a self-sustaining system of spiritual law. God conceived creation so that man's good comes not as a reward for his actions, but as a direct result of his actions. The same is true of the evil that overtakes a person. . . . Punishment is thus not an act of Divine retaliation, but the direct consequences of one's sin. . . . One's own deeds set up the mechanism whereby he is rewarded and punished. . . . A person must live with the baggage he carries, and exit through the door he entered. The system exists, and it is up to the individual to avoid being trapped by it. Just as God does not tamper with physical law, neither does He abrogate His moral law" (*The Handbook of Jewish Thought* II, 18:21).

The Slonomer Rebbe, *Shlita* cites the verse, "He (God) does not look at wrongdoing in Jacob, and He sees no vice in Israel. God their Lord is with them, and they have the King's friendship" (Numbers 23:21), then asks, "But how can it be said that God doesn't look at our wrongdoings?" After all, our sages pointed out (*Babba Kamah* 50A), 'Do not take God to be lenient (i.e., as one who just overlooks sins or ignores them) . . .' So what it means is that while God does punish those who sin, they are nonetheless not distanced from Him. For God is with them even after their sins. For just as He is in love with them before they sin, so too is He in love with them after they sin. Because in either case they are referred to as His children (cf. Exodus 4:22, "Israel is

My child, My firstborn"; and Deuteronomy 14:1, "You are God your Lord's children") (*Netivot Shalom, Avodat HaShem* 5).

The Baal Shem Tov pointed out, "When a father warns his child not to walk around barefoot because he might hurt his foot, and that if he does walk barefoot, he'll be punished, the child only fears the punishment he'd get for walking barefoot. Because he has no sense of the harm that could come to his feet. Only later, when the child grows up, does he, like his father, fear the harm to his foot. Likewise, God warns us not to sin, but to fear Him. We take that to mean that we shouldn't sin because we'll be punished if we do. But God knows that if we sin, we'll be separated from Him, which is the worst punishment" (*Sefer Ba'al Shem Tov Al Ha'Torah, Ekev* 27; cited in *Netivot Shalom, Yirat HaShem* 4:5).

And it could be pointed out that the numerical value of "punishment," *onesh*, is the same as for "inner," *toch* (426), which alludes to the internal, spiritual nature of punishment. For as it's said, "One instance of heartfelt self-reproach is more effective than many flagellations" (*Berachot* 7A).

4. "Worrying": See 1:16–20.

"Crying sorrowfully": See 1:15.

6. "Who sometimes slip and sin": See 3:143.

"Apostate in one area": See 1:38, 3:143, 146.

"Too great to condone": See 3:143, 209.

8. "Taking worthless oaths": See 3:45.

"Cursing . . . with the name of God": See 3:45–46

"Mentioning God's name either in vain . . .": See 3:44,61

"Closing their eyes to the poor": See 3:15, 67, 110, 117, 118, 183

"Slandering": See 3:200 to end of gate.

"Hating needlessly"; See 3:39, 223.

"Being haughty": See 3:34, 65, 163.

"Intimidating others": See 3:162–167.

"Staring at instances of nudity": See 1:35, 52, 3:64.

"Neglecting Torah study": See 3:17, 28.

"Write down in a book . . .": See *Sefer Chassidim* ¶21.

"Read from that book every day": See 1:36.

9. "Many degrees of tshuvah": See 1:13, 19.

"While you're young and vibrant": See *H. T.* 2:1.

"Prevail over your impulses": One couldn't have done anything all that serious while a child compared to what he's capable of doing as an adult. Apparently then, what the *Gemorrah* that Rabbeinu Yonah is citing here is implying, is that learning to control the yetzer harah—even before it fully actuates itself—is a form of tshuvah and of drawing close to God.

10. "For what use would all its accomplishments be if it were guilty in the eyes of its Master?": See 1:42.

"For the Creator breathed a living spirit into my nostrils . . .": See *Alei Shor* 1, 2:6, which underscores how important it is for a person to recognize the great heights he can reach before he can truly regret his failings. And that regret without that is based on hopelessness. In fact, Rabbeinu Yonah says as much in his opening words to *Shaarei Ha'Avodah*: that successful service to God "requires that the person serving (Him) know his own worth, 'recognize his own prominence and his ancestors,' as well as their greatness, importance, and preciousness. And know also how beloved they are to God . . . And then, when he starts to crave something and he comes up with the audacious idea of doing something unfitting, he can say to himself, 'How could a great and important person like myself, who has so many exalted and high good traits, who's the child of great people, ancient kings, do such a terrible thing as this today, and sin against God and my own ancestors?'"

"As I was created to do": See 3:17

"I haven't confronted the day of death": See 2:15–25

11. "Rid yourself of your wrongful ways and wholeheartedly resolve never to act that way again": Rabbeinu Yonah apparently joins together the principles of abandoning sin, and of taking it upon yourself not to sin that way again. See *H. T.* 2:2, where Rambam differentiates them.

"As bitter as gall": See Introduction to *Torat Avot* where the Slonomer Rebbe differentiates between "sadness" and "bitterness." Bitterness seems to be a strong distaste, while sadness seems to be a dull, flat reaction. See 1:18 (end).

"And agree to take upon yourself not to sin again": The *Daat Torah* counsels that the best way to avert such lapses in the future is to work at actively imagining yourself suddenly being in a spiritually challenging situation, and deciding then and there not to acquiesce.

". . . as long as he held onto the reptile and immersed": See 1:19. See *H. T.* 2:3.

12. "Impress upon yourself . . . grow heart-sad, let a storm brew . . . , moan bitterly": See 2:9.

"How could you have been so self-absorbed to have angered Him?": See *Sefer HaChinuch* (33) about being grateful. And see *Tomar Devorah* (Ch. 1, Trait 1) about how God continues to provide us with vitality despite our lack of appreciation.

13. "The bitterer and sadder you feel . . .": See 3:217 (end).

"How could I not feel for and have mercy . . .": Rabbeinu Yonah indicates that it's God's pity alone that allows for atonement. Compare that with Luzzatto in *The Path of the Just* (end of Ch. 4, p. 40 in this translator's edition) who says that it's the uprooting of the will to have committed the sin in the first place that's the mechanism.

14. "The only thing I long to do is serve You": See 2:18 for the opposite.

15. "'The heart and eyes are both agitators of sin' . . . 'Do not go about after your own heart and eyes'": Rebbe Nachman of Breslov likened the yetzer harah to someone running about through a crowd with a hand held tightly shut, giddily asking each one what they thought he might be hiding. Imagining his hand contained the very thing they wanted most, they chased after him. And when they caught up with him they were terribly disappointed to discover that his hand had been empty all along (*Sichot HaRan* 6, with thanks to Rabbi Ch. Freidman).

"Hence the sins they bring on . . .": See 1:35.

16. ". . . and only tribulations will purge.": See 4:2, 11–12.

17. ". . . whatever new waves the yetzer harah may roll over you": The idea of the yetzer harah overcoming a person like the sea was set out earlier on, in ¶11. But we'd use the concept another way now. And would say that if the yetzer harah comes in waves—i.e., in bunches, with respites in between—then the *yetzer hatov*, its opposite, should work that way, too. (In keeping with the Kabbalistic theme that a truth on one plane has its corresponding truth on the opposite one, based on the hidden import of "God has made this to correspond to that" [Ecclesiastes 7:14].) And we'd infer that the principles of tshuvah enunciated in this gate, and their concurrent emotions, are not to be dwelt on at great length at any one time. They're to be ingested as "waves" and roaringly so, at a certain point. Then they're to be slowly digested, at which point you're not to eat from them for a while. In keeping with, "And the living creatures *ran* and *turned back*" (Ezekiel 1:14).

18. "the righteous honor and respect people for all their good qualities, while wrongdoers always look for others' faults and mistakes": See 3:217. See also *Da'at Chochma U'Musar* (2:14) where Rabbi Yerucham affirms the simple implication that one who sees the good in others is righteous, and one who only sees the bad is a wrongdoer. And asserts that this is "the true test" and "the greatest proof" of one's righteousness.

"You're obliged to confess to them": See ¶40; see also *H. T.* 2:5.

"A person isn't forgiven until he returns . . . and until he asks for forgiveness . . .": See ¶44; and see *H. T.* 2:9.

"Because a person who sins publicly profanes God's name": See 1:47, 4:4–5.

19. "Essential principles to tshuvah—remorse, confession and ridding yourself of the sin": See *H. T.* 1:1 where Rambam stresses confession; and 2:2 where he expands upon the others. See *The Duties of the Heart*, Gate of

Repentance, Ch. 4 (p. 322 in this translator's edition), where Ibn Pakudah speaks of *four* essential principles.

". . . with a reptile in his hand, and thus immersed in vain": See 1:11.

20. "Constantly pray to Him for His help in tshuvah": See 1:41–43.

". . . you'd have been pretentious, . . . oblivious . . . taken no precautions against your impulses . . . , and would fall into their hands as a consequence": See 4:21.

21. "Because God is removed from your innermost being": In truth, God is very, very close to us. For He's the Essence of our essence, and what could be closer? (*Da'at Torah, Noach*).

As to the point that we might overlook God because He can't be seen, Rabbi Aryeh Kaplan, *zatz'al*, once noted, "God cannot be seen because there is no place empty of Him. The reason is very much like the reason that the air cannot be seen; it is an integral part of our environment, and this is all the more so true of God. The reason we cannot see God is not because He is too transcendent, but because He is too immanent. The only time we are aware of the air is when the wind blows. Similarly, we are only aware of God when He acts to manifest His presence." (*The Handbook of Jewish Thought*, Vol. 1, 2:43).

22. "Mortified": See 3:111, 139.

"A person who . . . is forgiven for all his sins": Being ashamed to do things in front of others often has nothing to do with an inner awareness of weakness or foolishness. It could be based on ego, and the wish not to lose respect in that person's eyes. But the kind of true shame spoken of here that will uproot your sins is rooted in holiness (*Da'at Torah, Yitro*). See *The Duties of the Heart*, The Gate of Reflection, p. 87, which discusses this trait, which we translated as "conscience" in that context.

"The Urim and Tumim": The oracle that granted a high degree of Divine Inspiration, which was placed on the High Priest's breastplate, and was consulted by Jewish kings (including Saul, hence the reference to it here), high public officials, and the Sanhedrin. It functioned until the destruction of the First Temple. For other references to it see Exodus 28:30, Leviticus 8:8, Numbers 27:21, Deuteronomy 33:8, Ezra 2:63, and Nehemiah 7:65. Also see *Yomah* 73B.

23. "Surrendering Wholeheartedly and Being Humble": See *The Duties of the Heart*, The Gate of Surrender, pp. 275–303.

25. "Act justly and to love kindness": See 3:13

"But let him who . . . that he understands and knows Me": See 3:34.

26. "To rid yourself of all the traits that caused you to sin and act defiantly": As to the place of character improvement in Torah, see Rabbeinu Yonah's commentary to *Pirke Avot* (Ch. 3), "You'd have to first correct your character for Torah to abide in you. For it will never abide in someone who hasn't a good character," and his comment to Proverbs 12:22 where he says that having a bad character "is worse than not observing a mitzvah." See R. Chaim Vital's *Shaarei Kedusha* (1:2): "it's more important to avoid bad character traits than it is to fulfill Torah imperatives or prohibitives. For, you'd easily keep all the *mitzvot* if you have a good character." See Rambam's *H. T.* (7:3), "One has to free himself from all his bad traits and do tshuvah for anger, hostility, envy, sarcasm, the pursuit of wealth or glory, the lust for food, etc. . . . For such transgressions are even more serious than the concrete ones." And see The Slonomer Rebbe's *Netivot Shalom* (Vol. 1, Intro. to *Netivei Taharat HaMiddot*), "Character traits are wings upon the wind of Divine service. And just as a bird could never ascend and fly without his wings, a person engaged in Torah and *mitzvot* could never merit soaring without having purified his character traits, which are the wings of spiritual winds."

27. "Arrogance": The *Da'at Torah* (*Achrei Mot*) explains that acknowledgment of one's own abilities isn't wrong. It's depending on them, or on anything else physical for that matter, rather than on God alone, that's the worse sin of all. Also see *The Path of the Just*, Ch. 11, pp. 98–100; and *The Duties of the Heart*, The Gate of Introspection, pp. 373–374, 380.

". . . who struck terror in the land of the living": See 3:163.

"When you're arrogant . . . And God doesn't help you then": See *The Duties of the Heart* (Introduction to The Gate of Trust in God, p. 173), "For if you do not trust God, you will inevitably trust someone or something else. God will then put you under the care of the one you trust rather than His own." Also see *The Path of the Just*, Ch. 2, p. 29 (at end).

28. "You'll avoid being angry at or short-tempered with others": Compare this with *Iggeret HaRamban*, which discusses avoiding anger and thus coming to humility which is "the best of all good character traits."

29. "These outward signs of surrender . . . will remind you to surrender your heart": See our note there about the twenty principles listed in this gate as not only prods to tshuvah, but as read-outs of just how successful you've been in your tshuvah, too. The idea of the needs for external prods to internal change is cited in *The Path of the Just* (Ch. 7, pp. 63–64); *Sefer HaChinuch* where it's first cited at Mitzvah 16, then reiterated at various points; and Rambam's *Hilchot De'ot* 1:7, *Sh'mone Perakim* 6, and *Moreh Nevuchim* 2:31. See Rabbi G. Appel's discussion of this in *Torat HaMitzvot Be'emunat Yisrael* pp. 78–79, which cites the latter sources.

As to the idea that these principles are marks and signs of just how much tshuvah you've done, that could be buttressed in a number of ways. First by comparing them to the symptoms of *tzora'at* (the so-called "leprosy" spoken of in Leviticus 13 and 14). Those symptoms showed up on their victim's person, on his clothing, and even on the walls of his house, depending on the depth of the sin that brought it on. In an analogous way, then, the appearance of "symptoms" of tshuvah as enunciated here in various corners of your being, would reveal the depths of your tshuvah.

It could also be extrapolated by a variant reading of the principles. They're expressed in the Hebrew "imperfect tense," which can either be read as a prediction or an order (E.g.., *yelech*, can be translated either as "He'll go" or "He should go"). So when it's written, "*v'yitcharet al maasav haraim*" (¶10), that could legitimately be translated as either "He *should* regret his wrongdoings" or as "He *would* regret his wrongdoings." Which would go for the other principles, as well. As such, the statements associated with the principles could read, "One who has truly done tshuvah *would* exhibit. . . ." rather than, "Exhibit these symptoms in order to do tshuvah." (See Rashi to Deuteronomy 16:15, "*ain zeh lashon tzivoi eleh lashon havtacha*" — "The language used implies a promise rather than a commandment.")

And lastly, it could be analogous to the description of "the grades and classes of people concentrating on the Torah" (p. 134) cited in *The Duties of the Heart*, pp. 131–134. Ibn Pakudah says there that his recitation of the degrees of success of those who study Torah "will help anyone searching for the correct path. (For) after determining the level he is closest to, he will be able to realize what is above it and try to reach that higher level" (p. 134). As such, Rabbeinu Yonah's list of the twenty principles of tshuvah could be a recitation of "the degrees of success" of those who do tshuvah.

30. "Overcoming Your Physical Cravings": See *The Path of the Just*, chapters 13–15, pp. 114–127; also *The Duties of the Heart*, The Gate of Abstinence, pp. 403–429.

". . . to satisfy your needs. . . . to fulfill the *mitzvot*": See Rabbeinu Yonah's comment to *Pirke Avot* 3:17 where he explains that it's important to practice restraint even when nothing prohibited is involved, simply because when you accede to physicality too much you "essentially separate yourself from your spirit and its elements, and incline your spirit toward the body and physicality." Which is to say, you distract your attention from the life of the soul, and have it concentrate too much on the physical, to your own spiritual detriment. This obviously acts as less of a moral statement about the "evils of the flesh" as Western minds might at first take it to be. And clarifies it as being the learned warning that it is.

Also see Rabbeinu Yonah's advice in his own *Yesod HaTshuvah* for the "weak, who can't endure difficult fasts, and are impelled by their cravings" (which would certainly include most of us). He cites the writings of Rabbi Avraham Bar David, "one of the world's (truly) pious individuals" who advises such a person to "*not* stop eating meat or drinking wine altogether, for it's enough for him to follow the prohibitions the Torah itself instituted." What he should do is "leave some (of what he's eating, and would still like to eat) behind, and to give honor to God through his cravings by not eating as much as he'd like." That is, one should purposefully stop himself when he'd rather not, expressly to draw closer to God. And Rabbeinu Yonah informs us there that that sort of conscious and purposeful self-control is even better than fasting.

34. "David would order . . . to be forgiven for the incident with Bathsheba": This alludes to "complete" tshuvah, which Rambam says in *H. T.* (2:1) is accomplished by being in the same situation one had been in when he'd sinned, being capable of sinning again, and not doing so. "So if, for example," he says, "one had once sinned with a woman, and after a time found himself alone with her, still in love and in full possession of his prowess, and in the same place he had transgressed" and he does not sin, he'd have accomplished full tshuvah. King David was not with Bathsheba in these instances, so he hadn't in fact accomplished full tshuvah. But he was nonetheless declaring and demonstrating that *were* he in the same situation he'd been in when he was with Bathsheba, he'd no longer sin. Since he'd overcome his cravings. Needless to say, it's ill-advised and forbidden to test oneself so (*Sanhedrin* 107A). Since few if any of us morally weak and "faint of heart" individuals could withstand such a challenge, and would more likely than not fail.

35. "If you've stared at instances of nudity . . . if you sinned by slandering someone": We'd expect Rabbeinu Yonah to suggest that we engross ourselves in Torah study if we'd stared at instances of nudity. Both because it would be a logical and good counteracting shift, but also because it's said later on that, "If you have 'a heart that plots sinister plans,'" which would certainly apply in this case, then you're to "keep words of Torah sequestered in your heart." And we'd expect him to counsel us to lower our eyes if we'd slandered. Since it's said later on that, "If you have 'an arrogant look' . . . lower your eyes," and slander is associated with arrogance in 3:206, 213. But Rabbeinu Yonah's point is that staring at nudity is an instance of high arrogance. Because we're often warned against staring licentiously at women (*histaklut b'nashim*, see *Nedarim* 20A, *Babba Battra* 57B, *Makkot* 24A) in less compromising positions. Staring at instances of nudity is audacious and nearly Godless, hence one guilty of that should learn to lower his eyes humbly. And his other point is that slander invariably involves "plotting sinister plans" as described below, on some subliminal level. Because slanderers feels threatened by their victims (and the only way they have to retaliate against them in many instances is to slander them). Hence they'd have to engross themselves in

Torah to affirm the wisdom of trusting in God, and to assure themselves that He'll always safeguard them.

The anonymous *Biur* to *Shaarei Tshuvah* (ad. loc.) equates this to Rambam's method (in *Hilchot De'ot* 2:2) of undoing a bad trait by going to the other extreme before returning to a golden mean.

36. "Let us scrutinize our ways": Rav Yechezkel Levenstein said that the whole point of Musar study is to bring yourself to self-examination in order to avoid duplicity (*Ohr Yechezkel*, Vol. 6). See 3:1–2.

"Confession is one of the principles of forgiveness": But isn't it one of the principles of tshuvah itself (see ¶40)? But it's also spoken of as being essential to forgiveness in ¶'s 41 and 45, so it's a principle of both, it's that important.

"Those sins . . . have become insignificant in your eyes": See 1:5.

"Your impulses would have had command over them": See 1:38.

37. "In order to weep bitterly . . .": See 3:1–2.

". . . forgiveness is held in abeyance . . . and only tribulations purge you of them": See *H. T.* 1:4. Also see 4:11–13, below.

38. "Concentrate . . . on the significance of the One who warned you about it": See 3:23, and *The Duties of the Heart*, The Gate of Repentance, Ch. 7, p. 331 for this same idea.

"Like a strand of delicate silk which becomes a thick cord": This idea can be found adjacent to the previous one cited in *The Duties of the Heart*.

"Apostates in one area": See 1:6.

39. "One who fears a mitzvah": In *Pri Ha'aretz* (*Noach*) Rebbe Menachem Mendel of Vittebsk speaks of the "fear of a mitzvah" in terms of a sudden stark and dumbfounded realization of the absolute holiness and Godliness of a mitzvah one is about to do, despite the physicality of it.

40. "Articulate your sins, as well as the sins of your ancestors . . ." See *Torat Avot* (*Lech Lecha*) where the enjoiner God made of Abraham to "Get out from your country, from your family, and from your father's house, to a land that I will show you" (Genesis 12:1) was made to underscore the fact that he must outgrow the influence of his background ("country"), his mother ("family") and his father ("your father's house") if he's ever to arrive at the "land that I will show you," which alludes to closeness to Him.

41. "Pray to God and ask to be mercifully forgiven for all your sins": Rabbeinu Yonah's prayer for tshuvah, in his *Yesod HaTshuvah*:

Please, God! I've been sinning accidentally, deliberately, and rebelliously from the day I was born to today. But my heart has now propelled me upward, and my spirit has persuaded me to return to You honestly, with the best of intentions and completely; with all my heart, soul, and might. In order to "admit and let go," to cast off all my acts of defiance; and in order to restore heart and soul, and be earnest in my devotion to You.

God! You who open Your arms to accept tshuvah and help those who come to cleanse themselves: Please open Your arms to accept my full tshuvah. Help me be firm in my fear of You, to resist the Antagonist who confronts me cunningly and wants to kill me, and to defy his command over me. Keep him from the whole of me, fling him into the depths of the sea, and order him never to set himself against me to antagonize me. See to it that I go in Your ways by replacing my stone heart with one of flesh.

Please, God! Hear out Your servant's prayers and pleas, and accept my tshuvah. Don't let any of my accidental or deliberate sins obstruct my tshuvah or prayer. And allow a sincere Advocate to offer my prayers to You, at Your Place of Honor. But if because of the number and seriousness of my sins I haven't a sincere Advocate, then dig down from beneath Your Place of Honor Yourself and accept my tshuvah. See to it that I never return wanting from before You, Who hears out prayers.

See The Invocation in *The Duties of the Heart* (pp. 467–476) for another moving prayer for closeness to God and tshuvah. See *H. T.* 2:4.

"Accept us graciously": Rav Yitzchak Hutner points out that prayer is so important in tshuvah because the fundamental outcome of sin is separation from God, while the fundamental function of prayer is coming close to God (*Pachad Yitzchak, Rosh Hashanna 5*).

"So when you do tshuvah your sins are forgiven, and the merit accrued from a mitzvah is bestirred": By virtue of the fact that sins *douse* but don't *extinguish mitzvot*, whose sparks are then bestirred through tshuvah, we see that sins act as a sort of sheath around your *mitzvot*, rather than the other way around, as we'd hope. But, apparently, as Rabbeinu Yonah says later on, your *mitzvot* nonetheless "shield you"—that is, they *do* act as a sheath about you—*after* you do tshuvah. And that's so important, that we're to pray to God for help in tshuvah for that to happen.

42. "Because God may not be pleased with you . . .": Apparently to offset any sense of discouragement such a statement might arouse in a sensitive soul, Rabbi Yechezkel Levenstein alluded to the idea that you nonetheless please God by trying to get close to Him against all odds, and despite all obstacles—regardless of whether you actually succeed or fail (cited in *Ohr HaTshuvah*, p. 87). Compare this to Rabbeinu Yonah's statement at the end of 3:148 to the effect that, "A person's status is determined by what he praises. If he praises good deeds, sages, and the righteous, you would know that he is himself good, and is basically righteous. . . . And while such a person may have committed some secret sins himself, he's nonetheless a lover of righteousness and is rooted in what's right. And he's a member of the community of those who honor God." Compare it as well with a similar statement in the anonymous *Biur*, in connection with the statement in this ¶ that, "That's why the only thing the righteous crave is God's approval and favor."

"And then he prayed . . . that God be as pleased with him as He was before he sinned": If the state of favor that one who does tshuvah wants to *return* to is one involving eternal life, being encompassed by God's light, and experiencing God's holy spirit, as well as glee, miracles, and salvation, as it's expressed shortly. Then obviously one of two things is implied here. Either that *The Gates of Repentance* is written for people already on that spiritual plane alone, and should be recognized as being such a work (which is unlikely). Or, that everyone experiences all that, on a very subliminal level perhaps, when they do tshuvah. And can come to experience it outwardly with deep and full tshuvah.

44. "Amending Your Misdeeds as Much as Possible": For circumstances that might thwart your chances of making amends with others, or from doing tshuvah in general, see the fourth chapter of *H. T.* And for an enunciation of the problems and solutions for them, see *The Duties of the Heart*, The Gate of Repentance, pp. 335–339.

". . . you're not atoned for until you ask your victim for forgiveness": See 4:18, and see *H. T.* 2:9.

47. "He will not be bribed by *mitzvot* to forgive or bypass sins": See our reference to tshuvah as a bribe in note 12 to 1:45.

"Whoever says that God overlooks sins will be overlooked by Him": See *The Path of the Just*, Ch. 4, p. 39, which cites this statement, and remarks that, "God . . . reckon(s) with each person according to his actions . . . in a most exacting way, whether good or bad." So, *nothing* is overlooked. Which gives hope to the efficacy of our long gone good deeds, and should give us pause about our forgotten wrongdoings—those sins we tend to "step over" (*Avodah Zarah* 18A) and disregard because we think them beneath our consideration.

"Profaning God's name": See 3:45, 61, 132, 134, 143 and 4:4–6, 16, 20. See *H. T.* 1:4

"And your tshuvah corresponded to your lapses": See 1:35.

48. ". . . or allow them to leave your heart till the day of your death": The original reads, "*milivavo lo y'chalphu ad bo chaliphato*." It should be pointed out that this reading is a minority one, not usually included in standard editions of *Shaarei tshuvah*. But it's found in the one published by The Institute for the Dissemination of Torah and Musar (Bnei Brak:1990), which is based on the first published edition of *Shaarei tshuvah*, on corroborated original manuscripts, and on citations by Torah greats approximately contemporary with Rabbeinu Yonah himself. (Though it's curious to note that the standard reading isn't included in the "Variant Texts" section in the back of that edition.)

The standard reading is "*milivavo lo y'chatphu ad bo chaliphato*," which would then have the sentence read, "It's important to always remember your sins, and to never forget them for the rest of your life *or seize them from your heart till the day of your death*." And that's usually explained to mean that the memory of your sins should never leave or be removed from your mind until the day of your death (see *Biur* and *Harotzeh L'tshuvah*).

There are a number of subtle problems with the standard reading, however. The phrase "*chataph mehalev*" is usually translated to mean "to be deceived," which would have the phrase read, "It's important to always remember your sins, and to never forget them for the rest of your life, or be deceived till the day of your death," which seems out of place and mostly irrelevant to the point. The term for death (*chalipha*) is also unusual (the usual term is "*mavet*"), and literally means to be supplanted, vanish, be displaced (as we indicated in our note), which would then have the phrase read, "It's important to always remember your sins, and to never forget them for the rest of your life, *or be deceived until you're displaced*." Hence, we feel confident in our choice of text.

We also feel justified in our choice in light of the wry play on words in the Hebrew, between one instance of *chalipha* and another (*lo yechalphu ad bo chaliphato*). That itself is very much in keeping with Rabbeinu Yonah's style, as is evidenced by a similar play on words in 1:10, "*v'eich hachlaphti beolam choleph olam omed lo'ad leolam*."

49. "Shunning a Sin When Faced With it and Still Fully Craving it": By virtue of the fact that you wouldn't want to satisfy your cravings in the first place if you'd already eradicated them, as you'd been instructed to in ¶31, we see that the twenty principles enunciated in this Gate are not in order. (After noting this we saw the same point made in *Me'or HaShaar* in relation to ¶40.)

". . . through the fear of God": We've defined "the fear of God" in the context of our comments as "the rank fear of a separation from the Beloved" (notes to ¶4), and as an expression denoting the need to "foster a deep and vital relationship with Him which we're to dwell on at all times" (notes to ¶10). And those definitions certainly hold true in this context as well. But it's defined elsewhere by others, as well as by Rabbeinu Yonah. See 2:25 and 3:23 here, for example. Also see Rabbeinu Yonah's *Sha'arei Avodah* 27, and his outright equating it there with serving God in ¶16. See *The Path of the Just*, Ch. 19, pp. 158–159, and Ch. 24 , pp. 210–211; *The Duties of the Heart*, The Gate of the Complete Love of God, p. 439; *H. T.* 10:1 as well as *Yesodei HaTorah* (2:2).

50. "Turning Others Away From Sin": See 3:19.

". . . you'll suffer the consequences of his sin": See 3:59, 72, 195–198.

52. "Twenty-four things hinder tshuvah": This list is also cited (with variations) in *H. T.* Ch. 4.; Rosh 8:18; Rokeach 28, 216; *Sefer Chassidim* 19; Meiri, *Chibur HaTshuvah* (1:4), *Reishit Chochma, Shaar HaTshuvah* 6; Maharal, *Netivot Olam*, Tshuvah 8. Also see *The Duties of the Heart*, The Gate of Repentance, pp. 335–337.

Gate Two

1. "By thus remembering your Creator": Rav Yechezkel Levenstein (cited in *Ohr HaTshuvah*) equates remembering God with *d'vekut*, alternately translated as the act of "clinging onto," "attaching yourself to," or, "devoting yourself utterly to" God. The concept is understood to represent the highest form of mystical contact with the Divine. On a simpler, experiential level, though, it also implies remembering God passionately and longingly. And devoting yourself to Him. Obviously, then, there are varying degrees of remembering God.

"If instead of being impelled . . . you were drawn to it of your own volition": See *The Duties of the Heart*, The Gate of Service to God, pp. 115–125 about self-motivation versus external motivation. And see *The Path of the Just*, Ch. 4, pp. 34–41, for the difference between those who are drawn to righteousness by merely remembering God and their obligations to Him, and those who come to it by other, less august means.

2. "For God criticizes those He loves, like a father does with a son He's pleased with": See 2:4 and 4:13.

"That happened to us by chance": See Rambam's *Hilchot Ta'anit* 1:3. This touches upon the subject of *Hashgacha*, Divine Providence—on how much input God has in the world. See *Babba Battra* 16A, *Breishit Rabbah* 13:9, *Moreh Nevuchim* 3:17. Rav Yechezkel Levenstein would often contrast the illusory belief in personal control (epitomized by the statement that "My power and the might of my hand has gotten me this wealth" [Deuteronomy 8:17]) with the existential reality of Divine Providence (epitomized by the declaration that "There is no other god" i.e., no one else in control, "but Him" [Ibid. 4:35]). See *Ohr Yechezkel*, Vol. 3, p. 181, and elsewhere in that volume.

3. "Physical ailments . . . heal your spiritual ailments": Rav Avraham Grodzinsky points out (*Torat Avraham, Sh'lemut V'yesurim*) that we can see

that troubles "heal spiritual ailments" rather than just atone for them from the fact that troubles alone—not tshuvah—cleanse a person of sins that incur excision or a court-imposed death sentence (see 4:11).

"Sins are spiritual ailments": See 4:1.

6. "Doing tshuvah on the day of your death": See *H. T.* 2:1, 3:14.

"When you'd realize that wrongdoing is coming to an end, and all hope is gone": See 2:17–20.

8. "There is not a man on earth so righteous that he does good without sinning": See 1:6.

9. "But those who are genuinely righteous and upright": The literal translation of this phrase reads, "Those who are righteous and upright *in their hearts*." Contrast that with the statement in 2:8, which we translated as, "people (who) . . . take themselves to be spotless and pure," but which would literally read, "people (who) . . . are spotless and pure *in their own eyes*." Rabbeinu Yonah is underscoring through his wordplay the fact that while the eyes can be allured by all kinds of delusions, the heart knows full well its own stature, and can't be fooled.

". . . find their thoughts roaring like a lion . . . , and thundering like the sea . . . about how negligent they'd been in their service to God" Compare that to their reaction to temptation in 1:11.

"God will overlook licentiousness and murder, but . . .": See 3:14.

"When you become elderly": Rabbi Aharon Luria remarked in his old age that "I see with my own eyes that even though the yetzer harah has weakened in old age, force of habit nonetheless grows stronger. And that (resisting that) entails an even greater battle. Because the yetzer harah's powers are rooted in thought, and thought can always be uprooted by (an alternate) thought. But habit is rooted in action, and has to be fought with alternate actions, which is particularly hard for a weak (old) man like myself" (*Avodat P'nim*, p. 190).

10. "You will go from darkness to great light in an instant": Compare this with 2:8's statement that "there are many from whom *the light of tshuvah* is withheld because they see themselves as spotless and pure." And with 2:9's suggestions that "since an old person can no longer enjoy the taste of what he eats or drinks . . . he should enjoy *the light of the sun*," and that he "find the *light of the sun* sweet in the face of the coming darkness." For just as your going from "darkness to great light in an instant" here alludes to transformation and the subsequent coming closer to God, your previously suggested search for light alludes to that as well. Compare this as well to *H. T.* 7:6, "Tshuvah brings those distant from God closer to Him—whereas heretofore they were repulsive to God, despicable, far removed and abominable, henceforward they are beloved and desired, close and intimate."

"You'd have exonerated yourself in short order": Compare this to the idea presented in 1:49 that you can accomplish full tshuvah, even if you don't prove your dedication to God before the most dire challenges, by constantly augmenting your fear of God. In both instances you'd act righteously from then on because of the person you'd become.

"Search for those who'd offer you criticism from that day onward, and learn from whoever would teach you": Rabbi A. Erlinger (*Me'Or HaShaar*) disagrees with our assertion that this is a stipulation to the guarantee presented before this. Instead, he sees it as an indication of success. For only someone who'd continue searching out teachers and critics would have truly taken what he'd heard already to heart.

11. "Because people sin when they're overtaken by their cravings and urged on by their yetzer harah": See 1:11.

"Because his hate for criticism implies a hate for the words of God": Despite our comment herein, Rabbeinu Yonah's statement here is still problematic. Since it seems to equate all of Torah with criticism. But isn't there so much of Torah that isn't reproachful, but rather quite uplifting, inspiring, enlightening, etc.? Apparently then *tochacha* (the original term, which is usually translated as "reproach," which we've translated as "criticism") is not what we take it to be alone. See 3:75 where we understand it to be an empathic warning; and 3:176 where it's taken to be sage advice. See our note to 3:3, as well.

12. "Solomon . . . couldn't possibly have included something as frivolous and worthless as this . . .": Compare this, which goes on to explain how Rabbeinu Yonah is about to explicate Solomon's seemingly meaningless statement here, with the assertion in 2:10 that, "For it's otherwise impossible (to explain how) a person (could) do more than he's aware of," which serves to explain how Rabbeinu Yonah arrived at his understanding of a seemingly inexplicable statement by the sages (see our note there). What the astute reader will find here is a clue to how the Masters come to their understandings of the meanings of cryptic statements in the Tradition. What they do when they come across a quote that seems initially untenable or banal, which thus puzzles them, is then factor in the basic "given" that so wise an individual as either Solomon or one of the sages *must* have meant something far deeper than appears to be. And they then strive to arrive at what that individual really meant. (As the expression goes, *hamaivin yavin*—"Whoever understands will understand.")

"If you're required to serve God with each one of your organs . . . then you're especially required to serve Him with the most valuable organ": Compare this with Ibn Pakudah's statement in his introduction to *The Duties of the Heart* (p. xxxii) to the effect that, "Since it is clear that God has obliged you in physical mitzvahs, it would not have been right of Him to leave out your soul and heart, your choicest parts, and not oblige them to serve Him as best as they can." Also see 3:201.

13. "How agreeable admonishment is": Admonishment is agreeable because it touches upon truth, and truth is sweet (*Biur*).

"You'd have defied God even more seriously if you don't dwell upon His word then": See our note at the beginning of ¶11.

"Behold, certainly the quill has written lies, and the scribes lied": That is, "The one who made the quill to write the Torah scroll made it for nothing; and the scribes who wrote the Torah scroll were there for no reason, since they didn't follow it" (*Metsudot*).

14. "Set aside periods of time in the course of the day and night to be alone in your room": See *The Path of the Just*, Ch. 14, p. 124 ; *The Duties of the Heart*, The Gate of Introspection, pp. 372–373.

"It's . . . a Torah imperative to rouse yourself to return to God on Yom Kippur": See 4:17, and *H. T.* 2:7.

15. "The 'whiteness' of your clothing refers to the personal purity that comes with tshuvah": See 1:9.

16. "Do new *mitzvot* every day since . . . whoever fulfills a mitzvah close to death . . .": See 1:49 where Rabbeinu Yonah counsels you to augment your fear of God daily. For that way you'll be accredited with having done full tshuvah, even when the opportunity for full tshuvah doesn't avail itself to you. The same principle apparently applies here. If opportunities to do certain rare and exceptional *mitzvot* don't present themselves to you in life, those rarer *mitzvot* will nonetheless be accredited to you when you increase in other *mitzvot*. Because God would note that you *would have* done them had they been available to you.

"Whoever fulfills a mitzvah close to death . . . While whoever commits a sin close to death . . .": The *Harotzeh B'tshuvah* points out that a person's character is defined by what he does and how he acts at the end. Consequently, if you're found to be doing *mitzvot* up until the end, you'll have proved yourself to have cared for God and His ways your whole life long. While the opposite is true, as well.

17. "The reality of their death doesn't occur to them until it comes upon them": How could a person possibly forget the reality of death? But see the very beginning of the introduction to *The Path of the Just* (p. 5) where Luzzatto declares that "what will be found in the great majority of what I have to say are things already known, and about which there is no doubt, but because they are so well-known and the truth of them is so self-evident, they are often hidden or completely forgotten." In fact, the same can be said about the reality of death. It's so well-known, such a "given" in the human situation, that it's overlooked.

"The Day of Judgment . . . The Resurrection of the Dead, "After twelve months . . .)": Rabbeinu Yonah says he'll be speaking about the Day of Judgment that will come in conjunction with The Resurrection of the Dead, *techiyat hamaitim*. Why does he then speak about the Day of Judgment that comes upon everyone after death? (As there are actually two Days of Judgment—one, after death, to determine one's status in The Soul World; the other, after the Resurrection, to determine one's status in The World to Come.) In fact, though, he may not be speaking of The Resurrection of the Dead when he refers to "*techiyat hamaitim*." He might instead be referring to "the coming to life which the dead experience" (another possible translation of, *techiyat hamaitim*). That's to say, he might be speaking about the sort of "life," that is, the sort of existence, the newly dead assume after their personal Day of Judgment.

18. "All wrongdoers ever want . . . is to satisfy their bodily cravings": See *H. T.* 3:1 for the more commonplace definition of a *rasha* as one who does more wrong than right, more bad than good. Also see 3:148, where Rabbeinu Yonah writes, "A person's status is determined by what he praises. If he praises good deeds, sages, and the righteous, you would know that he is himself good, and is basically righteous. . . . And while such a person may have committed some secret sins himself, he's nonetheless a lover of righteousness and is rooted in what's right. And he's a member of the community of those who honor God." Also see *Ali Shor* (Vol. 2, 571) where Rav Wolbe underscores the fact that one would only have to have experienced spiritual satisfaction over one mitzvah, or to have had one altruistic urge to do good in order to rise above this low status.

"All hope is lost when a wrongdoer dies": See 2:6.

19. "There are people who are secretly God-fearing . . .": But see Luzzatto's warning in *The Path of the Just* (Ch. 20, p. 175), "You are duty-bound to follow the *mitzvot* as strictly as possible, no matter who is watching you as you do, and are to neither be afraid nor embarrassed. . . . But even this requires discrimination and forethought, as it refers to those *mitzvot* which we are absolutely obligated to do. In regard to them you have to be as hard as flint. But as to those extra flourishes of piety which, when done in front of most people would cause laughter and mocking, and would have them sin and be punished because of the pious person's extra measures—the pious person should abandon such things, as they are not an absolute obligation upon him. . . . So many great pious people abandoned their saintly practices when they were among the common people when such acts would appear to be rooted in pride."

"If you're wise, you'll consider this world a temporary dwelling place, and will only make use of it to serve God . . .": The poor soul among you, dear readers, who feels as if he's been thrust in the mire of an ethic- and meaning-less morass of a world would do well to take time for himself, and concentrate upon this small "scroll" Rabbeinu Yonah has provided him. That is, he should meditate upon the text that begins with this paragraph and goes to the end of ¶21. And he will find his solace. In fact, the wise would review it weekly, or at least monthly.

21. Notice the parallels between elements of this ¶ (in the original) and the metaphor offered in ¶15 (about the sailor's wife awaiting his return at any time). It says there *v'shemen al roshecha*, while it speaks here of *simchat olam al rosho*. There it speaks of a sailor sent away on a mission for a king (refer to the commentaries to the original Midrash), just as here the object is to perceive yourself as being a messenger sent by a king. And it speaks there of his wife being *mitkashetet*, while the verse at the end of this ¶ refers to *keshet imrei emet*.

As a consequence we may infer that the sailor's wife in ¶15 represents what's referred to as the "highest soul" (the *yechida*) waiting in Heaven for the "lower soul" (the *neshama*) to return from its mission "across the ocean," i.e., in life. So the two can reunite in the End of Days, *ketz hayamim*—which is mentioned in this ¶.

22. "The day is short . . .": See 2:28.

25. "Observe three things . . .": See *The Path of the Just*, Ch. 23, pp. 199–200.

"Because death is also good—for humbling you, . . .": "A person comes to heartfelt humility and starts to curb his cravings when he sees (for himself) that there's death in the world, and he understands as a consequence that he's a created being. For without such thoughts he'd 'go about in this world thinking it will be his for generation upon generation,' as the Zohar put it. Because we instinctively think the world will be with us forever and ever. And that we're not mere created beings, utterly dependent upon God (as we are)" (*Ohr Yechezkel, Emunah*).

26. "But the wrongdoer's heart only listens . . .": Rav Yechezkel Levenstein differentiated the heart from the mind as follows. "In truth, comprehension isn't the main form of service to God. Since the human mind is a 'portion of God above,' and knows everything already from the womb [i.e., a part of the soul, which is itself a 'portion of God above,' the mind is inherently knowledgable, and need only be 'reminded' of things in life—a topic too recondite and complicated to discuss now— *YF*]. The difficult part of serving God involves having your heart understand and feel what the mind

knows. For man's heart is his toughest aspect, his heart is a heart of stone" (*Ohr Yechezkel*, Elul).

"So, you have to motivate *yourself*: Rav Shlomo Wolbe says, "It's possible to read a lot of Musar works quickly to little avail. What one should do is motivate himself through his studies by digesting the words well, and considering how relevant they are to him or how irrelevant (i.e., to reflect upon whether he exhibits the good qualities spoken of, or not). And he should then consider why they're irrelevant, whether he has the ability now to acquire them, how he would do that, or whether he still has to do other things beforehand" (*Ali Shor* 2:415). Also, see our reference to *The Duties of the Heart* in the supplementary note to 2:1 above about the primacy of self-motivation.

"We worked . . . and could not provide any more produce than this amount": See *The Path of the Just*, Ch. 26, p. 226, "I said that holiness ends up being a gift to you. That is necessarily so, because it is impossible for a human to place himself in this state which—because he is in truth physical, and flesh and blood—is so difficult for him. All you can do is make the effort . . ."

"It's not right . . . to postpone . . . efforts to improve myself": See 1:2–5.

28. "The day is short, there is a lot of work to do . . .": See 2:22. As Rav Reuven Malamed points out, "Don't be concerned that you'll never be able to complete the task. Because you're not asked to, you're asked instead to put all your energies into Divine service—which you can do" (*Ohr Hatshuvah*).

29. "You come upon transgression and stumble upon sins all the time when you postpone self-improvement": See 1:4.

31. "Let your garments always be white": See 2:15.

32. "Your transgressions will age if you postpone doing tshuvah . . .": See 1:5.

33. "you wouldn't earn as much merit . . . as you'd have earned . . . while you were young": See 1:9, and *H. T.* 2:1.

34. "It's important to find refuge for yourself as hastily as possible": See 1:2.

Gate Three

1. "You've already been warned to scrutinize your ways . . .": See 1:36–37, 2:15.

2. "In order to cover your face with humiliation when you ask for forgiveness": See 1:21–22

"And to see with your own eyes just how kind God is to forgive you": See 1:46.

". . . which is why we've included this introduction": If "this" alludes to all that preceded it in The Gates of Repentance, which then serves as an introduction to this crucial aspect of the book, as we conjectured in our notes, then we're reminded of Rashi's very first comment to the Torah. He asks there why the Torah didn't start with the first of the 613 *mitzvot*, which is its main thrust, rather than with the account of creation. We might likewise ask why Rabbeinu Yonah started his book with the details of tshuvah, rather than with an accounting of the *mitzvot* that people need to pay more attention to. But just as Rashi answers by saying that God started the Torah with the account of creation in order to justify His presenting the Jewish Nation with the Land of Canaan which they would turn into *Eretz Yisroel*, similarly Rabbeinu Yonah started this work with the details of tshuvah to allude to the great "Land of Canaan" we dwell in when we sin, which we can then overturn to a spiritual *Eretz Yisroel* when we do tshuvah.

"The death penalty": See 3: 107–118.

"excision": See 3:119–125.

6. "You'd be repeating your sin . . . (when . . . the consequences of a minor sin committed many times . . .": See 1:5, 7, 38–39.

7. "The decrees and precautions of the sages are the primary pathways to the fear God": See 3:156.

8. "The repercussions of being physical": See 2:1.

"Separating themselves from the ways of the community": See 3:168. Also see *H. T.* 3:11.

9. ". . . but you nonetheless prevailed over your impulses": See Rashi on *Kiddushin* 39B, "There's no greater mitzvah than prevailing over your yetzer harah when you're confronted with a sin."

10. ". . . they'd concentrate more on the trees that promised larger rewards than on the others, in order to get more": Compare that with the cooperation and non-competitiveness advocated in *The Duties of the Heart*, The Gate of Introspection, Ch. 3, p. 377 (22nd instance).

11. "One who takes an imperative lightly . . . has no portion in The World to Come, even if he has learned Torah and done good things": See 3:146, and *Pirke Avot* 3:11.

13. "While . . . , you can be benevolent with your very being as well as your money": See 3:53–54, 70 and 4:11 about offering advice as an act of benevolence.

". . . to do good for your people, . . . for another's welfare, whether he's poor or rich": Rav Yechezkel Levenstein (*Ohr Yechezkel, Midot*) cites the verse, "For Mordechai the Jew was second to the king Ahasuerus, and great among the Jews, and accepted by the multitude of his brothers, *seeking the good of his people, and speaking peace to all his brethren*" (Esther 10:3) as proof of the importance of acting out of kindness, and of the status it brings the person who practices it.

14. ". . . the sin of neglecting Torah study": See 3:177.

15. "Their fear of Me is a mitzvah of men learned by rote": See 3:169.

16. "The greater the mitzvah, the greater the consequences for not observing it": See the anonymous *Biur* who points out, "That accordingly explains the great consequences for not studying Torah, not giving charity or being benevolent, and not fearing God (discussed just previous to here). Because all of them are among the greatest and most significant *mitzvot*. It also serves as something of an introduction to ¶17, and informs us of the serious consequences to be suffered for not achieving the noble traits (discussed there)."

17. "Like the virtue of . . ." Rabbeinu Yonah addresses these major themes in various other works. For example, he discusses acting out of free will in his comments to *Avot* 7:2; following God's ways in *Avot* 1:18; complete trust in Proverbs 3:5–7, 9, 11, 22; reflecting upon God's greatness in Proverbs 2:5; "God chastises you the way a father chastises his son" in 4:13; fear in Proverbs 2:5; love in *Avot* 1:3; devotion in Proverbs 2:5; and see his comments to Proverbs 20:7 about fear, love and devotion together. It should be pointed out that a number of commentaries underscore the fact that *all* of us are obliged to strive for these ten noble traits, not just the especially righteous and pious. Because they are each *mitzvot*.

"Everyone called by My name I have created for My honor": See 3:143.

". . . if you don't put all your efforts and interests into the things you were created for?": See 1:10.

19. "You're required to be a dependable emissary and an adroit servant . . . to God.": See 2:21.

23. ". . . concentrate instead on the greatness of He who cautions you in it": See 1:48 and our note there.

24. "One who steals from a poor person is culpable for death by the hands of Heaven": See 3:110.

"Do not abuse one another": See 3:49.

25. "Taking interest on or profiting from a loan also involve prohibitions": See *Babba Metziah* 104A-104B for a discussion of *"Heter Iska,"* which allows for business transactions otherwise forbidden.

26. "People forget many of them . . . simply because they don't involve actions": Compare this to Luzzato's statement at the very beginning of his introduction to *The Path of the Just*. As he put it, "What will be found in the great majority of what I have to say are things that are already known, and about which there is no doubt; but because they are so well-known and the truth of them is so self-evident, they are often hidden or completely forgotten."

27. "Remember God at all times": Rav Reuven Malamud (*Ohr HaTshuvah*) offers three other ways of remembering God (aside from what Rabbeinu Yonah suggests). First, by sensing the soul within you and realizing that it, rather than your body, is primary, and yearning for The World to Come. Second, by affirming to yourself your whole life long that, "God is Lord; there is none other besides Him" (Deuteronomy 4:35). And third, by always recalling the miraculous history of the Jewish Nation (which would connect, in a more literal sense than how Rabbeinu Yonah uses it, with the very next mitzvah cited: "Watch out, and be very sure not to forget the things your eyes have seen").

"For the Nation of Israel can achieve all sorts of lovely traits, which will then distinguish it, when it remembers God": See 2:1.

28. "Hence the verse is only referring to one . . . and does not reflect on it all the time": See Rabbeinu Yonah's comments to *Avot* 3:8 where he says something contrary to what we say—that one is obliged to review *halachot* each and every day so as to never forget his studies.

30. ". . . after giving away some of your things . . . , and you even become poor as a result, don't resent God's admonishments": See *The Duties of the Heart*, The Gate of Introspection, p. 383, "Be introspective when your situation changes and the Creator decrees something for you that you do not want, after you trusted in Him and surrendered yourself, your money, your children, and everything else to Him," as well as Ibn Pakudah's sage insights there.

"For God only admonishes one He loves": See 2:4.

32. "Sense God's salvation in your heart, and . . . trust in it when you see trouble looming": Rav Rueven Malamud points out in *Ohr HaTshuvah* that the usual understanding of trusting in God involves belief in the fact that God will miraculously save. The truth is, though, that that's not the best form of trust, since you're not to depend upon a miracle. What you should do is proceed, and trust that everything that God does will be justified and for the good. (See *Avodat P'nim* 2:10.)

34. "Arrogance is one of the most significant sins, and it ruins and destroys souls": In fact, in his comments to *Pirke Avot* 4:4 Rabbeinu Yonah cites Rambam's declaration that arrogance is the root cause of most sins. See 1:26–27, 3:163.

39. "That comes to alert you to purge yourself of the trait of hatred": Rav Yechezkel Levenstein points out (*Ohr Yechezkel, Midot*) that Rabbeinu Yonah doesn't merely warn us not to express hatred. But rather to uproot it from our beings—which indicates that it's undeniably there, though sequestered away, in each one of us. And that hate will do what it will do unless you uproot it from your heart.

42. "That comes to alert you not to accept slander": Needless to say, the greatest work on the subject is *Sefer Chofetz Chaim* (or Rabbi Z. Pliskin's "Guard Your Tongue," in English, which is based on the former). See 3:211–213, 225.

43. "Do not covet your neighbor's house": See Ibn Ezra's comments to Exodus 20:14, where he asks how it can reasonably be expected of a person not to crave something not his own, and explains (in short) that you can manage to do that by perceiving things not granted you specifically by God as out of your realm and as being as unrealistic to expect as wings to fly with, etc.

45. "The consequences to suffer for profaning God's name are greater than for all other sins": See 1:47, 4:4–6, 16, 20. Also see *The Path of the Just*, Ch. 11, p. 96.

50. ". . . not to verbally encourage sinners, and not to join in with those who advocate wrongdoing": See 3:148, 190–191.

51. "It's forbidden to associate with wrongdoers in worldly matters": This would seem to make a nearly impossible demand upon us. For who among us isn't a wrongdoer from time to time? Rabbeinu Yonah himself cited the verse, "For there is not a righteous person on earth who does good and does not sin" (Ecclesiastes 7:20) in 1:6. But see the discussion in *Kiddushin* 40A about an "evil" wrongdoer versus one who isn't evil. As such we see that there are degrees of wrongdoing. Hence we're being warned here to avoid "evil wrongdoers"—a *rasha rah*, as it's worded in that Gemorrah, based on Isaiah 3:11—"*oy l'rasha rah*." (See citation in supplementary note to 3:125.)

52. "An accidental sin in instruction . . .": See *The Path of the Just*, Ch. 6, p. 57.

53. "To offer good advice . . .": See *The Path of the Just*, Ch. 11, p. 92.

54. "Benevolence": See 3:13.

57. "Do not acknowledge their charm": Some editions of *The Gates of Repentance* limit this injunction to praising those of the seven nations who originally occupied Canaan, as the verse would indicate (and which our note in the ¶ alludes to). But see *Yorah Deah* 151, *Sefer HaMitzvot* (*Lo Ta'aseh*) 3, *Hilchot Avodah Zarah*, Ch. 10:4 for dissenting, authoritative opinions. (Also see *Hagaot Maimon* to A.Z. 10:4, who cites the Tur and allows one to do so if he praises the Gentile in recognition of the fact that his beauty, like everything else, is God-given.)

58. "It's permitted to slander people who encourage conflict": The Chofetz Chaim warns, though, that certain conditions must be met before you can in fact do that: 1. you must know firsthand that the person is guilty of that, rather than depend on hearsay, 2. you must do so in order to improve him rather than out of sheer hatred, 3. there must be no other means of squelching the conflict, and 4. only if you can decide in all clarity, according to halacha, who the instigators are—otherwise it's best not to slander anyone involved (*Hilchot Lashon Harah* 8:8).

59. "Do not incur sin on his account": See 3:72.

"Do not fear any man": See 3:33.

". . . he sees leaders and authorities practicing deceit": See *The Path of the Just*, Ch. 19, pp. 167–168.

60. "But you can order a dishonest man to do whatever you'd care for him to do": This is the accepted *halacha*, as cited in Rambam's *Hilchot Avadim* 1:8.

61. ". . . about the cleanliness of their environment or their hands": See 3:44.

62. "Death and life are in the power of the tongue": See 3:210.

64. "(The) very important senses of seeing and of hearing": See 2:12.

". . . not to stare at a married woman, or at any other woman forbidden to you": See *The Path of the Just*, Ch. 11, pp. 85–88.

65. "Having upturned eyes . . .": See our Supplementary Note to 1:35 where we linked staring at women with arrogance and apply it to this ¶, the previous one, and the connection between the two.

66. "Profanity": See 3:229, as well as *The Path of the Just*, Ch. 11, pp. 88–89.

"Because doing so will protect you . . .": See 2:12, 3:198.

67. "Withdrawing your hand": See 3:9,15,36.

72. "Criticize your neighbor diligently . . .": See 1:50, 3:59, 195–196 (see the latter especially for certain warnings).

73. "It's important to appoint honest individuals . . . to thus eradicate wrongdoing": See 1:8, 3:2 for indications of how *The Gates of Repentance* itself is to serve this purpose in a sense. And see 3:75 for an allusion to that as well.

74. "For you know people forget things . . .": See *L'shon Chassidim*, p. 58, which cites the fact that we all forget things, and suffer spiritually as a consequence (see 3:27). The suggestion offered there is to always recall that you forget. And to thus allow for that, and to arrive at a means of compensating for it.

"Slander": See ¶'s 200–231.

75. "Those who criticize them . . .": See our Supplementary Note to 2:11, as well as the one to 3:73.

80. "Shaking a married woman's hand": See 3:138.

". . . from the mitzvah of *Nazir*": See *The Path of the Just*, Ch. 11, pp. 85–86.

82. "Anger": See *The Path of the Just*, Ch. 11, pp. 100–101; *The Duties of the Heart* 3:10, p. 162.

". . . not to expose our body to danger . . . troubled, angry, or mourning for your dead": See 1:13, 30–34. Also see Rabbeinu Yonah's comments to Proverbs 11:17, where he points out that if exposing anyone else to danger would be considered cruel, doing so to yourself would certainly be cruel as well. The astute reader would understand the ramifications of that principle as it touches upon other aspects of intra- and inter-personal relations, as well. Also see *The Path of the Just*, Ch. 9, p. 69, about exposing yourself to danger; and Ch. 13, p.122 for Luzzatto's explanation of detrimental forms of abstinence.

86. "Trust": See 3:17, 32.

101. ". . . a vicious dog or a defective ladder": The Hebrew for "a vicious dog" is *kelev rah* (literally a "bad" dog). And the term for "a defective ladder" is *sulam rauah* (literally a broken, or "bad" ladder). Hence we see that oftentimes in Hebrew the word for "bad" refers to meanness or defectiveness, or injuriousness and harmfulness (in fact, see *Hilchot Talmud Torah* 6:14, the seventh instance). Thus *rah* is often a statement about the effect something has on something, someone, or on mankind. And doesn't necessarily address a moral status. For dogs and ladders can't be "bad," since they're not subject to morality.

107. "The difference between death and excision . . .": See *H. T.* 8:1 where Rambam characterizes *karet* as exclusion from The World to Come alone.

"Death is more serious than excision . . .": Both the *Ohr HaTshuvah* and the anonymous *Biur* offer that a death sentence can be considered more merciful simply because death surrounds the individual before it strikes him. For that allows him time to do tshuvah. But Rabbeinu Yonah would clearly disagree, by virtue of the fact that he says outright that the death sentence "is more serious than excision."

109. ". . . afflict widows and orphans": See 3:24.

111. "The torment of humiliation": See 3:139, 200.

117. "Stealing gifts due the poor": See 3:24, 110.

119. "The one culpable for it and his descendants are excised": See 3:107.

120. "Those who cohabit with a menstruant": See 3:125.

122. ". . . to reward them in the world, yet bring them to ruin in The World to Come": See 3:159. Also see *Kiddushin* 40B; *The Duties of the Heart, The Gate of Trust in God*, pp. 210, 212–213; and Ramban's *Sha'ar HaGemul.*

123. "Because they might do tshuvah": See *The Path of the Just*, Ch. 4., p. 40.

125. "Woe to such a guilty wrongdoer": See Supplementary Note to 3:51 above about this citation. In point of fact, the modern reader would be stunned to find anyone guilty of what's perceived to be such a common, innocent sin (i.e., having relations with one's wife while she's yet menstruating) referred to as a "*rasha rah.*" But that bespeaks more of our naivete about matters of the soul than it does about anything else. And reminds us of how little of what we see before our eyes can be determined to be right or wrong, personally and universally constructive or destructive, without Torah's guidance!

126. "Sins culpable for stoning": See the others in this category in *Hilchot Sanhedrin* 15:10.

127. "Sins culpable for burning": Ibid. 15:11.

129. "Sins culpable for strangulation": Ibid. 15:13.

131. "You're to kill him as soon as you come upon him": The *Chazon Ish* addresses the issue of how taking it upon yourself to kill someone doing that, or punishing anyone else in so stringent a way in the name of God might appear in the eyes of others, and what it might be thought to say about Torah in general to the modern mind. So he offers (Y.D. 2:16) that the sentence of lowering anyone into a pit or, by extension, threatening anything which might appear to be "cruel and unusual punishment" in our eyes, "is only to be carried out when Divine Providence is as widespread as when there were open miracles and the voice of prophecy served, and when the righteous of the generation were obviously and personally guided by Divine Providence. Because then (it would be clear that) heretics were acting singularly deviantly by following their yetzer harahs and being wanton." He then went on to say that now, however, when the level of faith is so low in the world, it would do more harm than good to act that way toward heretics and renegades, and we should instead try as hard as we can to interact lovingly with them in order to bring them back to the ways of Torah. See Rambam's *Hilchot Mamrim* 3:3 as well.

138. "Shaking hands with a married woman": See 3:64, 80.

139. "The torment of blanching in shame is bitterer yet than death": See 3:111.

143. "We were created to bring honor to God": See ¶148 for further reference to this idea. But what about Luzzatto's revelation at the beginning of *The Path of the Just* that we were created to "delight in God and enjoy the radiance of His Divine presence" in The World to Come—which would seem to contradict this statement? And what of Rabbeinu Yonah's own mention of the great "glee and everlasting joy" we'll experience then (2:21), which would seem to bolster Luzzatto's idea? In fact, both are true. The point is that it is by experiencing such great glee and delight that we'll bring honor to God in a recondite and inscrutable way; and that bringing honor to God itself yields great glee and delight. (Based on the *Me'or HaShaar*.)

"Even the righteous stumble from time to time and sin": See 1:6, 2:9.

144. "One who says the Torah isn't from Heaven": See *H. T.* 3:8.

"Even if that person studied Torah and did a lot of good things, he nonetheless hasn't a place in The World to Come": See 3:160

145. "What good does it do us to have Torah scholars?": See 3:155–156.

146. "Doing work on the intermediate days": See 3:11. And see 3:4–8 about disregarding Rabbinic decrees, which this touches upon.

147. "Many sleeping hearts will be awakened" . . . : See *H. T.* 3:4.

148. "When you demean scholars and those who fear God": See 3:155, 4:19.

"That he himself is good and basically righteous": See 3:119.

"But one who praises terrible deeds . . . is (a) wrongdoer": See 3:190.

151. "People who associate with wrongdoers . . .": Also see 3:50–51, 59, 187–199

152. "For the only way the righteous will assume the honor due them is if the honor shown those wrongdoers is dashed": The original reads, *ain*

hatzlacha lekovod hatzadikim zulati acharei hashpalat kevodom, and can more literally be translated as, "The righteous will not achieve honor until *their* own honor is dashed." And that would allude to the more recondite idea expressed in Luzzatto's *Derech Hashem* that man's own lowliness will prove to be his greatness (*hashpalato tihiyeh hagbahato*), and his revelation in *Da'at Tevunot* that *hester panim* (Divine concealment) necessarily precedes *ha'arat panim* (Divine revelation).

153. "Those who discuss Torah in dirty alleyways": See 3:44.

"Those who are able to study Torah but don't": See 3:14, 177.

154. "Mention of the Resurrection of the Dead in the Torah": See Rashi's comments to *Sanhedrin* 90A, where he says that even if one believes in The Resurrection per se but denies that it can be found in the Torah he's nonetheless within this class. Because what would his faith be based on anyway? As to why The Resurrection of the Dead isn't stated outright in the Torah itself see *The Duties of the Heart*, The Gate of Trust in God, p. 212, where he explains why The World to Come isn't cited in the Torah itself, which can certainly be applied to The Resurrection of the Dead as well. See *Sanhedrin* 90B-92B. And see the seventh section of Saadia Gaon's *Emunot V'Deot* for a full discussion of the subject.

155. "One who does not exhibit fear and respect for Torah scholars . . .": As the *Harotzeh L'tshuvah* puts it, having respect for Torah scholars is analogous to having respect for God, whose Torah is in their hearts. So it's only logical that one who hasn't respect for them shouldn't enjoy The World to Come, since the essential experience of The World to Come is delighting in God and basking in the light of His presence.

". . . didn't have enough respect for the Torah to exhibit fear": See 3:121.

156. "Fearing them leads to the fear of Heaven": See 3:7.

158. "Our great obligation to sanctify God's name": See 3:45, 61, 132, 134, 143 and 4:4-6, 16, 20.

159. "God's enemies": The anonymous *Biur* points out that both this expression and "those who abandon God" in 3:169 are original with Rabbeinu Yonah, and are found nowhere else.

"God repays His enemies for the *mitzvot* they did while in this world . . .": See Ramban's *Shaar HaG'mul* for an extensive discussion of this issue. And see *The Duties of the Heart*, The Gate of Trust in God, pp. 210-213.

160. ". . . those who observe *mitzvot* and are careful to avoid all physical and verbal sins": The *Rotzeh B'Tshuvah* suggests these would be individuals who act out of fear of the consequences of not doing God's will, or who fulfill *mitzvot* externally and very superficially at that. *Da'at Torah* is stunned by the implications of Rabbeinu Yonah's charge, and wonders how many of us who appear to be loyal to God are in fact His enemies in our hearts. And he warns us to scrutinize our own motivations. The anonymous *Biur*, however, explains that the sentence that follows this one, which we've translated, "That is, when such individuals are troubled by and can't bear (the thought of) other people studying Torah" should read, "when such individuals are *in trouble* and can't bear . . .", which suggests that they only act the way they do when they're in travail. (And they apparently lapse into despondence and hopelessness—two emotions which thus prove to be such terrible, terrible pitfalls since they could lead one to lose his place in The World to Come!)

"Or if they admire the honor accorded wrongdoers . . ." See 3:187–193.

162. "Community leaders who evoke excessive fear for unholy reasons": See *H. T.* 3:13.

163. "The haughty are an abomination to God": See 1:27, 3:34.

164. ". . . to express the dread and fear of God in our hearts": The *Da'at Torah* asks how one could ever hope to *always* express the fear and dread of God. And he suggests that one can only be said to accomplish that when he tries as hard as he can to acquire the wherewithal to do that (which implies diligence in the study of Torah and Musar, as well as in prayer and communion with God). Also see 3:15.

168. "Those who separate themselves from the community": See 3:8. In *Rosh Hashanah* 17A, Rashi doesn't count "those who separate themselves from the community" as a separate class of individuals who don't have a place in The World to Come as Rabbeinu Yonah does here. Instead, Rashi understands the term to refer to the heretics, informers, etc., already discussed.

". . . demonstrating that he doesn't want to be their confidant": See 3:190.

169. "*Mitzvot* by rote": See 3:15.

170. ". . . broken utensils with pieces left intact, . . . 'demolished' and have no place in The World to Come": See 3:159.

171. "For if they turn from their wrongful ways, they'll escape destruction": See *H. T.* 3:14, and *The Duties of the Heart*, The Gate of Repentance, p. 339.

"Return, you faithless children, and I will heal your faithlessness": See 1:1.

172. "Four types never encounter the Divine Presence . . .": The question to be raised is, "Is 'not encountering the Divine Presence' and 'not inheriting a place in The World to Come' the same thing? And is this section thus a continuation of the previous one?" The answer isn't clear by any means.

The *Me'or HaShaar* points out that Rambam doesn't feature this class as being among those who haven't a place in The World to Come in *H. T.* (with the exception of slanderers—a major exception). The *Me'or HaShaar* consequently declares this section "Aggadic," with the implication that, in fact, it doesn't touch upon one's place in The World to Come; and *Maharsha* in *Sotah* 42A implies that these individuals do have a place in The World to Come (see more on this below). On the other hand, Zohar 1:219B equates The World to Come with encountering the Divine Presence, as do *Iyun Yaakov* (to *Ein Yaakov*), *Etz Yoseph* (Ibid.), and *Torat Avraham*, p. 384. And they would then seem to argue that Rabbeinu Yonah is continuing to discuss those who haven't a place in The World to Come

Nonetheless, Rabbeinu Yonah himself seems to conclude the issue of those who haven't a place in The World to Come by his "summing-up" language in ¶171, which comes right before the introduction of the Four Types. As such, it seems clear that not encountering the Divine Presence and either inheriting or not inheriting a place in The World to Come are two separate issues in his eyes. On the other hand, Rabbeinu Yonah uses certain terms in the course of this section that seem to echo themes raised in The World to Come section. As in, "How dreadful and lethal these traits are, . . . (which) all ultimately lead to death" (¶173); "Anyone with this trait is beyond hope" (¶176); "The habit of maligning only becomes a part of you when you cast off the yoke of Heaven" (¶177); and the citation of Psalm 5:7, "You destroy those who lie" (¶187). As such, there seems to be a "mixed message," if you will, as to whether or not the Four Types will inherit a place in The World to Come or will "merely" not encounter the Divine Presence.

Perhaps the solution can be found in the above-cited *Maharsha*, who indicates that one can be removed from the Divine Presence both in this world and in The World to Come. Which leads us to differentiate the two in our comment here, in the body of the work the following way: "Both the Four Types . . . and those . . . who haven't a place in The World to Come, are separated, perhaps even 'divorced' from God . . . But while the latter ruptured that relationship with their attitudes and decisions, those mentioned here are spurned by God Himself, because of the sorts of people they are."

175. "Arrogance": See 1:26–27, 3:34, 65, 163.

176. ". . . their habit of seeing themselves as sages": The parallel wording in the phrases, "This sort of maligner acquires that bad trait by considering himself a sage" (in the previous paragraph) and "What makes those in this category unable to take admonishment is their habit of seeing themselves as sages" here, seems to equate Torah and *mitzvot* with criticism and admonishment. See 2:11 and 3:75 where we discuss that correspondence.

"They malign every opinion other than their own": See *The Path of the Just*, Ch. 11, pp. 99–100.

177. "Are jolly and . . . sometimes a result of drinking": See *The Path of the Just*, Ch. 5, p. 44.

". . . once one casts off the yoke of Heaven, as a consequence of which he's made to bear the yoke of misfortune": Ibid., p. 45.

"Not to malign others casually or occasionally": See 3:217 where it's told that "a certain individual and a sage passed by a carcass, when the individual remarked, 'How putrid this carcass is!' to which the sage said, 'How white its teeth are!'"

179. ". . . for two reasons: for their lies, and for the damage that results from them": See 3:187

181. "They sometimes even make things up entirely": See *The Path of the Just*, Ch. 11, pp. 95–96 for a discussion of liars.

"Because he loves telling lies": Two points are to be made about this insight of Rabbeinu Yonah's. First, Rav Yechezkel Levenstein (cited in *Ohr HaTshuvah*) points out that this sort of person would even lie to God Himself! We might add that he'd certainly lie to himself, as well. And if that's so, we might wonder why lying isn't perhaps the most fundamental deterrent to tshuvah. And why it wasn't thus included among the other such traits at the end of the first gate? But see our second note to 2:8 and apply it here.

Second, notice how often "love" is used in this paragraph: this class of liars is said to be motivated by a "love of lies," they're said to "love committing" their sin and, again, we're told that such a person "loves tellling lies." Understand this in light of Rabbeinu Yonah's statement in 3:148 that one's stature is defined by what he praises, and thus by extension, by what he loves.

"We're permitted to tell such lies, however, in order to . . .": See *Babba Metziah* 23B as well. And see *Hilchot Deot* 5:7 and *Hilchot Gezella* 17:13.

182. "The fifth category consists of those who . . .": See the introduction to *The Duties of the Heart*, pp. xl–xli, about being a person of integrity, and doing what you say you're going to.

184. "We're obliged to remain honest, since honesty is an instinct of the human spirit": Citing a Midrash that addresses the issue, Rav Shlomo Wolbe (*Alei Shur* 2,:524) asks how it could ever be said that man is inherently honest, as this statement would seem to indicate? And he responds that while honesty is an instinct of the soul, as Rabbeinu Yonah points out here, it's nonetheless covered over and stifled by the cravings of the body. See note below.

186. "An honest person": The term used here for this (*ish emunim*) is to be found in Proverbs 20:6, where it's written, "Who can find an honest person?" But if, as the citation points out, an honest person is hard to find, then how can Rabbeinu Yonah say right after this in the text that honesty is "an instinct of the human spirit"? The answer apparently lies in what Rav Wolbe said in the previous entry.

188. "One sitting in judgment must never be afraid of any mortal man": See 3:33.

189. "The second . . . praises a wrongdoer. . . .": We've translated the term *rasha* here as "wrongdoer," as we have throughout the work (with an infrequent use of the term "guilty person," depending on context), rather than the more common "bad," "wicked," or "evil" person. Because in those other contexts Rabbeinu Yonah seems to be referring to someone who sinned in one or two instances, or more. Or who inclined toward wrongdoing. But who wouldn't ordinarily be taken as evil or wicked. But here (as well as in the previous ¶) Rabbeinu Yonah is indeed referring to an evil or wicked person—someone who might have done some good, but who's otherwise simply *bad*.

In fact, there have always been degrees of evil and wrongdoing. See for example *Kiddushin* 40A that, "*v'chi yesh rasha rah v'yesh sheaino rah? eleh rah leshamayim u'rah lebriot hu rasha rah; rah leshamayim vaino rah lebriot zehu rasha sheino rah*" — "Is there then a wicked man that is evil and one that is not evil? But one who is evil to Heaven and to man, is a wicked man that is evil. And one who is evil to Heaven but not to man, is a wicked man that is not evil."

Another point to be made about the idea of not praising wrongdoers is this. It's very hard for us of modernity to accept the idea that people shouldn't be praised for the good within them even if they're essentially bad. Because we claim to accept people in all their complexity. And have trouble designating a person "bad" when he's partially "good," too. But that might say more about us than about them. It might say that we're not willing to face our own badness. And that we tend to cover over badness with a sort of naive cheer that we take to be wisdom.

On the other hand, though, the point must be made that Rabbeinu Yonah is only warning us not to *praise* evil people. He isn't warning us not to love them for who they otherwise are, or to see them as immortal souls gone wrong, who can always do tshuvah. See Beruriah's response to Rebbe Meir to the effect that one must hate sin rather than the sinner (*Berachot* 10A). And see *The Path of the Just*, Ch. 19, p. 157, where it's pointed out that, "Divine retribution will come to one who . . . does not want to be benevolent. He will be judged according to the letter of the law because he acted that way (i.e., he judged others according to the strict letter of the law). And who is it that can withstand God's judgement of him according to the strict letter of the law?"

"Wrongdoers can be recognized by their speech and their conduct": In the text itself we took this to refer to the wrongdoer, whom the flatterer was complementing. Nonetheless it could also be understood to refer to the flatterer himself, who is also a wrongdoer. For he, too, can be recognized by his speech and his conduct—in keeping with what Rabbeinu Yonah pointed out in 3:148. That, "One who praises terrible deeds or compliments wrongdoers is himself an out and out wrongdoer. . . ."

190. "But if you aren't a confidant of the righteous, and you don't despise or curse wrongdoers, at least don't bless them": See 3:160, and 3:168 for use of the term "confidant." And see 3:218.

192. "And he'd never do tshuvah for his bad ways nor worry about his sins, because he'd think he's righteous": See *The Path of the Just*, Ch. 23, p. 201 (bottom).

"Only one outside the community of the righteous would say to himself, 'I always knew it!' when he's flattered": See 1:16.

193. "It is forbidden to stare at an evildoer": The *Magen Avraham* (as cited by the *Meor HaShaar*) points out that while it's forbidden to stare and dwell upon an evil person's visage and form at length, it's all right to look at him casually.

"How life-threatening it is to befriend wrongdoers": See *H. T.* 4:5.

196. "Just as it is a mitzvah to say something that will be listened to, so too . . .": See *The Path of the Just*, Ch. 20, p. 174.

198. ". . . you're obliged to stop associating with wrongdoers": See 3:193.

200. "A slanderer is worse than both": See 3:174.

201. ". . . that they themselves are in charge of their tongues": But see the ironic truth in 3:204.

". . . whose will all are bidden to carry out": See 2:12.

"Slander is more serious than . . . idol worship, illicit relations, and murder": The anonymous *Biur* cites Rabbeinu Gershom who understands the logic behind the fact that slandering is more serious than those other sins on the basis of a close reading of the verses cited. For it's said about idol worship, "Please, God, these people have sinned a great (*gadol*—in the singular) sin"; it's said about illicit relations, "How can I do something so (*gadol*—in the singular) wrong?"; and it's said about murder, "My sin is too great (*gadol*—in the singular) to bear." While it's said of slander, "God will obliterate all smooth lips, all tongues that speak arrogantly (*gedolot*—in the *plural*)."

202. "You're to give up your life rather than commit it": See 3:136–141.

204. "Second, it's very hard for a slanderer to do tshuvah": See 1:52, and *H. T.* 4:2.

"After having trained his tongue to speak lies . . . he can no longer control himself": See 2:30.

205. "When a fire-like sorrow burns . . .": See 1:13.

206. "A proud and haughty man . . . acts in arrogant wrath": See 3:174.

207. "Even if the slanderer were to do tshuvah, he'd have to ask forgiveness from everyone . . .": See *The Duties of the Heart*, The Gate of Repentance, p. 337.

208. "One who cites family blemishes will never be atoned for": See 3:111

"A heretic hasn't a share in The World to Come": See 3:155.

209. "One who casts off the yoke of the warning against sin": See 3:143.

210. "Talk about Torah, wisdom, and ethics. . . .": See 3:17.

211. ". . . to not even accept slander . . .": See 3:223 for an exception to this rule. For a full discussion of this, see the introduction to *Sefer Chofetz Chaim* (*Lavin #2, Be'er Mayim Chaim*). Also see *Clall* 6 in *Hilchot Lashon Harah*.

"Do not bear a false report": See 3:42.

"They . . . love finding fault, laying blame, and denigrating others": See 1:18.

212. "Even only inclining your ear . . . encourages people to speak against others": See *Hilchot Lashon Harah* 6:2.

214. ". . . whom our sages said, 'descend to *Gehenom* and never reascend' ": See 3:139–140.

"If you publicly discuss and relate the terrible things a person's ancestors did *out* of his presence": See *Hilchot Lashon Harah* Ch. 3 and 4:1 (and ¶1 of *Be'er Mayim Chaim* there).

". . . do not experience the Divine Presence": See 3:172.

215. ". . . if you see someone . . . and you reveal that in public, you'd be very wrong": See *Hilchot Lashon Harah* 6:4.

"The heart alone realizes its own bitterness": See 3:217.

"Report it to a discreet scholar . . .": See 3:220

". . . he's been bitter about it ever since": See 1:6.

217. ". . . and never praises anyone": See 3:226. But see 3:148 (at end) in conjunction with 3:128 (immediately following this) for a whole other depth of understanding.

". . . in books of ethics": See *The Duties of the Heart*, The Gate of Surrender, p. 291.

"Tshuvah is essentially effected by heartfelt bitterness": See 1:12–13.

218. ". . . expose his sins . . . to despise wrongful deeds": See *The Path of the Just*, Ch. 19, p. 168.

"A dishonest man is an abomination to the righteous": See 3:190 and our note there. As well as our reference in 3:217, above, and our note to the text itself.

219. "If the sinner is God-fearing . . . has certainly done tshuvah": See 3:116 (at end).

". . . and he's careless about a particular sin which everyone knows is a sin": See 1:6 and 3:143.

"But if the sinner is not God-fearing . . . it's permissible to humiliate and demean him": See 3:218 above.

"So, it's permissable to degrade the actions of one who doesn't follow the word of God . . .": See *Sefer Chofetz Chaim, Hilchot Lashon Harah, Be'er Mayim Chaim* 10:30.

"Even though Yehu fulfilled a mitzvah . . . he was just as defiant": See *Sefer Chofetz Chaim, Hilchot Lashon Harah* 10:3.

221. ". . . a single witness should testify. . . .": See 3:228, and *Sefer Chofetz Chaim, Hilchot Lashon Harah, Clall* 10, where seven prerequisites are offered.

224. "Instigating strife among relatives and friends . . . is the most serious one of all": The *Me'or HaShaar* explains it thusly: The fundamental damage done by slander is the fact that someone is given a bad name, harm is done to him, and hatred is stirred up. That's certainly all there when a person instigates strife among family members and close friends. But beside all that, the love those individuals once had for one another is thus reversed, which is doubly bad. For the hatred of a person you'd once loved is far worse than a stranger's. (See *Hilcot Richilut, Clall* 1, in *Sefer Chofetz Chaim*.)

225. "You're obliged to keep a secret . . .": See *Hilchot Lashon Harah* 9:6.

"For since he can't keep his lips from spreading rumors . . .": See 3:204.

"The Torah warned us never to accept slander": For the relationship between accepting slander and accepting rumors see *M'kor Chaim* in *Hilchot Issurei Rechilut* 5:1, and *Be'er Mayim Chaim* 1 there.

". . . to find favor in their master's eyes": See *The Path of the Just*, Ch. 23, p. 202.

226. "Most people stumble when it comes to theft, a few do when it comes to illicit relations . . .": See *The Path of the Just*, Ch. 11, pp. 82–89 for a full discussion of the ramifications of these first two faults.

"Honor is due those who search out honor": See 3:149. See 1:18, at the beginning, as well.

227. ". . . someone who praises another in a way that causes him harm": See *Hilchot Lashon Harah* 9. It's important to point out, however, that in his first comment in *Mekor HaChaim* there, the Chofetz Chaim cites sources that take such a statement to be out-and-out slander rather than its "dust."

228. "But you must first speak to him directly if you intend to reform him, since you just might divert him from his wrongful ways by criticizing him": See *Be'er Mayim Chaim* 10:7.

229. "Because you didn't close your ears . . .": See 2:12, 3:66.

231. "Fault-finders see everything as wrong rather than right. . . ." See 3:218.

"For a fault-finder will often scoff at favors done him, consider them disfavors, and do harm in exchange for good": *Me'Or HaShaar* cites *Sefer Hachinuch* (Mitzvah 33) who inserts the idea of recognizing favors done you in his discussion of respecting one's parents, and acknowledging all they've done for you throughout your lifetime. He says there that finding fault in your parents and taking what they've done for granted is "especially reprehensible" to God and to humankind. (*l'aliyat nishmat avi umori Yitzchak Hersch ben Daniel, alov hashalom*).

Gate Four

1. ". . . whose illnesses and diseases are its bad traits and sins": See 1:36, 2:3. And see the first supplementary note to 1:26 vis à vis bad character traits. Also see *Hilchot De'ot* 2:1. See 1:46 and our notes there about God's role as a Healer.

"Your sin wouldn't have been completely absolved until you'd been admonished. . . .": See 2:1–6.

2. "A sin offering was required for any sin committed accidentally . . .": See *H. T.* 1:1.

"God criticizes those He loves the way a father criticizes a son he is pleased with": See 2:2, 4.

3. "Since the actual atonement that comes with Yom Kippur comes after you've done tshuvah": See *H. T.* 1:3.

4. "Profaning God's name": Also see *H. T.* 1:4. Rashi (*Yomah* 86A) explains that profanation is so serious a sin because it causes others to sin as well. *Me'or HaShaar* offers that, "In the case of all other sins, atonement comes about as a result of what the body must endure, and its loss of physical prowess," which isn't the case when it comes to the profanation of God's name. But it's important for us to underscore, however, that not all sins are forgiven with death. For then everyone would die a righteous person, and all would be forgiven and overlooked. And there'd simply be no reason to have lived as a free agent. The point of the matter is that death (like the offering of sacrifices, the suffering of tribulation, and the experiencing of Yom Kippur) only forgives *after the sinner does tshuvah*.

5. ". . . since he'd thus acted so uprightly, in contrast to how foolishly he'd acted when he'd sinned": See 1:15, 35 and our notes there.

7. ". . . fantasies that arise in the mind, and . . . thoughts of sinning": See 3:40–41.

8. ". . . when you'll be made acceptable to God": See 1:42.

11. "Any sin you committed that incurs excision or a court-imposed death sentence. . . .": See 1:16.

"Benevolence": See 1:41–42 for a vital facet of this solution. And see 3:13, 36 as well.

"Sins are atoned for by kindness and truth": See 1:47.

12. "Also take fasts upon yourself, shed tears and deny yourself pleasures . . .": See 1:13, 15, 30–34.

"Accept those admonishments lovingly": See 2:3–4.

13. ". . . because God has been admonishing you . . . mercifully": See 1:45 (end) and 46. Also see *The Path of the Just*, Ch. 19. pp. 164–165.

Me'or HaShaar asks how it's possible to say that God doesn't have you suffer the consequences you deserve—after all, doesn't He administer justly? He offers the explanation presented at the end of the fourth chapter of *The Path of the Just*, where it's explained that, "According to the strict letter of the law, the sinner should be punished immediately, without any delay at all, upon the performance of a sin, and the punishment itself should be meted out with great anger, as we would expect in the case of one who rebels against the word of the Creator. . . . But in truth the Divine attribute of compassion obviates these points. It . . . allows for repentance for the sinner, so that the uprooting of the *will* to do is equivalent to uprooting the act itself."

"For when God admonishes His enemies . . .": See 3:159–160.

15. "Offense": See 4:22.

"If you sin, but your heart becomes preoccupied with what you did . . . God will forgive you for it": See 3:141, 205.

16. ". . . profaning God's name, which can't be atoned for by tribulations": See 4:4.

"The Tree of Life is a cure for the tongue": *Harotzeh B'Tshuvah* suggests that this refers to slander, which, the Chofetz Chaim points out, always involves the profanation of God's name. But see 3:209 where Rabbeinu Yonah points out that Torah study does *not* protect slanderers. Yet, if that's so, what does Rabbeinu Yonah mean here by "Torah is a cure for every grave affliction"? Isn't slander a grave afliction? Perhaps Rabbeinu Yonah is implying that slander is more than a grave affliction—it's a mortal, dread disease. For as he states in 3:200, "One who slanders acts as if he denies the existence of God," which is certainly worse than profaning His name.

17. "The imperative to do tshuvah": See 2:14.

18. "If you stole something from someone, you must first return the stolen object, then confess": See 1:44–45.

19. "You'd have to appease anyone you'd vexed": See *H. T.* 2:9.

"There's no remedy, however, for insulting a scholar, since you would have profaned the Torah": See 3:148, 155–158.

"But they mocked God's messengers, and . . . there was no remedy":
See 4:4.

20. "As soon as the fear of death overcame you": See 2:6.

21. "Those who are self-aware always catch sight of sins. . . .": See 2:2
(at end).

Index

Rabbi Yaakov Feldman

A student of the late Rabbi Aryeh Kaplan, and a leader in Jewish outreach, Rabbi Yaakov Feldman was the founder and director of *Machon Binah* (The Center for Understanding) in California, the director of other outreach organizations in New York, and a Hillel director at the State University of New York at Purchase. Rabbi Feldman serves on the board of directors of *Ohr Ki Tov* and is past chairman of the clergy committee of the Rockland Council on Alcoholism, a member of the clergy and ethics committees of Rockland County (New York) Hospice Association, and its Spiritual Care Coordinator. He had served for many years as a spiritual and addiction counselor. Rabbi Feldman has translated and commented on *The Duties of the Heart* by Bachya ibn Pakuda and *The Path of the Just* by Moshe Chaim Luzzatto (Jason Aronson Inc.). He has also written children's stories, and articles for Jewish journals, magazines, and newspapers. He lives with his wife, Sara, and their three children in Monsey, NY.